COMBAT
IN THE SKY

COMBAT
IN THE SKY

**Airpower and the Defense
of North Vietnam, 1965–1973**

Đồng Sỹ Hưng

Naval Institute Press
Annapolis, Maryland

Naval Institute Press
291 Wood Road
Annapolis, MD 21402

Library of Congress Cataloging-in-Publication Data
Names: Nguyễn, Sỹ Hưng, author.
Title: Combat in the sky : airpower and the defense of North Vietnam,
    1965–1973 / Đồng Sỹ Hưng.
Description: Annapolis, Maryland : Naval Institute Press, [2023] | Includes
    bibliographical references and index.
Identifiers: LCCN 2023003000 (print) | LCCN 2023003001 (ebook) |
    ISBN 9781612510279 (hardcover) | ISBN 9781612511153 (ebook)
Subjects: LCSH: Vietnam War, 1961–1975–Aerial operations, Vietnamese. |
    Vietnam War, 1961–1975–Aerial operations, American. | Vietnam War,
    1961–1975–Antiaircraft artillery operations.
Classification: LCC DS558.8 .N4973 2023 (print) | LCC DS558.8 (ebook) |
    DDC 959.704/348–dc23/eng/20230127
LC record available at https://lccn.loc.gov/2023003000
LC ebook record available at https://lccn.loc.gov/2023003001

Print editions meet the requirements of ANSI/NISO z39.48–1992
(Permanence of Paper). Printed in the United States of America.

31 30 29 28 27 26 25 24 23   9 8 7 6 5 4 3 2 1
First printing

In memory of
the heroes and martyrs
of the Vietnamese
People's Air Force,
who fought bravely
to protect the skies of
the fatherland.

Senior Colonel Vũ Chính Nghị, former MiG-19 pilot with the 925th FR, former head of Air Navigation Department of the VNP AD and AF Service.

Senior Colonel Nguyễn Văn Quang, former MiG-21 pilot with the 921st FR, former head of the Administration Office of the VNP AD and AF Service.

Senior Colonel Lữ Thông, former pilot and flight instructor at the AF Training School, former deputy director of the Pilot Training School (Vietnam Airlines).

─Translators─

Nguyễn Sỹ Hưng (Đồng Sỹ Hưng), BA (1981) and PhD (1988) in political science, Military-Political Sciences Academy, Moscow, Soviet Union; BA in English Language, Hanoi University of Foreign Studies (now Hanoi University), 1994.

Merle Pribbenow, BA in political science, University of Washington, Seattle, United States, 1968.

Nguyễn Huy Hiệu, MA in Teaching English to Speakers of Other Languages (TESOL), Canberra College of Advanced Education (now Canberra University), Australia, 1985; former head of Translation Section, English Department, Hanoi University of Foreign Studies (now Hanoi University).

Thomas Eugene Wilber, BA in Science and Mathematics, Pennsylvania University, 1977; MDiv, Education and Philosophy, United Theological Seminary, 1980; MBA, Supply Chain and Information Technology, Pennsylvania State University, United States, 1992.

Trần Văn, BA, Moscow State University of Geodesy and Cartography, 1981; PhD in economics, Institute of Market Problems and Economic-Ecological Research, Department of Economics, National Academy of Sciences of Ukraine, 1997.

Nguyễn Sỹ Thành, BSc in economics, London School of Economics, 2005; MBA, University of Westminster, United Kingdom, 2011.

Lieutenant Colonel Bùi Thị Thảo, BA in English Language, Foreign Language Institute, Hanoi National University, 2001.

CONTENTS

PREFACE

The aerial warfare in North Vietnam between the Vietnamese People's Air Force (VNPAF) and the combined airpower of the U.S. Air Force (USAF) and U.S. Navy (USN) lasted nearly eight years, with hundreds of thousands of combat missions carried out and more than four hundred fierce air battles fought. Over the past fifty years, a fair number of documents, books, articles, and studies on this aerial warfare have been publicized. However, the VNPAF's former leaders and fighter pilots and the Vietnamese aerial warfare researchers have long pondered the publication of a good book, both in Vietnamese and in English, on this air war. They wanted it to be compiled by the very pilots who fought in these air battles, in order to provide Vietnamese and international readers with an objective and multifarious view of the world's longest twentieth-century aerial warfare, which left a great number of historical lessons.

Besides several other books written by Vietnamese authors on the topic of the Vietnam air war, I coauthored, with other fighter pilots, the Vietnamese book entitled *Những trận không chiến trên bầu trời Việt Nam (1965–1975), Nhìn từ hai phía* (Air engagements over the skies of Vietnam (1965–1975), as viewed from both sides). This book, first published in 2013 and now on its third printing, has attracted a growing public interest, especially from the VNPAF's veteran pilots, as well as from Vietnam War students and researchers.

Enjoying support and assistance from many Vietnamese and American veteran pilots and friends, I embarked on writing a book in English on the same topic with newly acquired information. I collaborated with the Naval Institute Press, a reputable American publisher in the field of warfare, in order to get the English edition published, thereby making it accessible to readers around the world. Writing a book on this aerial warfare that lasted nearly eight years was a serious undertaking that included, among other things, collecting and studying a great number of documents from both sides, conducting meetings and interviews with former air force leaders and fighter pilots, staff officers, and ground control command officers, holding seminars, and analyzing advisers' remarks.

The book was given the title *Combat in the Sky: Airpower and the Defense of North Vietnam, 1965–1973*. It contains eight chapters depicting the events in chronological order from the first air battles, such as the one at Dragon's Jaw Bridge (April 1965), to the "Điện Biên Phủ in the Air" campaign (December 1972), then to the signing of the Paris Agreement on Ending the War and Restoring Peace in Vietnam (January 1973), and finally to the VNPAF's attacks on the parking area of South Vietnam Air Force aircraft at Tân Sơn Nhất airport (April 1975).

The aerial warfare over North Vietnam was the first modern warfare in which the two opposing sides used jet combat aircraft equipped with air-to-air missiles as the main weapons in battle. Therefore, the content of the book is not merely a chronological account of the events of the Vietnam air war, it also generalizes about most aspects of this longest air war in history. In this book, besides analyzing information about every air battle, the strategic calculations, the operations carried out, and the electronic characteristics of the weaponry used, I also analyzed the changes in tactics applied in each phase of this special type of war, in some detail. I devoted special attention to the battles, operations, and campaigns of strategic significance and importance, like Rolling Thunder, Linebacker I, Linebacker II, and the "Điện Biên Phủ in the Air" campaign.

This may be the first English version written by a Vietnamese author on the air war in Vietnam, and thus, I hope that it will help research-ers and read-ers who are interested in assessments of the results of the air battles from the

Vietnamese side. The postwar study of statistical documents shows that, in any war, the results claimed by one side often do not match those claimed by the other, and this disparity is unavoidable. With air battles, the disparity could be even greater. During the air war, both sides employed rigorous and accurate victory-confirming procedures for every claim before awarding kills. If the USAF and USN had their own procedures and mechanism for air combat credit, with requests to submit to the Enemy Claims Evaluation Board within twenty-four hours,[1] the VNPAF had its own procedures for air combat credit for MiG pilots, based on reports from a pilot claiming a kill, from his AF regiments, then AD and AF Service HQ would finally decide to credit (or not) the aerial combat victories. The problem is that each national army has its own procedures and mechanism to verify its pilots' claims of victories. But, as the saying goes, any analysis of the combat results is only theory on paper. In reality, engagements are complex occurrences and there are still many disparities. Thus, there are many different reasons for those disparities. Much has been written in documents on the topic of the Vietnam air war regarding the reasons for different assessments. Following are some of the author's analyses from the Vietnamese side of the reasons why there are different assessments.

First, one of the main reasons for this is that air battles are always very fierce, they take place in a very short time and with a high degree of maneuverability, and in most cases they are performed far from each side's air bases. In many such cases, some of the pilots who took part in these battles were listed as killed in action (KIA) or missing in action (MIA) far from the base. This made it difficult to collect the necessary information about them, and in some cases it took a decade or even, in one case, as long as thirty-two years.

Second, there are reasons related to the tactical methods and maneuvering techniques applied by pilots of both sides in battle. In some circumstances in battle, the pilot of one side thought that he was being attacked by the other side, or that his aircraft was hit by the other side's shell or missile, but it was only smoke or minor damage. He then dove down to evade through the clouds, then flew away and landed safely. It was at that point that the attacker thought he had shot down the aircraft of the other side and it could be claimed as a victory.

Third, there is the psychological reason. In acknowledging that one or some of their aircraft were shot down in North Vietnam (NVN), some U.S. pilots said that they were shot down by the surface-to-air missile (SAM) or antiaircraft artillery (AAA) units, rather than admitting that they were shot down by MiGs. The USAF and USN usually believed that they had a superior airpower that was the world's most powerful, with modern and sophisticated aircraft, and with experienced and well-trained pilots, while the VNPAF was a newly founded AF, with fewer and antiquated types of aircraft, which were piloted by young and inexperienced pilots. So such belief could make it difficult for some U.S. pilots to admit that their aircraft were shot down by MiGs. Especially in those cases in which NVN coordinated its forces, including SAMs, AAAs, and MiGs to fight against the U.S. aircraft at the same time, which caused some specific U.S. aircraft to crash. This would make it somewhat difficult for the U.S. pilots to confirm which of the above force actually shot down such aircraft.

Fourth were reasons related to statistical listing and gathering techniques and mechanisms; sometimes the difference in time zones also affected the statistical results. In addition, there were quite a large number of those deaths caused by non-air combat, including unforeseen incidents, friendly fire, ejecting as fuel ran out, and in some cases in battles, the aircraft of one side had been hit and was badly damaged but only crashed far away when flying back to its air base, so the other side did not know about that kill.

It should be noted at this point that some U.S. publications also give the reason why the win/loss ratio in the Vietnam air war was not as high as that in the Korean War. In the Korean War in particular, the North Korean (NKR) and the Chinese pilots' main objective was to shoot down the enemy's aircraft. But in the Vietnam air war, the VNPAF pilots, with their deep understanding of the characteristics of their aircraft fleet and with the application of their tactical policy, had as their primary mission to shoot down the enemy's bomber and attacker aircraft. As such, the MiG flights (each with a small number of aircraft) always avoided direct engagements with the enemy's fighter aircraft. Therefore, the U.S. fighters had less chance in the Vietnam air war to chase and shoot down MiGs than they had in the Korean War with NKR's and China's air forces.[2]

In a seminar that took place in San Diego in September 2017, with participation by a number of Vietnamese and American researchers and authors, some said that despite the unavoidable differences, the number of casualties suffered by each side were almost accurate because one could not deny the fact that in such-and-such a battle when some aircraft was/were shot down, the pilot(s) could have been killed or could have parachuted down and been either captured, killed, or rescued. In relation to the Vietnamese side, if a MiG aircraft was shot down in a battle, we would confirm the loss without evading the fact. If American documents claim that one or more MiGs were shot down in certain air battles but in fact the MiG(s) that took part in these battles landed safely at their base, based on information I have from NVN sources, I will analyze and give my opinion about the differences in assessment from both sides.

As analyzed above, there are differences in statistical figures between the two sides about the results of air engagements, and there may be some concern that the disparities mentioned in this book could became a potential matter of heated debate among researchers and enthusiasts. Although each side has and believes in its own sources of information, I believe that, since more than fifty years have passed, the statistics of the results of the air battles are only meaningful for researchers' references, which may add one or more points of view on the Vietnam air war, and which does not mean to prove anything conclusively or to confirm absolute figures. Recently, Vietnamese researchers and readers have read numerous U.S. books and articles on the Vietnam air war, in which American authors give their opinions about the results of air battles, which do not match the Vietnamese side's records. However, most Vietnamese readers and historians consider this as a second source of information, giving them a different perspective on the air war in Vietnam.

Hopefully, the contents of this book will provide American readers and researchers with an account of the Vietnam air war based on the Vietnamese side's sources, which they have previously not been able to access.

As soon as diplomatic relations between Vietnam and the United States were normalized, many former U.S. pilots traveled to Vietnam to visit the country and their old battlefields, and also to meet their adversaries of almost fifty years earlier. Besides personal trips, there were three historic meetings between delegations of veteran pilots from VNPAF and USAF/USN. At some meetings organized recently between Vietnamese and American veteran pilots, the pilots, who fought against each other almost fifty years earlier, had chances to get to know each other, and the idea of writing a book in English on the air war in Vietnam was greatly welcomed by the participants. In the meetings organized in Hanoi and San Diego, I was able to get a fair amount of important information from both sides, which helped me and interested researchers very much in enriching the knowledge of the past air war. In this book more information collected in the three meetings mentioned above has been added and updated. Moreover, in the process of my structuring of this book, some of my American friends also helped me by reading the manuscript and offering practical advice on the use of English, for which I would like to extend my deep thanks to them.

The author and the members of the VNPAF Advisory Committee and the VNPAF Pilots Editorial Advisory Board do hope that this book will have a growing readership and thus there will be more meetings in the future between veteran pilots of the two sides, which will contribute to the further development of the relationship between the Vietnamese and U.S. veteran pilots.

It has been more than fifty years since the end of the war and while only a limited number of meetings and interviews have been organized, there has been a very great amount of available documents and references, which has caused me some difficulties in my expression. Therefore, I would welcome all suggestions and comments from the readers for future editions.

ACKNOWLEDGMENTS

There are many people to thank.

Preparing this book in English has been hard but interesting work. At the very first moment when I hit upon the idea of writing and publishing this English edition, I was inspired, encouraged, and supported by many people. In particular, I give my deep thanks to the legendary pilots in the VNPAF Veterans Liaison Committee, such as Lieutenant General Trần Hanh and Major General Phạm Ngọc Lan.

My special thanks go to members of the VNPAF Advisory Committee, such as Lieutenant General Nguyễn Đức Soát, Lieutenant General Phạm Phú Thái, and Senior Colonel Nguyễn Văn Chuyên. Also to members of the VNPAF's Pilots Editorial Advisory Board and to other former VNPAF commanders, veteran pilots, and the ground control officers for their very valuable assistance in the preparation of the early manuscripts, and for the documentations, experiences, and knowledge of the Vietnam air war they shared with us in more than fifty interviews during the process of writing this book.

I am also extremely thankful for the enthusiastic encouragement and assistance I received from those VNPAF veteran commanders and pilots who are among the main characters of the book but who regrettably passed away in recent years. They are Heroes Phạm Ngọc Lan, Nguyễn Ngọc Độ, Lâm Văn Lích, Nguyễn Văn Bảy (A), Nguyễn Nhật Chiêu, Lưu Huy Chao, Nguyễn Hồng Nhị, Nguyễn Tiến Sâm, and also dedicated contributor Lữ Thông, who was a veteran pilot.

I would like to show gratitude to the leaders of the VNPA's AD and AF Service, its departments and units, and also other related departments that facilitated the writing and publishing of this book. I am also thankful to the AD and AF Service's museum photographers, who willingly gave me permission to use their photos in this book.

My thanks go to the representatives of the VNPAF pilot martyrs' families for cooperating with me in including the stories of the heroic lives and deeds of these pilot martyrs in this book.

Regarding assistance and encouragement from American friends, my sincere thanks go to Col. Charlie Tutt, USMC, and all members of the Vietnam and U.S. veteran fighter pilots' delegations at the three VN/U.S. meetings, who encouraged me to write the book in English. In particular, I would like to express my special thanks to Ambassador Douglas Brian "Pete" Peterson for his constant support and encouragement throughout this project. My special thanks also go to Mr. Merle Pribbenow, who kindly and generously helped me during my structuring of this book in English.

My thanks also go to Col. Marshall Michel III, a Vietnam air war veteran pilot who took the time to read the manuscript and gave me his valuable advice and comments on editing and publishing this work. I also would like to especially thank Mr. Thomas Eugene Wilber, Mr. John Mollison, and Mr. Joe Babcock, who helped me so much in commenting on and editing this English version, as well as allowing me to use their artwork and illustrations on the topic of the Vietnam air war.

I would also like to thank James Hoogerwerf, a U.S. veteran pilot, Susan Brook, Padraic "Pat" Carlin, and other relevant members of the Naval Institute Press for their kind help, valuable advice, and cooperation in publishing this book in the United States. At the same time, I would like to thank Dr. Brian D. Laslie and Dr. Michael Hankins for taking the time to read the entire manuscript and giving me valuable comments and advice. Dr. Laslie kindly wrote an introduction specifically for this English-language version of my book, which surely will help American readers better understand the content, and the disparity between Vietnamese and American sources of information mentioned in this book.

Any comments and recommendations for the book are gratefully welcomed and will be well received, especially those for amending the contents for further accuracy.

ABBREVIATIONS

A1C	Airman 1st class
AAA	Antiaircraft artillery
AB	Air base
ABC	Airborne mission commander
ACM	Air combat maneuvering
ACS	Air commando squadron
ACW	Air commando wing
AD	Air Defense
AF	Air Force
AFB	Air force base
AIM	Air intercept missile
ARRS	Air rescue and recovery squadron
AWACS	Airborne early warning and control system
AWC	Air war commander
B1 network	AD and AF Service's long-range radar network
BARCAP	Barrier combat air patrol
BDA	Bomb damage assessment
BS	Bomb squadron
BVR	Beyond visual range
BW	Bomber wing
CAAV	Civil Aviation Administration of Vietnam
CBU	Cluster bomb unit

CINCPAC	Commander in Chief, U.S. Pacific Command
CO	Commanding officer
CSG	Combat support group
EW	electronic warfare
FIS	Fighter interceptor squadron
FR	Fighter regiment
FW	Fighter wing
GCI	Ground controlled interception
HQ	Headquarters
IFF	Identification Friend or Foe
IKO	индикатор кругового обзора (*indikator krugovogo obzora*) [round view indicator], MiG-21 onboard radar viewfinder
JCS	Joint Chiefs of Staff
KIA	Killed in action
MAG	Marine aircraft group
MANPAD (A-72)	Soviet-built shoulder-launched missile
MATR	Military air transport regiment
MIA	Missing in action
MiG	MiG (15/17/19/21): Types of Soviet-made aircraft widely used as fighter aircraft interceptors in the Vietnam air war, manufactured by Russian aircraft manufacturer Mikoyan Gurevich
MiGCAP	MiG combat air patrol, a U.S. mission aimed at suppressing MiGs
MZ	Military zone
MZ4	Military Zone Four, one of four military zones of North Vietnam, including the provinces of Thanh Hóa, Hà Tĩnh, Nghệ An, Quảng Bình, and the Vĩnh Linh District of Quảng Trị
NAS	Naval air station
NKAF	The North Korean Air Force, which had a unit stationed at Kép airfield in the fall of 1966–67
NKR	North Korean Republic
NVN	North Vietnam

PACAF	Pacific Air Forces
PIRAZ	Positive identification radar advisory zone
POW	Prisoner of war
PTT	Post-target turn
R-3S/RS-2U/K-13	Soviet-made air-to-air missile armed in MiG-21s
RESCAP	Rescue combat air patrol
ROE	Rules of engagement
RP	Route package
RVAH	Heavy reconnaissance bombers
SAC	Strategic Air Command
SAM	Soviet-made surface-to-air missiles
SAR	Search and rescue
SEA	Southeast Asia
SOD-57	Equipment to amplify feedback signal between MiGs and the radar of the defense system; it helped to distinguish friend from foe and to identify friendly aircraft
SVN	South Vietnam
SW	Strategic wing
TAC	Tactical Air Command
TEWS	Tactical electronic warfare squadron
TFS	Tactical fighter squadron
TFW	Tactical fighter wing
TRW	Tactical reconnaissance wing
UAV	Unmanned aerial vehicle
UMiG	MiG with two cockpits, used specifically to train pilots/cadets
USAF	United States Air Force
USMC	United States Marine Corps
USN	United States Navy
USS	United States Ship
VA	Attack aircraft (USN)
VAH	Heavy attack bombers (USN)
VF	Fighting squadron, combat aircraft unit stationed on a USN aircraft carrier
VMA	Attack aircraft (USMC)

VMFA	Fighter aircraft (USMC)
VMGA	Aerial refueler (USMC)
VNP	Vietnamese People's
VNPA	Vietnamese People's Army
VNPAF	Vietnamese People's Air Force
WVR	Within visual range
X-1/X-2/X-3	Code names of the VNPAF's ground control stations in MZ4

Introduction

On 12 January 1973, the final air-to-air engagement occurred between the American armed forces and the People's Air Force of North Vietnam. In that engagement an American F-4J of the United States Navy's VF-161 fired an AIM-9 Sidewinder heat-seeking missile and downed a MiG-17. At least this is what American sources tell us. The author of this book, Đồng Sỹ Hưng (Nguyễn Sỹ Hưng), notes that an earlier engagement that occurred on the night of 8 January 1973, in which MiG-21 pilot Bùi Doãn Độ of the 921st Fighter Regiment was shot down by a missile fired by an American Air Force F-4 of the United States Air Force's 4th Tactical Fighter Squadron, was the last time a MiG aircraft fell from the skies due to an American weapon.[1] The pilot of the MiG ejected safely and lived to tell his story. Lieutenant Bùi Doãn Độ became the last MiG pilot, according to Vietnamese sources, who was shot down by an American aircraft.

Those who are in search of answers to the tragedy in Vietnam might not find them here. It is difficult to form a synthesis history that bridges the differences in both sides' sources. The average American's understanding of the air war over North Vietnam, Laos, and Cambodia is likely to remain, much like the entire war itself, as described in Secretary of Defense Robert McNamara's retrospective on the war called *Argument without End: In Search of Answers to the Vietnam Tragedy*. However, this book directly addresses the issue of the discrepancy in statistics from the North Vietnamese and American sources, and the author, in conjunction with other

Vietnamese and American scholars, has come as close as is possible to bridging the differences in the two sides' reporting. The numbers and claims of aircraft downed will never be completely resolved, but this work comes as close as possible while at the same time preserving the unique perspective of the North Vietnamese pilots.

Did the last air battle of the Vietnam War occur on 12 January or 8 January 1973? Some might see it as a question of semantics and the "true" answer largely depends on whose sources you want to believe: American or Vietnamese. Either date concludes one of the longest air wars in history. Beginning in 1965 and lasting until this final engagement, the air forces of the United States fought a back-and-forth battle with the MiG pilots of North Vietnam. Two distinct countries went to war, and that war defined both countries in the succeeding years after that conflict.

Between 1965 and the last engagement of 1973, American F-8 Crusaders, F-4 Phantoms, and F-105 Thuds fought MiG-17s, MiG-19s, and MiG-21s in hundreds of engagements. These "tussles" and "dogfights" often ended with one side or another claiming an aerial "victory" for shooting down the other side's aircraft. Most of those Americans who were "lucky" enough to eject safely were quickly captured and would spend the remainder of the war in one of the numerous prisoner-of-war (POW) camps in North Vietnam, the most well-known being the Hoa Lo Prison, known to the Americans as the Hanoi Hilton. The Vietnamese pilots who survived their ejections were shortly returned to combat.

It has been fifty years since the last missiles left the rails of American or Vietnamese aircraft. Fifty years since American fighters and North Vietnamese tumbled, dueled, and killed one another in the skies over North Vietnam. Since that time hundreds of books on the war in Vietnam have been published. Less has been written about the air war than the ground war, but it remains a verdant field with new books and memoirs published every year. That being said, there has been a considerable dearth of published material from the Vietnamese side, at least material that is readily available in English. In my own study of the air wars that occurred during the Vietnam conflict, *Air Power's Lost Cause: The American Air Wars of Vietnam*, I lamented the lack of access to the archives of Vietnam and the lack of available sources written from the perspective of the pilots of North Vietnam. Both of those thorny problems have been solved by this book.

The author of this book, with the support and cooperation of his comrades including members of the Vietnam People's Air Force Advisory Committee and VNPAF's Pilots Editorial Advisory Board, men with first-hand experiences in these battles, presents this history with forthrightness and candor. He has struggled to de-conflict the perspectives of the participants and what both countries believed to be "true." In the 1983 film *Star Wars: Return of the Jedi*, Jedi Master Obi-Wan Kenobi told Luke Skywalker that "you are going to find that many of the truths we cling to depend greatly upon our own point of view." Nowhere is that truer than in the aftermath of a conflict, and historians delving into archives should take the Jedi Master's words to heart.

In this book, *Combat in the Sky: Airpower and the Defense of North Vietnam, 1965–1973*, Đồng Sỹ Hưng (Nguyễn Sỹ Hưng) has wrestled with and reconciled many of these points-of-view problems. The result is a book told from the perspective of a pilot "who was there," but also from the perspective of someone with a firm grasp of the importance of historical narrative, historical methodology, and historiography. I hope the readers of this book will find valuable perspectives previously not accessible to the American researcher or history buff. It is a book that has been needed for many years, and it more than deserves a place on the bookshelf of anyone who wants to better understand the Vietnam War.

To the combatants on both sides of this conflict, thank you for your respective service to your countries.

—Brian D. Laslie
United States Air Force Academy
March 2022

1

Prelude

U.S. Airpower in Southeast Asia before the War

During the Cold War from the end of World War II, 1945, until the early 1990s, Western countries pursued a general strategy aimed at preventing the influence of the Soviet Union and the spreading of socialism to other countries around the world. There were "hot spots" in some areas in the world, known as local wars, among which the most notable was the involvement of the United States and some Western countries in the war in Vietnam (1964–73).

On August 5, 1964, after the Gulf of Tonkin incident, the Johnson administration authorized a retaliatory strike against naval bases and oil depots in North Vietnam (NVN), starting the U.S. war of destruction against NVN, which would last almost eight years.

In all of the United States' strategic calculations, military campaigns, and operations in Vietnam, and in many cases, even the decisive ones including the ending of the war, U.S. airpower (the USAF and the USN) had important roles to play. Some U.S. presidents, under some political schemes, decided to launch major air operations. Several American authors have mentioned that no other U.S. presidents had ever taken an interest in target selection as Lyndon Johnson did. He personally scrutinized lists of proposed targets, and the targeting, the tactics, and the rules of engagement were put under the White House's direct control, and were determined at the White House's regular Tuesday luncheons.[1] During eight years of war, the United States launched a number of air campaigns, including major ones such as Rolling Thunder (1965–68) and Linebackers I and II (1972).

UNITED STATES AIR FORCE, ORDER OF BATTLE

Shortly after the Gulf of Tonkin incident, the USAF strengthened its forces in Southeast Asia (SEA) and South Vietnam (SVN). Many USAF units were assigned and deployed in the Vietnam air war from 1964 to 1973. These were its higher-echelon units, 7/8/13 AFs, and some air divisions as well as several tactical wings/squadrons, with thousands of tactical aircraft. There were also deployments of some strategic wings (SWs) and bomb squadrons (BSs), with deployed B-52s, including five SWs attached to or deployed with KC-135A tankers. To support combat operations, there were many combat support groups with supporting aircrafts, and helicopters directly engaging in air combat missions in the skies of North Vietnam. In addition to the forces mentioned above, a number of units of the Pacific Air Forces (PACAF) also participated in combat and support operations.

During wartime, the Air Coordinating Committee, which was chaired by the commander in chief of the Seventh Air Force, coordinated between the USAF and the USN. The Seventh Air Force Command was the headquarters (HQ) of all air attack operations in NVN. In order to simplify and make clear the command arrangements of air strikes, Adm. U. S. Grant Sharp Jr. decided to allocate the targets by dividing NVN into seven geographical areas or "Route Packages" (RPs). The USAF took responsibility for RPs 1, 5, and 6A, while the USN took responsibility for RPs 2, 3, 4, and 6B, which were areas where the aircraft launched from the U.S. carriers in the Gulf of Tonkin could reach without air refueling.[2]

These USAF units were deployed at ten air bases (ABs) in South Vietnam and seven ABs in Thailand. In addition to these ABs, the USAF also occasionally used some ABs in Guam, Japan, the Philippines, and Taiwan to conduct air combat operations and support the attacks against North Vietnam.

During the war, the USAF used thousands of its most modern strategic and tactical combat aircraft. In the first stage of the war, F-4s and F-105s were mainly used in air engagements. In the second stage (1972), the USAF's F-105s were rarely used. Instead, F-4s were used as both fighters and attackers. During Linebacker II (December 1972) many B-52s were used for strategic bombing. Regarding armaments, U.S. combat aircraft were chiefly equipped with air-to-air missiles AIM-4/7/9 in various models. Besides air-to-air missiles, some types of combat aircraft (including USAF F-4s from May 1967) were also equipped with 20-mm M61A1 cannon/M3 machine guns.

UNITED STATES NAVY AVIATION, ORDER OF BATTLE

During the Vietnam War, the USN sent many aircraft carriers to take part in the Vietnam air war over NVN. At the beginning of the war, the carriers USS *Bonhomme Richard*, USS *Constellation*, USS *Ticonderoga*, and USS *Kearsarge* were ready off the NVN coast. During nearly eight years of war, seventeen USN aircraft carriers close to the Vietnamese coast conducted battle activities with a rotating period of as few as five days to as many as 208 days each. Numerous carrier-based squadrons—attack aircraft (VA), fighters (VF), heavy attack bombers (VAH), and heavy reconnaissance bombers (RVAH)—deployed with their air wings on the aircraft carriers. This wide-ranging mix of aircraft joined the air battle missions over NVN.

From March 1965, Task Force 77 developed an operating area they named "Yankee Station," located off the coast of Quảng Bình down to Đà Nẵng, so that USN aircraft could take off to attack the targets in NVN with minimal refueling while flying in and out of the battle areas. On 20 May 1965 another operating area nicknamed "Dixie Station" was established one hundred miles off Cam Ranh Bay. Other USN land-based squadrons were deployed in Thailand, SVN, and some other countries.

During the first stage of the war (1965–68) the USN mainly used F-4 B/Js and F-8s for BARCAP (barrier combat air patrol) missions. Meanwhile, aircraft including A-1, A-4, A-6, and A-7 were used to carry out attack missions. But during the second stage of the war (1972) the USN's F-8s were rarely used for combat missions. For some technical reasons, USN F-4s were not equipped with the USAF 20-mm gun pods during the war.

UNITED STATES MARINE CORPS AVIATION, ORDER OF BATTLE

The United States Marine Corps (USMC) Air Command sent numerous squadrons in rotation to participate in the Vietnam War. These forces included squadrons of attackers (VMA), fighters (VMFA), aerial refuelers (VMGR), and several squadrons of reconnaissance and supporting groups. Marine units primarily deployed Marine Aircraft Groups (MAG) at airports in SVN, air bases in Japan, and on board some U.S. aircraft carriers. During eight years of war, there were not many air engagements between USMC aircraft and VNPAF MiGs as compared with those between USAF and USN aircraft with VNPAF MiGs.

The VNPA's Vision: The Air Defense and Air Force Service before the War

With strategic vision, President Hồ Chí Minh and other leaders of NVN had predicted that sooner or later, when faced with a strategic impasse, the United States would use its airpower to attack targets deep inside NVN, even directly attack Hanoi City, the capital of Vietnam. Therefore, in the early days before the war, the Vietnamese government and the Vietnamese People's Army (VNPA) had made careful preparations and initiated plans and were ready for the fight against the U.S. special air war of destruction, and this was known to be completed by the Vietnamese government and the VNPA at a very early time.

Besides sending cadets to pilot training colleges in the Soviet Union and China, the Ministry of National Defense gave directions on and presided over the establishment and the organizational structure of the Air Defense and Air Force (AD and AF). The most important first step was the decision to establish the AD and AF Service. On 3 March 1955, Vietnam's minister of national defense, General Võ Nguyên Giáp, signed Decision No. 15/QĐA on the establishment of the Airfield Research Department under direct control of the General Staff of the VNPA. On 24 January 1959, the Ministry of National Defense issued Decision No. 319/QĐ on the establishment of the Air Force Department, and on 1 May 1959 the 919th Military Air Transport Regiment was established.

On 22 October 1963, the Ministry of National Defense issued a decision to establish the AD and AF Service, headed by Senior Colonel Phùng Thế Tài (who later became a 3-star general) as the commander in chief, Senior Colonel Đặng Tính as political commissar, and Colonel Nguyễn Quang Bích as the service's chief of staff.[3] This was the core of the national air defense system, which commanded the activities of all AD and AF units against the U.S. war of destruction in NVN.

Before and during the war more than twenty groups with more than one thousand flight cadets were sent to the Vietnamese pilot training school (the 910th AF Regiment) and pilot training schools in the Soviet Union, China, Poland, and other countries. Among them, more than four hundred pilots served at VNPAF units after graduation.[4] Before becoming fighter pilots (available to stand in combat alert duty), they had to complete the pre-air home-base combat training program in maneuverability in air engagement, using weapons to be qualified for assignment to air combat alert duty. On average, a flight student had to complete about 180–200 hours of flying time in order to graduate.[5]

By the time he joined the first combat sorties (April 1965), a VNPAF fighter pilot would have had only about 250–300 hours of flight and would still have not experienced real air-borne combat. The MiG pilots had to be ready to take off to fight against the U.S. strikers on the one hand and had to draw experience and lessons from the fights on the other, in order to adjust their operational tactics to Vietnamese conditions.

As for aircraft engineering, more than seven hundred technicians were sent to the Soviet Union and China to study how to do technical service on MiGs.

AVIATION INFRASTRUCTURE: AF INVENTORY, AIRPORT SYSTEM
AND GROUND CONTROL INTERCEPTION SYSTEM

At the end of 1965, the VNPAF had received more than twenty-eight MiG-17F aircraft equipped with targeting radars. By early 1966, MiG-21s were added to the VNPAF inventory and took part in the combat alert duties from March 1966. Besides three series of MiG-17 aircraft (A, F, and PF) during the war, the VNPAF had in its fleet several series of MiG-21 aircraft, including PF-76, FL-13, PFM-94, MF-96 series, and the last one was MiG-21bis. It should be noted that although inferior to the F-4 in speed, combat range, and firepower, the MiG-21 was a small single-seat (very difficult to spot at a distance) that did not leave a smoke trail when afterburners were switched on, was modified with better acceleration to climb up very fast to the higher altitudes, and had good maneuverability in function.

Some foreign documents gave information about the number of MiG aircraft that the VNPAF had in its combat inventory during the war.[6] Although the number of fighter aircraft of the VNPAF at any given time was very limited, even in difficult times there were only a few combat aircraft left in the fleet that were able to participate in the battles. But throughout the war, the VNPAF had in its combat inventory about 360–400 MiG-21s and MiG-17s from the Soviet Union, and about 100–140 MiG-17/19s from China (not counting UMiGs, which had two cockpits and were used for training).[7] With regard to the armaments, MiG-17s/19s were armed with 23-, 30-, and 37-mm guns. The MiG-21s were armed with R-3S, RS-2U air-to-air missiles, 23-mm (for F-96, Bis series), and 30-mm (for F-13 series) cannon. In some battles, the unguided rockets were installed in MiG-21s, but the effect of rockets was very limited. In order to test the newly equipped missiles to increase the attack power of the MiG-19, in mid-1972 some MiG-19s were modified to be able to carry two A-72 manpad-shoulder-fired missiles in some air battles.

During the war, the VNPAF had the ground control interception (GCI) system with three levels, from the AD and AF headquarters (HQ) down to AF FRs and front command posts, which were flexibly located in the main directions of battle areas. To support the GCI system, the Vietnam AD system also gradually developed a system of long-range outer perimeter radar nets (B-1 net) to scan all over the skies of NVN, and navigation ground control radars were directly located near the AF FR's command post.[8]

The building of the system of airfields located in NVN was also given urgent priority. At that time the airfields in the system included Gia Lâm, Đa Phúc (Nội Bài), Kép, Yên Bái, Kiến An, and Thọ Xuân. Besides the basic airfield system, some secondary airfields such as Anh Sơn, Hòa Lạc, Vinh, Đồng Hới, Gát, and Cẩm Thủy were also built.

It should be emphasized that the VNPAF was not alone in the war of resistance against the USAF and USN. Together with the AD forces, the AF was one of the core response elements of the People's AD system. Its units fought in very tight coordination with forces of surface-to-air missiles (SAM) (from July 1965) and antiaircraft artillery (AAA) of all types. In order to ensure better command and coordination in combat, the Air Defense System (MiG-SAM-AAA) divided the combat area into four combat zones (four perimeters of firepower): (1) AAA perimeter closest to Hanoi and some big cities, (2) combat zone for MiG-17 aircraft, (3) SAM perimeter, and (4) outer combat zone for MiG-21 aircraft. It should be noted, however, that the coordination between MiG-17 and MiG-21 aircraft in some air battles was not limited to their combat zones but also extended to the altitude and their mission.

THE 921st FR: THE RED STAR GROUP

The 921st FR was established by Decision No. 18/QĐ, signed by Vice Minister of National Defense Lieutenant General Hoàng Văn Thái on 30 May 1963. The core force of this unit was the flight trainees and technician trainees of the first training group sent to China for training. The day that the establishment of the regiment was officially announced was 3 February 1964 when Major General Trần Qúy Hai, the vice chief of the General Staff, officiated at a ceremony in which he read the Ministry of National Defense order establishing the 921st FR (Red Star Group). The regiment's first commander was the pilot Lieutenant Colonel Đào Đình Luyện; the political commissar was Major Đỗ Long; the vice political commissar was Major Chu Duy Kính; pilot Major Trần Mạnh was the deputy regiment commander; and Major Lê Văn Thọ was the chief of staff and concurrently the chief of rear services.

With regard to personnel, all of the pilots who graduated from the first flight training course in China were assigned to the regiment with a total of seventy pilots, thirty of whom had satisfactorily completed the entire training course and were able to perform combat alert duty. The other pilots were graduates from later courses and were qualified to fly the MiG-15bis and were waiting for conversion training to be qualified to fly the MiG-17. In terms of the regiment's aircraft, in accordance with an agreement signed by the governments of Vietnam and the Soviet Union on 12 April 1963, the Soviet Union had turned over to Vietnam thirty-six jet aircraft (thirty-two

MiG-17As and four UMiG-15s trainer aircraft). The main mission of the 921st FR was to join and coordinate with the AD forces as the core force of the national air defense system against the U.S. war of destruction in NVN.

On 2 August 1964, the NVN People's Navy torpedo boats clashed and exchanged fire with USS *Maddox* to defend the territorial waters of Vietnam in what would be a much disputed incident. On 4 August 1964, the crew-members of the *Maddox* mistook their own sonar's pings off rudder for the NVN People's Navy's torpedoes, and fabricated the story of the Gulf of Tonkin incident. On 5 August 1964, the Johnson administration, having received this information, used it as an excuse to launch the war of destruction against NVN,[9] with the goal of destroying the economic and military potentials of NVN and preventing NVN military aid to SVN and, as Gen. Curtis LeMay aggressively declared, bombing NVN back into the Stone Age.[10]

On 6 August 1964, thirty-two MiG-17A aircraft of the 921st FR were mobilized from Mông Tự airport in China to Đa Phúc airfield in Vietnam and on the same day took the air combat alert duty at the airport immediately.[11]

The first commander of the 921st FR was Lieutenant Colonel Đào Đình Luyện (born in 1929, participated in Điện Biên Phủ Campaign, 1954), who later became a VNPA three-star general, commander in chief of the AD and AF Service, and chief of the General Staff of the VNPA. He retired in 1997 and died in 1999.

2

1965

THE AIR FRONT
OPENED UP

On 13 February 1965, President Johnson allowed Operation Rolling Thunder to be carried out, to strike the most important targets in North Vietnam. The operation lasted until 30 October 1968.

During the first stage of the operation, until early April 1965, USAF and USN aircraft encountered only AAA and ground antiaircraft guns at low altitudes. But from 3 April 1965, VNPAF MiGs engaged the air front and initiated encounters with U.S. aircraft. From July 1965 the U.S. forces were also confronted by SAMs. Even though the VNPAF and its fighter pilots were very young and had less airborne combat experiences, they skillfully and courageously fought against very well-trained and experienced U.S. pilots. These air engagements between VNPAF and the USAF and USN in April 1965 were very fierce.

3 April 1965: Opening Up the Air Front

On 1 February 1965, General Võ Nguyên Giáp, Vietnam's minister of national defense, and General Văn Tiến Dũng, the chief of the General Staff, were briefed with a report from the AD and AF Service Command on the VNPAF readiness situation. By the end of February 1965, the pre-air combat training program of the 921st FR was completed and most of the MiG pilots were qualified and available to stand on combat alert duty. The commander of the 921st FR, Lieutenant Colonel Đào Đình Luyện, officially reported to the AD and AF HQ about the combat readiness of the regiment.[1]

From March to early April 1965, after analyzing the strategic intelligence reports and the operating patterns of the USAF activities, the AD and AF Service HQ predicted that after the bad weather season, in about early April, the USAF would bomb Hàm Rồng (Dragon's Jaw) Bridge and targets north of the twentieth parallel. The 921st FR decided to choose 3 April 1965 as the date of the first battle with which the air front would open up. On the evening of 2 April 1965, Lieutenant Colonel Đào Đình Luyện assigned the regiment's flights the combat mission duty.

Exactly as the AD and AF Service had predicted, on 3 April 1965 the USAF strike formation flew in to attack targets in the area of Hàm Rồng Bridge in Thanh Hóa Province. The strike formation consisted of a total of more than seventy aircraft, including forty-six F-105 Thunderchiefs assigned to bomb the targets, twenty-one F-100 Super Sabres assigned to suppress the MiGs (MiGCAP), two RF-101 Voodoos to fly reconnaissance, and ten KC-135 aerial tanker aircraft. Meanwhile, on 3 April 1965, the USN aircraft including thirty-five A-4s, sixteen F-8Es, and four F-4Bs from the aircraft carriers USS *Hancock* and USS *Coral Sea* conducted two strike missions against bridges in Thanh Hóa.

Because of the significance of this first battle, which would successfully open up the air front, almost all high-level officers of the AD and AF Service Command were present at the HQ command post. Around the command table were the commander in chief, Senior Colonel Phùng Thế Tài, together with Senior Colonel Đặng Tính, the service's political commissar, and the service's deputy chief of staff Hoàng Ngọc Diêu. The duty ground control interception (GCI) officers were Trần Quang Kính and Đào Ngọc Ngư. At the 921st FR command post, Regiment Commander Đào Đình Luyện supervised the operations. The regiment's GCI officers were Bùi Quang Liên and Phạm Minh Cậy.

Based on the analysis of the situation and the activities of the USAF during the preceding days, the AD and AF Service Command post issued the following combat orders to the 921st FR: a flight of two MiG-17s would fly a supporting diversionary mission at an altitude of 20,000 feet, while the primary attack flight of four MiG-17s would attack the enemy attack bombers whose targets were Hàm Rồng Bridge and Bìm Sơn areas in Thanh Hóa

Province. The combat order was disseminated to the fighter companies during the night of 2 April. At 0500 hours on 3 April 1967 the combat alert duty flights were all ready. The battle plan called for the use of six MiG-17As in the following manner: (1) The attack flight consisting of four MiG-17As (without afterburner): Phạm Ngọc Lan, No. 1 (aircraft No. 2310); Phan Văn Túc, No. 2 (aircraft No. 2118); Hồ Văn Qùy, No. 3 (aircraft No. 2312); and Trần Minh Phương, No. 4 (aircraft No. 2318). (2) The diversionary flight consisting of two MiG-17As to attract the enemy fighters and be prepared to support and cover the attack flight: Trần Hanh, No. 1 (aircraft No. 2316) and Phạm Giấy, No. 2 (aircraft No. 2416). The weather in the designated battle area was predicted to be three-tenths cumulus cloud covering an altitude of 1,000 feet. Visibility after 1000 hours was predicted to be more than 6.5 miles with a layer of mist between 700 feet and 9,000 feet.

This would be the battle in which the VNPAF would open up the air battle front, and for that reason everyone from the senior command officers down to the pilots and support personnel were all very resolute and determined. At 0700 hours the USN sent an aircraft in to conduct weather reconnaissance and to reconnoiter the key targets. After this flight, the area around Hàm Rồng Bridge became very quiet. At the command post everyone felt very tense. No one knew exactly which area would be the focus of the USAF's primary attack. This would be the first time that the service HQ command post commanded an air battle between the VNPAF and the world's most powerful AF. At 0940 hours the service command post and the visual observation posts detected U.S. aircraft flying in to attack the bridges along Route 1 (Hàm Rồng, Tào, and Đò Lèn Bridges). The attack group was led by the commander of the 67th TFS (Tactical Fighter Squadron), Lt. Col. Robinson Risner.

From the very first moments of the U.S. aircraft's attack wave, on the Vietnamese side, the antiaircraft guns of the 234th AAA Regiment and those of the local air defense forces fought courageously. They shot down one USN A-4C and captured its pilot, Lt. Cdr. Raymond Arthur Vohden of VA-216 based on the USS *Hancock*. The two-aircraft diversionary flight took off at 0947 hours and flew on a heading of 190° to Ninh Bình at an altitude of 19,000 feet. One minute later the attack flight took off, penetrated the cloud layer, and was directed to fly on a 210° heading.

A few minutes later, the flight was ordered to turn to a heading of 70°. Just after that, Trần Minh Phương reported that he had spotted a target—the formation of F-8s on the right heading straight toward his flight while a number of other enemy aircraft were attacking AAA positions around Hàm Rồng Bridge. This was a formation of four F-8Es escorting a group of six A-4Es and A-4Cs that were assigned to attack targets in the area of Hàm Rồng and Đò Lèn Bridges. Meanwhile, high overhead were F-4Bs assigned to intercept MiGs. At that time, a second formation of F-8s led by Lt. Cdr. Spence Thomas was in the process of making their attack dives against the target from an altitude of 10,000 feet.

The MiG lead shouted an order: "Drop external fuel tanks, increase speed and engage the F-8 formation." Exactly acting upon the combat plan, the flight split into two sections. After making a tight turn to chase the target, when Phạm Ngọc Lan ordered his wingman to attack, No. 2 immediately made a hard turn toward the F-8s. Having realized that the MiGs were chasing them, the F-8 pilot made a hard turn to engage in a dogfight. After evading the MiG attack, the lead F-8 pulled up in a climb to 10,000 feet and looked for his No. 2, who had disappeared in the clouds. At that moment, Phạm Ngọc Lan quickly got on the F-8's tail and brought it into his sight and when the range was right, pressed his trigger. The F-8 was hit, began to burn, and dove toward the ground. The time was 1014 hours on 3 April 1965. This was a historic moment when a VNPAF MiG for the first time shot down a U.S. aircraft, a USN F-8, in an air battle in the sky over North Vietnam.

Realizing that his aircraft had been hit, Lieutenant Commander Thomas initially thought he had been hit by antiaircraft guns from the ground, but as soon as he turned to look to the rear, he saw four MiGs chasing his aircraft. The MiG-17's shells had hit the wing and the tail fin, and damaged the aircraft's hydraulic system, causing the F-8 No. 1 to fall out of the sky. Just after that, when he spotted the F-8 No. 2, Phan Văn Túc quickly approached it from the rear and above, then he dove and fired a burst. The F-8 was hit, began to burn, and dove into the ground. Coinciding with the air activities of the two lead MiGs, Hồ Văn Qùy in No. 3 pursued the other F-8 of the second section ferociously and fired two long bursts from his guns, but the range was too great so the enemy aircraft fled to escape back out over the sea.

When the command post gave the order to break off the engagement, Hồ Văn Qùy joined up with MiGs No. 2 and No. 4 to fly back to land at Đa

Phúc airfield. As for MiG No. 1, because he had run out of fuel he decided to make a forced landing on a sand bar along the banks of the Đuống River. The pilot was not injured and the aircraft was later recovered, repaired, and was in good condition again

In summary, during the battle of 3 April 1965 the flight of four MiG-17s shot down two USN F-8s.[2] This was the VNPAF's first battle and its first victory, thereby successfully opening up the air front. Thus began the air war in Vietnam, which would last more than seven years.[3]

Pilot Phạm Ngọc Lan, lead of the MiG-17 flight that opened up the air front with the battle on 3 April 1965, was later promoted to the rank of major general and appointed deputy director of the VNP Army's Operational Training Department. He was awarded the honorable title VNP Armed Forces Hero.

MiG-17s IN THE CONFLICT

The first batch of MiG-17 aircraft that VNPAF received in mid-1964 consisted of thirty-two MiG-17As and four UMiG-15s, which were then assigned to the 921st FR. In September 1965 when the 923rd FR was established, its fleet was equipped with, among other things, all MiG-17s. According to some foreign sources, during the war, the VNPAF had in its fighter aircraft inventory more than three hundred MiG-17s with three series: A/F/PF. With regard to the armaments, a MiG-17 was equipped with only two 23-mm guns and one 37-mm gun, was not equipped with air-to-air missiles (AIM), and was technically backward in comparison with the U.S. modern types of aircraft such as the F-4, F-105, and F-8. However, during the war, pilots of MiG-17s shot down 118 U.S. aircraft (including nine unmanned aerial vehicles, UAVs). Six of the VNPAF aces were MiG-17 pilots. Beside air combat records, MiG-17 pilots Lê Xuân Dỵ and Nguyễn Văn Bảy (B) accomplished a mission to attack the USS *Higbee* and USS *Oklahoma City* on 19 April 1972 and forced them to go back to Philippine Bay for major repair.

4 April 1965: First Clash between MiG-17s and F-105s

Right after the first victory in the air battle on 3 April 1965, on the night of the same day, the 921st FR held a review of its victorious first battle in order to draw combat experience, strengthen its determination to fight, and work on the development of combat tactics for the next day's battle. The AD and AF Service HQ anticipated that since the USAF had not been able to destroy Hàm Rồng Bridge, it would attack this target again. Also it was believed that after this first aerial engagement the Americans did not yet take the VNPAF seriously and that they would not have had time to change their methods of countering the MiGs. Even though the VNPAF did not expect to repeat the element of complete surprise it had adapted in the first battle, the experience drawn after the first battle was that the VNPAF still could gain the element of surprise by selecting the right time to take off, by employing a diversionary flight, and by coordinating its efforts with the AAA forces, by having the AAA units encounter the enemy first, and then VNPAF fighter aircraft would make their appearance.

The combat plan devised by the AD and AF Service Command was as follows: because on 3 April the VNPAF MiGs had come in from the west to attack the USN strike formation, the U.S. forces would probably have their fighters assigned to suppress the MiGs that were in a holding pattern and waiting in the west. The AD and AF Service Command decided to have a diversionary MiG-17 flight fly at an altitude of 25,000 feet to entice the U.S. fighters to stay in the west. Meanwhile, after taking off, the attack flight would fly in from the southeast at a low altitude. Only when the flight reached the designated combat area would the fighters climb up to an altitude favorable for a tactical advantage. At the Service's command post, Deputy Service Commander Colonel Nguyễn Văn Tiên was in charge of the command duty team, and the GCI's officers on duty were Trần Quang Kính and Đào Ngọc Ngư.

In the early morning of Sunday, April 4, many USN aircraft flew in to reconnoiter the Thanh Hóa area and check the weather conditions. In an attempt to knock down Hàm Rồng Bridge, the USAF strike force was increased to a total of forty-eight F-105Ds accompanied by ten F-100Ds as fighter escorts. Squadron Commander Lt. Col. Robinson Risner would again lead the strike formation. In addition, more than thirty USN F-4Bs were assigned to provide air cover support if and when needed. The weather on 4 April was bad, with a thick layer of dry haze between 12,000 and 15,000 feet in altitude, which meant that the attack bombers would have to circle in a holding pattern south of Hàm Rồng Bridge in order to attack the target by one aircraft after another.

The 921st FR assigned the primary attack mission to a flight consisting of pilots Trần Hanh, Phạm Giấy, Lê Minh Huân, and Trần Nguyên Năm. The diversionary flight, piloted by Lê Trọng Long, Phan Văn Túc, Hồ Văn Qùy, and Trần Minh Phương took off at 1020 hours, teamed up after penetrating the top of the cloud layer, and then flew over the area south of Vụ Bản at an altitude of 26,000 feet in order to deceive the enemy, to lure the U.S. fighters in from the west, and to be ready to support and cover the attack flight. The attack flight took off at 1022 hours and flew on a heading of 230 degrees before suddenly turning down to the southeast and heading to the designated battle area. At 1030 hours all of the pilots reported spotting enemy aircraft flying in from the east. The MiG lead Trần Hanh spotted four F-105Ds (with two rear aircraft flying 1.2 miles behind the two lead aircraft) pulling up in a climb after dropping their bombs. This was a formation of F-105Ds from the 354th TFS (Tactical Fighter Squadron) of the 355th TFW (Tactical Fighter Wing), assigned to the bomber mission as part of the F-105 strike formation assigned to attack targets in the area of Hàm Rồng Bridge. It became clear that the USAF had learned lessons from the air battle of 3 April because on 4 April it had assigned ten F-100Ds to escort the attack bomber aircraft. The F-100Ds were split into two four-aircraft formations, with the two remaining aircraft assigned to the bomb damage assessment (BDA) reconnaissance and weather check mission. Because the F-105Ds were so heavily loaded and because they had to fly in a holding pattern to wait for their turn to drop their bombs, all of them were flying at speeds of between 370 and 400 mph. That was not a good speed for them if they had to shift to air combat mode. The F-100Ds assigned to escort duties had to reduce their speed in order to stay with the F-105Ds. For that reason, when they spotted the MiGs it would take them some time to gain sufficient speed to engage in air combat against the MiGs.

Meanwhile, Trần Hanh's flight of MiG-17s had skillfully slipped in between the formation of F-105Ds and that of F-100s in order to get into position to attack the USAF attack bombers. The MiG pilots looked around and saw a formation of four F-105s that was circling in a holding pattern at an altitude of 16,000 feet and a speed of 370 mph. (This might have been the formation that was flying in the center of the attack formation.)

Seeing that the F-105 flying in the lead position had lost altitude and was climbing, Trần Hanh decided to pursue this aircraft. After ordering his wingman to cover him, Trần Hanh got on the tail of the F-105D. Just at that moment, the F-105s had begun their circular holding pattern (orbit) to wait for their turn to drop their bombs. The F-105 No. 3 reported that he spotted two unidentified aircraft making a diving approach about two miles behind the F-105Ds. When the two aircraft were 0.8 miles away, the F-105 pilot realized that they were two MiGs and saw that they were getting into firing position to attack the two lead F-105s. The pilots of the F-105 No. 3 and No. 4 called out a warning to the two lead F-105s, but they did not see any reaction from them. Trần Hanh's MiG began to get into attack position, and when the range to the target was down to 450 yards, he fired two bursts from his guns. He missed, but he then calmly took aim a third time. When the range was just 160 yards he squeezed the trigger, firing all three of his cannon, and he saw his shells hit both wings. The F-105 began to smoke, flipped upside down, exploded, and fell toward the ground. Trần Hanh's MiG-17 flashed right past the nose of the now-burning F-105. The pilot of the F-105D that Trần Hanh shot down was Maj. Frank Everett Bennett from the 354th TFS of the 355th TFW.[4] Bennett's aircraft had been hit and although the pilot tried to fly back out to the sea, the aircraft crashed eighteen miles from Thanh Hóa, near Hòn Mê Island. Bennett was able to eject and parachute into the water, but he drowned before the rescue forces arrived. This was the first F-105 Thunderchief (sometimes called the "Thud") shot down by MiGs in the air war over North Vietnam.[5]

At the same time, Lê Minh Huân, supported and covered by Trần Nguyên Năm, opened fire at the F-105D flying in the No. 2 position. A number of cannon shells hit the fuselage of the F-105D flown by Capt. James A. Magnusson of the 354th TFS of the 355th TFW, causing the Thud to crash twenty miles south of Thanh Hóa. Almost immediately after firing, Lê Minh Huân made a hard turn because he was worried that a USAF F-100D might be chasing him. When the GCI gave the order to break off the engagement, MiGs No. 3 and No. 4 responded, "There are too many enemy aircraft. We can not break away," and the two pilots resolved on fighting to the end. MiGs No. 3 and No. 4 fought a ferocious turning dogfight against a large number of F-100Ds in the skies over Hà Trung–Lạch Trường–Nga Sơn.

Shortly after shooting down the F-105 and turning away to break off the engagement, Trần Hanh saw some F-100Ds closing in behind him. When an

F-100D pilot launched a missile, he immediately flipped his aircraft upside down and pulled his aircraft into a very high-G dive. Just as the nose of his aircraft was about 30 degrees below the horizon, two Sidewinder missiles flashed past his aircraft. Trần Hanh's maneuver was so violent that his landing gear popped out of its locked position and his gyrocompass system was damaged, which made it impossible for the pilot to determine his location thereafter. The MiG flight was now split into two sections. The first one, consisting of Trần Hanh and Phạm Giấy, fought the F-100Ds that were assigned to MiGCAP duty south of the Hàm Rồng Bridge, while Lê Minh Huân and Trần Nguyên Năm engaged in dogfighting against another formation of F-100Ds north of Hàm Rồng Bridge.

After hearing the warning calls from the MiGCAP formation, the four F-100Ds assigned to rescue combat air patrol (RESCAP) duty spotted one MiG-17 (this might have been Trần Hanh's MiG-17) right in front of them and headed straight toward it. When discovered that two more MiGs were chasing behind, the F-100D No. 1 had only enough time to warn his No. 2 and shouted, "Switch to afterburner and turn hard!" The F-100Ds made a sharp turn that caused the two MiGs to pass right by and get ahead of them. At that moment, however, the MiG, using a skillful maneuver, made a hard turn and got right on the tail of the F-100D No. 1, which was out ahead of the rest of its formation. The F-100D pilot then suddenly had to climb to break off the attack because his altitude was already so low.

As for Trần Hanh, after breaking off and exiting the battle area at a low altitude, he found that he had lost radio contact with the GCI post, that he could not determine his exact position, and that his fuel tanks were almost dry (he had only a little over 100 liters of fuel left). He decided to eject and abandon his aircraft, but then he saw a level, flat area below him, changed his mind, and decided to try to land in a valley at Kẻ Tằm village in Nghệ An Province. After touching down next to a small stream, he saw a high earth mound ahead of him so he stomped on his rudder pedal in order to turn his aircraft sideways. The aircraft slid some distance farther and then came to stop in the middle of a rice field with mud that was about six inches deep. The pilot passed out for a moment. When he came to consciousness again, he found himself sitting behind the control stick.[6]

Pilot Trần Hanh, the lead of the MiG-17 flight, who was the first pilot to shoot down one USAF F-105, was later promoted to the rank of lieutenant general and appointed commander in chief of the VNP AD and AF Service, and then vice minister of national defense. He was awarded the honorable title VNP Armed Forces Hero.

THE FIRST TWO AIR ENGAGEMENTS: ASSESSMENT AND ANALYSIS

The engagement between MiG17s and F-8s in the skies over North Vietnam on 3 April was a surprise to American pilots. Two MiG-17s shot down two F-8s and none of the MiG aircraft were shot down. As MiG No. 1 ran out of fuel, the pilot decided to make a forced landing at Đuống River. All four pilots returned to base safely. This was a very effective victory, with a score of 2–0 in favor of the VNPAF.

A number of American documents on the 4 April 1965 battle stated that three F-105Ds had been lost, but the third F-105 loss was probably due to ground fire, although this was not confirmed.[7] When those records were made, the Vietnamese did not know about that information. Based on an analysis of the actions of the MiGs during this air battle, this third F-105D may have been shot down by either Phạm Giấy or Trần Nguyên Năm. The results of the first two battles were that the USAF lost five aircraft, without any victories, regardless of Capt. Donald W. Kilgus' claim that he shot down a MiG-17. The United States did not officially give Kilgus credit for this kill, and only recorded "possibly shot down/possible kill."[8] However, the VNPAF has publicly acknowledged that three VNPAF pilots were killed in this battle (Phạm Giấy, Lê Minh Huân, and Trần Nguyên Năm).[9]

For the VNPAF, before the first two engagements, the MiG-17 pilots had had no airborne combat experience, but during these two engagements they had good tactical sense. They promoted their own strength in horizontal maneuvers, they were close shot by guns, they had good cooperation between the attack and the support flights (diversionary aircraft), and they managed to shoot down five U.S. aircraft. However, in the first two battles, the 921st FR lost five aircraft, and three pilots were killed in action.

Obviously, the first two air battles gave VNPAF pilots valuable lessons in aerial combat. At the same time, these two victorious air battles successfully launched the aerial front against the U.S. war of destruction in NVN. Also, on 5 April 1965, Minister of National Defense General Võ Nguyên Giáp visited the AD and AF HQ to hear the report on the results of the first two air battles. He also highly appreciated the success of the 921st FR and ordered the continuation of the training program while constantly maintaining a readiness to accomplish all air combat missions.

Air Engagement on 4 June 1965

After scoring victories in its first two battles on 3 and 4 April 1965, but also suffering heavy losses in these two battles (losing five aircraft and three pilots), the 921st FR decided to temporarily suspend combat sorties in order to reorganize its forces, draw lessons from the first encounters, work out suitable combat tactics, and conduct additional training. Many different plans for attacking the U.S. fighters and attack bombers were discussed and began to take shape. The MiG pilots who were there recalled that, at the very start of the war, numerous "open tactic discussion-seminars" were held.[10] At these conferences officers at the command level and the pilots who had personally participated in the battles carefully analyzed the different combat situations and actions, successes and mistakes made during the course of these battles, and suggested new battle plans.

In the period between April and June 1965, the USAF escalated their attacks, striking many places in North Vietnam. In the early morning of 4 June, the USAF attack aircraft flew in to attack Route 15 in the Quan Hóa–Bá Thước (Thanh Hóa Province) area and then expanded their attacks from Suối Rút stream out to Thiệu Yên. Anticipating that the USAF would conduct armed reconnaissance missions, the AD and AF Service Command decided to use MiG-17s to take the Americans by surprise by attacking the reconnaissance flights as they were headed back home after completing their mission. The 921st FR entrusted this combat mission to a four-aircraft flight consisting of Lâm Văn Lích, Nguyễn Nhật Chiêu, Hồ Văn Qùy, and Trần Minh Phương.

The fighter flight took off at 0555 hours, climbed to gain altitude, and headed for Nho Quan–Ninh Bình Province. Five minutes later the flight made a hard right turn to a bearing of 340 degrees. At that time the GCI's post picked up a group of F-4s (fighter escorts for the F-105s) that was turning left to head for Quan Hóa–Thanh Hóa Province. The command post issued an order to change the plan of attacking the reconnaissance aircraft, and instead ordered the flight to fly toward the Hồi Xuân ferry crossing in order to intercept the F-4s and F-105s. Seeing that the enemy aircraft were 4.5 miles ahead, MiG No. 1 ordered the flight to turn left to pursue the targets. Having realized that MiGs were pursuing them, the F-4s immediately began making a "Figure S" weaving maneuver along Route 15. However, the MiGs continued to stay right on the tails of the American aircraft. Hồ Văn Qùy checked the rear and saw two enemy aircraft heading toward the MiGs. Seizing this opportunity, he turned back to the rear, got into attack position, and fired. His first burst of shells missed, falling behind the tail of the enemy aircraft, but his second burst hit the F-4. The damaged F-4 tried to make it to the coast but it crashed when it was ten miles east of Thọ Xuân. The MiGs formed into two two-aircraft sections, returned to Đa Phúc airfield, and landed safely.[11]

17 June 1965: First Engagement between MiG-17s and USN F-4s

After a period (from 4 to 16 June) of temporary suspension of Operation Rolling Thunder, on 17 June the USAF again sent in strike forces to attack Hàm Rồng Bridge. In order to support the attack strikes the United States sent in EC-121D aircraft equipped with airborne early warning and control systems (AWACS) to Saigon to provide direct command over USAF and USN air operations. They also committed EB-66 and EA-1F EW aircraft to the battle to try to jam the NVN AD command's radar network.

Due to the great significance of the battle, the 921st FR decided to set up a forceful formation consisting of the senior officers of two fighter companies on combat alert duty. The pilots were Lâm Văn Lích (regimental chief of flight techniques), Cao Thanh Tịnh (commander of the 3rd Fighter Company), Lê Trọng Long (deputy commander of the 1st Fighter Company) and Nguyễn Nhật Chiêu (platoon commander from the 1st Fighter Company). This formation of four MiG-17s was given the mission of attacking the enemy attackers, but after taking off and flying toward Ninh Bình, the formation unexpectedly encountered a formation of USN F-4 fighters in the skies over Nho Quan, Ninh Bình. Meanwhile a strike formation of fourteen A-4 Skyhawks from the aircraft carriers USS *Midway* and USS *Bonhomme Richard* were flying in to attack Hàm Rồng Bridge. The USN had assigned six F-4Bs from VF-21 (the unit that had clashed with the Chinese AF near

Hainan Island on 9 April) from the USS *Midway* to provide support and suppress the MiGs. This fighter formation was led by VF-21's executive officer Cdr. Louis Page (with Lt. John C. Smith Jr. in the backseat) in an F-4B.

Having spotted the F-4s at a range of four miles heading toward the MiGs, Lâm Văn Lích ordered his formation to drop their external fuel tanks and to turn toward the F-4s. The air battle between the MiGs and the F-4s lasted only two minutes. Pilots Lâm Văn Lích and Lê Trọng Long each shot down one F-4.[12] Realizing that four MiGs were heading to attack his aircraft, the F-4 No. 1 ordered his pilots to shift to combat formation to engage the MiGs. However, fearful of misidentifying other American aircraft, which might have led to shooting down friendly aircraft by mistake, the formation did not dare to attack immediately. During this period the USAF and USN followed the rules of engagement (ROE). Then F-4 No. 1 increased speed and flew ahead in order to visually identify the target.

After identifying the other aircraft as MiGs, the F-4B No. 1 got in behind the MiG No. 2 and fired a missile at him. At the same time, the F-4 No. 2 launched two AIM-7 missiles and shot down MiG No. 4. The MiG pilot bailed out and descended safely to the ground. Just at that very moment, the two remaining MiGs turned hard to get on the tails of the F-4Bs. The two F-4Bs switched on their afterburners, pulled into a climb, flew into the clouds, then rolled back over and increased speed to escape. While maneuvering in a ferocious dogfight with the F-4s, Lê Trọng Long bravely and skillfully maneuvered against several USN F-4s and shot down one F-4B, but after that he was killed while pursuing the second F-4.

That left only MiG No. 1, Lâm Văn Lích, who was able to return and land safely at Đa Phúc airfield. According to the records of the 921st FR, the reason for these losses was that the MiGs were not able to reach the enemy attack bombers and instead were drawn into an air battle against the USN fighters. During the air battle on 17 June, MiG-17 pilots for the first time shot down two F-4Bs.[13] However, the VNPAF also publicly acknowledged that three MiGs were lost. Two pilots ejected and parachuted safely (Nguyễn Nhật Chiêu and Cao Thanh Tịnh), but Lê Trọng Long was killed. This was another air battle in which the VNPAF suffered heavy losses. As for the USAF and USN, this was the first time that the USN shot down a MiG.

The American pilots only claimed credit for shooting down two MiG-17s but some thirty-two years later, in 1997, based on information from NVN admitting that three MiG-17s were shot down on 17 June 1965,[14] and after analyzing the declassification of documents relating to the 17 June 1965 engagement, Lt. Jack E. D. Batson Jr. and Lt. Cdr. Robert B. Doremus were credited with shooting down one more MiG-17 (this meant that these pilots were credited with shooting down two MiGs). The F-4B pilots described that the two MiG were flying close together and MiG No. 3 had been damaged by ingesting debris from his wingman's exploded aircraft, after which it was hit by the F-4's Sparrow, then the second MiG also crashed.[15]

Although Lieutenant Batson's report was only examined thirty-two years later as part of the effort to confirm this claim, it seems more logical than the theory that Lê Trọng Long flew into a mountain, because he was an excellent pilot and the possibility that he flew into a mountain while making hard turns at low altitudes is very unlikely.

20 June 1965: MiG-17s versus A-1Hs

On 20 June 1965, while a number of F-4C formations attacked targets in Sơn La, an F-4C flown by Capt. Paul Anthony Kari and back-seater Curt H. Briggs was reported to have been shot down by a MiG-17 near Điện Biên Phủ in northwestern Vietnam (the Vietnamese side had no information about this engagement). Captain Kari was captured but Captain Briggs escaped and was rescued a few days later.

After Kari's F-4C was shot down, the USN sent a formation of four A-1H Skyraiders, propeller-driven aircraft of the VA-25, which took off from the aircraft carrier USS *Midway* to carry out a search and rescue (RESCAP) mission. The four A-1Hs, led by Lt. Cdr. Ed Greathouse, flew in a formation of two two-aircraft sections in order to support each other if attacked by MiGs.

Guessing that the USAF and USN would again attack the targets in Quan Hóa–Bá Thước–Thanh Hóa Province, the AD and AF Command ordered the 921st FR to arrange for its MiG-17s to intercept and engage the USN attack bombers. Two MiG-17 pilots, Mai Đức Toại and Nguyễn Văn Lai, were ordered to take off and then directed to fly on a heading of 230 degrees. When the A-1Hs were flying fifty miles northwest of Thanh Hóa, A-1H No. 1 spotted two MiG-17s above to the right at a bearing of 90

degrees. Realizing that the two MiGs had flown right past the A-1H formation, the GCI officer Nguyễn Văn Chuyên ordered the MiGs to turn left to
a heading of 170 degrees and turn in to approach the A-1H formation from
the right-hand side (this occurred at the very time that the American pilots
decided that the MiG-17s had not seen them when flying past them overhead). Even though the MiGs had lost the element of surprise, they still saw
the A-1Hs as they performed a 50-degree dive and leveled off at an altitude
of five hundred feet above the surface of the river, which ran in between two
parallel mountain ranges. The two MiG-17s resumed the chase and both aircraft simultaneously fired two volleys. Nguyễn Văn Lai got on the tail of the
A-1H No. 1, and opened fire at a range of approximately 120 yards. The formation of four A-1Hs was flying above the river on a heading to the southeast, with mountains between 450 feet and 1,600 feet high on both sides
(based on the description of the U.S. pilots this may have been the stretch of
Mã River between Bá Thước and Cẩm Thủy–Thanh Hóa Province). Since
the A-1Hs were hemmed in by the mountains they could neither turn
left to evade the attackers nor turn in a circle between the two mountain
ranges. They then split into two two-aircraft sections and maintained an extremely low altitude hedge-hopping above the mountain slopes on the right
in the hope that the MiG-17s would not be able to achieve a good firing
angle on them.

Having a stable sight of the A-1Hs, the MiG-17 lead Mai Đức Toại began
firing, but because the A-1Hs were making such extreme evasive maneuvers
the MiG-17's shells skipped along the surface of the water in front of the target. When the MiG-17 pulled up to gain altitude in order to make another
attack dive on the target from the left-hand side, A-1H No. 1 was forced to
make a hard, high G turn in between two mountain peaks at an extremely
low altitude. Acknowledging that they could not continue to make tight
turns at low altitudes while carrying all the ordnance under their wings, the
A-1H No. 1 pilot ordered his formation to jettison all of their bombs, even
though they had not yet accomplished their mission.

While chasing the A-1H formation flying low along the river and not
daring to make any extreme maneuvers, Nguyễn Văn Lai took advantage of
the opportunity by shooting down one of the U.S. aircraft.[16] As the MiG-17
pilot focused on the target in front of him, he did not see two A-1Hs flying

behind and above him. After attacking the two A-1Hs in front of him, the MiG-17 pilot pulled up into a climb at an angle of 90 degrees to an altitude of 600 feet where he was right in the middle of the gun sights of the two A-1Hs behind him. Both A-1Hs opened fire, firing long bursts at extremely close range.

Nguyễn Văn Lai was killed because he tried to turn too hard to avoid the enemy's guns while he was at a low altitude and so close to the mountains.[17] According to the U.S. authors,[18] the two A-1Hs that fired their cannon and shot down Nguyễn Văn Lai's MiG were piloted by Lt. (jg) Charles W. Hartman III and Lt. Clinton B. Johnson from VA-25, USS *Midway* (each credited with half a kill). Realizing that the situation had become difficult, the command post ordered Mai Đức Toại to break off the engagement.

On April 2016, Clinton Johnson visited Hanoi to attend a Vietnam/U.S. veteran pilot meeting, where he met Senior Colonel Mai Đức Toại. They both recalled what had happened in that engagement.

10 July 1965: Faced with the "Feather Duster" Tactic

On the morning of 10 July, the early warning radar network picked up a large-scale formation of USAF aircraft coming in from the Laotian-Vietnamese border. These F-4Cs of the 45th TFS/15th TFW were assigned to provide MiG suppression and fighter escort support to attack bombers that were coming in to attack targets in the Yên Bái area. The USAF fighters (call sign Mink) were deployed in two sections, one formation of eight F-4s flying south of the Tam Đảo mountain range with another formation of six F-4s splitting into two-aircraft sections flying in a holding area north of the Tam Đảo mountains. Knowing that MiGs usually attacked the tail-end formation of attack bombers (F-105s), the F-4Cs decided to masquerade as F-105Cs by flying at the same altitudes and speed as the F-105s did, so that they would appear to be the final group of F-105Cs heading in to bomb the target. A two-aircraft flight from the 921st FR piloted by Phan Thanh Nhạ and Nguyễn Cương was ordered to take off to intercept and engage the attackers in the Yên Bái area, but because the MiGs encountered the U.S. fighters that were waiting for them in the area over Tam Đảo mountains, the battle was fought out toward the direction of Phổ Yên.

At that time, the F-4s were almost out of fuel and decided to make a turn to the left before turning back for home when Mink No. 1 spotted MiGs on his radar. He ordered the F-4s to deploy into an extended horizontal line formation and to turn to meet the MiGs head-on. By using this formation the F-4Cs hoped to be able to spot the MiGs visually before the MiGs were able to open fire.

As for the VNPAF, after a number of air engagements with the F-4s from the first battles in April, the MiG-17 pilots knew that the tactical scheme employed by the F-4C formation was to split into two two-aircraft sections separated by a distance of approximately ten miles. If they identified the pursuing aircraft as MiGs, these two aircraft would break away by climbing and moving to a safe range to allow the F-4C No. 3 and No. 4 to launch their AIM-7 missiles straight at the oncoming MiGs. As the four aircraft flew right past each other from opposite directions, the two F-4Cs utilized their tremendous engine power to increase speed and get farther ahead of the MiGs. They then used the "Feather Duster" tactic, a dive and roll technique to reverse positions, and attacked the MiGs, but for some reason they were not able to launch their missiles. During this ferocious and unequal air battle, Phan Thanh Nhạ shot down one F-4 but was then hit by an F-4's missile. The F-4C flown by Capt. Kenneth E. Holcombe and Capt. Ronald C. Anderson was able to carry out a Feather Duster tactic by extending the range from the MiG-17 No. 1, then rolling upside down and diving to fire four missiles, one after another, and pilot Phan Thanh Nhạ was killed.[19]

When chased by MiG No. 2, the pilot of the F-4C No. 4 also used the tactic of increasing his speed and pulling up to an altitude of 13,000 feet in order to get farther and farther ahead of the MiG-17. When the F-4 pilot saw that the MiG was losing speed, could not chase him any longer, and was beginning to lose altitude to prepare to break off the engagement, the F-4 pilot immediately flipped his aircraft upside down and reversed the direction to get on the MiG's tail. When the range to the target was down to one mile, the F-4C fired two Sidewinder missiles. These two missiles missed, but the third missile hit the target. The F-4 No. 4 fired a fourth missile which hit the MiG in the tail. Having been hit by the F-4's missile, Nguyễn Cương ejected unsuccessfully and was killed. After this engagement Capt. Thomas S. Roberts and Capt. Arthur C. Clark were credited with shooting down MiG No. 2.

During the 10 July 1965 air battle the VNPAF lost two MiG-17s. However, the records of the 921st FR stated that only one MiG-17 was shot down by the F-4's missile and that the other aircraft was lost in an accident during air combat. After this air engagement, VNPAF HQ decided to temporarily suspend combat sorties of MiG-17s, spend time studying the lessons of this battle, and conduct additional training to cope with the enemy's tactics in the future.[20]

DEPLOYMENT OF SAMS

The SAM-2 was the Soviet Union–built surface-to-air missile. In the USSR it was called the S-75 Dvina, and the NATO reporting code name was the SA-2 Guideline. The SAM-2 had a combat range of twenty-five miles, and could reach an altitude of twelve miles. Their Mach number was 3.5. After a visit by the USSR premier Alexei Kosygin in February 1965, the USSR agreed to help the Vietnamese People's Army (VNPA) with modern MiG-21s and surface-to-air-missiles (SAMs).[21]

After some months of training SAM crews and after receiving SAMs to assemble, from July 1965 SAM sites were ready to fight against U.S. aircraft. And on 24 July 1965, VNPA SAMs made a surprise attack in their first battle and shot down one U.S. F-4 aircraft. From that day, besides AAA forces and MiG fighters, SAMs became a very important and efficient weapon in the air defense system, and they proved their highest efficiency when they shot down B-52s in Operation Linebacker II. To deal with SAMs, the USAF and USN were forced to deploy F-105G and F-105F aircraft, each equipped with two air-to-ground missiles, the AGM-45 Shrike, to suppress SAM sites. As such, the U.S. attack formations then also consisted of these aircraft, code named Wild Weasels.

Throughout the time of their participation in the air war, SAMs fought about 3,542 battles, fired 5,885 missiles, and shot down 788 American aircraft of various types, including forty-three B-52s.[22] Toward the end of the war, SAM-3s were already in Vietnam, but for some reason they had not been used.

THE FORMATION OF THE 923RD FIGHTER REGIMENT

In mid-1965 the second group of fighter pilots came back home after completing their flight training in the Soviet Union and in China. As a result of that, the 921st FR received thirty new pilots, doubling the regiment's original size. The regiment also received significant numbers of additional aircraft and equipment. In August 1965 modern MiG-21s provided by the Soviet Union began to arrive. These aircraft were assembled and issued to the 921st FR. The regiment's MiG-17s were gradually replaced by newer and more capable MiG-17Fs, and twenty-eight MiG-17PFs equipped with targeting radars to serve as night fighters. During this period Kép airfield in Bắc Giang Province, which was at that time being used by the 919th Military Air Transport Regiment's helicopter units, was improved so that it could be used by MiGs.

In accordance with a Ministry of National Defense decision, on 4 August 1965, a second VNPAF FR was founded. The new regiment was given the designation of the 923rd FR (in the code: Lam Sơn Group). This regiment was given the mission of using MiG-17s to defend the skies northeast of Hanoi. Lieutenant Colonel Nguyễn Phúc Trạch was appointed commander of the new FR. Lieutenant Colonel Nguyễn Ngọc Phiếu was the regiment's political commissar, Major Lê Oánh and Major Đào Công Xưởng were the regiment's vice commanders. The FR initially had two MiG-17 fighter companies. The 923rd FR's pilots, mechanics, and support personnel were transferred from the 921st FR.[23]

At the same time, a number of NVN's best pilots of the first group of MiG-17s (Trần Hanh, Phạm Ngọc Lan, Nguyễn Ngọc Độ, Nguyễn Nhật Chiêu, Đồng Văn Đe, and others) were selected for conversion training to fly MiG-21s.

Air Engagement on 20 September 1965

September 1965 was considered a "hard month" for the USAF and USN. During the first half of the month, a number of American aircraft were shot down by SAMs and AAA units. Among the American pilots who were shot down and captured during this period were some of America's best-known and most experienced pilots. The commander of Carrier Air Wing 16 on board the carrier USS *Oriskany*, Cdr. James Bond Stockdale, who had led the aircraft that attacked North Vietnamese combat vessels during the August 1964 USS *Maddox* incident, was shot down on 9 September 1965. He bailed out and was imprisoned at Hanoi Hilton until 1973. Lt. Col. James

Robinson Risner, the commander of the 67th TFS/18th TFW (who flew 110 missions with the F-86 during the Korean War and shot down eight MiG-15s during that conflict) was shot down on 16 September 1965.[24]

In September 1965 the USAF intensified their bombing attacks of road traffic and lines of communications from Hải Phòng, Lào Cai, and Lạng Sơn to Hanoi and from Hanoi, down to the provinces of Military Zone Four (MZ4). By making sure to protect the bomber attack forces, the USAF and USN focused a great deal of attention on tactical measures to deal with North Vietnam's MiGs, SAMs, and AAAs. With regard to tactics, the U.S. aircraft usually used "pop-up tactics," meaning they flew in over the coast in Hòn Gai area at low altitudes, after which the A-4 attack bombers would climb up over the Yên Tử mountains and head for the area of the Bắc Lệ railroad yard and the Hóa River Bridge to conduct their attacks. The F-4 escort fighters would wait in the Nhã Nam area.

After temporarily suspending combat operations for almost two months to reorganize and conduct additional training, in early September 1965 the General Staff of the VNPA and the AD and AF Command ordered the MiGs to prepare to resume combat operations. This combat mission was assigned to a flight of four MiG-17s flown by Phạm Ngọc Lan, Nguyễn Nhật Chiêu, Trần Văn Trì, and Nguyễn Ngọc Độ. The battle plan recommended by the ground control team and approved by the commander called for a change in the sector from which the fighters would approach the target. Instead of flying toward Hiệp Hòa-Bắc Ninh to reach a battle area over Kép, as the pilots had done in a number of previous engagements, in order to gain the element of surprise after taking off, on this air battle, the MiG-17s were directed to make a turn past Phổ Yên–Thái Nguyên and then fly on a heading of 350 degrees toward Thái Nguyên at an altitude of 1,600 feet. Almost at the moment the MiGs were passing Chợ Mới, it was calculated that the F-4s were leaving the area of Nhã Nam, flying at an altitude of 13,000 feet and a speed of 500 mph. Judging that the F-4s perhaps had not yet detected the presence of MiGs in the area, the command post ordered the flight to immediately turn right to a heading of 150 degrees and increase the speed to 560 mph. Within minutes the MiG pilots spotted a formation of American aircraft 30 degrees to their right and ahead at a range of ten miles. Nguyễn Nhật Chiêu quickly turned in and got behind the F-4 formation.

After a number of earlier air battles against the F-4s, the VNPAF pilots had slowly become familiar with the battle tactics used by this type of aircraft and had found their weaknesses, which the MiG-17s could exploit in order to gain the upper hand. After entering into an air battle with MiG-17s, the F-4s usually tried to increase speed and turn hard to escape the MiGs behind them, after which they would split their formation and head in different directions.

Seeing that one F-4 was banking with the intention of escaping into a cloud in front of him, Nguyễn Nhật Chiêu swept in and turned to the other side of the cloud in order to confront the F-4 in a favorable position when it flew out of the cloud at the other side. When the F-4 emerged from the cloud, before it had time to increase speed and make a hard turn, Nguyễn Nhật Chiêu got on his tail and calmly brought the target into his sights, then squeezed the trigger, firing two bursts from his guns that shot down the F-4.[25] After hearing an order from the command post to break off the engagement, the attack flight broke off the engagement and landed safely back at Đa Phúc airfield.

7 October 1965: First Air Combat of Nguyễn Văn Bảy (A)

None of the Vietnamese records make any mention of an air battle fought on 6 October 1965. However, after conducting interviews with Colonel Nguyễn Văn Bảy (A) about an air battle on 7 October, many of the details of Colonel Nguyễn Văn Bảy(A)'s story matched the American descriptions of the 6 October battle. This could have been the result of the fact that the two organizations (Vietnamese and American) that maintained the daily combat logs were writing in different time zones.

From Nguyễn Văn Bảy(A)'s combat diary:

On 7 October, when flying over Yên Thế area at an altitude of 10,000 feet, the MiG lead [Trần] Huyên was the one who first spotted the U.S. aircraft and he requested permission to attack them. I immediately dropped my external fuel tank and increased speed in order to cover my fellow pilots. However, as soon as I banked to turn I saw an F-4 behind me that was launching a missile. I immediately pulled my stick into a hard turn, but because the range was so close the missile exploded right next to my aircraft on my right side, flipping my aircraft upside down. A piece of shrapnel hit my canopy, cutting a hole in the canopy and causing my cockpit to lose pressure. At that very moment I looked up through the top of the canopy and saw a huge aircraft flying right over my head. I wanted to pursue him, but because my aircraft had been damaged and my speed was much less than his, I could not catch him. I looked over my aircraft and saw that there were many shrapnel holes in the fuselage. My aircraft was shuddering and unstable, so I requested permission to return and land.

After landing, the mechanics counted eighty-four holes in my MiG. Everyone who saw it was amazed because none of them believed that such a badly damaged aircraft could come back and landed safely.[26]

This was the first time Nguyễn Văn Bảy (A) engaged with U.S. fighters in the skies of North Vietnam.

Air Engagement on 6 November 1965

On 14 October the USAF lost two F-105Ds, both from the 36th TFS/6441st TFW. The American side stated that Capt. Thomas William Sima was shot down by 37-mm antiaircraft guns about fifty miles east of Hanoi. An F-105D flown by Capt. Robert Harry Schuler went down and Captain Schuler was killed. One U.S. document stated that this aircraft was the victim of a MiG.[27] However, the VNPAF has no information about an air engagement on 14 October. It is likely that this F-105D was shot down by the ground-based AD forces.

On 6 November a flight of MiG-17s consisting of Trần Hanh, Ngô Đoàn Nhung, Phạm Ngọc Lan, and Trần Minh Phương was scrambled to intercept American aircraft flying in to search for and rescue a U.S. pilot in the area of Routes 12A and 21A in Hòa Bình Province. The American pilot whom the USAF tried to find and rescue was Lt. Col. George Carlton McCleary, who was shot down on 5 November, and was the third F-105 squadron commander to be shot down.

After taking off, the MiGs were vectored down toward Mỹ Đức (Sơn Tây Province). The GCI officer twice directed the flight to intercept the target at an intercept angle of almost 90 degrees, but both times the MiG pilots were unable to spot the target. The third time, the command post directed the MiG pilots to turn back and almost immediately they met the target head-on. Having received a few oral guidance commands, Ngô Đoàn Nhung saw a target at a range of six miles. He moved into a very precise attack position, aimed, and fired at the target at a low altitude just above the mountain jungle terrain. He shot down a CH-53 helicopter. The helicopter crashed on the spot six miles southwest of Chợ Bến. This was the first American helicopter shot down by VNPAF MiG-17s.

Some Assessments of the Air Battles of 1965

As for the VNPAF, from its first battle on 3 April 1965 through 31 December 1965 its MiG pilots flew hundreds of combat sorties and fought dozens of air battles against USAF and USN aircraft. Twenty-five pilots fired their guns in these battles, and they shot down fourteen American aircraft of different types. The VNPAF recorded the loss of eight MiG aircraft, and eight Vietnamese pilots were killed.[28] The VNPAF successfully completed the mission to open up the front in the air, but because the VNPAF was very young with only thirty MiG-17s, which belonged to an old type, they did not cause much trouble to the USAF when they attacked the targets.

Meanwhile a number of American records reported that the United States had shot down seven MiGs (and one probable),[29] and admitted that four American aircraft were shot down by MiGs. However, they stated that other aircraft were either shot down by SAMs or antiaircraft guns or that the aircraft were just damaged and then crashed on their way back to their base. After suddenly engaging with MiG-17s in some initial encounters, the USAF had drawn experience in launching the Feather Duster tactic to deal with MiG-17 tactics.

On 24 December 1965, President Lyndon Johnson announced the temporary suspension of bombing in North Vietnam untill 31 January 1966. Both sides then continued to prepare for air operations that start in early 1966.

3

1966
THE DEPLOYMENT
OF MiG-21s

The year 1966 began with three notable events. First, after fighting dozens of air battles in 1965, the VNPAF completed its first stage of development, accumulating airborne combat experiences. Second, the VNPAF deployed more modern fighter aircraft (MiG-21s) equipped with air-to-air missiles, which were in technical terms comparable to U.S. aircraft of a similar generation at that point in time. Third, the organization of the VNPAF took a new step in its development by adding one more fighter regiment, with many more fighter pilots to be assigned to combat alert duty, especially the group of MiG-21 pilots led by pilot Nguyễn Hồng Nhị (who later became a VNPAF ace). At the same time, the USAF made some changes in their organization in the Vietnamese theater (the 2nd AD was redesignated as the 7 AF), as well as changes in weapon use, tactics, and countermeasures. Consequently, air battles over North Vietnam in the year 1966 were expected to be even fiercer!

3 February 1966: First Nighttime
Combat Victory of MiG-17

By the end of 1965 the VNPAF combat fleet had received additional aircraft including twenty-eight MiG-17PFs (equipped with a targeting radar for use in night fighter engagements) and twenty-six MiG-17Fs. Although these two new types of MiG-17s were armed only with three guns, the thrust of their engines was significantly greater because they had afterburners. These

MiG-17PFs had much greater maneuverability and acceleration for use in air combat. A number of the 921st FR's pilots received conversion training to fly these night fighters and were assigned to a new night fighter company. Two days after the temporary Christmas bombing halt ended, the USAF and USN resumed their bombing attacks against important targets in North Vietnam.

Pilot Lâm Văn Lích (the 921st FR's chief of flight techniques) was assigned to combat alert duty on the night of 3 February. Having detected by the radar net that USN A-1H aircraft were approaching Hòa Bình, and anticipating that these aircraft intended to attack Route 15A between Suối Rút and Quan Hóa and Route 21A between Hòa Bình and Tân Lạc, Colonel Nguyễn Văn Tiên decided to order Lâm Văn Lích to take off all alone and climb into the winter night sky. This was the first night mission with a MiG-17, so Lâm Văn Lích was a little bit nervous. Within minutes, the command post ordered him to climb to an altitude of 15,000 feet and to turn left to chase a formation of U.S. attack bombers that was operating over Tân Lạc and Suối Rút. The command post ordered Lâm Văn Lích to turn and fly one complete circle, which enabled the pilot to get into a position behind the American aircraft. When he was above Mộc Châu, Lâm Văn Lích decided to turn on his aircraft's on-board radar. Almost immediately he saw the American aircraft five miles in front of him on the radar screen. Having closed in to a range of 0.5 miles, he pushed his throttle forward to accelerate, planning to fire his guns when the range closed to 0.25 miles.

As he was scanning the sky visually he suddenly saw a black enemy aircraft flying just in front of him, below the front of his MiG's wing. He reduced speed and decreased altitude to get into attack position. Fortunately, at that moment the American aircraft switched on their navigation lights. Only then did Lâm Văn Lích realize that in fact there were two U.S. aircraft in front of him. He calmly took aim at the target, centering his aim between the lights on the tips of the enemy's aircraft's wings. He fired a long burst and his shells headed straight into the enemy aircraft.

When he turned his MiG to break off he saw one more enemy aircraft on the right, and he immediately turned his aircraft to pursue it. Excited at the success of his first attack, he aimed at the second aircraft and fired a long burst from his guns. His shells hit the target. This was the first victory for a MiG-17 in nighttime combat.[1]

Lâm Văn Lích was directed to break off by turning back toward Hòa Bình, then descended to a safe landing at Đa Phúc airfield.

4 March 1966: The First Victory of the MiG-21

The first wagons that carried component parts of the first series of MiG-21s arrived at Đa Phúc airfield around the end of 1965. They were immediately assembled and were ready to be in the combat fleet. In order to prepare MiG-21 pilots for their first battle, the AD and AF Command decided to have the MiG-21s fight a few trial battles in order to learn lessons and gain air combat experience. The best targets for these initial trial battles were either enemy attack bombers or reconnaissance drones. The honor of flying the first MiG-21 combat mission was given to Nguyễn Hồng Nhị, the lead of the first VNPAF MiG-21 trainee course.

The opportunity for the MiG-21's first battle arrived. From 3 March 1966, taking advantage of good weather, the USAF repeatedly sent high-altitude reconnaissance drones in to overfly Thái Nguyên, Hải Dương, and the outskirts of Hanoi. Their tactic was to send several flights of two aircraft each in different directions. On that day, Colonel Nguyễn Văn Tiên was in charge of the command duty team and the GCI officers were Nguyễn Văn Chuyên and Trần Quang Ngư. At 1353 hours on 4 March 1966, the radar detected a high-altitude reconnaissance aircraft target flying in over Việt Trì, Thái Nguyên, and headed toward Route 1 North. The AF HQ discovered that this was a drone and ordered Nguyễn Hồng Nhị to be ready to take off. It should be noted that this presented difficulties for the MiG-21 pilot, who was about to fly his first combat mission, because the drone was flying at an altitude of more than 58,000 feet. At that altitude, the MiG-21's maneuverability was very poor.

At 1401 hours Nguyễn Hồng Nhị was ordered to start his engine and take off immediately, then he was directed to fly on a heading of 270 degrees. When Nguyễn Hồng Nhị reached an altitude of 20,000 feet, the command post instructed him to drop his auxiliary fuel tank, turn to a heading of 310 degrees and switch on full afterburner, accelerate to a speed of Mach 1.8, and climb to an altitude of 55,000 feet. Knowing that controlling the aircraft at an altitude of 55,000 feet was very difficult, he had to make careful calculations and control his aircraft with great precision in order to reach the required altitude and speed. Almost at the very moment when he was informed that the range to the target was twenty miles, he spotted a white contrail on his left, twelve to twenty miles away. Having judged that this was the target he decided to pursue it, and when he got close to the target, he recognized it as a drone aircraft with long and dihedral wings. Even though at such high altitude the air was thin and it would be more difficult to maneuver his aircraft, with well-practiced flying skills Nguyễn Hồng Nhị closed to the target.

When the range to the target was ten miles, Nguyễn Hồng Nhị switched on his aircraft's radar, closed to the target, and turned his radar sight upward in preparation for locking onto the target at a range of 4.5 miles. When he had a good audible signal from his missile's heat-seeker, at a range of two miles and a speed of Mach 1.7, he fired his first missile. To make sure he hit the target, almost immediately he fired his second missile. Nguyễn Hồng Nhị reported to the command post, "I have drunk all the beer," a coded message meaning that two missiles had fired. The command post told him that the target had disappeared from their radar screen and ordered Nguyễn Hồng Nhị to return to the airfield to land.[2]

The date and the time, 1421 hours on 4 March 1966, went down in the history of the VNPAF as the time that MiG-21 pilot Nguyễn Hồng Nhị pressed the button to fire his first missile and destroyed a reconnaissance drone. This missile firing signaled the appearance of a new type of weapon and a new generation of pilots. It opened up a new page in the history of the VNPAF in its air battles against the USAF and USN aircraft.

Later, pilot Nguyễn Hồng Nhị became the first commander of the 927th FR (1972). When the war ended he was credited with eight victories. As a VNPAF ace he was given the honorable title VNP Armed Forces Hero, promoted to the rank of major general, and appointed chief of staff of the VNPAF. In 1988 he was appointed general director of the Civil Aviation Administration of Vietnam (CAAV), remaining there until his retirement in 1998.

It must be remarked that, although the first victory over U.S. aircraft was scored, the MiG-21 pilots understood that this was just an initial exercise because the target was just a reconnaissance drone. However, the important point was that this initial victory had a very good psychological effect on the

Vietnamese pilots. They now had full confidence in this new weapon and in the new missiles, and more importantly in their ability to master the new technology.

The day of 4 March 1966 saw more action for the MiGs when, at 1514 hours, radar picked up a group of American aircraft twenty-five miles southeast of Sam Neua, crossing the border and heading toward Mộc Châu and Yên Bái. Anticipating that the USAF might conduct reconnaissance in preparation for attacking the railroad line from Yên Bái to Thanh Ba, the command post, under the command and direction of the AD and AF Service commander Senior Colonel Phùng Thế Tài, decided to order a flight of four MiG-17s from the 923rd FR to take off. The MiG-17 flight, with Phạm Thành Chung, Ngô Đức Mai, Trần Minh Phương, and Nguyễn Thế Hôn, took off at 1542 hours and then headed toward Mộc Châu.

When the radar net picked up a formation of four F-4s twelve miles east of Vạn Yên at an altitude of 14,000 feet, and which was turning to head to the northwest, the command post ordered the MiG flight to turn right into a position to intercept the F-4s. At 1600 hours, the MiG lead reported that he had spotted the F-4s at a range of seven miles. He ordered his wingmen to drop their auxiliary fuel tanks and deploy into a combat formation, then split up to chase the U.S. aircraft. The two lead MiGs flew straight at the closest pair of F-4s, then MiG No. 1 brought a U.S. aircraft into his gunsight and fired, but the F-4 was able to take violent evasive action and his shells missed. Seeing that No. 2 was in a favorable attack position, MiG No. 1 turned back into a covering position, allowing his wingman to push his throttle forward, aim at the F-4 No. 2, and open fire. Seeing that the first burst of cannon fire hit the enemy aircraft, but the F-4 was still able to fly, MiG No. 2 Ngô Đức Mai moved closer, and when the range was down to 0.125 miles he fired two more bursts of shells. The F-4 caught fire and dove toward the ground in the Vạn Yên–Mộc Châu area.[3] At this point, the command post spotted another formation of four F-4s that were chasing the second section of MiGs and were launching missiles. Under the warning instruction from the command post, those two MiGs took evasive actions to avoid the missiles and supported each other as they turned to launch a counterattack. After a ferocious dogfight that lasted for four minutes, with neither side being able to get into position to fire, the two MiGs decided to break off the engagement.

That day, 4 March 1966, was a memorable one for the VNPAF. On the same day the VNPAF's MiG-21s scored their first victory and the newly formed 923rd FR also scored its first victory. Even though the 923rd FR MiG-17s only shot down one U.S. aircraft, this air battle was especially significant. It bolstered the morale of the 923rd FR and continued the VNPAF's tradition of winning victory in the first battle.

Air Engagements on 23 April 1966

On 23 April 1966, the 923rd FR launched three missions. The first one was at 1120 hours when the flight piloted by Hồ Văn Qùy, Lưu Huy Chao, Nguyễn Văn Biên, and Trần Triêm took off from Đa Phúc airfield. The second mission, a flight consisting of Mai Đức Toại, Võ Văn Mẫn, Nguyễn Khắc Lộc, and Đỗ Huy Hoàng, took off from Kép airfield at 1300 hours. After climbing to a high altitude, the flight flew toward Bình Gia–Bắc Sơn area. Just two minutes later, the pilots saw some targets at a range of ten miles. The duty watch team at the AD and AF Command post believed that this was a group of F-4Cs from the 555th TFS/8th TFW, which was supporting F-105s that were attacking targets along Route 1 in the Bắc Giang area and bridges located northeast of Hanoi. As on the U.S. side, after spotting the MiGs at a range of ten miles, the lead of the F-4C formation sped up in order to visually identify the MiGs (as was required by the USAF rules before missiles could be fired). The two lead F-4Cs fired two AIM-7 missiles, hoping to force the MiGs to take evasive action to avoid the missiles and thereby shatter the MiG flight formation. But at that moment, MiG No. 3 Nguyễn Khắc Lộc quickly cut across and got right on the tail of the F-4C No. 2 and fired his guns. Seeing that the F-4 No. 2 had a MiG on his tail, the two F-4Cs of the second section, one flown by Capt. Max F. Cameron and 1st Lt. Robert E. Evans, and the other one by Capt. Robert E. Blake and 1st Lt. S. W. George, launched missiles from a long range to try to save No. 2. They then swept in to get on the tail of the MiG, but Nguyễn Khắc Lộc was faster: he opened fire and shot down the F-4C No. 2. The command post ordered the pilots to break off the engagement and all eight MiG-17s that took off that day landed safely at Đa Phúc airfield without any loss.[4]

In the afternoon, the radar net picked up a number of the USAF reconnaissance aircraft flying at an altitude of 65,600 feet over the Điện Biên area of Lai Châu Province, and then at 1332 hours the radar picked up a group of six to eight enemy aircraft south of Nọng Hét flying toward Yên Bái–Bắc Cạn at an altitude of 29,000 feet. The AD and AF Command decided to launch two MiG-21s flown by Nguyễn Đăng Kính and Đồng Văn Song at 1356 hours to intercept and attack these USAF aircraft over the Yên Bái area. A few minutes later, while flying at an altitude of 19,000 feet, two MiG-21 pilots spotted a target nine miles away. This was a formation of F-105s that was flying in to attack Phủ Lạng Thương Bridge. When he heard the order to break off the engagement, Nguyễn Đăng Kính made a sharp turn to head back to the Đa Phúc airfield. Suddenly, he noticed that his aircraft turned on its side without any action on his part. When he was on his landing approach and lowered his landing gear, Nguyễn Đăng Kính saw that his hydraulic system pressure was too low. While he was still at an altitude of 1,300 feet he noticed that his aircraft's sideway tilt was increasing and that he could no longer control his aircraft. Nguyễn Đăng Kính decided to eject at an altitude of 650 feet. He parachuted safely to the ground in Ninh Giang Village, Kim Anh District. We cannot find any record on the U.S. side about this victory.

26 April 1966: MiG-21 First Encounter with EB-66

Analyzing all the pieces of information received, including those about the enemy's activities during the previous days, the AD and AF Command predicted that the USAF would send in a number of diversionary flights and that it would use small strike elements to attack transportation targets. The AD and AF Command's battle plan was to use four MiG-17s to attack enemy strike groups approaching the Bắc Sơn–Võ Nhai area. Meanwhile two MiG-21s would fly in a holding pattern at an altitude of 13,000 feet north of Đa Phúc airfield to be ready to join in the air battle.

In the afternoon, the USAF sent F-105Ds into North Vietnam's airspace to attack the section of Route 1B between Bình Gia and Bắc Sơn and to attack the Lạng Sơn–Hanoi railroad line. At the same time, F-4Cs assigned to provide fighter support flew in a circular holding pattern east of Chợ Mới. Accurately assessing the situation, the AD and AF Command decided to put into effect a plan for coordinating the efforts of MiG-17s and MiG-21s.

After the first attempt to shoot down an EB-66 EW aircraft on 24 March failed, the 921st FR continued to draw up plans to destroy EB-66 EW aircraft over North Vietnam. At 1340 hours the intelligence reported that forty F-105s taking off from Thailand would fly in to attack Route 1. Just at that moment the R-35 radar site picked up a target over Bắc Cạn–Thái Nguyên, and a flight of MiG-21s was ordered to take off at 1412 hours. After leaving the runway, the pilots flew on a heading of 320 degrees while climbing to an altitude of 20,000 feet. The pilots were then ordered to drop their auxiliary fuel tanks, switch to full afterburner, and climb to an altitude of 25,000 feet. Actually, on 26 April 1966 two EB-66 EW aircraft that flew into NVN were very closely defended by F-4C fighters. When the American pilots saw MiG-21s on a bearing of 30 degrees speeding directly toward them at very high speed, the F-4Cs dropped their auxiliary fuel tanks and engaged the MiG-21s to protect the EB-66s. The F-4Cs fired many Sidewinder missiles but none of the missiles hit their targets.

Taking advantage of the fighting between the MiGs and the F-4Cs, EB-66's crew turned away from the battle area and flew back to the Vietnam–Laos border. As the MiGs saw the formation of F-4s, they sped forward to attack. Nguyễn Hồng Nhị in MiG No. 1 decided to chase one F-4 on the left, but the pair of F-4s accelerated and escaped. Just when he was planning to pull up to gain altitude, MiG No. 1 saw a streak of light flash past his cockpit. He turned to look to his rear and his sides and saw many F-4s all around. Realizing that he was trapped in the middle of a formation of F-4s, he quickly turned his aircraft on its side, intending to chase an F-4, but then he felt his aircraft shudder slightly and found that it was hard to maintain his turn. He decided to level out and pushed his throttle forward to 100 percent power to return to the air base. Unfortunately, his aircraft continued to lose speed and altitude and his hydraulic system's low pressure warning light came on. When his altitude was down to 10,000 feet and he realized that he could no longer control his aircraft, Nguyễn Hồng Nhị decided to eject. According to information from both sides, it is likely that the F-4 that fired the missile that hit Nguyễn Hồng Nhị's MiG-21 was an F-4C flown by Maj. Paul J. Gilmore and 1st Lt. William T. Smith from the 480th TFS/35th TFW.[5]

A flight of four MiG-17s flown by Hồ Văn Qùy, Lưu Huy Chao, Nguyễn Văn Bảy (A), and Trần Triêm from the 923rd FR took off from Kép airfield at 1431 hours. The MiG-17s were directed to fly on a heading of 360 degrees while climbing to an altitude of 11,000 feet, then the pilots were vectored toward Bắc Cạn. At that very moment, when the pilots spotted the target off to the left at a range of three miles, they dropped their auxiliary fuel tanks and pursued the enemy aircraft. Almost immediately, Lưu Huy Chao swept down to attack and shot down one U.S. aircraft. Coinciding with this, the two MiGs of the second section were ordered by the flight lead to attack the lead enemy group. Even though the two F-4s turned very sharply, Nguyễn Văn Bảy (A) was able to shoot down one F-4. This was the first American aircraft shot down by Nguyễn Văn Bảy (A). After ordering the pilots to break off the engagement, the command post directed them back to a safe landing at Đa Phúc airfield at 1451 hours.

Air Engagement on 29 April 1966

In the afternoon, the USAF sent in an RF-101C reconnaissance aircraft to take photographs, in order to assess the results of the previous attacks by F-105s against the Thái Nguyên steel mill complex. At 1430 hours two groups of USAF aircraft flew in from southern Sơn La, flew past Bảo Hà, and headed toward Bắc Cạn in order to attack targets in the Bắc Cạn–Phủ Lạng Thương area.

At 1535 hours a group of American aircraft was detected flying over the Mai Châu–Hòa Bình area. After concluding that these might be slow, propeller-driven aircraft flying at altitudes between 10,000 and 12,000 feet searching for a downed pilot (the GCI's officers at the command post believed that the aircraft might be A-1Hs), the AD and AF Command ordered a flight of four MiG-17s to take off to attack them. The MiG-17s flight, piloted by Bùi Đình Kình, Bùi Văn Sưu, Nguyễn Hữu Tào, and Nguyễn Xuân Nhuần, took off at 1545hours, and then was directed to a heading of 240 degrees.

After turning to a 360-degree heading to the battle area over Mai Châu–Hòa Bình, the MiG pilots spotted the target at a range of 2.5 miles. The target in fact was a group of A-1E Skyraiders. The group was escorting HH-53 helicopters that had been sent in to locate Maj. Albert Runyan, the pilot of the RF-101 that had been shot down. As they crossed the Vietnam–Laos border two A-1E Skyraiders were attacked by two MiG-17s. Seeing that the American aircraft were flying at a higher altitude than the MiGs, MiG-17 lead Bùi Đình Kình ordered his flight to drop their auxiliary fuel tanks, switch on their afterburners, and pull into a climb to attack the enemy aircraft. The MiG lead turned to pursue an A-1E. When the range was right, Bùi Đình Kình opened fire and shot down the A-1E, which was flown by Capt. Leo Sydney Boston from the 602nd ACS (Air Commando Squadron)/14th ACW (Air Commando Wing). Captain Boston was declared missing in action and was later reclassified as killed in action. The command post ordered the MiG flight to break off the engagement and return to land.

At 1620 hours, the scramble order was given again and a flight of three MiG-17s flown by Nguyễn Khắc Lộc, Lưu Huy Chao, and Nguyễn Văn Bảy (A) took off to intercept a formation of F-4Cs over Bắc Giang. This was a formation of four F-4Cs from the 555th TFS/8th TFW, which was conducting a MiGCAP mission to support F-105s that were bombing Bắc Giang Bridge. The MiG-17 pilots fought a ferocious dogfight against the F-4s, and during the fight MiG No. 1 Nguyễn Khắc Lộc was hit by a missile fired by an F-4. The MiG pilot bailed out and parachuted safely back to the ground.

30 April 1966: A Hard Day for MiG-17s

During the early morning hours, the radar network detected a formation of four F-105s that was divided into two two-aircraft sections and circling over the Quang Minh–Hòa Bình area. After receiving approval from the AD and AF Command, the 921st FR gave the order to a combat alert flight piloted by Phạm Ngọc Lan, Bùi Văn Sưu, Trần Tấn Đức, and Nguyễn Quang Sinh, who took off from Đa Phúc airfield at 0735 hours then flew up toward Nghĩa Lộ. At 0754 hours the pilots spotted the target at a range of 3.5 miles. The MiG lead ordered his wingmen to drop their auxiliary fuel tanks, switch on afterburners, and turn sharply to begin the attack. The target was a mixed formation including both F-105s and F-4Cs that were supporting a RESCAP mission northwest of Hanoi.

Realizing that MiGs were chasing at their six o'clock, the F-105s decided to switch on their afterburners to escape. When he saw two F-4s heading straight toward him, nose to nose, MiG No. 1 decided to make a hard turn to chase these two F-4s. Seeing that the MiG was behind them, the two F-4s split up. Phạm Ngọc Lan decided to chase the F-4 on the right and fired his guns at it, but he missed, as he was too far away. He continued to increase his speed. Unfortunately, when the range was down to 0.28–0.31 miles and he was preparing to fire, he felt his aircraft suddenly shaking violently. It began to spin and became uncontrollable. He then decided to eject, and his parachute brought him down to the ground safely. Based on the details of this air engagement, it is very likely that the F-4C that fired the AIM-9B missile that hit MiG No. 1 was the one flown by Capt. Lawrence H. Goldberg and 1st Lt. Gerald D. Hardgrave of the 555th TFS/8th TFW.[6]

At the same time, MiGs No. 2 and No. 4 were chasing another F-105, but the F-105 switched on its afterburner and sped away, eastbound to the sea. MiGs No. 2 and No. 4 dove toward the ground and flew into a cloud. Realizing that their speed was still very great and that they were flying in an area of high mountain peaks, the two MiGs then sharply pulled up again above the clouds, and turned back to land. As for Trần Tấn Đức's MiG, according to what his fellow pilots observed, he pursued an F-105 at extremely low altitudes. He fired his guns, but because his speed was so great his aircraft flashed right past his target and he was killed in an area of mountain peaks near Bắc Yên District, Nghĩa Lộ Province. The details provided by other MiG pilots are quite similar to the reports of a clash between an F-4, flown by Capt. Larry R. Keith and 1st Lt. Robert A. Bleakley of the 555th TFS/8th TFW, and a MiG-17 on 29 April 1966. Captain Keith said that during a ferocious air battle, the MiG flew into a mountain.[7] The difference in the dates recorded in the reports may have been the result of being in different time zones, but it could also have been that the individuals who wrote the reports may have made a mistake about the date of the battle.

12 June 1966: Low-Altitude Battle between MiG-17s and F-8s

After a long period of fighting air engagements at medium altitudes, the MiG-17 pilots held a review of their battle experiences. During the discussion, many of the pilots said that they could fight more effectively if they could bring the American pilots down to fight at low altitudes where the MiG-17s' superior horizontal maneuverability and turning capabilities could be better utilized. After reaching this conclusion, the MiG-17 pilots conducted additional training to prepare for the next round of battles.[8]

Based on the intelligence reports that on 12 June 1966 the USN would probably send in low-level reconnaissance aircraft and attack targets along Route 1, the AD and AF Command ordered the 923rd FR to intercept and engage the U.S. aircraft at low altitudes as they were approaching from the direction of the sea. The 923rd FR decided to employ a flight of two MiG-17s to fight the air battle at low altitudes.

At 1441 hours, some USN aircraft flew in at an altitude of 6,000 feet from the direction of Cái Bầu Island. Having received information that the U.S. aircraft were crossing the Yên Tử mountain range, then descending to low altitudes, Lê Quang Trung and Võ Văn Mẫn were ordered to take off at 1443 hours from Kép airfield. A little more than two minutes later, the command post directed the pilots to circle over Kép airfield at an altitude of 3,000 feet. Almost immediately, MiG No. 1 spotted two F-8s six miles east of Lục Nam. These were two of four F-8s assigned to support a formation of eight USN A-4 attack bombers led by Cdr. Harold L. Marr from the USS *Hancock*. It was remarked that the weather in the air battle area was cloudy, with broken clouds at an altitude of 6,500 feet. When the A-4s reached the target area, they turned in to attack their target while the F-8s split off and established a patrol circular holding MiGCAP pattern between Chũ and Kép airfield in order to block any MiGs. Facing this situation and utilizing their new low-altitude (1,500 feet to 2,000 feet) battle tactics, the MiG-17s dropped their auxiliary fuel tanks, switched on their afterburners, and maneuvered at low altitudes to pursue the A-4 attackers, even though they were outnumbered by the F-8 escort fighters that were flying very close to the attack bombers. The F-8 No. 1 turned back hard and chased the MiGs. At this point the two MiG-17s, flying in a rather close formation, swept in directly at the F-8s, confronting them virtually nose to nose. Taking their altitude advantage, the F-8s got into position to attack. Then, however, MiG No. 1 turned hard and made two complete left-hand circles before breaking away. The F-8s and the MiG-17s split into two groups and fought a ferocious turning dogfight in the skies over Hà Bắc. Lê Quang Trung stuck right on his target's tail, calmly took aim, and destroyed one F-8 in the skies over Mai Sưu–Chũ (Hà Bắc Province).

As an ace with five victories during the war, Major Lê Quang Trung, the first commander of the 925th FR, was given the honorable title VNP Armed Forces Hero.

After being informed that three more groups of American aircraft were heading for the area of the air battle from the direction of Route 18, at 1453 hours the 923rd FR command post ordered a flight consisting of Phạm Thành Chung and Dương Trung Tân to take off to provide cover and support, and ordered the flight consisting of Lê Quang Trung and Võ Văn Mẫn to return and land.

The information reported by the two sides about the results of the 12 June battle is contradictory. Cdr. Harold L. Marr, flying an F-8E from VF-211 off the USS *Hancock*, reported that he had shot down two MiG-17s. Right after the battle the pilot reported that he had not seen whether or not his cannon shells had brought down the second MiG-17 so he was only credited with a "probable kill," but later Commander Marr was officially credited with shooting down two MiG-17s during the 12 June 1966 air battle.[9] However, according to the archived files and the combat log of the 923rd FR, all four MiG-17 pilots who participated in the 12 June 1966 air battle returned and landed safely.[10] Therefore the information stating that Cdr. H. L. Marr shot down two MiG-17s is incorrect.

This was an air engagement fought at low altitudes (600 feet to 2,000 feet) in the midland area where there were hills and mountains, but because of excellent preparations the MiG-17 flight won this air battle. As for the USN, they were probably surprised when they found that they had been forced to fight the MiGs at low altitudes, so the effectiveness of their missiles was low, perhaps because the missiles' heat-seekers were less effective at low altitudes. Apparently, after the 12 June 1966 air battle, the USAF and USN had to conduct a study of the effectiveness of their missiles at low altitudes.

21 June 1966: Furious Dogfight between MiG-17s and Crusaders

On 21 June 1966, the USAF conducted three waves of attacks against targets deep inside NVN territory. In the first wave, from 0645 to 0800 hours, a formation totaling thirty USAF F-4s and F-105s flew up from Thailand, crossed over Yên Bái, and attacked the Hóa River Bridge and Kép airfield. The second wave, a total of twelve aircraft, attacked Phú Lương Bridge. The third wave, consisting of two flights (four aircraft each) of F-4s flew in from the ocean over southern Tiên Yên.

Meanwhile the USN sent in a strike formation of twelve aircraft from the USS *Hancock*. The strike formation was divided into two separate groups. A group of two Crusaders consisting of an RF-8A reconnaissance aircraft, escorted by one F-8E fighter, was assigned to fly a photo-reconnaissance mission along the railroad line northeast of Hanoi. The main strike formation, consisting of six A-4s, was escorted by three F-8s from VF-211. When the formation of A-4s were approaching the target area, an RF-8A reconnaissance aircraft flown by Lt. Leonard Corbett Eastman was shot down. After covering the A-4s during their attacks on the targets, the F-8s turned back to try to find the pilot of the RF-8 that had been shot down. The two lead F-8s circled to look for the downed pilot and mark the location where the pilot had ejected while the remaining F-8 joined up with the F-8 that had been escorting the RF-8 reconnaissance aircraft. In other words, the four F-8Es formed two sections of a new combat group. All four F-8s remained at altitudes of 1,600 to 2,000 feet right over the spot where the RF-8 had been shot down.

While carrying out their search for the downed pilot the F-8s had to face AAA, SAMs, and MiGs. A flight of four MiG-17s constituting the main attack element, and made up of pilots Phạm Thành Chung, Dương Trung Tân, Nguyễn Văn Bảy (A), and Phan Văn Túc, took off from Kép airfield and flew at low altitudes to the combat area in the airspace between Kép and Chũ.

At 1426 hours, the MiG-17 flight took off then flew on a heading of 110 degrees. A few minutes later all four pilots spotted four F-8s flying in an extended trail formation. The F-8s were constantly circling in the sky to look for the downed pilot. The AD and AF Command's post informed the MiG pilots that a number of F-8s were flying back toward the ocean (perhaps the F-8s were low on fuel and were flying to their aerial refueling area), but two other F-8s continued to circle at an altitude of 4,000 feet to look for the downed pilot. At this very moment, four silver MiG-17s swept out of the clouds and headed for the F-8s at an intercept angle of 30 degrees. Actually, the F-8s and the MiGs were in a very close confrontation as they raced toward each other.

The MiG pilots dropped their auxiliary fuel tanks to attack. The MiG lead ordered his No. 3 to attack the F-8 No. 2 while he attacked the F-8 No. 1. The F-8 No. 2, on afterburner, headed virtually straight toward the MiG and fired two bursts of 20-mm shells. The two groups of aircraft engaged in a close dogfight that lasted a little more than two minutes. At 1437 hours, after making many circles and turns, MiG No. 1's shells hit one F-8. At that moment two other F-8s—which had just been refueled and which might have heard the radio call about the MiG attack—and the F-8 No. 3 all saw the F-8 No. 1 being hit and set on fire by shells fired by a MiG-17. This was an F-8E flown by Navy Lt. Cdr. Cole Black from VF-211 off the USS *Hancock*.[11] Lieutenant Commander Black ejected and was captured. The F-8 No. 2 from the Nickel formation (Nickel 102) turned back to look for his flight lead but he could not see him. After getting close to the MiGs, the newly arrived F-8s No. 3 and No. 4 almost immediately turned hard to join the air engagement, but the range was too short and their aircraft were in such high G turns that they could not get into attack positions. At this time the MiG lead Phạm Thành Chung was ferociously chasing the F-8 No. 4. This F-8 was damaged and did not dare to get involved in a dogfight, so the pilot used his afterburner to extend the range and try to escape out to sea.

Having received the order to break off the engagement, MiG No. 2 headed back toward the airfield. While he was turning, however, he felt his aircraft suddenly shaking violently. He found that he could not control the aircraft's altitude. Realizing that his aircraft was no longer controllable and that he was at an altitude of only 1,200–1,600 feet, Dương Trung Tân decided to eject and safely landed. Based on the details of the reports about this air engagement, the F-8E that attacked and hit Dương Trung Tân's MiG most likely was flown by Lt. Eugene J. Chancy of VF-211 off the USS *Hancock*. Lieutenant Chancy did not see the MiG crash and so only claimed a "probable shoot-down." Later the Americans credited Lieutenant Chancy with shooting down this MiG.[12]

The two MiGs of the second section were in a ferocious dogfight with the F-8Es when they heard the command post order to break off, so they turned away and headed for the airfield. On their way back No. 4 saw that an F-8 was chasing them. Waiting until the F-8 pulled up into a climb from a low altitude, No. 4 aggressively turned, swept in, and fired his guns, hitting the F-8 and causing it to start to burn. MiGs No. 1, 3, and 4 landed safely at 1445 hours. The Navy F-8 pilots claimed they shot down two MiG-17s on 21 June 1966, but according to the records of the 923rd FR, only one MiG was shot down while the other three MiGs returned and landed safely.

SUSPENDING MiG-21 OPERATIONS TO FIND
NEW COMBAT TACTICS

By the end of June 1966, the 921st and 923rd FRs had fought fourteen air battles and shot down thirteen American aircraft. However, a review revealed that all of the victories were scored by MiG-17s. The MiG-21s participated in a number of air battles but they ran into trouble in each battle. Aside from the reconnaissance drone shot down by Nguyễn Hồng Nhị on 4 March 1966, the MiG-21s did not shoot down any other American aircraft. Meanwhile two MiG-21s were lost. The AD and AF Command HQ and the 921st FR HQ held a review of the air battles. During the review it was pointed out that the MiG-21's combat efficiency was low, aircraft were lost, and, most importantly, they still had not found a proper tactic for MiG-21s, which had been built as a high-speed fighter-interceptor designed to fight at high altitudes.

The AD and AF Service Command decided to temporarily suspend MiG-21 combat operations for almost two months, in order to review battle experiences, learn lessons, determine the causes of the problems, and identify the most suitable tactics and fighting procedures.[13] In their presentations and "open tactical discussion," the pilots who had personally participated in air battles provided detailed briefings on every phase of the battle and their assessments of the enemy's tactics and tricks. During these discussions the pilots took the first step toward concluding that the primary reason for the MiG-21's lack of success was that they had not fully exploited the advantage of the aircraft's capabilities (it was originally a fighter-interceptor) and that they had not yet identified the most suitable attack tactic for the MiG-21 in the conditions of Vietnam.

A number of pilots had employed MiG-17 combat tactics (maneuvering dogfights) in their MiG-21s but were not yet proficient in their use of the aircraft's weapons, and the pilots were still unsure of whether they should use missiles or unguided rockets. There were even some pilots who wanted to ask the Soviet Union to provide Vietnam with the type of MiG-21 that was armed with guns like the MiG-17. Based on the conclusions of these sessions, many new additions were made to the MiG-21's combat procedures and tactics. A round of supplementary training for MiG-21 pilots in the new battle methods was hastily carried out.[14]

In early July 1966 the MiG-21s began to be placed on combat alert duty again and stood ready for new air battles using their new battle plans.

29 June 1966: First Wave of Battles to Defend Hanoi

While the MiG-21 pilots temporarily suspended their combat missions in order to review their experiences and conduct additional training, the USAF continued to expand the war and escalated its attacks by attacking targets in the Hanoi area, including the Đức Giang fuel storage depot. In the morning of 29 June, a U.S. four-aircraft armed reconnaissance formation flew into the area of Việt Trì–Phú Thọ. Then at about noon time, a formation of American aircraft consisting of twenty-four F-105s, escorted by sixteen F-4s, flew in from the direction of Mộc Châu, Phù Yên, and Yên Bái, and then flew down along the southern slopes of the Tam Đảo mountains (the Thud Ridges) and turned to bomb the Đức Giang fuel storage depot. Maj. James H. Kasler, the operations officer of the 354th TFS and a USAF "hero" during the Korean War, planned and led this attack. (Later, Major Kasler's aircraft suffered serious damage in a fight against two MiG-17s flown by Võ Văn Mẫn and Nguyễn Văn Biên on 19 July 1966.)

The F-4s flew over Đa Phúc and Kép airfields to suppress the VNPAF fighter aircraft based there. In order to support the ground air defense units, the 923rd FR command post ordered a flight of four MiG-17s to take off to intercept and attack the USAF bombers on Hanoi's outer defense perimeter. The MiG-17s, flown by Trần Huyền, Võ Văn Mẫn, Nguyễn Văn Bảy (A), and Phan Văn Túc, were scheduled to carry out this mission. The flight was ordered to take off from Đa Phúc airfield and then turn left to a heading of 270 degrees. When the MiG pilots reached an altitude of only 1,600 feet, they were informed that their target was twelve miles in front of them. At that very moment the flight spotted four F-105s, which were assigned to conduct an air defense suppression mission (Iron Hand). Trần Huyền ordered his wingmen to drop their external fuel tanks and switch to afterburner in preparation for the attack. When the F-105 pilots spotted four MiG-17s closing on them very fast, they just split up the formation and jettisoned their bombs in order to engage the MiGs.

The two lead MiGs made an inside turn and fired a burst at the F-105D No. 3. The Thud was damaged and its canopy was shattered. The MiGs and the F-105s made many turning circles in this dogfight and both MiG-17s fired their guns, but all were out of gun range. The F-105 was only damaged and it was able to switch on its afterburner and escape. At the same time, the two MiGs of the second section turned left and got on the tails of the two lead F-105s. Knowing that they had MiGs on their tails, the two F-105s made very sharp turns with a violent series of evasive maneuvers. Nguyễn Văn Bảy (A) pursued the F-105 No. 2, turned inside the F-105's turn, and fired two bursts from his guns. The shells hit all over the nose of the F-105, and it began to burn. When he spotted F-105 No. 1 right in front of him, Phan Văn Túc immediately pursued it and fired two bursts from his guns at a firing angle of 40 degrees and range of 1,600 feet, and hit that F-105.

Therefore, in this battle against the F-105s, MiG-17s No. 3 and No. 4 shot down two F-105Ds in the skies over the Tam Đảo mountains, and the rest of the enemy attackers hastily jettisoned their bombs and turned away to flee. Because the auxiliary command station informed the MiGs that U.S. aircraft were still overhead and threatening Đa Phúc airfield, the four MiG-17s diverted to Gia Lâm airfield, where they all landed safely. This was the opening battle in a new wave of VNPAF battles to defend Hanoi, the capital of the country. It should be remarked that a number of U.S. records stated that an F-105D flown by Maj. Fred L. Tracy of the 421st TFS/388th TFW shot down a MiG-17 with his 20-mm cannon.[15] However, the Vietnamese records stated that all four MiG-17 pilots returned and landed their aircraft safely.[16]

7 July 1966: A MiG-21's Victory Using Unguided Rockets

The air battle on 7 July 1966 marked a notable occasion when a MiG-21 for the first time used unguided rockets to shoot down U.S. aircraft. After suspending combat operations for a period to review experiences and conduct additional air combat training, in early July the 921st FR was again ready for battle. While analyzing and monitoring the activities of the USAF, the 921st FR command post (under the leadership of regiment commander Trần Mạnh) and MiG-21 pilots came to identify the standard pattern of operations used by the USAF aircraft flying from Thailand to attack the Thái Nguyên area. The USAF strike groups regularly flew in over Phú Thọ, then north of the Tam Đảo mountains, and sometimes they even flew over Đa Phúc airfield where a large number of MiGs were on combat alert. The 921st FR decided to draw up a plan to attack the USAF aircraft in the air over Đa Phúc, an area whose terrain all Vietnamese pilots knew very well and where there were supplementary ground control observation stations to provide ground control directions that could help put the pilots in a favorable attack position.

On the morning of that day, the AD and AF Service's radar network picked up many groups of USAF aircraft that had taken off from Thailand and were heading toward Thái Nguyên Province. The 921st FR ordered a flight of two MiG-21s flown by Nguyễn Nhật Chiêu (armed with R-3S missiles) and Trần Ngọc Síu (armed with unguided rocket pods) to take off. After reaching a desired altitude, the two MiG-21s were directed to a holding combat area to patrol the airspace directly over the airfield.

Just as anticipated, the F-105Ds from Thailand flew along the Tam Đảo mountains and passed over the Đa Phúc airfield. Suddenly two MiG-21s appeared and turned hard to chase the F-105s from the air holding area. Having spotted a group of F-105s to his left rear flying on a heading of 340 degrees, MiG No. 2 immediately informed No. 1 of his sighting and then made a sharp turn to the right and cut in behind two F-105s. Now in a favorable attack position, Trần Ngọc Síu skillfully centered the target in his sights and fired a volley of rockets at a range of 0.31 miles. He then closed to 0.09 miles and fired a second volley of rockets that hit one F-105's wing, causing it to go nose down toward the ground. The two MiG-21s accelerated and turned away, leaving the battle area before the F-4 escort fighters had time to react.

The VNPAF credited pilot Trần Ngọc Síu with the first shooting down of an F-105. This was the first victory of a MiG-21 after almost two months of suspending combat activities. With regard to the type of weapon used to shoot down this F-105D, after interviewing MiG-21 pilots who personally either commanded or participated in the fighting at that time, it can be confirmed now that in the air battle on 7 July 1966, pilot Trần Ngọc Síu for the first time used unguided rockets to shoot down an American F-105.[17]

Air Engagement on 11 July 1966

On 11 July 1966 the USAF sent a large number of F-105s escorted by F-4s over the Yên Bái–Bắc Cạn area to attack the railroad line from Kép up to Lạng Sơn. The VNPAF HQ decided to use a flight of two MiG-21s to intercept the USAF bomber strike force between Tuyên Quang and Thái Nguyên. To check the effective use of weapons, the command post decided to use both air-to-air missiles and unguided rockets for the flight of two MiG-21s, with Vũ Ngọc Đỉnh and Đồng Văn Song. This battle would be another opportunity for MiG-21 pilots to gain experience and learn lessons for determining the most appropriate attack methods and weapons to be used.

In the morning, while attacking targets north of Kép airfield, two F-105Ds were shot down by the AAA units near Vũ Chúa Bridge. At 1355 hours the VNPAF HQ ordered the flight of MiG-21s to take off, fly two complete circles over the airfield, and then turn left to a heading of 310 degrees at an altitude of 6,500 feet. Almost immediately the command post informed the pilots that the target was 30 degrees to their front at a range of ten miles. After No. 2 reported that he had spotted a formation of F-105s flying below and in the opposite direction, the MiG lead gave the order to drop auxiliary fuel tanks and increase speed. The pilots then made two hard turns to the right and got on the tails of the F-105s. MiG No. 2 sped forward to a range of 0.31 miles and fired two volleys of rockets. Both volleys missed, exploding in front of the target. No. 2 adjusted his sight, brought the target into its center, and fired a third volley of rockets at a range of 0.18 miles. The F-105 began to smoke, rolled upside down, and dove toward the ground. The F-105 hit by Đồng Văn Song's rockets crashed in the area of Sơn Dương, Tuyên Quang Province. The F-105D's pilot most likely was Maj. W. L. McClelland of 355th TFW.[18]

After two victories in a row, the 921st FR conducted a review session to determine the proper attack method to be adopted by MiG-21s. The procedures for intercepting the target, getting into attack position while still far from the target to give the pilot time to gain airspeed, and aiming and firing techniques were initially affirmed. However, in order to perfect the MiG-21's proper attack method and to determine the effectiveness of the MiG-21's air-to-air missiles, additional trials needed to be carried out in future air battles.

13 July 1966: Dealing with USN Strike Formation

During the month of July 1966 the 923rd FR's MiG-17s fought a number of victorious air battles with six victories. Also during this period the MiG-17s usually conducted combat intercept missions using flights of two aircraft each, in order to have more freedom to maneuver during engagements. As the situation developed, some MiG-17 flights moved to Gia Lâm airfield to stand on combat alert duty there, so that they could participate in the battles in defense of Hanoi.

On the morning of 13 July, two U.S. aircraft flew in to conduct their reconnaissance of the AD forces and AAA positions in Thái Bình–Hưng Yên area. Thereafter, the USN aircraft formed up into an Alpha Strike consisting of A-4Ds and F-8s escorted by F-4 fighters, and flew in to attack the railroad line and Cổ Trai Bridge. At the same time, four F-4Bs assigned to the MiGCAP mission circled over an area south of Hanoi to support the bomber strike formation.

At 0958 hours the scramble order was given and Phan Văn Na and his MiG-17 flight (Nguyễn Thế Hôn, Trần Triêm, and Lưu Huy Chao) took off to intercept and attack the attack bombers south of Hanoi. Five minutes later, the pilots spotted two A-4Ds to their left front at a range of four miles. Phan Văn Na gave the order to drop auxiliary fuel tanks and prepare to attack. He then turned sharply, closed with the A-4s, and fired two bursts that hit an A-4D in the lead enemy formation.

At the same time, Nguyễn Thế Hôn pursued a formation of F-8s and fired three bursts from his guns. He saw his shells hit the left wing of the F-8E, which dove toward the ground and crashed. The two MiGs of the second section turned and engaged in a turning dogfight against the F-4 escort fighters. It was very likely that the A-4D pilots called for the F-4Bs assigned to MiGCAP duty to come to their rescue. In order to take up a favorable position, the F-4Bs fired a number of AIM-9 Sidewinder missiles at the MiG-17s. According to the reports provided by the MiG No. 4 pilot and by local residents, when the MiG-17 flight broke off the engagement to return to base, Trần Triêm saw that F-4s were following him, and he turned back and engaged in a turning dogfight at very close range (0.11–0.17 miles). Then, just as he had leveled off to turn back to the airfield, his aircraft was hit by a missile fired by an F-4. The MiG lead shouted for him to take evasive maneuvers but his wingman did not reply. When he saw that the MiG No. 3 had been hit by a missile, MiG No. 1 shouted for the pilot to eject, but he did not see any response on the part of the pilot. Phan Văn Na descended to an altitude of 400 feet, flew back to the airfield, and landed.

14 July 1966: Change of MiG-17 Tactics

After accurately analyzing the engagements in the first half of July 1966, the 923rd FR decided to make a number of changes in its flight formations and fighting tactics. One of the most important changes was that the regiment shifted to the use of flights of two aircraft each, which would fly into the designated battle area at low altitudes, select an appropriate combat zone, and resolutely attack the bomber groups in the USAF and USN strike formations.

In the morning, a formation of F-8Es from the aircraft carrier USS *Oriskany* was supporting the attack aircraft assigned to bomb a fuel storage depot on the outskirts of Nam Định City and targets in the Hưng Yên area. At 1100 hours, after detecting many enemy formations continuing onward to attack Kép airfield, the 923rd FR ordered a flight piloted by Lê Quang Trung and Ngô Đức Mai to take off. During a ferocious dogfight with the F-8s, Ngô Đức Mai cut inside an F-8, which most likely was flown by Cdr. Richard M. Bellinger of VF-162 from the USS *Oriskany*, at a point twenty-five miles southeast of Hanoi, and opened fire. Bellinger's right wing suffered severe damage. Commander Bellinger ducked into the clouds and turned south. Perhaps because he knew that his hydraulic system was leaking badly, Commander Bellinger did not return to his ship but instead diverted to Đà Nẵng air base. However, unfortunately, because he could not deploy his aircraft's aerial refueling probe, Bellinger was forced to eject when his aircraft was twenty miles from Đà Nẵng. The pilot was picked up by a rescue helicopter.

After the MiG-17s left the patrol area and flew to the battle area to intercept the USN aircraft southwest of Hanoi, the AD and AF Command ordered two MiG-21s of the 921st FR, flown by Hoàng Biểu and Tạ Văn Thành, to take off. Just a moment after takeoff, when they were at an altitude of only 450 feet the command post ordered the pilots to drop their external fuel tanks and make a hard left turn to close with a formation of four F-105s that was flying over the area of Đa Phúc airfield. MiG lead Hoàng Biểu made an inside turn and got on the tail of the enemy aircraft No. 4. After hearing a good sound signal from the missile, Hoàng Biểu launched his missile at a range of 1.2 miles. However, right after he pushed his missile launch button the F-105 made a hard turn and the missile missed, flying past the nose of the target aircraft. While No. 1 was pursuing the F-105 to try to bring it into his sights again, he heard an explosion. His aircraft shook hard and he momentarily lost consciousness. When he regained consciousness, he initiated the ejection process and touched down safely. Also Tạ Văn Thành was hit by a missile and ejected over the Đại Từ area in Thái Nguyên Province.[19]

Unfortunately First Lieutenant Tạ Văn Thành was killed (his parachute failed to open and the pilot's seat failed to separate from the canopy). Later on, the new model of MiG-21 was modified in such a way that the canopy could slide backward to give space for the pilot to eject from the aircraft instead of opening upward as in the old model of MiG-21 (F-76).

19 July 1966: An Encounter with a U.S. Korean War Ace

After a series of open tactical discussion seminars among VNPAF fighter pilots, in which attendants presented analyses and reviews of combat experiences, the MiG-17 pilots of the 923rd Regiment determined how to fight effectively in low-altitude turning dogfights, thereby winning many battles. On 19 July the American strike formation led by USAF "Ace" Maj. James H. Kasler flew in to bomb the Đông Anh fuel storage facility. James H. Kasler was a famous pilot who had fought in the Korean War and whom American pilots called a "pilot with a sixth sense," "Astronaut No. 1," and "a legendary figure in the USAF." He also was the pilot who had led the attack on the Đức Giang fuel storage facility on 29 June 1966.

Early in the afternoon, having received reports that many groups of F-105s were flying low down the Tam Đảo mountain range, the 923rd FR command post came to the conclusion that as a routine pattern the F-105s would fly in from northern Tuyên Quang down the north side of the Tam Đảo mountain range (Thud Ridge) and conduct their bombing attack using "fly low then climb high" with "pop-up" tactics, using the Tam Đảo mountains to hide from the air defense radars of Đa Phúc airfield and Hanoi's northern air defenses. Even though the air defenses were very thick, the F-105D flight formations were able to reach the Đông Anh fuel storage facility. A MiG-17 flight consisting of Nguyễn Văn Biên and Võ Văn Mẫn was ordered to take off and fly in a holding pattern directly over the airfield. The guiding concept for the MiG-17 tactic was to keep the American aircraft at low altitudes and fight the air battle in the area of the airfield, in order to take advantage of the support from the visual ground control stations around the airfield and the supporting fire of the antiaircraft positions deployed in the area of the airfield. At this time, the supporting ground control station on Hàm Lợn Mountain sent in an urgent report stating that three formations of F-105s had appeared from the end of the Tam Đảo mountain range and were heading toward Đa Phúc airfield. Lieutenant Colonel Trần Mạnh ordered the two MiG-17s to be ready to intercept and attack the F-105s at low altitudes using the plan that had been prepared beforehand.

Acting upon the AF command post's concept of air combat tactics, the two MiGs flew diagonally across the airfield to intercept the F-105 formation. At this time the F-105s were flying in stairstep formation, with the trailing two aircraft about 1.1 miles behind the leading two aircraft. When Kasler's formation was almost in its target area where it would drop its bombs, the American pilots suddenly spotted two MiGs speeding in to attack the F-105s. Realizing the threat from the MiGs, Major Kasler ordered two F-105s to turn back to engage the MiGs while the rest of the F-105s continued to carry out their bombing mission. After climbing to reach the best altitude, Nguyễn Văn Biên quickly increased speed, got on the tail of his target, brought the aircraft into his sights, and fired his guns when the range was 0.23 miles. Guessing that they were in danger, the two F-105s hastily put their aircraft into a side-slipping turn, rolled upside down, and dove to a low altitude. When he saw the two F-105s dive to low altitudes, Nguyễn Văn Biên knew that his opponent was doing exactly what the regiment's battle plan wanted the enemy to do. At low altitudes the MiG-17 was almost as fast as the F-105 but more maneuverable and could perform sharper turns, while the F-105s would consume more fuel and quickly run out of it.

The two swallow-shaped MiG-17s and the two needle-nosed F-105Ds fought a turning dogfight directly over the airfield. The four jet aircraft turned round and round in circles, like leaves in a tornado, each trying to get on the next one's tail. The roar of jet engines and the occasional streaks of flame when guns were fired left trails of smoke against the azure July sky. After making many turns in the sky without either side being able to gain an advantage, the swirling air battle gradually moved into the range of the antiaircraft guns protecting the airfield, just as the MiG-17 pilots intended. Unable to stand the tension of the whirling dogfight and the threat from the antiaircraft guns on the ground, the pilot of the F-105D No. 2, 1st Lt. Stephen

Whitman Diamond, decided on his own initiative to break off and flee the battle area. Võ Văn Mẫn immediately recognized the F-105 No. 2's desire to flee, quickly reduced the tightness of his turn, and got right on his target's tail. Just as Diamond leveled his wings, Võ Văn Mẫn squeezed his trigger to fire two bursts, which hit the F-105D, causing it to suddenly go nose up and then nose down, then it dove into the ground. The pilot was able to eject, but he was killed.

With the two MiGs squeezing him between them like the jaws of a vise, the surviving F-105 had to call for the lead formation of F-105s to turn back to save him. The lead formation of F-105s turned back and headed for the two MiGs but their way was blocked by the fire of the airfield's antiaircraft guns. One of the F-105s was damaged and the F-105s had to spread out their formation. The two MiGs flown by Nguyễn Văn Biên and Võ Văn Mẫn continued to dogfight against Kasler's F-105. The two MiGs skillfully pushed Kasler onto the defensive and repeatedly attacked him, forcing Kasler to use every bit of his more than two decades of air combat experience to evade the determined attacks by Nguyễn Văn Biên and Võ Văn Mẫn. Using bold and creative air combat maneuvering (ACM) techniques, two MiG pilots took turns attacking Kasler's solitary F-105D. A burst of shells fired by Nguyễn Văn Biên hit the F-105D's right wing. Kasler hastily rolled upside down, nosed his aircraft into a dive, and then accelerated and headed straight for the border. (On 8 August 1966 James Helms Kasler was shot down by antiaircraft guns.)

Nguyễn Văn Biên and Võ Văn Mẫn landed safely at Gia Lâm airfield after performing skillfully in this ferocious air battle against a formation of F-105s. After this battle, MiG-17 pilots further reaffirmed the belief that the low-altitude turning dogfight was a tactic that best increased the strengths of the MiG-17.[20] Obviously, this war-combat tactic is the most flexible element of the art of air operations; the tactic used by one type of aircraft is not unchangeable. Tactics and techniques must be constantly studied, modified, and improved in order to be able to deal with the opponent's new tactics and new weapons.

The VNPAF credited the flight composed of Nguyễn Văn Biên and Võ Văn Mẫn with shooting down two F-105Ds, without loss to themselves in the air battle of 19 July 1966. It should be noted that this air battle was fought directly over the airfield where the ground control tower and the auxiliary ground control stations not only provided timely information to the two MiGs but also became stations that provided instructions to the pilots to maneuver, to select targets, and to make counterattacks. Even though pilot Võ Văn Mẫn constantly made excellent evasive maneuvers during the air battle, after he landed it was found that there were many holes in his wings from enemy cannon shells.

Senior Lieutenant Võ Văn Mẫn died in a battle on 14 May 1967. As an ace with five victories to his credit, he was posthumously awarded the honorable title VNP Armed Forces Hero.

29 July 1966: A U.S. Reconnaissance Aircraft Killed

The U.S. RC-47D regularly flew reconnaissance missions near the Vietnamese border and occasionally even crossed the border into Vietnamese territory, because the USAF were sure that there were no MiGs or AAA units in the area. On 29 July 1966 an RC-47D aircraft from the 606th ACS/634th CSG (Combat Support Group), based at Nakhon Phanom air base in Thailand, flew a reconnaissance mission over the Sam Neua area into Vietnam. The aircraft was commanded by Capt. Bernard Conklin and Capt. Robert Eugene Hoskinson, and carried six additional flight personnel. As the RC-47D was flying from Hồi Xuân up to Yên Châu in Sơn La, the duty watch team at the AD and AF Service Command post was monitoring it closely.

After assessing the situation, the AD and AF Command ordered two MiG-17s of the 923rd FR, flown by Trần Huyền and Võ Văn Mẫn, to take off at 1455 hours. They were directed to fly on a heading of 240 degrees at an altitude of 10,000 feet. A little more than two minutes later MiG No. 1 saw a target aircraft twelve miles ahead. Because the target aircraft was flying very slowly, the MiG pilots were certain that it was an RC-47D reconnaissance aircraft. The MiG-17 flight decided not to drop their auxiliary fuel tanks but reduced speed to approach the target from the rear at a 10-degree angle. When the range to target was 0.51 miles, Trần Huyền fired a first burst from his guns. Then, after closing in, he fired a second burst at a range of 0.23 miles, his shells hit the American aircraft's left wing, and it caught fire. His aircraft was too close to the enemy's, so after firing two bursts he swept past the target, and taking advantage of his speed he quickly turned back, aimed at the target again, and fired a third burst at a range of 0.45 miles.

Trần Huyền saw the RC-47D burst into flames. After they were certain that the RC-47D had crashed, the two MiGs broke off the engagement and flew back to Đa Phúc airfield, landing at 1515 hours. All crew members of the RC-47D aircraft were listed as killed in action.

The USAF believed that the VNPAF had scored a significant success by shooting down such an important aircraft in a daring and skillful attack, and the Americans also suffered a great loss with the loss of the entire crew of eight officers and flight personnel. According to witnesses, only one parachute opened but the pilot who used this parachute died after one day undergoing treatment in hospital.[21]

12 August 1966: Coordination of Two Types of MiG

On the basis of the evaluation of the high combat effectiveness of the MiG-17's fighting at low altitudes and the excellent performance of the MiG-21 in fighting at medium altitudes, in May 1966 the VNPA AD and AF Service Command issued a directive on air combat operations, which stated that flights with small numbers of aircraft should be used in future combats. In addition to the use of only one type of aircraft in future combats, pilots of both types, MiG-17 and MiG-21, were to be trained to gradually become able to coordinate well with each other in future combat where MiG-21s would be armed with both missiles and rockets for fighting at medium altitudes while MiG-17s would fight at low altitudes.[22] The AD and AF Command post and the regimental command posts also prepared plans for both fighter types to simultaneously join the battles when they were on duty either at the same air base or at different air bases.

In the afternoon of 12 August, having received information that American aircraft would attack targets in the Hanoi and Hải Phòng areas, Colonel Nguyễn Văn Tiên ordered several flights of MiG-17s and MiG-21s to stand by for takeoff, and to fight using a plan for coordination of the two types of aircraft in a single battle. According to the battle plan, a flight of MiG-17s from the 923rd FR would act as the primary attack element to intercept and attack the formation of American aircraft flying in from the direction of Yên Châu up to Yên Bái–Tuyên Quang, while a flight of MiG-21s would provide support and cover.

At 1637 hours a target group appeared on the B1 long-range radar net heading toward Nghĩa Lộ. As was scheduled, a flight of two MiG-17s piloted by Phan Văn Túc and Lưu Huy Chao took off from Gia Lâm at 1649 hours, gained altitude, and flew up along the Red River past Sơn Tây to Thành Sơn and then to the battle area located fourteen miles southeast of Nghĩa Lộ. A little more than five minutes later a flight of two MiG-21s assigned to provide support took off from Đa Phúc airfield and hedgehopped along the eastern slopes of the Tam Đảo mountain range up to Sơn Dương.

After the flight reached the battle area, the command post guided it to an angle of approach of 30 degrees to attack a formation of F-105Ds flying in to attack the fuel storage areas around Thái Nguyên. The MiG pilots intensified their scan of the skies, and when No. 1 spotted the target aircraft at a range of ten miles, he ordered his wingman to immediately drop the auxiliary fuel tanks and swept in to attack. The two MiGs coordinated with one another expertly, covering each other and simultaneously attacking and dogfighting against four F-105Ds at altitudes between 1,600 feet and 3,200 feet. During the dogfight, Lưu Huy Chao shot down one F-105D and then broke off and flew away at low altitudes.[23] At that same time, two MiG-21s were vectored up from the area over Sơn Dương to a point south of Yên Bái to cover the MiG-17s as they returned to land at Đa Phúc airfield.

Air Engagements on 17 August 1966

One day before, on 16 August, a flight of two MiG-17s flown by Mai Đức Toại and Nguyễn Văn Biên from the 923rd FR fought an air battle against eight A-4s in the Đồng Giao–Bỉm Sơn area. During this air battle against the USN aircraft, even though only two MiG-17s were involved in the battle, the MiG-17s pilots fought bravely and pilot Mai Đức Toại shot down one A-4.

On 17 August, the USAF sent two groups of attackers in from two different directions. The first group approached over Phủ Lạng Thương–Đáp Cầu to attack Đuống Bridge. The second group approached via the Tam Đảo mountains north of the Đa Phúc airfield. The AD and AF Command post ordered the 923rd FR to launch aircraft and fight the enemy directly over the airfield, to simultaneously defend both the airfield and the Đuống Bridge. Previously, during the course of the review of MiG-17 combat experiences, the pilots of the 923rd FR had proposed a plan in which two flights of two MiG-17s each would take off from different airfields and then fly in to fight in the same battle area.

Keeping in mind the combat plan and tactic for the battle, two flights of MiG-17s, one consisting of Lê Quang Trung and Ngô Đức Mai and the other piloted by Nguyễn Văn Biên and Phan Văn Túc, took off at 1352 hours from Gia Lâm and Đa Phúc airfields to fight a coordinated battle to protect Hanoi. After takeoff, the two flights flew out to Bắc Ninh to attack the group of enemy aircraft flying down from Phủ Lạng Thương to bomb Đuống Bridge. Having spotted the target, the two MiG flights took turns to attack a formation of F-105Fs, which had split into small sections and flown in at a low altitude to make surprise bombing attacks in the Đuống Bridge area. The appearance of two flights of MiG-17s, one after another, prevented the F-105Fs from being able to concentrate on their bombing mission. Instead they were forced to engage in air combat against MiG-17s at low altitudes. During the air battle, Lê Quang Trung shot down one F-105F. When the command ordered the pilots to break off and return, all aircraft turned back and landed safely.

At the 921st FR, two MiG-21s flown by Đồng Văn Đe and Nguyễn Văn Cốc were ordered to take off at 1407 hours to intercept and attack the enemy attackers approaching from the west to attack Hanoi. Within minutes, while climbing to an altitude of 1,600 feet, the MiG lead saw one F-105 to the north and flying eastward across the Đa Phúc airfield area. After leveling out at an altitude of 10,000 feet, when the two pilots saw that the F-105 was still flying straight and level, Đồng Văn Đe decided to pursue this target. When he reached a range of 1.8 miles and his speed was 500 mph, he placed his target designator firmly on the target and pressed his missile firing button. Seeing the missile warhead detonate above the target, he kept his target designator on the enemy aircraft and fired his second missile. This time the missile warhead detonated directly beneath the belly of the F-105. Đồng Văn Đe quickly turned right and then circled around to the west end of the Đa Phúc airfield runway and landed.

5 September 1966: MiG-17s versus F-8s at Low Altitudes

In order to intercept and attack the many USAF formations of F-105s flying in to attack targets north of Hanoi, on 18 and 22 August, the 923rd FR command ordered four flights with two MiG-17s each to take off. The MiG-17 flights fought bravely and forced the F-105s to jettison their bombs prematurely before they reached the target, and turn away to escape. But during these battles, Senior Lieutenant Phạm Thành Chung, a company's deputy commander in the 923rd FR, was killed, and First Lieutenant Nguyên Kim Tu was killed because he ejected at an altitude that was too low (about 300 feet) after his aircraft was damaged. U.S. documents contained no reports of shooting down any MiGs during the air battles on 22 August 1966.

From early morning of 5 September, the USN sent in four separate attack waves to bomb targets in the Nam Định–Thái Bình area. On that day the 923rd FR placed a flight of two MiG-17s at Gia Lâm airfield, piloted by Nguyễn Văn Bảy (A) and Võ Văn Mẫn, as the primary attack element. In the morning, the primary attack flight went to the first level of combat alert twice and took off once to move to another airfield. In the afternoon, the AF's HQ decided to use two MiG-17s to attack enemy attackers at low altitudes, while two MiG-21s flew a covering mission at high altitudes.

The flight of two MiG-17s took off at 1630 hours, and flew on a heading of 210 degrees. When the flight reached Chi Nê in Hòa Bình Province the pilots spotted a target to their right front at a range of approximately sixteen miles, and they dropped their auxiliary fuel tanks and switched on their afterburners to close with the target. Realizing that there were MiGs in the area, two F-8s switched on their afterburners and flew through a cloud to escape. Nguyễn Văn Bảy (A) decided not to pursue them, instead flying in between two clouds to meet them when they came out of the cloud. As he expected, right after he flew through a hole between two clouds, the F-8 No. 2 arrived, Nguyễn Văn Bảy (A) immediately turned in and chased the F-8. When the range was approximately 0.28 miles, he fired his guns, but his shells missed to the left. He fired two more bursts and saw his shells impact around the cockpit of the F-8, which then turned onto one side. Nguyễn Văn Bảy (A) valiantly swept forward and fired another burst. At that time he saw that the F-8 was on fire. The F-8 dove straight into the ground near Ninh Bình City. The pilot of this F-8E most likely was Capt. Wilfred Keese Abbott, USN, from VF-111 of USS *Oriskany*.[24] The pilot ejected and was captured.

At the same time, Võ Văn Mẫn turned and got on the tail of the F-8 No. 1. When the range was 0.4 miles he fired two bursts from his guns, but he missed. Võ Văn Mẫn continued to close in on his target and fired three more bursts. The F-8 burst into flames, rolled upside down, and dove toward the earth.

DESCRIPTION BY PILOT NGUYỄN VĂN BẢY (A)

I made some quick calculations and ordered my wingman to accompany me in taking a shortcut to meet the enemy aircraft when they flew out of the cloud. The two F-8Es continued their combat weave in order to keep a lookout and cover each other, but this slowed them down. I decided to chase the second F-8. When the range was down to 0.18 miles, I fired a burst of shells at the American aircraft. The shells hit the cockpit and the aircraft began to burn. The pilot ejected from his aircraft. Because I was so close when I fired, a piece of plastic from the F-8's cockpit was ingested into my MiG-17's air intake nozzle.

Right after I fired, I rolled onto one side and turned to one side to allow [Võ Văn] Mẫn to make his attack. Võ Văn Mẫn chased the F-8 No. 1 and fired his guns. Mẫn's shells hit the F-8's cockpit, severely injuring the pilot. The F-8 caught fire and the pilot ejected. Our flight, both of us, returned and landed safely.[25]

After his seventh victory, Nguyễn Văn Bảy (A) was released from combat duty status by an order from his superiors in July 1967. Senior Colonel Nguyễn Văn Bảy (A) became a MiG-17 ace with a top score of seven victories (he didn't parachute at any time during the war), and was awarded the honorable title VNP Armed Forces Hero. After the war, Nguyễn Văn Bảy (A) was appointed vice chief of staff of the AD and AF Service. When he was more than eighty years old, he attended all three Vietnam/U.S. veteran pilot meetings in Hanoi and San Diego. It should be noted that several U.S. veteran pilots paid visits to his farm in Đồng Tháp Province and they were amazed at the idyllic life of this legendary ace, who was now an old farmer in the southern countryside, and they took many photos with him.

16 September 1966: A Savage Dogfight over the Skies of Hải Dương

After the radar picked up an American strike formation composed of six F-105s and eight F-4C fighter escorts flying in from the sea to attack targets in the area of Phả Lại, Đông Triều District, Hải Dương Province, a flight of four MiG-17s piloted by Hồ Văn Qùy, Đỗ Huy Hoàng, Nguyễn Văn Bảy

(A), and Võ Văn Mẫn was ordered to take off from Gia Lâm airfield to intercept the American strike formation in the skies over Phả Lại. As the MiGs were flying past Phả Lại the pilots spotted the targets, both F-105s and F-4Cs at an altitude of 2,200 feet. During this period the USAF aircraft usually flew in from the sea at very low altitudes in order to avoid detection by the radars. MiG lead Hồ Văn Qùy ordered his wingmen to drop their auxiliary fuel tanks in order to make the attack. Exactly following the combat plan, the flight split into two sections, with two MiGs of the second section engaging in a dogfight with the F-4s while the two lead MiGs chased the F-105 bombers.

The fighter aircraft from both sides intermingled as they chased one another and fought a swirling, savage dogfight in the skies over Nam Mẫu. Exploiting their superior weapons, the F-4s repeatedly fired their missiles, but the MiGs were able to avoid all eight of the missiles. Meanwhile, seizing an opportunity, pilots Hồ Văn Qùy and Nguyễn Văn Bảy (A) made tight inside turns, kept on their opponents' tails resolutely, and shot down one F-105 and one F-4C.

The F-4C flown by Maj. John Leighton Robertson and 1st Lt. Hubert Elliot Buchanan from the 555th TFS/8th TFW was attacking a target in the Đáp Cầu area when it engaged with a MiG-17. This was Nguyễn Văn Bảy (A)'s MiG, as moving toward the Phantom, he saw the F-4 turning left. That turning maneuver allowed the MiG to cut the diameter of the circle and close the distance to the opposing aircraft to 0.07 miles, to achieve an appropriate angle of attack. He fired his 37- and 23-mm cannon at the Phantom and destroyed it in an area twenty miles southeast of Kép airfield. Major Robertson's ejection was unsuccessful and he was killed. First Lieutenant Buchanan ejected and was captured, then was taken to the Hanoi Hilton.

In September 2017, in the VN/U.S. meeting in San Diego, when U.S. pilot H. Buchanan met an old Vietnamese pilot, he asked if that pilot had fought the air battle on 16 September 1966 and the answer was "Yes." After recalling the air combat situations and actions on that day, the two pilots Nguyễn Văn Bảy and H. Buchanan recognized each other as having been opponents more than forty years earlier. The two old veteran pilots then hugged each other very tightly and that moment was very emotional.[26]

On 16 September 1966, the Americans credited an F-4C flown by 1st Lt. Jerry W. Jameson and 1st Lt. Douglas B. Rose from the 555th TFS/8th TFW, with shooting down one MiG-17 with an AIM-9B missile.[27]

However, according to the combat log of the 923rd FR, following the air battle on 16 September 1966, all four MiG-17s that had taken off returned and landed safely.[28]

20 September 1966: MiG-17s versus F-105s

After having a discussion about the situation and coming to the conclusion that the USAF would focus its attacks on targets in the Hanoi area, on 20 September 1966 the AD and AF HQ ordered the 921st and 923rd FRs to plan to fight a battle with the coordinated actions of both types of aircraft, MiG-17 and MiG-21.

Headquarters received the information about a formation of F-105s, escorted by F-4s, that was flying in from Yên Bái and northern Tuyên Quang then turning down and flying along Thud Ridge northeast of the Tam Đảo mountain range to attack the Hanoi area. At 1530 hours, the flight of MiG-17s designated as the primary attack element was ordered to take off from Đa Phúc airfield. The flight, composed of Lê Quang Trung, Hoàng Văn Kỷ, Trần Minh Phương, and Lưu Đức Sỹ was vectored to fly along the west side of Route 3 at an altitude of 10,000 feet, then was ordered to turn right and head toward the Võ Nhai area to intercept a group of F-105s. Two minutes later, Lê Quang Trung saw a formation of the USAF aircraft approaching at a range of five miles, and he ordered his wingmen to drop their auxiliary fuel tanks and accelerate to attack the enemy aircraft. During this engagement, Lê Quang Trung shot down one F-105 and damaged another one.

Meanwhile, Hoàng Văn Kỷ also shot down one F-105. Seeing that the MiGs were attacking the F-105s, the F-4s turned back and headed toward the four MiG-17s. Having assessed the situation and determined that it was becoming unfavorable, the command post ordered the flight to break off the engagement. The entire flight of four MiG-17s flew toward Đại Từ, returned to Nội Bài, and landed.

21 September 1966: Coordinated Actions of Two Types of MiG

On 21 September, the weather in the battle area was very bad, with thick cloud cover. In the morning a formation of the U.S. strike force, composed of forty F-105s and eight F-4s, flew in from the sea and across the Yên Tử mountains to attack Đáp Cầu Bridge in Bắc Giang Province. The AD and AF Command's post decided to again employ the plan for coordinated actions by MiG-17s and MiG-21s to intercept the American strike group.

In order to carry out the combat missions, the flight of four MiG-17s piloted by Nguyễn Văn Bảy (A), Đỗ Huy Hoàng, Lưu Huy Chao, and Võ Văn Mẫn took off from Kiến An airfield at 0858 hours to intercept the USAF strike group. The flight was directed to fly at a low altitude past Kinh Môn to Đông Triều and then to turn left, climb, and approach the target. A few minutes later, after scanning the sky, the pilots spotted F-105s at a range of nine miles but also saw F-4s farther away.

Precisely following the battle plan, the flight of MiG-17s decided to attack the F-105 bombers, but before they could get close to the bombers a group of F-4 escort fighters swept in and engaged the MiGs at an altitude of 3,000 feet. Faced with this development, the MiG-17 flight changed the initially designed plans and began a circling, swirling dogfight with the F-4s. By the end of the eight-minute air engagement, pilot Võ Văn Mẫn had shot down one F-4. This was most probably an F-4C flown by Capt. R. G. Kellems and 1st Lt. J. W. Thomas from 433rd TFS/8th TFW.[29] Captain Kellems tried to fly his aircraft out to sea but the aircraft crashed; both pilots were rescued. Meanwhile, Đỗ Huy Hoàng was hit by a missile fired by an F-105 and the pilot was forced to eject.

Taking advantage of the dogfight between the F-4s and the MiG-17s, the two MiG-21s flown by Lê Trọng Huyên and Trần Thiện Lương swept in to attack the formation of F-105s that was heading directly toward the MiGs at a range of ten miles. The two MiG-21s switched on their afterburners and chased the F-105s at an altitude of 6,500 feet, and a savage air battle raged between the two MiG-21s and the F-105s. The American pilots believed that this chaotic air battle was due to the foggy weather as well as limited air control guidance. This was the most ferocious air battle fought between the United States and the VNPAF up to that point of time.

During this battle the MiG-21 pilots displayed the superior capabilities of their aircraft in air combat against the F-105s. When F-105s got on his tail, Lê Trọng Huyên took drastic action. He quickly dove, built up air speed, and then suddenly pulled up above the F-105s. Before they had time to react, Lê Trọng Huyên had completed his climb maneuver, rolled upside down, got into an attack position behind an F-105, and fired a missile at it. The F-105 hastily dove and tried to escape but Lê Trọng Huyên was able to pursue it, and shot it down near Bắc Ninh. As a result of the 21 September 1966 air battle the USAF recognized the tremendous effectiveness of the MiG-21 equipped with R-3S air-to-air missiles, and realized that this battle signaled a new era in the air war over North Vietnam.

One difference in the assessment of the air engagement on 21 September 1966 was that the VNPAF claimed that it shot down one F-4C and one F-105, while some U.S. authors said that only the F-4C was shot down in the air engagement and that the F-105 was shot down by AAA units. On 21 September the USAF's pilots claimed they shot down two MiG-17s. In reality, however, the VNPAF records revealed that only one aircraft went down (Đỗ Huy Hoàng ejected and parachuted to earth safely) and the other aircraft all returned and landed safely.

5 October 1966 : The Atoll Missile's Effectiveness

Based on intelligence information and the result of the analysis of the activities of U.S. aircraft some days earlier, the AD and AF Command came to the conclusion that on 5 October the USAF would probably send EB-66s in to operate over the northwest region, and send in fighters as a diversion and to escort and cover the EB-66s. Guessing that the EB-66s would fly in across the border to conduct an electronic jamming mission, the AF Command decided to use two flights of two MiG-21s each to intercept and destroy the EB-66s. Actually, a long time before that point, four of the 921st FR's best pilots had been selected for a special training course for this mission. The two flights composed of Bùi Đình Kình and Nguyễn Đăng Kính (the primary attack flight), and Nguyễn Nhật Chiêu and Đặng Ngọc Ngự (the support flight), were placed on combat duty alert.

Two flights took off at 0735 hours, turned left, and were vectored to the battle area. At 0743 hours the primary attack flight saw a target 25 degrees to their front at a range of fifteen miles and an altitude of 20,000 feet. In fact, the target was a group of four F-4Cs flying in a spread-finger formation, and was assigned to escort two EB-66 EW aircraft that were jamming Vietnamese electronic signals in order to prepare for a strike group to bomb a bridge thirty-five miles southwest of Yên Bái. The MiG lead gave the order to his wingmen to drop auxiliary fuel tanks and attack, then he chased to attack the F-4C escort fighters himself to allow his No. 2 to attack the EB-66s.

Being surprised by the MiGs' attack, the F-4C escort fighters hastily made a violent maneuver to be able to avoid the attack and turn back to counterattack. Bùi Đình Kình got on the tail of the F-4C No. 3 flying in the rear. He quickly closed the range, got into the attack position, and when the range was 1.6 miles he fired his first missile. However, the F-4 continued to fly straight and level. Undaunted, Bùi Đình Kình continued to chase his target and fired his second missile at a range of less than 1.3 miles. The F-4 began to burn and dove toward the ground. Apparently, the F-4C went down so fast that the other F-4 pilots and the crew of the EB-66 did not know why the F-4C No. 3 had gone down. The F-4C that was shot down by Bùi Đình Kình's R-3S missile was flown by 1st Lt. E. W. Garland and Capt. William Richard Andrews of the 433rd TFS/8th TFW. Both pilots ejected, but only First Lieutenant Garland was rescued by an HH-3 helicopter. Captain Andrews was listed as killed in action.

It should be remarked that Bùi Đình Kình was the first pilot to shoot down an F-4C with an R-3S air-to-air missile (which NATO called the Atoll) and this signaled the beginning of a new era in the air combat history of the MiG-21. First Lieutenant Garland himself confirmed that his Phantom was hit by an R-3S missile fired by a MiG-21. This was the first F-4 shot down by a MiG-21 with an air-to-air missile.[30]

This victory not only helped MiG-21 pilots affirm the armament plan for using R-3S air-to-air missiles, it also provided ideas for the VNPAF's HQ to resolve the question of how to direct and control the MiG-21s in order to intercept and close with the target from afar, just to give the pilot time to get into attack position, exactly as the MiG-21 had been designed to do as an interceptor.

Air Engagement on 8 October 1966

At 1130 hours, three groups of U.S. aircraft were detected over the northwest region, flying past Phú Thọ, Yên Bái, and Tuyên Quang. At 1414 hours four more groups of U.S. aircraft flew in from the direction of Sam Neua and flew over Yên Châu and Yên Bái, then headed toward the Tam Đảo mountains and Đông Anh. The AD and AF Command decided to use both

MiG-17s and MiG-21s in coordinated actions to disrupt the enemy's strike formation and force them to jettison their bombs before they could reach the target.

As was scheduled, a flight of two MiG-21s (Trần Ngọc Síu and Mai Văn Cương) took off at 1438 hours. While they were still gaining altitude, the MiG pilots spotted a formation of four F-105s east of the airfield. The MiG lead shouted an order to drop auxiliary fuel tanks and sped forward to attack. Almost immediately, when the MiG No. 1 turned in to get on the tail of the two lead American aircraft, the F-105s No. 3 and No. 4 quickly got on the tail of the MiG No. 1. Without hesitation, MiG No. 2 immediately got on the tail of the two trailing F-105s. When the MiGs turned back the pilots spotted four more enemy aircraft that were turning away after bombing Đông Anh. No. 2 immediately chased them and shot down one F-105 over Vĩnh Yên. The AD and AF Service Command ordered the pilots to break off the engagement and return to land at 1502 hours.

9 October 1966: First Clash of MiG-21s with USN Aircraft

Toward the end of 1966, the USAF and USN continued to escalate the war by attacking targets around Hanoi City and many other important targets deep inside North Vietnam. The VNP AD and AF units continued to score successes and shot down many U.S. aircraft. While the MiG-17s of the 923rd FR took off constantly and scored several victories against the USAF and USN, the MiG-21s continued to experience problems and still had difficulty with their tactics. The MiG-21 pilots of the 921st FR, therefore, needed to win more victories to affirm the new tactics that were best suited to the MiG-21.

At 0649 hours on 9 October, USN aircraft flew in over the Đáy river-mouth up to Nam Định and Phủ Lý. A formation of four USN F-8Es flew a MiGCAP patrol, supporting A-4 attack bombers coming in at a low altitude to bomb targets in the areas of Phủ Lý in Ninh Bình Province and Vụ Bản in Nam Định Province. During the attack the USN aircraft used a new tactic by including in the formation an E-1B early warning aircraft to provide information to the F-8E fighters about the appearance of MiGs in the area.

The AD and AF Service's HQ decided to use MiG-17s supported by MiG-21s to make a surprise attack on the USN strike formation during the second wave of bombing attacks in the area of Giẽ Bridge, with the goal of disrupting the USN aircraft's attacks on transportation targets. To carry out the command's tactical intentions, the 921st FR placed a flight of MiG-21s, piloted by Phạm Thanh Ngân and Nguyễn Văn Minh, on combat alert duty. To check the effectiveness of weapons used on MiG-21s, in this battle MiG-21 No. 1 was armed with R-3S missiles while No. 2 had rocket pods. The 923rd FR MiG-17 pilots on combat alert duty were Lê Quang Trung and Trần Minh Phương.

Going ahead with the plan of coordinated actions in battle, at 0740 hours the two flights, one consisting of two MiG-21s and the other of two MiG-17s, took off and flew on a heading of 210 degrees to the battle area. A moment later, when Nguyễn Văn Minh reported that he had spotted the target, Phạm Thanh Ngân gave the order to drop auxiliary fuel tanks and make a sharp turn to the right to pursue the target, which was a formation of the enemy aircraft approaching to bomb the Phủ Lý–Giẽ Bridge area. Phạm Thanh Ngân saw two F-4s in front of him and two more aircraft farther away that were in a climb southwest of Mỹ Đức in Hà Tây Province. These aircraft were a formation of F-4Bs assigned to escort A-4s attacking targets southwest of Hanoi. Briefly assessing the situation, Phạm Thanh Ngân decided to turn hard to get on the tail of the aircraft on his right and in the trailing section. When the range was down to between 0.6 and 0.9 miles and he had his target designator stabilized on the target, just as he was preparing to press his missile firing button he saw that his wingman was firing rockets at the F-4s. MiG No. 1 decided to turn away and drop back to cover No. 2's attack. Phạm Thanh Ngân heard Nguyễn Văn Minh shout over the radio, "I hit him!" When the command post gave the order to break off the engagement, No. 2 did not reply. Phạm Thanh Ngân looked for his No. 2 for a while and then turned back and landed at the airfield.

While covering the MiG lead, Nguyễn Văn Minh spotted F-4s behind them that were firing missiles at the MiGs. He made a sharp turn to confront the F-4s virtually head-on. When the F-4s accelerated to try to get away, Nguyễn Văn Minh got on the tail of the lead F-4 and fired a volley of rockets from a range of around 0.24 miles. He saw the rockets hit the fuselage of the F-4. After this firing attack, he broke off the engagement and turned away to return to land. About 25 degrees into his turn, he felt his aircraft suddenly shake very hard. Realizing that his aircraft had been hit by a missile, he decided to eject and parachuted safely to the ground.

The aircraft that shot down Nguyễn Văn Minh's MiG-21 was most probably an F-8 that had approached at a low altitude so that the search and early warning radar network had not detected it and had not been able to warn the MiG-21s. The F-8 fired two Sidewinder missiles, and the second one hit the MiG-21's tail. This was the first time that a Navy F-8 shot down a MiG-21 with an air-to-air missile. The F-8E that shot the MiG down most likely was flown by Cdr. Richard M. Bellinger of VF-162 off the aircraft carrier USS *Oriskany*. Bellinger was a veteran pilot who had fought in three different wars (World War II, the Korean War, and the Vietnam War).

During the same day, a flight of MiG-17s flown by Lê Quang Trung and Trần Minh Phương was ordered to take off to intercept a formation of A-1Hs from VA-176 of the USS *Intrepid*, which was flying in to search for a downed pilot in the Vụ Bản area of Hà Nam. A ferocious air battle ensued. In spite of the fact that there were a large number of American aircraft and that the A-1Hs were covered by F-8 escort fighters, Lê Quang Trung was able to shoot down one A-1H. During a dogfight against the enemy aircraft, Trần Minh Phương's aircraft was hit and he was forced to eject. It was most likely that the aircraft that shot down Trần Minh Phương's MiG-17 was an A-1H flown by Lt. (jg) William T. Patton from VA-176 off the USS *Intrepid*.

In summary, during the battle of 9 October 1966 MiG flights shot down two F-4Bs and one A-1H. The VNPAF also acknowledged that one MiG-17, flown by Trần Minh Phương, and one MiG-21, flown by Nguyễn Văn Minh, were shot down. Both pilots ejected and survived.[31] At the same time, the USN claims credit for shooting down one MiG-17 and one MiG-21.[32]

5 November 1966: A Hard Day for MiG-21s

In early November 1966 the MiG-21 pilots of the 921st FR were still continuing to hone their skills, test their strength, and try to find and reaffirm the most appropriate fighting tactics for the MiG-21. Obviously, one of the most important missions that the regiment's pilots worked very carefully to prepare for was a plan to attack and destroy EB-66 EW aircraft, a target that the MiG-21 pilots had failed to kill a number of times before. On the morning of 5 November, a Saturday, a formation of four F-4Cs from the 480th TFS/366th TFW was escorting an EB-66 that was supporting a bombing strike against targets in RP 6 north of Hanoi.

Two skilled pilots, Bùi Đình Kình and Đồng Văn Song of the 921st FR, were assigned to take off and attack this target. After taking off, the two MiG-21s were directed up to intercept the flight path of the EB-66. In spite of the presence of the F-4C fighter escorts, the MiG-21 pilots bravely aimed their attack at the intended target. When the two MiG-21 pilots spotted the EB-66 and its escort fighters, they ignored the F-4Cs and approached the EB-66 from the rear very quickly. At a reasonable firing range one of the pilots fired one R-3S missile at the EB-66. At that moment the F-4C No. 1 shouted a warning to the EB-66: "Make a hard turn to the right!" The EB-66 turned sharply to the right, dove, accelerated, and fled from the area. Meanwhile the F-4Cs swarmed in to engage the MiG-21s, resulting in a swirling, turning dogfight.

Based on the recorded notes and on interviews of the pilots and the GCI officers, the picture of the air battle between the two MiG-21s, the EB-66, and the F-4s can be reconstructed.[33] While the MiG No. 1 chased and fired a missile at the EB-66, the F-4C No. 1, flown by Maj. James E. Tuck and 1st Lt. John J. Rabeni, got on the tail of the MiG No. 1, but the MiG No. 2 quickly swept in and got on the tail of the F-4C No. 1. Meanwhile the F-4C No. 2 (flown by 1st Lt. Wilbur J. Latham Jr. and 1st Lt. Klaus J. Klause) was pursuing the MiG No. 2. At that time the air engagement turned into a circle with all aircraft in right-hand turns and each aircraft determinedly chasing the next. Obviously, it was clear that the MiG No. 1 Bùi Đình Kình had accepted the risk (because he had to reduce speed to get behind and target the EB-66) and was determined to chase and destroy the EB-66. Meanwhile, the two F-4Cs had to maintain the correct closing speed in order to choose the proper time and range at which to fire their missiles in order to avoid the possibility that their missiles might hit the EB-66.

Even though the F-4 No. 1 repeatedly launched a series of AIM-7 and then AIM-9 missiles, none of the missiles hit their target. Ignoring the threat from the F-4 fighters, the MiG-21 continued to chase the EB-66. The EB-66 flew into a cloud at an altitude of 10,000 feet to hide itself. Suddenly, when the MiG turned hard to the right to try to intercept the EB-66 after it emerged from the cloud, the MiG pilot found that it was hard to control his aircraft. Realizing that his aircraft had been hit by a missile, Bùi Đình Kình decided to eject. In the meantime the MiG-21 No. 2 had also been hit by a missile fired by an F-4 and its pilot, Đồng Văn Song, was also forced to eject.

It was likely that the crew of the EB-66 and the pilots of the F-4s coordinated the timing of the EB-66's sharp turn in order to provide the two F-4s with an opportunity to fire missiles.[34]

During the open tactical discussion seminars held after the battle, the MiG-21 pilots said that the reason for the loss on their part was that they had been so eager to attack the EB-66 that they had not kept close enough track of the U.S. fighter aircraft behind them. The MiG-21 pilots, in the discussion, did not try to evade drawing experience from the reasons for their losses in this battle. The important thing was to learn lessons from this experience and to come up with a new plan to destroy an EB-66 in the next battle.

It was interesting when, in October 2018, Col. W. J. Latham and Colonel Đồng Văn Song, two attendants of the third VN/U.S. veteran pilots meeting in Hanoi, met each other, discussed their respective experiences, and talked about what happened in that air engagement.

Air Engagement on 2 December 1966

Vietnamese records affirm that as many as twelve U.S. aircraft were shot down on 2 December 1966, during what was called Operation Rolling Thunder-Alpha 52. Some foreign authors described 2 December 1966 as "Black Friday" because of how the USAF and USN suffered that day, with the loss of seven aircraft acknowledged.[35]

From 2 December to 24 December 1966, the USAF and USN used a force of 280 aircraft sorties to conduct large-scale bombing strikes against targets in the Hanoi area, including the Gia Lâm railroad factory, Yên Viên and Văn Điển railway stations, and so forth. They also attacked Đa Phúc airfield to prevent Vietnamese fighter aircraft from taking off. During this period the AD forces shot down a total of twenty-six U.S. aircraft.

Focusing on the most important missions, the pilots of the 923rd and 921st FRs took the initiative in preparing plans to protect Đa Phúc airfield and targets in the Hanoi area. Having resolved to accomplish the AD and AF Service Command's battle intentions, on that day the two FRs carried out a coordinated plan: MiG-21s would fight at altitudes above 6,500 feet when the U.S. attackers flew in to attack the targets, while MiG-17s would fight at altitudes below 6,500 feet when the U.S. attackers flew out. A flight of MiG-21s flown by Vũ Ngọc Đình, Nghiêm Đình Hiếu, Lê Trọng Huyên, and Trần Thiện Lương was ordered to take off, then flew to the battle area. As they spotted the target, which consisted of both F-4s and F-105s, Vũ Ngọc Đỉnh ordered the pilots to drop their auxiliary fuel tanks and speed in to attack. The four MiG-21s split into two two-aircraft sections, each of which then turned inside and got on the tails of the F-105 attackers that were turning away after completing their dive-bombing. After making one complete circle in a turning dogfight with the range to the target steadily decreasing, at a range of 1–1.2 miles, Lê Trọng Huyên fired a missile that shot down the F-105 No. 1.

On 2 December 1966, the United States lost eight aircraft, including five F-4s, one F-105, and two A-4Cs.[36] There are many details about the loss of an F-105D, flown by Capt. Monte Larue Moorberg, shot down eighteen miles west of the Đa Phúc airfield, which matches the Vietnamese side's information about the F-105D shot down by Lê Trọng Huyên, over Nội Bài airfield.

4 December 1966: Battles over MiG Valley

Previously, on 22 November and 2 December 1966, the USAF had conducted a series of attacks against the airfields in North Vietnam but failed to suppress them. Therefore, in early December, they again conducted intense attacks against the airfields, using an average of fifty sorties per day. The AD and AF's HQ came to the conclusion that on 4 December the USAF would again attack targets in the Hanoi area and would also attack the airfields used by the MiGs.

The area south of the Tam Đảo mountains, where the Đa Phúc and Kép airfields were located, and a large area in the Red River delta were put together and nicknamed "MiG Valley" by some unknown U.S. pilots.[37]

The AF Command ordered the 921st and 923rd FRs to coordinate their combat efforts to protect the main airfields, Đa Phúc and Kép, located within the area of MiG Valley south of the Tam Dao mountains, and targets in the Hanoi area. A battle plan was approved for the use of a large number of combat sorties (fourteen MiG-17 sorties and ten MiG-21 sorties). The weather over the airfield was good, with six-tenths altocumulus cover at an altitude of 10,000 feet and visibility of more than twelve miles. The 921st FR had four MiG-21 flights (two aircraft in each flight) on combat alert duty at the airfield. According to a project to reaffirm the effectiveness of weapons (air-to-air missiles or unguided rockets) to be used in this battle, within each flight aircraft No. 1 was armed with R-3S missiles and the No. 2 with rocket pods. At 1500 hours, when the radar net picked up a group of U.S. aircraft approaching from Sam Neua and preparing to cross Route 2, the first flight of MiG-21s (pilots Đồng Văn Đe and Nguyễn Văn Cốc) was ordered to take off. When the flight was over the west end of the airfield the pilots spotted four F-105s that had just bombed area C (the location of the 921st FR HQ) and were climbing away. The MiG lead immediately gave the order to drop auxiliary fuel tanks and pursue this target. However, when the F-105s saw that MiGs were behind them they accelerated to escape.

Meanwhile, Nguyễn Văn Cốc continued to chase the two F-105s on the left. When the range was 0.5 miles he fired seven rocket volleys. The rockets exploded behind the enemy aircraft. Although he saw smoke trailing from one F-105, the F-105 continued to fly.[38]

The flight piloted by Nguyễn Ngọc Độ and Phạm Thanh Ngân took off at 1525 hours. As the pilots were climbing out after takeoff, a formation of F-105s that had finished their bombing runs was flying away. While circling in the holding pattern at an altitude of 6,500 feet, the pilots spotted four F-105s approaching at low altitudes to attack Area E (where the 921st FR's pilot housing and hidden bunkers were located). Nguyễn Ngọc Độ decided to dive after the first F-105, but the F-105 made a very sharp turn so he decided to attack the F-105 No. 2. After firing the missile, he quickly pulled his stick hard to the right to break away, so he did not see the results of his attack.

In summary, on 4 December 1966, four flights of MiG-21s took off to engage American aircraft in the area over Đa Phúc airfield. The pilots fired five missiles and two full loads of rockets (sixty-four rockets). Even though no American aircraft were shot down on the spot, the MiGs forced the U.S. aircraft to jettison their bombs to escape, foiling the American plan to destroy the target.

Based on the situation and the requirement to coordinate their combat efforts with the MiG-21s, the 923rd FR assigned three flights to combat alert duty that day. The first flight, consisting of Trần Huyền, Trương Văn Cung, Ngô Đức Mai, and Hoàng Văn Kỷ, took off at 1530 hours and flew toward Đa Phúc airfield. At the moment it reached the end of the airfield, it encountered a group of F-105s flying in from the direction of Phúc Yên straight down the runway and headed directly at the four MiG-17s. The MiG pilots pulled up and climbed to attack the enemy bombers. When they realized that they were being chased and attacked by MiGs, the four F-105s immediately split into two sections. Trần Huyền decided to chase the section that was heading west. He fired his guns at the lead enemy aircraft at a range of 0.18 miles, but he missed. The two F-105s accelerated and fled, so Huyền decided to turn back to the airfield. When he saw four more F-105s making dive-bombing runs against the airfield, he quickly turned toward them and fired three bursts from his guns at the tail-end F-105 at a range of 0.8 miles, but he missed again. When he returned to the airspace over the airfield, he saw more aircraft flying over Hàm Lợn Mountain. He sped forward to attack. Repeatedly, Huyền fired his first burst at a range of 0.10–0.12 miles, his second burst at a range of 0.08 miles, and his third burst at a range of only 0.06 miles. He saw his shells hit both wings of the U.S. aircraft and he saw smoke begin to stream from the enemy aircraft. The flight of MiG-17s returned and landed at Đa Phúc airfield.

5 December 1966: Air Battle over Thud Ridge

After the AD and AF Service HQ approved a new intercept tactic for MiG-21s, MiG-21 pilots vigorously joined the training exercises and were prepared to carry out the new combat plan once the U.S. attack bombers appeared.

Exactly as the AF Command had predicted, on the morning of 5 December the radar net picked up a formation of twelve F-105Ds flying in from Thailand. They were divided into three groups flying in trail formation, one behind the other, and they were maintaining a steady altitude and combat formation. As planned, two pilots, Nguyễn Đăng Kính and Bùi Đức Nhu, were ordered to take off and vectored to fly in a holding pattern over Sơn Dương to intercept the F-105s. Keeping in mind the regiment's battle plan and new tactic, both MiG-21s were armed with R-3S missiles. After flying one complete circle in the holding area, the MiG-21 pilots spotted the F-105D groups flying in extended trail formation. Almost immediately, the pilots were ordered to drop their auxiliary fuel tanks and get into position to attack.

Seeing the two MiG-21s chasing them, the startled F-105D pilots jettisoned their bombs and tried to escape, but it was too late. Nguyễn Đăng

Kính's MiG-21 was already on the tail of one F-105, and when the range was right and he had a good audible signal from the missile's heat-seeker, he fired an R-3S missile at the tail-end F-105, causing it to crash on the spot.

On the afternoon of that day a group of twenty-four F-105Ds flew in, using the old, standard flight path. Two flights of MiG-21s, one piloted by Lê Trọng Huyên and Trần Thiện Lương, the other by Vũ Ngọc Đỉnh and Nguyễn Đăng Kính, took off and were vectored to the skies south of Sơn Dương to intercept the F-105Ds. As soon as they reached the battle area the MiG-21 pilots spotted their target. The MiG lead Vũ Ngọc Đỉnh calmly got into the attack position, adjusted his sights precisely, and fired two R-3S missiles at one time that shot down one F-105D. Vũ Ngọc Đỉnh recalled that he saw the missile hit the tail of the enemy aircraft and saw the aircraft trailing smoke. Then he saw more aircraft in front of his MiG, so he told his wingman to attack them because he had already fired both of his missiles.[39] The entire USAF F-105D formation disintegrated. The pilots jettisoned their bombs and fled. The two flights of MiG-21s returned and landed safely at Đa Phúc airfield.

On 5 December an F-105D from the 421st TFS/388th TFW flown by Maj. Burriss Nelson Begley was approaching its target when it was shot down by a MiG-21.[40] The F-105D was hit in the tail and crashed twenty-five miles from Thud Ridge. Major Begley tried to make it to the Laos border, but a few minutes later he was forced to eject, and was later listed as killed in action. Eventually, both of that day's battles fought using the new MiG-21 intercept tactic were successes. Even though this was just the first step, it was very significant in the process of finding and reaffirming the tactics and fighting method that the MiG-21s should use. It should be noted that after these two victories on 5 December, during the rest of December MiG-21s scored victories in many other battles by using the tactic of intercepting the target at long range. The AD and AF Command ordered MiG-21s to attack the enemy aircraft at even longer ranges in order to disrupt the enemy bomber attacks on the outer perimeter of its defenses.

Air Engagement on 8 December 1966

Since the weather in the Hanoi area that day was poor, the USAF shifted its strike targets. Instead of attacking targets in the Yên Viên area, they attacked railroad targets and fuel storage facilities in Thái Nguyên. When the lead formation of four F-105Ds were still sixteen miles from the target, they were attacked by two MiG-21s piloted by Trần Ngọc Síu and Mai Văn Cương from the 921st FR. An F-105D flown by Lt. Col. Donald Henry Arise was chased by a MiG-21 and forced to try to hide itself in a cloud during a ferocious dogfight. Having been hit by a MiG's missile, the F-105 dove down into an area of heavy antiaircraft fire. Within moments, the pilot lost control of his aircraft when one of the external fuel tanks under one of his wings could not be jettisoned while the aircraft was at a low altitude. Don Arise's damaged aircraft may have flown into the ground. The F-105s of the Kingpin formation lost radio contact with Kingpin 03 after hearing a short "beep."[41] At the time he was shot down, Lieutenant Colonel Arise was the commanding officer of the 354th TFS/355th TFW deployed at Takhli air base.

The VNPAF records state that the pilot who shot down the F-105D flown by Lt. Col. Don Asire was Captain Trần Ngọc Síu.

14 December 1966: A Successful Day for MiG-21s

The air engagements that were fought on 14 December 1966 in the skies northwest of Hanoi resulted in a great deal of information that is found in the records of both the VNPAF and the USAF. A large number of aircraft from both sides participated in this air battle.

Having reviewed the air battles that had taken place shortly before, the AD and AF HQ had the idea that, because the VNPAF had fought a number of battles directly over the airfield and over the Tam Đảo mountain range during the previous days, it was very likely that on 14 December the USAF, having learned its lesson, would change its tactics and the type of combat flight formation it would use. For that reason, the AF Command decided to send MiG-21s from the 921st FR out to the Văn Yên–Yên Bái area to intercept the USAF strike formations at long range, in order to create the element of surprise. The 921st FR placed two flights of four MiG-21s each on combat alert duty. The first flight was piloted by Nguyễn Nhật Chiêu, Đặng Ngọc Ngự, Đồng Văn Đe, and Nguyễn Văn Cốc, and the second flight consisted of Phạm Thanh Ngân, Hoàng Biểu, Trần Ngọc Síu, and Mai Văn Cương.[42] As an element of the project to recheck the effectiveness of the weapons, in this battle all of the MiG-21s flying in No. 2 and No. 4 positions were armed with rocket pods.

After the B-1 radar net picked up jamming signals from EB-66 EW aircraft, the AF Command predicted that this was an indication that bomber aircraft would soon appear, so it ordered a number of MiG-21 and MiG-17 flights to stand by to take off. At 1455 hours a flight of four MiG-21s from the 921st FR took off and was vectored to a holding area over Hòa Bình–Vạn Yên. Just after making three complete circles, the MiGs pilots spotted twenty F-105s flying in spread-finger formation along the northern slopes of the Tam Đảo mountains and heading toward Hanoi. The MiG-21s immediately dropped their auxiliary fuel tanks and exploited their altitude advantage to sweep in to attack the bombers.

Quickly turning hard, Đặng Ngọc Ngự got on the tail of one group of F-105s while Nguyễn Nhật Chiêu flew behind him to cover and support him. Realizing that MiG-21s were chasing them, the F-105s jettisoned their bombs, accelerated, and turned away. While two lead MiGs were attacking the third group of F-105s, pilots Đồng Văn Đe and Nguyễn Văn Cốc turned to the right to chase the fourth F-105 group. Having discovered that MiGs were behind them, the F-105s jettisoned their bombs and turned to escape. In accordance with the battle coordination arrangements, the MiGs did not chase the enemy aircraft very far before turning to fly back and circle over the airfield. While the flight was returning, the two MiG pilots spotted four more enemy aircraft in front of them. Đồng Văn Đe got on the tail of the tail-end F-105D and, at the range of 1.3 miles and with a stable sight picture, he fired a missile. He saw the missile warhead exploding under the tail of the target. He then pushed his stick over to the left to turn away. Seeing another F-105 flying directly in front of him, he decided to attack this aircraft. When the range was right and he had a good sight picture, he fired his second missile, which flew straight and exploded right next to the target's left wing. As he broke off the engagement to fly back to the airfield, he saw a white parachute hanging in the sky below him. This may have been the parachute of Capt. Bob "Spade" Cooley of 357th TFS/355th TFW. Captain Cooley was flying in the No. 3 position in the Fosdick formation, assigned to attack a target north of Đa Phúc airfield. Captain Cooley was rescued by HH-53 helicopter escorted by four A-1s.[43]

At the same time, Nguyễn Văn Cốc chased the F-105 No. 2 on the right and fired a volley of rockets. He saw the rockets exploding behind the target.

The F-105 accelerated to flee. Following an order given by the command post, the two MiGs broke off the engagement and returned to land. During his return, Nguyễn Văn Cốc saw the F-105, having been hit by MiG No. 3, burning fiercely, and he saw one parachute floating down toward the ground. The flight returned and all pilots landed safely.

The USAF and USN had a hard day on 14 December, when U.S. pilots did not claim to have shot down any MiGs, while seven U.S. aircraft were lost. Of the seven losses, two were USN aircraft reported to have been shot down by SAMs while conducting an Iron Hand missile suppression mission in the Văn Điển area.

Air Engagement on 19 December 1966

On 19 December the USAF sent in a strike formation consisting of thirty-two F-105s escorted by F-4s to attack the Vĩnh Yên area and Đa Phúc airfield. In order to protect these facilities, the AD and AF HQ ordered the 921st FR to launch MiG-21s to intercept the U.S. strikes. After taking off, the command post directed the flight to fly to the battle area in northwestern Vĩnh Yên. When the pilots saw the target at a range of seven miles, Nguyễn Hồng Nhị gave the order to drop auxiliary fuel tanks and made a surprise attack by coming in to attack the F-105 formation from behind. Having his orders from the MiG lead, Vũ Ngọc Đỉnh chased the F-105 No. 4. When the range was right, he calmly adjusted his target designator and launched a missile that shot down one F-105.

During just the single month of December 1966, MiG-21s and MiG-17s shot down a total of eleven U.S. aircraft. Even the American pilots acknowledged that in just twelve days in December 1966 ten F-105s were lost, seven pilots were killed or listed as missing in action, five pilots were captured, and three pilots were rescued.[44]

1966: Statistics and Tactics Analyzed

In 1966 the VNPAF flew 623 combat missions and fought more than 60 air engagements against the USAF and USN aircraft. The MiGs opened fire 109 times and shot down 54 American aircraft (including 6 UAV), 45 of which crashed on the spot. Meanwhile, 17 MiGs were lost, with 12 pilots ejecting and parachuting to the ground successfully and 6 MiG pilots killed.[45]

In 1966 the USAF and USN acknowledged the loss of 538 aircraft of all types. The U.S. side acknowledged the loss of only 14 American aircraft to MiGs.[46] At the same time the United States claimed to have shot down 19 MiG-17s, 5 MiG-21s, and 2 An-2.[47] Until December 1966, the MiG-21 was still in the test phase of the new intercept tactic. After several meetings, research, and studies, the 921st FR's commander and pilots concluded that MiG-21s should be interceptors with air-to-air missiles, so they could be directed to intercept the enemy's aircraft from afar instead of engaging in dogfights above the airport.

The air victories of December 1966 proved the validity of these arguments, but this was only the beginning step. The MiG-21 pilots of VNPAF had to undergo hard trials and several fierce air raids in 1967 to perfect this new tactic. However, with regard to the use of weapons (the percentage of aircraft armed with missiles as opposed to those armed with rockets), this was still a test period, so half of the MiG-21s continued to be armed with unguided rockets while the other half were armed with R-3S missiles. A number of young pilots requested that their aircraft should be armed with missiles for their combat missions.[48]

After several air battles during December 1966, in which MiG-21s had eleven victories, USAF and USN pilots were forced to re-analyze and change their tactics to deal with the MiGs. Perhaps this was the reason that Col. Robin Olds drafted a plan for a special campaign called Operation Bolo, with the purpose of killing MiGs at MiG Valley, and then submitted it to Gen. William W. Momyer, who endorsed it and approved it. This operation was launched in January 1967.

4

1967

AIR BATTLES OVER MiG VALLEY AND MiG INTERCEPT TACTICS

If the year 1966 was called by the media as the year of Lyndon Johnson's war, 1967 would be called the year of the "U.S. war of escalation" in Vietnam. At the beginning of the year, the Joint Chiefs of Staff (JCS) ordered the beginning of Operation Rolling Thunder to directly attack the military, transportation, and industry targets of all six "route packages," including targets inside Hanoi and Hải Phòng. In 1967, the USAF made staff changes in the most senior posts of the Pacific Armed Forces (PACAF) and the Seventh/Thirteenth AF Combined Command. Meanwhile, the USAF deployed both aircraft and weapons with improved technical characteristics, as well as air combat tactics to better deal with the MiGs of the VNPAF.

The VNPAF also changed and strengthened its organization. It established the 371st Air Fighter Division (code name F-371), added new series of MiG-17s and MiG-21s to the combat inventory, and improved its readiness to accomplish air combat missions. Meanwhile, the number of VNPAF combat pilots increased with the arrival of newly graduated pilots from pilot training schools. The year 1967 also witnessed the growth of the combat operational capabilities of VNPAF and the development of MiG intercept tactics.

So air battles over MiG Valley in 1967 were expected to be very fierce. And from the beginning of January 1967, VNPAF pilots were faced with the challenges of the USAF's Operation Bolo.

Air Battles on 2 January 1967: Operation Bolo

By the end of 1966, at a conference in Luzon, Philippines, Col. Robin Olds, the 8th TFW commander, proposed to Gen. W. W. Momyer, Seventh AF commander: "Sir, the MiGs are getting frisky up north and beginning to go after the Thuds. I have an idea on how to counter their threat."[1] A few days later, General Momyer called Colonel Olds to come to Saigon to talk about his idea. Colonel Olds' overall objective was to mount a typical large strike using the F-105 call signs, ingress routes, altitudes, airspeeds, timings, and communications, even the same tanker track, as were used daily by the Thuds strike forces (the routine stuff that the North Vietnamese were used to seeing in the predictable bombing raids by the Thuds). But instead of using F-105 Thuds, the "striking force" would be F-4s armed with air-to-air missiles instead of bombs. Flights of Phantoms would come in from different directions and orbit the VNPAF airfields. In order to accomplish the combat plan, the first thing was emulating a strike making the NVN side think the approaching force (the F-4 fighters) was a typical strike package made up of F-105 attackers—but the plan depended on luck and the cloud cover.[2] That meeting was the first step in completing the plan for Operation Bolo, which was to begin on 1 January 1967. However, on that date, the weather over North Vietnam was bad, with thick layers of clouds, and the operation was postponed to the next day.

As it became clear that the weather would be better, although with extensive cloud cover, on 2 January 1967 the USAF decided to perform the missions that were drafted in the general plan for Operation Bolo. About midday on 2 January 1967 a strike formation led by Col. Robin Olds (West Force) flew into NVN airspace. The attack formation had a total of ninety-two aircraft, consisting of fifty-six F-4Cs, twenty-eight F-105s assigned to suppress SAMs, and eight F-104 Starfighters. Additionally, almost one hundred more aircraft (including EB-66s, EC-121s, A-1 Skyraiders, and helicopters) were used to support this strike. Keeping their part in the combat plan, the F-4s flew along the northern corridor of RP 6 at the same altitude and speed as was usually flown by F-105 bombers, in order to make North Vietnam radar net mistake them for F-105s.

Five minutes later, another strike group (East Force) led by Col. Daniel "Chappie" James Jr. (who was Olds' deputy commander on this operation and who later became the USAF's first African American four-star general) flew in toward the battle area. A number of the F-4 flights in Colonel Olds' formation flew toward Đa Phúc airfield and were navigated down along the northern portion of RP 6 while another group of F-4s flew at low altitudes to a holding position north of the Tam Đảo mountains. Meanwhile, an EC-121 aircraft equipped with an air search radar flew over the Gulf of Tonkin to provide advance information of MiG-21 takeoffs and to alert the F-4s to sweep in to attack as soon as the MiGs broke through the top of the cloud layer, before they had a chance to form up together and while their speed was still low.

On that day the 921st FR's commanding officers on duty were Lieutenant Colonel Trần Mạnh and Major Đỗ Hữu Nghĩa. The regiment's GCI officers on duty were Lê Thành Chơn and Lê Thiết Hùng. At midday, many U.S. aircraft were picked up on radar flying toward Phú Thọ and possibly planning to attack Hanoi. The first MiG-21 flight, piloted by Vũ Ngọc Đỉnh, Nguyễn Văn Thuận, Nguyễn Đăng Kính, and Bùi Đức Nhu, was ordered to take off at 1346 hours. For this engagement, all of the MiGs were armed with R-3S missiles. Shortly after climbing through the cloud layer and reaching Phù Ninh District, the MiG pilots intensified their scan of the sky and spotted four F-4s approaching from the direction of Phú Thọ. The flight pursued these aircraft to a point west of the airfield when it encountered four more F-4s. MiG lead Vũ Ngọc Đỉnh switched on his afterburner to pursue this target, but the F-4s immediately initiated a violent combat weave maneuver, making it impossible for Vũ Ngọc Đỉnh to get into position to fire a missile. A moment later, when Vũ Ngọc Đỉnh decided to turn to the left to return to the airfield, he saw that two F-4s behind him had fired missiles at him. Unfortunately, Vũ Ngọc Đỉnh did not have time to take evasive action before his aircraft was hit by an enemy missile. The aircraft shuddered and became uncontrollable. Vũ Ngọc Đỉnh decided to eject. The F-4C that hit Vũ Ngọc Đỉnh's MiG with an AIM-7E missile may have been the F-4C flown by 1st Lt. Ralph F. Wetterhahn and 1st Lt. Jerry K. Sharp of the 555th TFS/8th TFW.[3]

At that moment, Nguyễn Đăng Kính had seen another flight of four F-4s and decided to chase them. Based on the details of the descriptions, this was probably the flight of four F-4s led by Col. Robin Olds, which had been lying in wait above the cloud layer over the area of the Tam Đảo mountains. When the group of F-4s commanded by Colonel James had gotten into an attack position, one of the pilots in the call-sign Ford formation told Colonel Olds that he saw MiGs. Colonel Olds also spotted a MiG and chased it. When Nguyễn Đăng Kính had just pulled his stick to turn back to his rear he saw three or four black spots heading at him from the rear. In the blink of an eye Nguyễn Đăng Kính's MiG was shaken very hard. He realized that his aircraft had been struck by a missile and decided to eject. According to the detailed descriptions of the battle, it is likely that Colonel Olds' F-4 had launched two AIM-7 missiles that had missed their target, so Olds flipped his firing switches to fire a heat-seeking missile and launched an AIM-9B. This was the missile that exploded right next to Nguyễn Đăng Kính's aircraft.[4]

MiG-21s No. 2 and No. 4 pursued and engaged in a dogfight with the F-4s, but regrettably, because there were so many F-4s and because the F-4s fired so many missiles at them, both MiGs were hit by the enemy missiles, and both pilots ejected safely. The two F-4C pilots from the 555th TFS/8th TFW who shot down these two MiG-21s were a flight crew made up of Capt. Walter S. Radecker III and 1st Lt. James E. Murray III, and another flight crew made up of Capt. Everett T. Raspberry and 1st Lt. Robert W. Western.[5] In summary, after the flight of MiG-21s popped through the top of the cloud layer it was caught in the middle between the groups of F-4s, which constantly fired missiles at the MiG-21s. As a result all four MiG-21s were hit by the enemy missiles but all four pilots were able to eject safely and survived.

At 1355 hours the 921st FR's command post ordered a second flight of MiG-21s, flown by Nguyễn Ngọc Độ, Đặng Ngọc Ngự, Đồng Văn Đe, and Nguyễn Văn Cốc, to take off. Having broken through the top of the cloud layer as the flight at an altitude of 10,000 feet, Nguyễn Ngọc Độ spotted enemy planes and called his flight to drop external fuel tanks and turn left. Nguyễn Ngọc Độ decided to pursue the two lead enemy aircraft. When the range was down to 1.3 miles and he had a stable sight picture, he fired one missile. Almost immediately after he launched the missile, he felt his aircraft become unstable, and the aircraft went into a side-slip spin and began dropping. Nguyễn Ngọc Độ decided to eject. He landed safely in Nam Liên Hamlet, Sơn Dương District, Tuyên Quang Province. It is likely that the F-4 that damaged Nguyễn Ngọc Độ's aircraft and forced him to eject was an F-4C No. 1 (call sign Ramble 01) flown by Capt. John B. Stone and 1st Lt. Clifton P. Dunnegan Jr. who were from the 433rd TFS/8th TFW.[6] All three remaining MiG-21s turned back and landed safely at their base.

Account by pilot Vũ Ngọc Đỉnh:

> I do not know why the weather on 2 January was so unfavorable for
> our side. The clouds were thick, with the bottom of the cloud layer at
> 650 feet and the top of the cloud layer at 1,800 feet. This made it easy
> for the USAF to conceal their forces so that they could ambush our
> MiGs above the clouds. Because we had not figured out the enemy's
> plan, after we took off and popped through the top of the cloud layer,
> all four of our aircraft were shot down, but all four of our pilots were
> able to eject and land safely. This is because the Americans were able
> to keep their plan totally secret, and we were not able to learn much
> from our intelligence reports about the American tactical schemes. In
> any case, we learned lessons from our experiences in this battle, and
> all four of us emerged unhurt so that we were able to rejoin the fight
> within a few days.[7]

The U.S. side documented that in the air battles of 2 January 1967 seven MiG-21s were shot down,[8] but the 921st FR's battle log recorded only five MiGs crashed, that all five pilots safely parachuted, and within a couple of days all of them were available to once again undertake combat flight duty.[9]

6 January 1967: An Unsuccessful Day for MiG-21s

The weather over Đa Phúc airfield on 6 January 1967 was quite bad, with the bottom of the cloud layer at 900–1,300 feet and the top of the cloud layer at 1,900 feet. The commanding officer of the 921st FR on duty that day was the deputy regiment commander, Đỗ Hữu Nghĩa. After reviewing and learning lessons from the air battles of 2 January 1967, the AD and AF HQ came to a point of view that on 6 January 1967 the USAF would again attack targets in the Hanoi area and suppress MiG operations at Đa Phúc airfield. In fact, on that day, Col. Robin Olds, the commander of the 8th TFW, again led his formation, applying a new tactic in which the USAF would use a group of F-4Cs of the 555th TFS/8th TFW, led by Capt. Richard M. Pascoe, to fly in an extremely tight formation along a flight path similar to that used by a reconnaissance aircraft. The intent was to make North Vietnam's radars mistakenly believe that this was a flight of U.S. reconnaissance aircraft in order to entice MiGs to take off to intercept the flight.

Shortly after the radar net picked up the target and guessed that this was a flight of reconnaissance aircraft, at 0924 hours the 921st FR ordered a flight of four MiG-21s, consisting of Trần Hanh, Mai Văn Cương, Đồng Văn Đe, and Nguyễn Văn Cốc, to take off from Đa Phúc airfield to intercept the enemy aircraft. Meanwhile, four F-4Cs had been alerted by the air controller in the EC-121 and had turned back, switched on their radars, and tracked the MiGs. Realizing that the flight was in an unfavorable position, Trần Hanh immediately shouted, "Make a hard right-hand turn!" At the same moment Trần Hanh also saw six missile smoke trails headed from the F-4s straight toward his flight. Two F-4s had locked onto Đồng Văn Đe's MiG-21 and fired three AIM-7 missiles at it. The first missile, fired by Captain Pascoe, hit its target. The MiG-21 burst into flames. Đồng Văn Đe ejected, but his attempt to parachute down was unsuccessful and he was killed. Later, an investigation on the scene revealed that because the order to take off had been so sudden the pilot had not secured his parachute harness locking mechanism.

When Trần Hanh shouted to dive back under the clouds, MiG No. 2 Mai Văn Cương was flying back through the clouds when his MiG was hit by a missile fired by an F-4. Realizing that his aircraft was uncontrollable, Mai Văn Cương decided to bail out. He landed safely on the ground. The F-4C that fired the AIM-7E missile that hit Mai Văn Cương's aircraft was probably the F-4 flown by Maj. Thomas M. Hirsch and 1st Lt. Roger J. Strasswimmer from the 555th TFS/8th TFW.[10]

In summary, in two battles on 2 January and 6 January 1967 the VNPAF suffered total losses of seven MiG-21s and one pilot killed, without being able to shoot down any enemy aircraft. The death of Đồng Văn Đe was a tremendous loss because he was an outstanding pilot. After learning the cause of Đồng Văn Đe's death, the 921st FR supplemented its pre-flight procedures by adding the line, "Before closing the cockpit canopy, the mechanics must personally check to confirm that the parachute harness is securely fastened."

After these two battles in early January 1967 in which the VNPAF suffered losses, MiG-21s suspended their combat flight operations in order to conduct reviews, learn lessons, seek suitable combat tactics, and conduct additional training.[11] MiG-21s did not resume combat operations until 23 April 1967, and in the battle fought on 28 April 1967 they scored a clear, clean victory with their new tactics.

21 January 1967: The First MiG-17 Victory of the Year

During this time period, the USAF continued its attacks against Đa Phúc and Kép airfields and targets along Route 1. On 21 January 1967 several groups of F-105s and F-4s from the 355th TFW at Takhli AB, the 388th TFW deployed at Korat, and the 366th TFW stationed at Đà Nẵng took off to attack Kép airfield and targets in the Thái Nguyên area. As planned, a flight of four MiG-17s, flown by Hồ Văn Qùy, Phan Thanh Tài, Nguyễn Văn Bảy (A), and Võ Văn Mẫn, had secretly moved down to Kép airfield in order to attack the F-105s outside the perimeter of the ground-based air defense umbrella in the Đông Triều, Phả Lại, and Chũ sectors. The AD and AF Command believed that, since the VNPAF had not flown any combat missions during the previous days, the USAF might have become complacent and would, therefore, only assign a small number of escort fighters. In addition, MiGs seldom operated in this particular area so there would be the element of surprise.

The flight of MiG-17s was ordered to take off at 1456 hours, then was navigated to fly on a 220-degree heading. The flight was informed that the target was six miles away to the flight's left front. At that moment, the MiG lead Hồ Văn Qùy, and Võ Văn Mẫn both saw a formation of twenty F-105s. When they noticed that the MiGs were at their six o'clock, the F-105s hurriedly jettisoned their bombs and deployed into combat formation. The F-4 escort fighters turned back and fired missiles at the flight of MiGs. Seeing that there were so many U.S. aircraft, Hồ Văn Qùy ordered the flight to turn left, push down to low altitudes, and draw the F-105s toward the direction of Chũ District. Nguyễn Văn Bảy (A) got on the tail of one F-105, and when the range was down to 0.3 miles he fired five or six quick bursts from his guns. The F-105 burst into flames and crashed half a mile from the auxiliary ground control station. After firing his guns, Nguyễn Văn Bảy (A) broke away, returned to the airfield, and landed.

Also on that day, another F-105D flown by Lt. Col. Eugene Ogden Conley, the CO of the 354th TFS/355th TFW based at Takhli, was shot down while flying at an altitude of 13,000 feet. Conley did not have a chance to eject and was listed as killed in action. He was the second CO of the 354th TFS to be shot down and killed in the space of only two months (Lt. Col. Don Asire, the previous squadron CO, was shot down and killed on 8 December 1966).[12]

24 MARCH 1967: ESTABLISHMENT OF VNPAF CORPS

On 24 March 1967, General Võ Nguyên Giáp, the minister of national defense, signed Decision No. 014/QD-QP to establish the VNPAF Corps, under the umbrella of the AD and AF Service. Colonel Nguyễn Văn Tiên was appointed its first commander, Colonel Phan Khắc Hy was appointed its first political commissar, Colonel Hoàng Ngọc Diêu was appointed its chief of staff, and Colonel Đào Đình Luyện was appointed its deputy commander. The AF Corps' code name was F-371.[13] It consisted of two FRs, a military air transport regiment, and a flight training school. The establishment of the F-371 proved that VNPAF was growing and becoming an important force of the AD and AF Service. From that time, the AF Corps' command post directly controlled all air activities of its fighters.

Colonel Nguyễn Văn Tiên (b. 1924) later became a lieutenant general and the vice commander in chief of the AD and AF Service, then was appointed vice chief of the Technical General Department of the VNP Army, and dean of the Technical University of the VNP Army. He retired in 1996 and died in 2003.

Air Engagements on 26 March 1967

In the morning, the AD and AF Command provided an alert notice, which argued that because the weather was good it was likely that the USAF would conduct large attacks and that in particular the attacks would focus on targets northwest of Hanoi near Hòa Lạc airfield. The AF Command directed all forces to maintain a high state of combat readiness. At 1453 hours, the radar net picked up four groups of U.S. aircraft approaching from three directions: one in the Hòa Bình–Suối Rút sector that was turning up to attack Hòa Lạc airfield; one approaching in the Nghĩa Lộ–Sơn La–Yên Châu sector and headed toward the area northwest of Hanoi; and another one in the Ba Vì–Viên Nam sector and flying down along the Đà River.

The primary USAF strike group, which consisted of twelve F-105s escorted by a flight of four F-4Cs, was led by Col. Robert R. Scott, the commander of the 355th TFW, and was approaching on a suppressive mission in the area of the Hòa Lạc airfield in Sơn Tây. After concluding that the Hòa Lạc airfield was the primary target of the U.S. strike formation, the AD and AF Service Command ordered the 923rd FR to use its MiGs to attack the USAF strike formation in order to block the attack. At 1500 hours the flight flown by Ngô Đức Mai, Vũ Huy Lượng, Phan Thanh Tài, and Trương Văn Cung took off from Đa Phúc airfield to attack a group of F-105s that had just bombed the target and was flying past Hòa Lạc airfield. At 1509 hours, when the flight was in a holding pattern over Hòa Lạc airfield, the pilots spotted four F-105s. Ngô Đức Mai shouted to the flight to drop external fuel tanks and then sped forward to engage the flight of F-105s.

Having realized that they were under attack, the other F-105s jettisoned their bombs and turned west to flee. At this time, the F-4C escort fighters that were circling over the airfield swept in toward the MiGs. MiG-17s No. 1 and No. 2 immediately made an inside turn and chased two F-4Cs at an altitude of 2,000 feet. At a range of 0.2 miles Vũ Huy Lượng fired a long burst at the F-4. The F-4 shuddered in flight, and then it dove down toward the ground on the other side of the Ba Vì mountains. The F-4C that was hit by Vũ Huy Lượng's MiG was most likely flown by Lt. Col. Frederick Austin Crow and 1st Lt. Henry Pope Fowler of the 433rd TFS/8th TFW.[14] Both pilots were captured. Even though U.S. authors state that Lieutenant Colonel Crow's F-4C was shot down by a SAM-2, many details of this battle indicate that in fact this is the aircraft shot down by Vũ Huy Lượng.

While he was attacking a second F-4, Vũ Huy Lượng's aircraft began acting unusually. It rolled first to the left and then to the right, and then it dove toward the ground. The auxiliary ground control station saw this and shouted to the pilot to eject, but the pilot was unable to bail out of the aircraft. It was most likely that the American pilot who hit Vũ Huy Lượng's MiG with 20-mm cannon shells was Col. Robert R. Scott, the commander of the 355th TFW.[15]

The 923rd FR's report on the 26 March 1967 battle states that Vũ Huy Lượng died because he attempted a maneuver that was too violent after his aircraft had been damaged, and as a result his aircraft stalled. The three other MiG-17s returned and landed safely at Đa Phúc airfield.

19 April 1967: An Active Day for MiG-17s

Some years, due to some unusual weather conditions, the northeast monsoon in North Vietnam would last longer than usual until April. During the spring of 1967 the weather over North Vietnam was very bad. After 18 April 1967 there were many sunny days, signaling that the remaining days of April would become one of the most ferocious periods of the bombing campaign. The U.S. side realized during this period that North Vietnam's entire AD system and the MiGs made advancements in comparison with the previous months. The MiGs became more dangerous and more effective. MiGs intercepted and attacked American flight formations both during their approach to the target and during their withdrawal after their attacks.

In order to deal with the new tactics being used by MiGs and the ground-based air defense units, the USAF made a number of changes in its tactics. Consequently, from early April, F-4s were used more extensively to carry out bombing attacks, which meant that fewer F-4s were assigned to the MiGCAP mission, and the F-105s began carrying AIM-9 missiles so that, when necessary, they could engage MiGs in air combat. On the afternoon of 19 April, the long-range intelligence net detected many F-105s approaching Hanoi from the southwest. At 1552 hours the AD and AF Service's commander in chief, Phùng Thế Tài, issued an order directing the MiG-17s of the 923rd FR to take off. The 923rd FR ordered three flights (a total of ten aircraft) to take off from Gia Lâm and Hòa Lạc airfields.

The flight piloted by Võ Văn Mẫn, Hà Đình Bôn, Phan Văn Túc, and Nguyễn Bá Địch took off from Gia Lâm airfield at 1556 hours. When he spotted six F-105s flying in attack formation, Võ Văn Mẫn led his flight in to attack. Having seen the MiGs approaching, the F-105s jettisoned their bombs and turned to engage the MiG-17s. After two minutes of dogfighting against the six F-105s, which were now acting as fighters, Nguyễn Bá Địch cut inside the turn of the F-105s and got one F-105 in his sights. When the range was right, he opened fire and shot down this F-105. The F-105 that was shot down by Nguyễn Bá Địch was flown by Maj. Thomas Mark Madison and Maj. Thomas James Sterling,[16] and was part of a flight of F-105s carrying out Operation Iron Hand to support attack bombers assigned to bomb targets in the Xuân Mai area, twenty miles northwest of Hanoi. Two other F-105s were damaged and forced to return to their base. All of the MiG-17s broke off the engagement and returned and landed safely.

As was determined in the combat plan, the AF Command ordered another flight of MiG-17s (Lê Quang Trung, Nguyên Văn Thọ, Nguyên Xuân Dung, and Dương Trung Tân) to take off from Hòa Lạc airfield and fly to the Hòa Bình area in order to be prepared to support the primary attack flight. At 1718 hours the command decided that the support flight would now become the primary attack flight, and GCI officers ordered this flight to make a hard turn to a heading of 210 degrees.

After the F-105 flown by Major Madison and Major Sterling was shot down in the Xuân Mai area, a number of A-1E Skyraiders flew in to conduct a search and rescue (SAR) operation. At 1721 hours, after picking up two additional flights of enemy aircraft approaching western Vụ Bản, the AF Command ordered the flight to make a right turn to a heading of 250 degrees in order to close with the F-105s from an intercept angle of 140 degrees. When they spotted two flights of F-105s (eight aircraft) and two A1-Es at a range of four miles, Lê Quang Trung immediately ordered his flight to split up into two sections to engage the two groups of U.S. aircraft. During this air engagement with the MiG-17s, an A-1E flown by Maj. John Smith Hamilton (from the 602nd ACS/56th ACW) was shot down by the MiG-17 flown by Nguyễn Văn Thọ (923rd FR) with a burst of 37-mm gunfire. The A-1E crashed in the Xuân Mai area. No parachute was seen and Major Hamilton was listed as killed in action.

SOME DIFFERING ASSESSMENTS

In the battle of 19 April, pilots of F-105s of the 354th TFS/355th TFW reported that they had shot down four MiG-17s. In addition, these pilots reported that two more MiGs may have also been shot down but these could not yet be confirmed.[17] However, the report that F-105s from the 354th TFS/355th TFW shot down four MiGs has a big question mark.

According to the combat logs of the VNPAF, no MiG-17 was shot down during the battles of 19 April 1967 and all ten MiG-17s that had taken off returned and landed safely.[18] The records of one VNPAF unit state: "Between 19 April 1967 and the end of the month, in battles fought on six separate days the 923rd FR fought twelve air battles, shooting down fourteen American aircraft while preserving our own forces."[19]

24 April 1967: Some "Unexpected Meeting" Air Engagements

On 24 April, the USAF continued their attacks on targets around the Hanoi area and the Kép and Hòa Lạc airfields. On that day a number of "unexpected meeting" air engagements took place between U.S. aircraft and VNPAF's MiGs. At 0915 hours the 923rd FR command post ordered a flight consisting of Mai Đức Toại, Lê Hải, Phan Văn Túc, and Hoàng Văn Kỷ to take off from Gia Lâm airfield. The flight split into two two-aircraft sections, separated from one another by a distance of 0.9 miles, and was directed to fly toward Xuân Mai in Hòa Bình Province with the intention of intercepting an approaching group of F-105s.

Remarkably, the weather was very foggy that morning and visibility was limited, especially at altitudes below 6,500 feet. When the MiGs were flying at an altitude of 6,500 feet and a speed of 430 mph, before they were totally out of the layer of fog and mist, Hoàng Văn Kỷ spotted a group of F-105s escorted by F-4s below and to the left, flying along the course of the Đáy River. Obviously, this was a standard tactic of the USAF, utilizing the cover of terrain on one side that consisted of a range of sheer, high limestone mountains to avoid detection by radars. Only when they were close to the objective would they pull up to higher altitudes in order to bomb their target. It was clear that these F-105s were heading toward Hanoi.

Although the MiGs' flight had not yet reached the designated battle area, in light of the urgent situation caused by this unavoidable "unexpected meeting," the MiG lead decided to order the entire flight to drop their external fuel tanks and to head straight for the U.S. aircraft. The MiG-17 flight split into two combat sections. The two lead MiGs headed in to chase and engage the F-105s while the two MiGs of the second section intercepted the F-4s in order to enable the two lead MiGs to attack the enemy attackers. While flying at low altitudes down in the valley, with a line of limestone mountains on one side, the F-105 pilots spotted the four MiG-17s. They immediately jettisoned their bombs in order to shift over to the fighter role and then began turning and maneuvering, looking for an opportunity to attack. This "unexpected encounter" took place at low altitudes and it was very difficult for both sides to get into firing position. Even though this was Lê Hải's very first battle, he was able to skillfully get on the tail of an F-105, and at the appropriate firing range he pressed his trigger. But because he was still inexperienced he held the trigger down for more than five seconds, firing his entire load of ammunition in front of the F-105D. Ultimately, after a two-minute dogfight, the USAF F-105D formation fled from the battle area and the command post ordered the flight of MiG-17s to break off the engagement and return to base. Because of the violent turns at a low altitude, Lê Hải's gyrocompass was providing incorrect readings and the flight lead sent Phan Văn Túc back to guide Lê Hải back to the airfield to land.

In this "unexpected meeting" air engagement, even though the flight had shot down only one F-4 (shot down by Phan Văn Túc), the most significant outcome of the engagement was that the flight had successfully disrupted a surprise bombing attack by a large formation of USAF aircraft against targets in the Hanoi area. It should be emphasized that this air battle marked the beginning of the heroic combat career of ace pilot Lê Hải.

Continuing the eventful day, on the afternoon of 24 April 1967 another flight of MiG-17s, composed of pilots Võ Văn Mẫn, Nguyễn Bá Địch, Nguyễn Văn Bảy (A), and Nguyễn Thế Hôn, took off flying in two-plane sections in trail formation at an extremely low altitude (320 feet). Flying in complete radio silence, they landed secretly at Kiến An airfield in order to ambush and intercept USN strike groups coming in from the sea.

It should be emphasized that two days earlier the USAF and the USN had bombed Kiến An airfield in preparation for a new wave of attacks against Hải Phòng City. But amazingly, in an incredible achievement, the soldiers and civilians of Hải Phòng had filled in the bomb craters and repaired the damage in a single night, just in time to allow the flight of MiG-17s to land. U.S. intelligence had not discovered the unprecedented repair activities, and believed that Kiến An airfield was still unusable. The flight waited in ambush at Kiến An throughout the day on 23 April, but the USN did not attack Hải Phòng that day as the AF command post had anticipated.

During the afternoon of 24 April 1967 many flights of USN F-4s flew in from the sea to attack the Đông Triều–Quảng Yên area, and another group of aircraft flew in to attack Kép and Hòa Lạc airfields. Under the direction of the AF command post, the flight of MiG-17s had taken off a few minutes earlier and had approached the F-4s from the direction of the sun, making it easy for the MiG pilots to spot their targets. When they spotted the F-4s at a range of six miles from the target, Võ Văn Mẫn ordered the flight to split into two sections and got inside to attack.

When the surprised Navy F-4B flight realized that they were being chased by MiGs, they turned back toward the sea and split into two sections, with one section diving down to prevent it from being chased. However, it was too late. Võ Văn Mẫn ordered No. 2 to cover him and then quickly got behind an F-4B. When the range was down to 0.24 miles he opened fire. The F-4B was hit and exploded. At that time the four F-4Bs and two MiG-17s were chasing each other in an intermingled, confused situation. Nguyễn Văn Bảy (A) was on the tails of two F-4Bs trying to attack them while at the same time there were two more F-4Bs right behind him and pursuing him. With a second burst from his guns, Nguyễn Văn Bảy (A) shot down one F-4B and then made a quick, hard turn to avoid another F-4B that was right on his tail. It was probable that the F-4B that Nguyễn Văn Bảy (A) shot down was being flown by Navy Lt. Cdr. Charles Everett Southwick and back-seater Ens. Jim W. Laing from VF-114 of the USS *Kitty Hawk*.[20] Both pilots were picked up and rescued. (Southwick had taken part in the bombing attacks on North Vietnam during the Gulf of Tonkin incident in August 1964. After the 24 April 1967 air battle, on 14 May 1967 Southwick flew into North Vietnamese airspace again and was shot down and captured.)

The 923rd FR's command post ordered the flight to break off the engagement and all aircraft landed safely back at Kiến An airfield. In a battle that lasted for less than four minutes, the flight of MiG-17s shot down two F-4s while losing none of their own aircraft. After the four MiG-17s landed safely at the airfield, the ground technical personnel immediately hauled the aircraft to a hidden parking area at the foot of a mountain. Immediately thereafter, a group of twenty A-4s and F-4s arrived and savagely bombed the airfield. The buildings that housed pilots and mechanics were completely destroyed and the runway was hit by nine bombs that created bomb craters more than 33 feet wide and 16 to 23 feet deep. The Americans were certain that this time Kiến An airfield had been rendered completely unusable. However, once again the soldiers and civilians of Hải Phòng City repaired the damage in a single night, and by dawn the runway was ready to allow the MiGs to take off. The USN was once again surprised when, on the morning of 25 April, the four MiG-17s took off again from Kiến An airfield, intercepted American aircraft, and shot down three more American planes.

During two air engagements against USAF and USN pilots, the MiG-17 pilots of the 923rd FR won victory with a score of 3–0. Of special note, during this day's battle the VNPAF claimed the 1,800th American aircraft shot down over North Vietnam.

According to U.S. documents, during the battle on 24 April 1967 the USN shot down two MiG-17s with AIM-9D missiles.[21] However, the records of the VNPAF reveal that on 24 April all eight MiG-17s from both flights returned to base and landed safely without any loss.[22]

It is interesting that on July 2015, Lt. (jg) Charles Plump, one of the USN F-4 pilots who had fought this air battle, made a visit to Vietnam and a special visit to Nguyễn Văn Bảy (A)'s farm in Đồng Tháp Province. Two veteran pilots, who had been involved in an air battle more than forty-eight years earlier over the skies of Kiến An, met each other and revived their memories of that battle.

25 April 1967: The MiG-17's Ambush and Intercept Tactics

It should be noted that all throughout the night of 24 April 1967 the soldiers and civilians of Hải Phòng worked to fill in the bomb craters and repair the airfield to prepare it for the MiGs to take off. At 1004 hours, a 923rd FR's MiG-17 flight, consisting of Nguyễn Văn Bảy (A), Hà Đình Bôn, Nguyễn Thế Hôn, and Nguyễn Bá Địch, which had been standing combat alert duty at Kiến An airfield, was ordered to take off and then fly along the course of the Văn Úc River. Just after the flight had climbed to 4,500 feet it was informed by the GCI that "the enemy aircraft are in front of you." At that very moment the pilots spotted the target. Nguyễn Văn Bảy (A) ordered the entire flight to drop their external fuel tanks and head for the U.S. aircraft. Taken by surprise by the sudden appearance of MiGs that had taken off from Kiến An airfield, the attack bombers hastily jettisoned their bombs and turned to flee while the F-8 fighter escort turned back to intercept and conduct a dogfight against the MiGs.

While the F-8s were still accelerating on their way back to engage the MiGs, the flight of MiG-17s had been able to close in on the attack bombers. Hà Đình Bôn chased an A-4 that was trying to escape out to sea. When closing to a range of 0.25 miles, he fired a burst, the A-4 caught fire, and it dove toward the ground. The pilot ejected right over the mouth of Văn Úc River. The A-4C shot down by Hà Đình Bôn most probably was flown by Lt. (jg) Charles David Stackhouse from Squadron VA-76, based on the USS *Bonhomme Richard*.[23] At the same time, seeing an A-4 right below him, Nguyễn Bá Địch pushed his stick forward, placed the A-4 in the center of his sights, and pulled the trigger, causing the A-4 to catch fire. This A-4E was flown by Lt. Cdr. F. J. Almberg of VA-192 based on the USS *Ticonderoga*, who was assigned to attack SAM launch sites in the Hải Phòng area. A SAM exploded very close to him but his aircraft was not damaged. Immediately thereafter, however, Almberg saw another missile explode right next to his aircraft, damaging his aircraft's hydraulic system.[24] It is very possible that this was the moment when Almberg's aircraft was in fact hit by the shells fired by the MiG-17. Based on the detailed report of this air engagement, it is possible that this A-4E was actually shot down by Nguyễn Bá Địch.

At that time the F-8s had turned back and swept in to engage the MiG-17s. Just at that very moment, Nguyễn Thế Hôn saw an F-8 fire missiles at two MiGs ahead of him. He shouted a warning that enabled his fellow pilots to evade the missiles in time. While the F-8 was concentrating on pursuing the two MiG-17s in front of him, Nguyễn Thế Hôn pursued the F-8, and when he got into firing range, he opened fire. The F-8 was hit, exploded in mid-air, and then dove down to crash along the coast. The terrified surviving U.S. aircraft turned and fled out to the sea, but the SAM and AAA units shot down three more U.S. aircraft.

In a little over two minutes of air combat against the USN aircraft, the MiG-17s of the 923rd FR won a victory by shooting down three U.S. aircraft.[25] The flight flew up along the course of the Red River, flying over a field of blossoming corn, and landed safely at Gia Lâm airfield. This victory provided the VNPAF with more experience in fighting "surprise approaching-ambush tactic" engagements by taking off from an airfield that the Americans had just bombed and that they thought had not yet been repaired. The MiGs intercepted the Americans from a direction least expected by them and used tactics best suited to the MiG-17, an aircraft that was armed only with guns, making it most suitable to close-in air combat tactics.

When the first flight was preparing to break off the engagement and return to land, the second flight of MiG-17s, piloted by Mai Đức Toại, Lê Hải, Lưu Huy Chao, and Hoàng Văn Kỳ, was ordered to take off from Gia

Lâm airfield and attack the American strike formation, and to cover the first flight as they returned to land. Mai Đức Toại led his flight to attack a group of F-105s. During this dogfight, Mai Đức Toại shot down one F-105 just south of Gia Lâm airfield. After the first flight landed safely and the U.S. aircraft had exited the area, flying back out to the sea, the second flight returned to the airfield and landed.

28 April 1967: The MiG-21 Back in Action

Having received advance warning from the B-1 net that the USAF would attack targets in an arc west and southwest of Hanoi, the commander in chief of the AD and AF Service, Senior Colonel Phùng Thế Tài, ordered MiG-21s to intercept the U.S. aircraft approaching at low altitudes in the Tuyên Quang sector and ordered that MiG-17 flights attack the enemy aircraft flying in from the Suối Rút–Hòa Bình area. The 923rd FR's command post ordered the MiG-17s flight, flown by Mai Đức Toại, Lê Hải, Lưu Huy Chao, and Hoàng Văn Kỷ, to take off from Gia Lâm airfield at 1425 hours and directed them to fly to the designated battle area over Chương Mỹ, Hà Tây Province. A few minutes later another flight of MiG-17s, flown by Dương Trung Tân, Phan Điệt, Phan Thanh Tài, and Nguyễn Văn Thọ, took off from Hòa Lạc airfield and also flew toward its designated battle area west of Ba Vì. In terms of tactics, in this battle the AF HQ coordinated between aircraft of the same type but which had taken off from two different airfields. The idea behind this was for the MiGs to approach from different directions to attack the enemy unexpectedly. In this air battle pilots Lê Hải and Phan Thanh Tài each shot down one F-105. All MiG-17 aircraft of both flights returned and landed safely.

At 1534 hours a flight of MiG-21s flown by Đặng Ngọc Ngự and Mai Văn Cương took off and was navigated to fly along the northern slopes of the Tam Đảo mountains. This was the MiG-21's first return to action after more than three months of suspending combat operations. Arriving at a point nine miles north of Sơn Dương, the flight was ordered to turn left to Vạn Yên, and then to turn up north of Nghĩa Lộ to intercept a group of F-105s that were exiting Vietnam after completing their bombing attack. When he spotted the target 30 degrees to his left front at a range of 2.4 miles, the MiG lead Đặng Ngọc Ngự accelerated to pursue the target, and at an appropriate range he fired an R-3S missile, but the missile missed. When No. 1 shouted that there were two aircraft to the right, Mai Văn Cương quickly got on the tail of another F-105. At a speed of 680 mph, an altitude of 8,000 feet, and a range of 0.9–1.2 miles, Mai Văn Cương fired a missile that shot down one F-105. The F-105D that was hit by the missile fired by Mai Văn Cương's MiG-21 may have been flown by Capt. Franklin Angel Caras of the 44th TFS/388th TFW.[26] The F-105 exploded in an area twenty miles east of Nà Sản. The pilot was listed as killed in action. After the attack, two MiGs used their high speed to pull into a climb to break off the engagement and then returned and landed safely. This was the first MiG-21 victory recorded after almost three months of its temporary suspension of combat operation.

Air Engagements on 29 April 1967

At 1500 hours four F-105Ds of the 44th TFS/388th TFW flew into NVN airspace on a mission to suppress SAM sites and support a bomber strike formation assigned to attack targets in the Hanoi area. At 1528 hours a group of F-4s assigned to the MiG suppression mission arrived in the battle area, and one minute later a group of F-105 attack bombers flew over Long Viên, headed toward bombing targets in the area southwest of Hanoi.

The combat alert flight of four MiG-17s on duty, consisting of Nguyễn Văn Bảy (A), Lê Sỹ Diệp, Võ Văn Mẫn, and Trương Văn Cung, was scrambled to intercept the F-105 attack bombers in the Hòa Lạc–Ba Vì area when the bombers were exiting the area after their attack. However, when the MiG-17 flight was approaching the USAF bomber formation it encountered four F-4s assigned as fighter escorts for the attack formation. The GCI post believed that this flight of four F-4s had taken off from Đà Nẵng air base, assigned to provide fighter escort to F-105s carrying out bombing attacks against targets southwest of Hanoi. When the MiG-17s appeared and swept in to attack, the flight of F-4s immediately split up into two-aircraft sections that came in flying at separate altitudes, one 3,200 feet above the other. The MiG-17s dropped their external fuel tanks and turned to fight the F-4s. Nguyễn Văn Bảy (A)'s MiG quickly turned and got on the tails of the F-4s No. 2 and No. 3. The F-4s also dropped their external fuel tanks and engaged in a dogfight with the MiGs. However, the MiG-17 pilots quickly gained the advantage by maneuvering ferociously, and forced the F-4s to break off and flee. Nguyễn Văn Bảy (A) shot down one F-4C over the Ba Vì area.

It should be remarked that VNPAF documents on this battle only record a battle by MiG-17s against USAF F-4s and contain no record of any MiG-21 combat sorties on this date. However, in addition to the F-4C that was shot down, American authors also record a battle on 29 April 1967 in which two F-105s were pursued by MiG-21s and that one F-105 was shot down by a MiG.[27] But the VNPAF's pilots did not claim to have shot down any F-105s on this day.

30 April 1967: A Day of Impressive Victory for MiG-21s

Toward the end of April, the USAF and USN continued to send a large number of aircraft to attack several targets in the Hanoi area. The day of 30 April 1967 was a Sunday. On that day, the officers on duty in the 921st FR command post were Lieutenant Colonel Trần Mạnh and his deputy, Major Trần Hanh. At 1450 hours, after receiving a report from radar net that a number of flights of USAF aircraft were approaching to attack targets in the area southwest of Hanoi, the 921st FR's commander Trần Mạnh decided to launch MiG-21s.

Two pilots, Nguyễn Ngọc Độ and Nguyễn Văn Cốc, took off at 1459 hours and flew on a heading of 260 degrees to an area south of Mộc Châu. A dozen minutes later the regiment's radar picked up a target flying up from the south toward Yên Châu. The GCI decided to have its two MiG-21s attack this target. When he spotted a formation of F-105s at an altitude of 13,000 feet, Nguyễn Ngọc Độ ordered to drop external fuel tanks and told his wingman to support and cover him. The target was a formation of four F-105s that was part of a formation of twenty F-105s and eight F-4s from the 355th TFW. The U.S. aircraft formation, led by Col. Jack Broughton, was flying in to attack the Yên Phụ electrical power plant in Hanoi. (Later Colonel Broughton wrote a book entitled *Thud Ridge* in which he described this Sunday as "the longest mission").[28]

After seeing their target, the two MiG-21s switched on their afterburners and slashed toward the flight of F-105s, assigned to the mission of suppressing the SAM sites. Seizing a favorable moment, Nguyễn Ngọc Độ pushed his stick forward to chase the F-105 flying in the No. 3 position of the bomber formation. When the range was 0.6–0.9 miles and he heard the sound of the missile warhead indicating that it had locked onto the heat source properly, Nguyễn Ngọc Độ launched his Atoll missile and hit the F-105, causing it to burst into flames. The F-105F that was shot down by Nguyễn Ngọc Độ was probably the aircraft flown by Maj. Leo Keith Thorsness and Capt. Harold Eugene Johnson from the 357th TFS/355th TFW (Major Thorsness was the pilot who claimed that he had shot down one MiG-17 in a battle on 19 April 1967). Both pilots successfully bailed out and both were captured.[29]

Just before the F-105 flight had time to recover from its shock, youthful pilot Nguyễn Văn Cốc managed to capture the moment by quickly increasing speed to shoot forward and get on the tail of the F-105D No. 4. Calmly keeping his aircraft stable, Nguyễn Văn Cốc brought the target into his sight and launched his missile at a range of 1.2 miles, and it flew straight at the F-105. The aircraft caught fire and dove toward the ground in the Thành Sơn area.[30] The F-105 that Nguyễn Văn Cốc shot down was flown by 1st Lt. Robert Archie Abbott of the 354th TFS/355th TFW.[31] The pilot was able to eject and was captured. The F-105s, surprised by the appearance of the MiG-21s and the sudden loss of two of their number, hastily jettisoned their bombs and fled. The regimental GCI ordered the flight to return and land at their air base. This was the first of a total of nine U.S. aircrafts that Nguyễn Văn Cốc shot down during the war.

During wartime, Nguyễn Ngọc Độ was credited with six victories and was given the honorable tittle VNP Armed Forces Hero. Later, he was promoted to the rank of major general and was appointed as chief of staff of the AD and AF Service and then as head of the AF faculty at the National Defense Academy.

After the two F-105s were shot down, the news of their sudden loss was transmitted through the air early warning net (Red Crown) and SAR aircraft were immediately deployed. The lead of the strike formation decided to abort the bombing mission and instead concentrate his entire strike formation on the effort to rescue the pilots who had just been shot down. At this point, apparently Colonel Broughton, the strike formation commander, ordered Maj. Ed Dobson's Tomahawk flight to switch to the RESCAP mission (suppressive cover for the rescue of the pilots). Maj. Albert J. Lenski, flying the No. 3 aircraft in the Tomahawk flight, later described the unusual rescue effort in the well-known book *Magic 100*.

Terribly shocked by the loss of two F-105s in quick succession and anxious to rescue the pilots, eight other F-105s immediately swept in to bomb the Thành Sơn area. The first A-1 Sandies immediately thereafter joined the search effort. Having argued that this was an excellent opportunity to intercept the enemy bombers, at 1629 hours the 921st FR ordered two MiG-21s flown by Lê Trọng Huyên and Vũ Ngọc Đình to take off. While waiting for the SAR aircraft to arrive (they took off one hour after Thorsness was shot down), the two aircrafts flown by Maj. A. J. Lenski and Capt. Joe Abbott were almost out of fuel. Just as the two F-105s were flying toward the aerial refueling position they were attacked by the MiG-21s flown by Lê Trọng Huyên and Vũ Ngọc Đình. The aerial engagement caught the F-105s by surprise. In just one minute Lê Trọng Huyên and Vũ Ngọc Đình shot down one F-105 and heavily damaged one other. Capt. Joe Abbott's F-105 (Tomahawk 04) was hit by Vũ Ngọc Đình's MiG missile, caught fire, and dove toward the ground. The pilot ejected and was captured. Maj. A. J. Lenski's F-105 was heavily damaged but the pilot strove to make it to the aerial refueling area so that he could return to land at Udorn. Following the new tactics method, the two MiG-21s then pulled up into a climb, quickly broke off the engagement, returned, and landed safely in the airfield. The U.S. aircraft assigned to the SAR effort failed to accomplish their mission. Both the "Jolly Green" helicopters and the A-1 Sandies experienced mechanical problems. All four American pilots were captured, even though during the days that followed the USAF devoted a large number of resources to the unsuccessful SAR effort.[32]

This meant that during just this single afternoon on 30 April 1967 two flights of MiG-21s, totaling four aircraft, shot down three F-105s and damaged another one; all four MiG-21s returned to base and landed safely. This was a clear victory for MiG-21s after a long period during which flight operations were suspended in order for the MiG pilots to review experiences and learn lessons from mistakes. These victories highlighted the advances of new tactics and provided further confirmation of the proper new MiG-21 intercept tactics, which were to ensure the element of surprise, to catch the enemy unaware while closing from long range, gaining a favorable attack position and achieving a significant speed advantage, getting in close and firing accurately, attacking quickly, and breaking off quickly. The engagements on that day confirmed the dramatic change of MiG-21 intercept tactics.

Maj. A. J. Lenski later became a brigadier general and in October 2018, when he was eighty-eight years old, he went to visit Vietnam as a member of a U.S. pilot veterans group that was meeting with VNPAF pilot veterans. At this meeting he met Senior Colonel Vũ Ngọc Đình (then seventy-eight years old) who, fifty-one years before had shot down his wingman, Capt. Joe Abbott. The two pilot veterans, formerly adversaries and now friends, discussed what had happened more than fifty-one years in the past.

1 May 1967: One of the Longest Air Engagements

At the International Labor Day celebration on 1 May, the commanding officer on duty at the 923rd FR was the deputy regiment commander Lê Oánh. Early that morning a flight of four MiG-17s of the 923rd FR, piloted by Nguyễn Văn Bảy (A), Lê Sỹ Diệp, Võ Văn Mẫn, and Nguyễn Bá Địch, was on combat alert duty at Gia Lâm airfield.

In the morning the radar net detected three groups of USAF aircraft flying in from Sam Neua and over Mộc Châu, headed to attack Hòa Lạc airfield. Other groups of enemy aircraft, totaling approximately twenty planes, were also approaching from the west. These aircraft consisted of both F-4s and F-105s that were flying in standard four-aircraft flight formation in extended trail, with each flight flying at a different altitude so that after conducting their bombing attack they could shift to serving as fighters. Having analyzed the developing situation and the deployment pattern of the enemy aircraft, the VNPAF command post concluded that apparently this time the USAF planned to fight a big battle against MiGs to "seek vengeance" for the defeats they had suffered in late April 1967.

At 0858 hours the MiG-17 flight took off and then was vectored on a heading of 240 degrees and an altitude of 3,280 feet to the designated battle area, the Suối Rút area of Hòa Bình Province. Five minutes later, the command post warned the flight to keep an eye out for enemy aircraft on the flight's right-hand side, range 6.5 miles. Immediately thereafter the MiG pilots spotted two F-105s that had completed their attack and were exiting the area. The MiG lead ordered his flight to drop their external fuel tanks and chase the F-105s to the area south of Thành Sơn but was unable to catch the enemy aircraft. The command post immediately ordered the MiG-17 flight to turn left to a heading of 180 degrees to return to the Hòa Bình area. There the flight flew three circuits in order to watch for American aircraft in a formation and be ready to engage the enemy aircraft (a number of American authors call this MiG-17 tactic the "wagon wheel" or "low altitude defensive wheel"—flying in a level horizontal circle to keep watch and to fight at low altitudes).[33] The American pilots considered this tactic to be very effective because it allowed the MiGs to protect one another while at the same time be ready to shift over to the attack.

When Nguyễn Bá Địch reported that he had seen a flight of U.S. aircraft to his flight's right rear, the MiG lead ordered the entire flight to make a hard turn back in the other direction and saw many flights of U.S. aircraft approaching. The leading flight consisted of four F-4s and the next flight consisted of four F-105s. Approximately twenty more U.S. aircraft followed behind these two flights. Nguyễn Bá Địch chased two F-4s to an area south of Hòa Bình, opened fire, and shot down one F-4. Almost immediately after this success, however, four more F-4s pursuing him fired missiles at Nguyễn Bá Địch's MiG. MiG-17 No. 4 was hit and Nguyễn Bá Địch was killed. It is likely that the F-4C that fired the missile that hit Nguyễn Bá Địch's MiG was flown by Maj. Robert G. Dilger and 1st Lt. Mack Thies of the 390th TFS/366th TFW. Major Dilger's F-4C fired one AIM-7 missile and three AIM-9 missiles before finally hitting the MiG.[34]

When Lê Sỹ Diệp got in range less than 0.25 mile from the two F-4Cs, he fired an accurate burst from his guns into one F-4C in the skies over southwestern Hòa Bình. The F-4 shuddered and dove toward the ground. After pulling back up to watch the F-4C that had been hit, Lê Sỹ Diệp saw four more enemy aircraft flying below him. He dove at them determinedly and fired his guns, but a flight of F-4Cs in his rear immediately fired missiles at him. Initially he felt his aircraft shake, but after testing his stick and finding that he could still control his aircraft, he decided to turn back toward Viên Nam Mountain in order to break off the engagement and return to land. At that instant, however, he spotted four more F-4Cs. Even though he was almost out of fuel, employing the tactic concept of using offense as a defense (the best defense is a good offense), Lê Sỹ Diệp flew into the middle of the formation of F-4s and fired a burst from his guns. The F-4Cs were taken by surprise and they turned and fled. Lê Sỹ Diệp landed at Hòa Lạc airfield at 0925 hours. This was perhaps one of the longest air engagements in the history of the air war over Vietnam (eleven minutes). During this dogfight Lê

Sỹ Diệp and Nguyễn Bá Địch were each able to shoot down an F-4C, but after his success Nguyễn Bá Địch was hit by a missile and was killed. The other MiGs flew back and landed safely at Gia Lâm airfield.

On that same day, sixteen USN Skyhawks from the aircraft carrier USS *Bonhomme Richard* conducting an "Alpha Strike" flew in to bomb Kép airfield. The USN pilots reported that they had destroyed three MiG-17s and damaged at least one more while the MiGs were parked at Kép airfield. Additionally, an A-4C flown by a former F-8 pilot, Lt. Cdr. Theodore R. Swartz, had shot down one MiG-17 as it was on its final approach to land at Kép airfield. Swartz became the only A-4 Skyhawk pilot to shoot down a MiG-17 during the entire war. Of particular interest, Swartz reported that he shot the MiG-17 down using Zuni rockets (the Zuni was an air-to-ground rocket). Lt. Cdr. Marshall O. Wright, piloting an F-8 from VF-211 on board the USS *Bonhomme Richard*, reported that he had shot down one MiG-17 over the Bắc Giang area while he was conducting a mission in Operation Iron Hand. In addition, according to Maj. R. G. Dilger, when his F-4C fired a second AIM-7 missile, a MiG-17 trying to evade the missile made too violent a maneuver and crashed into the ground.[35] However, on this date the VNPAF has records of losing only one MiG-17 and the other three MiG-17 pilots were able to land safely back at their airfield.

During this period of time, the North Korean AF unit was stationed at Kép airfield,[36] so it is very likely that these were the results of air engagements between the North Korean AF unit and USN aircraft. Two North Korean MiG-17B pilots are listed as having been killed on this date: Senior Captain Pac Dong Dun and Captain Ly Txang Il.

4 May 1967: An Encounter between Two Legendary Aces

Even though during the first days of May the weather was usually good, on 4 May the weather over the airfield was cloudy. The flight of the 921st FR flown by Phạm Thanh Ngân and Nguyễn Văn Cốc was ordered to take off from Đa Phúc airfield at 1331 hours and intercept the F-105s and F-4s at long range in the Nghĩa Lộ-Tam Đảo area, beyond Hanoi's AAA and SAM umbrella. However, because they took off late from Đa Phúc airfield, the battle was fought near the airfield. After taking off, the flight turned left to a heading of 350 degrees. A few moments later, Phạm Thanh Ngân spotted a group of U.S. aircraft, which consisted of twelve F-105s and eight F-4s. The F-4s had been given the dual mission of bombing the target while at the same time providing fighter escort to the bombers. The lead of this strike group was Col. Robin Olds, the commander of the 8th TFW, who had commanded Operation Bolo on 2 January 1967. Seeing that three four-plane flights of F-105s, flying in a spread-finger formation, were four miles from the MiGs, Phạm Thanh Ngân ordered his wingman to increase speed in order to attack. When he had reached the proper range and heard a good signal from his missile's heat sensor, Phạm Thanh Ngân launched one R-3S missile. As soon he was beginning his break-off maneuver, he heard Nguyễn Văn Cốc shout, "Make a hard left turn!" Phạm Thanh Ngân immediately made a turn to the left. Having almost turned back he saw three more enemy aircraft. He decided to cut inside and pursue these three aircraft. Closing the range to 0.7 to 0.9 miles, Phạm Thanh Ngân launched his second missile, which shot down one F-105. Phạm Thanh Ngân broke off the engagement to return to the airfield to land. When he was making the third point of his landing approach to the airfield, he saw that his No. 2 was also returning to land.

At the moment when Nguyễn Văn Cốc pulled his stick hard to the left to follow his flight lead to break off the engagement, he heard a loud explosion right behind him. Guessing that it was an air-to-air missile fired by one of the F-4s and that his aircraft had been damaged, he checked his aircraft. Finding that it was still flyable, he decided to head for home and make a direct landing at Đa Phúc airfield. When he was on his fourth landing turn his speed was still 210 mph and as he passed the far navigation tower (two miles from the end of the runway) he still had not lowered his landing gear. Immediately thereafter, he began to lose altitude rapidly and his speed was only 190 mph. Just before he reached the close navigation tower (0.9 miles from the end of runway) his altitude was down to 350 feet and his speed had fallen to 161 mph. Realizing that he could not land on the runway, he decided to pull his aircraft up to more than 350 feet and then he ejected. His parachute landed him safely near the airfield's far navigation tower and his aircraft crashed 0.3 miles away.

The detailed report of this air engagement (the times, the location, the intercept angle, etc.) reveal that it is likely that the F-4C that fired the missile at Nguyễn Văn Cốc's MiG was flown by the commander of the 8th TFW, Col.

Robin Olds. Olds launched two AIM-7 and two AIM-9 missiles at Nguyễn Văn Cốc's aircraft, but none of these missiles hit the target. Finally, the next AIM-9 missile he fired exploded just a few feet beneath the MiG's tail.[37]

Of particular interest was the fact that during his air combat term in Vietnam, Colonel Olds engaged many times in the skies with several pilots who later became the aces of VNPAF. During air battles on 2 January 1967, he engaged with Mai Văn Cương (eight victories), Nguyễn Đăng Kính (six victories), Nguyễn Ngọc Độ (six victories), Vũ Ngọc Đỉnh (six victories), and Nguyễn Văn Cốc (the top-scorer, with nine victories). In air engagements on 4 May 1967, USAF ace Olds engaged with two VNPAF aces: Phạm Thanh Ngân (eight victories) and Nguyễn Văn Cốc for a second time. Later, in the air engagement on 23 August 1967, he would engage also with Nguyễn Nhật Chiêu (six victories) and Nguyễn Văn Cốc again. That means he and Nguyễn Văn Cốc had engaged each other three times in the sky.

Unfortunately, Colonel Olds returned to the United States in about October–November 1967, and he and Nguyễn Văn Cốc, two legendary pilots of the USAF and VNPAF, did not have the chance to meet each other again in the skies of North Vietnam, nor to meet on the ground postwar in a peaceful atmosphere. However, at the Vietnam/American fighter pilots' meeting in San Diego in September 2017, Colonel Olds' daughter, Christina Olds, kindly presented copies of her father's book, *Fighter Pilot*, to each member of the VNPAF delegation.

Also on 4 May 1967, the 923rd FR ordered a two-aircraft flight, piloted by Cao Thanh Tịnh and Hoàng Văn Kỷ, to intercept eight F-4Cs and sixteen F-105s flying in to bomb Hòa Lạc airfield. In this engagement Hoàng Văn Kỷ shot down one F-4C in the skies over Hòa Lạc.

12 May 1967: A Great Victory Day for MiGs

A few days earlier, on 5 May, two MiG-21 pilots, Nguyễn Ngọc Độ and Đặng Ngọc Ngự of the 921st FR, were ordered to intercept an F-105 attack group in the Sơn Dương–Tam Đảo area. In that air battle Nguyễn Ngọc Độ shot down an F-105. Also on that day the USAF lost three F-105s, including the F-105 operated by Lt. Col. James Lindberg Hughes from the 469th TFS/388th TFW. Although the United States only recorded that the F-105 was hit by missiles without mentioning whether the missile was an Atoll air-to-air or a SAM, based on the details of the battle, the F-105 was most likely hit by the Atoll missile from Nguyễn Ngọc Độ's MiG-21. In addition, on 5 May 1967, the aircraft of Lt. Col. Gordon Albert Larson, commander of the 469th TFS/388th TFW, was shot down by a SAM.

The month of May also witnessed more successes when, on 12 May, MiGs encountered and shot down five U.S. aircraft. Following the plan to attack targets in the Hanoi area and Hòa Lạc airfield, on the afternoon of that Friday a large number of American aircraft approached from the southwest and headed to the battle area. The AF HQ command post ordered the MiG-17s to make the first attack on the inside perimeter by intercepting the USAF attack in the Ba Vì–Hòa Bình area, then the MiG-21s would attack the American formation when it exited the target. Determined to accomplish the HQ's combat intent, the 923rd FR command post decided to place a strong flight, piloted by Cao Thanh Tịnh, Lê Hải, Ngô Đức Mai, and Hoàng Văn Kỷ, on combat alert duty.

The flight was ordered to take off from Gia Lâm airport at 1532 hours, then directed to climb to an altitude of 11,500 feet and fly west to the battle area. Just at the moment that the flight had almost reached Hòa Lạc airfield it encountered a formation of U.S. aircraft. This was a flight of F-4s from the 366th TFW that was led by Col. F. C. Blesse. It should be noted that this battle was the first time the 366th TFW's F-4s, carrying M-60 20-mm cannon pods, were to fight against MiGs. Besides that, many of the F-105s were only carrying air-to-air missiles in order to engage MiGs. The U.S. formation was approaching the airfield from the east, flying along the side of Viên Nam Mountain. Almost immediately, Cao Thanh Tịnh spotted F-4s and F-105s at a range of four miles, and at the same time the U.S. planes also spotted the MiG-17s. The battle fought over Hòa Lạc between the USAF and the VNPAF MiGs lasted for four minutes.

During their close approach to the MiGs, the F-4s and F-105s fired missiles repeatedly, and the F-105s also fired their guns at the MiG formation. Under the direction of the auxiliary command station the MiG-17s split up into two sections and fought a ferocious dogfight against the U.S. aircraft in the skies over Hòa Lạc. The MiG lead Cao Thanh Tịnh and No. 2 Lê Hải fought F-105s at low altitudes. After chasing his targets for several minutes, Cao Thanh Tịnh opened fire at an F-105 but missed. Shortly after breaking off this attack, Cao Thanh Tịnh spotted two more F-4s in front of him. He pursued them and when the range was right he opened fire and shot down one F-4.

Coinciding with the two lead MiGs, while flying at a lower altitude, Ngô Đức Mai spotted an F-4C popping out from under a cloud and he immediately jumped on it. This was the F-4C flown by Col. Norman C. Gaddis. During this battle, Colonel Gaddis was flying as wingman for Colonel Blesse in the MiG suppression role. At a range of 0.2 miles and an altitude of 4,500 feet Ngô Đức Mai fired two bursts at Gaddis's F-4. Because the aircraft of both sides kept popping in and out of the clouds, Gaddis did not have a chance to look around to see where the MiG-17 was before he was hit by Ngô Đức Mai's second burst. The F-4C caught fire and crashed twelve miles from Hòa Lạc airfield. Colonel Gaddis ejected and was captured.[38] The aircraft's other pilot, 1st Lt. James Milton Jefferson, also ejected but was classified as killed in action.

When Hoàng Văn Kỷ spotted a group of F-105s escorted by F-4s flying above him, he quickly pulled up into a climb and chased them. Because the USAF aircraft outnumbered him and repeatedly fired missiles at him, Hoàng Văn Kỷ was forced to make continuous violent evasive maneuvers, but he still had time to get on the tail of an F-4C and open fire, shooting this F-4C down. During this dogfight all four members of the MiG-17 flight fired their guns and they shot down three F-4s. All MiG-17s returned to Gia Lâm and landed safely there.

While the air battle was raging in the area of Hòa Lạc airfield, another flight of MiG-17s piloted by Dương Trung Tân, Phan Trọng Vân, Trương Văn Cung, and Nguyễn Văn Thọ took off from Đa Phúc airfield and flew to the designated battle area of Vĩnh Yên–Phúc Yên to intercept a group of U.S. aircraft flying in along the western slopes of the Tam Đảo mountains. At an intercept angle of 100 degrees and a range of three miles, the flight spotted a large group of F-105s. The F-105s hastily jettisoned their bombs and turned to fight the four MiG-17s. During this engagement Phan Trọng Vân positioned his aircraft behind a flight of F-105s and shot one of them down.

Continuing the eventful day of combat, at 1640 hours, a MiG-21 flight with pilots Lê Trọng Huyên and Đồng Văn Song was ordered to take off from Đa Phúc airfield, and then navigated to the designated battle area of Mai Châu–Vạn Yên to intercept F-105s when they were about to fly back to their home base. After launching one Atoll missile but missing the target, the MiG lead called for No. 2 Đồng Văn Song to make his attack. Đồng Văn Song swept in close and got into a favorable position then fired an R-3S missile that shot down another F-105. Đồng Văn Song immediately pulled up his stick to climb to break off the engagement, then landed safely at 1659 hours.

> In October 2018, after attending the VN/U.S. veteran pilot meeting in Hanoi, Col. David E. Vipperman visited Colonel Nguyễn Văn Bảy (A)'s Farm. Nguyễn Văn Bảy asked Colonel Vipperman to deliver to General Gaddis his regard. When Colonel Vipperman returned to the United States and spoke with General Gaddis about the Hanoi meeting, Gad-dis was interested and asked him to send back to Nguyễn Văn Bảy a message with a picture from his 95th birthday celebration, and he wanted Nguyễn Văn Bảy to know that his left engine had ingested some debris from an earlier missile explosion and flamed out when he engaged the afterburner.[39]

13 May 1967: A Great Discrepancy

Having analyzed intelligence input information that USAF aircraft would fly in behind the Tam Đảo mountains and would then turn south to attack Đông Anh, Hanoi, the Hòa Lạc airfield, and Đuống bridge, the AF HQ sent an order to the 923rd FR to launch MiGs to intercept the enemy bombers. Two MiG-17 flights of the 923rd FR were placed on combat alert duty at Gia Lâm airfield to carry out this mission. Another four-aircraft flight was on combat alert at Đa Phúc airfield, ready to take off when needed.

The first MiG-17 flight, piloted by Cao Thanh Tịnh, Nguyễn Phi Hùng, Phan Thành Tài, and Nguyễn Văn Phi, was ordered to take off at 1455 hours and then fly on a heading of 260 degrees. According to the combat plan the flight was directed in to attack the U.S. aircraft flying in toward Hòa Lạc from the southwest. But when they learned that the U.S. strike formation was heading toward Tuyên Quang, the AF HQ assumed that the USAF strike formation would utilize the cover of the Tam Đảo mountain range to fly in to attack Hanoi. Realizing the new threat, it ordered the flight of MiG-17s to turn and fly on a heading of 360 degrees up to Sơn Dương to intercept this formation. Just as it almost reached Sơn Dương, the flight was making a left-hand turn when it spotted a group of F-105s escorted by

F-4s. Cao Thanh Tịnh ordered his pilots to drop external fuel tanks and to split into two two-aircraft sections. The two lead MiGs climbed to attack the F-105s, while the two MiGs of the second section engaged the F-4s flying at lower altitudes.

Upon realizing that the MiGs were closing in, the F-105s dropped their external fuel tanks, jettisoned their bombs, and turned to flee. At the same moment, the F-4s swept in, firing missiles to protect the F-105s. However, by making violent maneuvers, the MiGs were able to evade the missiles and then aggressively swept forward to engage the F-4s in a dogfight. MiG pilots No. 1 and No. 2 both turned inside the formation of the U.S. aircraft, got into a firing position, and fired their guns at the F-4s, but they both missed. Seeing that they were low on fuel, both MiGs decided to break off the engagement and returned to base. When Nguyễn Văn Phi spotted a flight of F-4s, he quickly turned and got on the tail of the F-4 No. 4. When he closed the range to 0.3 miles, Nguyễn Văn Phi fired a long burst that hit the fuselage of the F-4. The command post ordered him to break off the engagement, and he returned and landed at Đa Phúc airfield.

It should be noted that there is a tremendous discrepancy between the figures recorded by the two sides with regard to the 13 May 1967 engagements. The USAF claimed to have shot down seven MiG-17s (one document said that it was six MiG-17s) and said that the USAF did not lose any aircraft. The USAF assessed the battle of 13 May as a bigger "victory" even than Operation Bolo on 2 January 1967. Additionally, some American authors have written that in this battle F-105s shot down five MiG-17s for the first time, including two shot down by using M61A1 guns.[40]

The American pilots who participated said that in this battle the MiG-17s had changed their tactics. Instead of using horizontal level defensive circle, or wagon wheels, this time eight MiG-17s formed two circles, one above the other, in the hope that they could more easily engage the American fighters in the space between the upper and lower levels,[41] and the American pilots concluded that this tactic was not effective.

However, according to the accounting records and combat logs of the 923rd FR (including interviews of veteran pilots), the VNPAF did not suffer any losses during the battle of 13 May 1967 and all ten MiG-17 pilots who took off on that day returned and landed safely.[42] In fact, No. 4 Nguyễn Văn Phi is credited with shooting down one F-105. It is also very unlikely that the

USAF engaged MiG-17s from the North Korean unit, because the records of the North Korean AF unit also do not indicate any losses on 13 May 1967.

For many different reasons, differences in the records of the two sides and the results claimed by each side in a number of air battles are unavoidable, but the very great difference in the records of the two sides regarding this air engagement is unusual.

14 May 1967: A Difficult Sunday for MiG-17s

Between 1430 and 1500 hours on 14 May, the radar network picked up two groups of USAF aircraft flying into the Mai Châu–Hòa Bình–Suối Rút area. Believing that the USAF would attack Hòa Lạc airfield and targets west of Hanoi, the AF HQ ordered MiG-17s to take off and fly toward Hòa Bình–Suối Rút to intercept enemy bombers on the outer perimeter. The 923rd FR placed two flights of MiG-17s on combat alert duty. The first flight consisted of Võ Văn Mẫn, Hà Đình Bôn, Nguyễn Thế Hôn, and Lê Hải. The second one was flown by Ngô Đức Mai, Phan Điệt, Hoàng Văn Kỷ, and Nguyễn Quang Sinh.

The first flight took off at 1505 hours and was navigated toward Hòa Bình. Ten minutes later, the MiG pilots spotted targets at an altitude of 11,500 feet. This was an F-4 group of the 366th TFW from Đà Nẵng, which was escorting F-105s coming in to attack targets in the Hà Đông area. VNPAF HQ also received reports indicating that the escort F-4s had been modified to carry 20-mm M61 Vulcan cannon to engage MiGs in air combat. When they realized that four MiG-17s were chasing two F-105s, the escorting F-4 formation split in two sections. One group flew high above the clouds and the second flew just above the top of the cloud layer. Two F-4s turned in to engage the leading section of two MiG-17s. Immediately the MiG lead Võ Văn Mẫn ordered his flight to drop their external fuel tanks and switch on their afterburners to attack the F-105 bombers.

In fact, the four MiG-17s were fighting against more than twenty F-4s under the cloud layer, and below them was a range of high mountain peaks, so the MiG pilots were not able to carry out their favored MiG-17 tactic of forcing their opponents down to low altitudes to dogfight there. While Hà Đình Bôn was sticking with No. 1 to cover him in attacking an F-4 in front of them, he heard No. 1 shout, "He's burning!" That was the moment that pilot Võ Văn Mẫn shot down one F-4. Immediately thereafter, Hà Đình Bôn saw an F-4 to the rear firing a missile that hit Võ Văn Mẫn's aircraft. He immediately shouted, "Eject!" However, unfortunately, Captain Võ Văn Mẫn did not have time to eject and was killed after shooting down one F-4. Coincident with that, MiGs No. 3 and No. 4 were engaged in a dogfight against a flight of F-4s. Nguyễn Thế Hôn got in close and shot down one F-4. Just after shooting down the American aircraft, Nguyễn Thế Hôn's MiG was hit by a missile fired from an F-4 and First Lieutenant Nguyễn Thế Hôn was killed. Knowing that the situation was unfavorable, the command post ordered No. 2 and No. 4 to break off the engagement, turn back, and land at Gia Lâm and Hòa Lạc airfields.

19 May 1967: MiG-17s versus USN aircraft

In the early morning hours of that day, a large number of U.S. aircraft flew in from the direction of Hòa Bình Province and then flew onward to attack Hanoi. AF commander Nguyễn Văn Tiên decided to use MiG-17s to engage the enemy attackers in the southwestern sector and to use MiG-21s to engage the enemy in the northwestern sector. In the afternoon, USN aircraft flying in a large strike formation approached to attack Hanoi (focusing their attacks on the Yên Phụ electrical power plant). This was a formation of Navy F-4Bs, F-8s, and A-4s from the aircraft carriers USS *Enterprise* and USS *Kitty Hawk*, and it was their first bombing attack against targets in the Hanoi area. The F-8s and A-4s were assigned to suppress SAM and AAA sites while the F-4Bs were assigned to conduct the bombing attack. At 1624 hours the AF command post ordered a flight of MiG-17s piloted by Trần Minh Phương, Nguyễn Văn Thọ, Dương Trung Tân, and Nguyễn Văn Phi to take off from Gia Lâm airfield. Two minutes later, a two-aircraft flight consisting of Phan Thanh Tài and Phan Điệt took off as well. Both flights turned, flying toward Văn Điển, and climbed to an altitude of 3,200 feet. Maintaining a speed of 460 mph, they flew to the designated battle area at Thanh Oai–Quốc Oai.

Minutes later the lead flight reported that it saw the target, consisting of Navy F-4s, F-8s, and A-4s, at a range of four miles. The two flights of MiG-17s were ordered to drop their external fuel tanks and engage the U.S. aircraft. An extremely ferocious battle between the six MiG-17s and elite USN fighter pilots raged for seven minutes. During that fight, Phan Thanh Tài and Phan

Điệt each shot down a Navy F-4B. Numerous other F-4s swarmed around the two MiG-17s and fired missiles at them repeatedly. Phan Thanh Tài and Phan Điệt were able to avoid many of the missiles, but because they were so heavily outnumbered, both Phan Thanh Tài's and Phan Điệt's aircraft were hit by enemy missiles. Phan Thanh Tài tried to eject but he was killed. Phan Điệt ejected at a low altitude and hit the ground hard, so he suffered rather serious injuries.

Afterward, the USN lost another F-4B. This was an F-4B flown by Lt. (jg) Joseph Charles Plumb and Lt. (jg) Gareth Laverne Anderson from VF-114 of the USS *Kitty Hawk*. This aircraft was shot down ten miles southwest of Hanoi. Both pilots were captured. Unfortunately, during the air combat against USN F-8s, Trần Minh Phương and Nguyễn Văn Phi from the first flight of MiG-17s were hit by U.S. air-to-air missiles and were killed. An F-8C flown by Navy Lt. Cdr. Bobby C. Lee and an F-8C flown by Lt. Phillip R. Wood from VF-24 of the USS *Bonhomme Richard* reported that they had fired AIM-9D missiles, which had hit MiG-17s during a ferocious dogfight. However, Lieutenant Wood's F-8C suffered heavy damage from shells fired by Trần Minh Phương during the air battle and was unable to return to the *Bonhomme Richard*. Wood was forced to land on the *Kitty Hawk* with many shell holes in his aircraft's fuselage.[43]

To summarize, during an unequal aerial battle, the MiG-17 pilots shot down two F-4s and damaged an F-8, but four MiG-17s were lost and three pilots were killed, including some very experienced pilots. AD and AF Command decided to temporarily suspend MiG-17 combat operation for reviewing and learning lessons from the unsuccessful battle of 19 May.

20 May 1967: A Clash between U.S. Aircraft and Some "Strange" MiG-17s

Around noon on Saturday, 20 May 1967, the VNPAF command post reported that after 1500 hours the USAF would send a large formation to attack Hanoi and would suppress air operations at Đa Phúc airfield. In fact, the USAF sent two groups of F-4Cs led by Col. Robin Olds, commander of the 8th TFW, into NVN to provide fighter cover for the F-105s of the strike group assigned to attack Kép airfield.

When the formation of F-4s, coming in from the northwest, flew near the target, it encountered two flights of MiGs (the American pilots said that these were MiG-17s). Almost immediately, the F-4s split into two groups to fight against the two flights of MiGs. Apparently in this battle the F-4s used a new tactic to deal with the "low-altitude horizontal level circle (wagon wheel) tactic of the MiG-17s. This new tactic was to pull up and then dive to make the attack while another pair of F-4s tried to attack the MiG wheel from below. Using this tactic, two F-4s, No. 1 (Maj. Phillip P. Combies and 1st Lt. Daniel L. Lafferty, call sign Ballot) and No. 3 (Maj. John R. Parddo and 1st Lt. Stephen A. Wayne, call sign Tampa), reported shooting down one MiG-17 each with Sidewinder missiles, while the F-4 flown by Col. Robin Olds and 1st Lt. Steven B. Croker (Tampa 01) reported shooting down two more MiG-17s with Sparrow missiles, raising Colonel Olds' MiG kills total in the Vietnam air war to four.[44]

A number of other publications state that the U.S. F-105s and F-4s encountered a large group of more than twenty MiG-17s sent up to intercept them,[45] and in this battle the USAF and USN aircraft shot down five MiG-17s and two MiG-21s.[46]

However, according to archival documents and interviews of veteran pilots of the 923rd FR, it should be confirmed that on 20 May 1967 no MiG-17s flew combat missions and that the MiG-17s did not clash with either F-4Cs from Thailand or Navy F-8s coming in from the ocean. It should be noted that on 20 May 1967 the MiG-17 pilots all stood down from combat flight operations to review the battle of 19 May 1967 in an effort to learn lessons from that unsuccessful battle and conduct additional training,[47] so the statement by U.S. pilots that their F-4s encountered a large formation of MiGs-17 is groundless. This raises some questions about the five MiG-17s that the USAF and USN pilots claimed to have shot down in this engagement. It is possible that the USAF and USN aircraft clashed with aircraft from the North Korean fighter unit based at Kép airfield.[48]

The 921st FR commander Lieutenant Colonel Trần Mạnh assigned the intercept mission of the day to two flights of MiG-21s standing combat alert duty. In the afternoon a flight of two MiG-21s, piloted by Nguyễn Nhật Chiêu and Phạm Thanh Ngân, took off at 1526 hours. Another flight, piloted by Vũ Ngọc Đỉnh and Nghiêm Đình Hiếu, took off four minutes later. After forming up with one another, Nguyễn Nhật Chiêu and Phạm Thanh Ngân were directed to fly on a heading of 320 degrees. When they were about to pass the Tam Đảo mountains they saw a USAF strike group consisting of F-4 escort fighters and two flights of F-105s, 45 degrees to their left front at a range of five miles. The MiG lead gave the order to drop external fuel tanks, and pushed forward to attack the first flight. Closing the range down to 1.2 miles and with a good sound signal from the missile's heat sensor, Nguyễn Nhật Chiêu suddenly heard his wingman shout, "Enemy aircraft behind you. Take immediate evasive action!" Nguyễn Nhật Chiêu pulled up hard to the right, and then he turned hard to the left and dove. Then he pulled up to an altitude of 11,500 feet and pursued the flight of F-4s. Having a favorable position, he took aim at aircraft No. 3 in the flight. After launching a missile, Nguyễn Nhật Chiêu immediately broke off to the left above the Tam Đảo mountains.

According to a post-mission analysis of the details of this air engagement and the results of the debriefings of captured American pilots, the F-4C that was hit by the missile fired by Nguyễn Nhật Chiêu was flown by Maj. Jack Lee Van Loan and 1st Lt. Joseph Edward Milligan from the 43rd TFS/8th TFW.[49] Both pilots ejected and were captured.

Meanwhile after taking off, the flight consisting of Vũ Ngọc Đỉnh and Nghiêm Đình Hiếu also flew up to the Tam Đảo mountains about nine to twelve miles behind the first flight of MiG-21s. When Vũ Ngọc Đỉnh flipped his aircraft onto its left side to scan the area he saw four F-4s pursuing them, about 2.5 miles to the rear. Realizing that the F-4s were already in a position to fire their missiles, Vũ Ngọc Đỉnh shouted to his wingman to take immediate evasive action and then immediately turned to the left. When he leveled out to change course, he saw two F-4s flashing over his head and found that his aircraft was difficult to control (perhaps the two F-4s had fired missiles down at him from above). His damaged aircraft dropped its left wing and began to spiral downward. When he saw that there was a lot of smoke in his cockpit, Vũ Ngọc Đỉnh decided to eject. When his seat shot him out of the aircraft, Vũ Ngọc Đỉnh lost consciousness for a second. When he came to his senses, he saw that his parachute lines were tangled. Vũ Ngọc Đỉnh calmly untangled the lines so the chute could open properly and landed safely. The F-4 that had chased Vũ Ngọc Đỉnh's MiG and fired the missile that downed it may have been the F-4C flown by Maj. Robert D. Janca and 1st Lt. William E. Roberts Jr. from the 389th TFS/366th TFW.[50]

When Nghiêm Đình Hiếu saw a flight of two F-4s, he decided to pursue the enemy aircraft. When his MiG closed in to a proper range, he fired one missile at an F-4. He quickly broke off the engagement and then looked for his flight lead in order to form up and fly back to land. At that moment, First Lieutenant Nghiêm Đình Hiếu's aircraft was hit by a missile. He ejected, but he suffered severe injuries and died. It is likely that the F-4C that engaged and shot down Nghiêm Đình Hiếu was flown by Lt. Col. Robert F. Titus and 1st Lt. Milan Zimer from the 389th TFS/366th TFW.[51]

Regarding the results of engagements fought on 20 May 1967, the MiG-21s of the 921st FR shot down two F-4s, but two MiG-21s were lost and one pilot was killed.

Air Engagements on 22 May 1967

The day of 22 May 1967 is Buddha's birthday according to the Buddhist calendar. In spite of the holiday, however, ferocious air battles were fought on that day. A short time after noon, the AF HQ issued a warning stating that some time after 1500 hours the USAF would conduct a large air strike and requested the regiments to be ready to launch four MiG-21s to attack the U.S. strike formation in the Tuyên Quang–Phú Thọ sector. At 1452 hours, the 921st FR ordered a flight consisting of Trần Ngọc Síu and Đặng Ngọc Ngự to take off. Within minutes, seeing four F-105s five to six miles to his left front, with a flight of four escorted F-4s, Đặng Ngọc Ngự requested permission to drop external fuel tanks and attack. The flight of two MiG-21s flew straight in, right past the F-4s, and swept into the middle of the formation of F-105 bombers.

Just after seeing that the MiGs were chasing the F-105 formation, the F-4 flight immediately split into two two-aircraft sections and sped forward to protect the F-105s. The MiG lead Trần Ngọc Síu spotted four more F-4s chasing him about four miles to his rear. Realizing that it would not be a good idea to continue to chase the two F-105s, Trần Ngọc Síu pulled up into a left climbing turn and then rolled his aircraft upside down. The F-4s were unable to match his maneuver. Then Trần Ngọc Síu descended to an altitude of 1,600 feet, made a straight-in landing approach, and landed safely. Shortly after pulling up in a climb to 21,000 feet, Đặng Ngọc Ngự saw four

F-105s flying in a trail formation. Đặng Ngọc Ngự fired one missile into the formation of F-105s and then put his aircraft into a dive. As he pulled up he was surprised to find that his aircraft was in the middle of a formation of twelve F-4s assigned to escort the F-105s. Since it appeared that the F-4s did not realize that there was a MiG in their midst, Đặng Ngọc Ngự got the trailing F-4 in his sights, and when the range was 0.62–0.9 miles he adjusted his sight picture and fired a missile that sped straight toward the F-4, causing it to burst into flames.

After evading four missiles fired by the F-4s chasing him, Đặng Ngọc Ngự made a hard turn, climbed to an altitude of 25,000 feet, and then rolled his aircraft upside down and dove to an altitude of 10,000 feet. He switched on his afterburner to escape back to the airfield, but his afterburner would not light and his speed and altitude began to drop rapidly. As he was trying to get the MiG back to the airfield, when his altitude was down to 1,000 feet and his speed down to 186 mph, the command post told him to eject. In order to avoid having his aircraft crash in a populated area, he put his aircraft into a turn and ejected at an altitude of 650 feet. He landed in the middle of the Red River in the area of Phúc Thọ District, Sơn Tây Province.

During wartime, Captain Đặng Ngọc Ngự was credited with seven victories and later was posthumously awarded the honorable title VNP Armed Forces Hero.

APRIL AND MAY: SOME ASSESSMENTS

The compiled figures and result-counting reports revealed that the aerial engagements of May 1967 were ferocious. However, the summary assessments concluded that during the first half of May 1967 American aircraft repeatedly changed their tactics in order to counter MiGs. They conducted air ambushes, and in particular they used the two-level flying (two different altitudes) tactic to disrupt the defensive horizontal wheel tactic of MiG-17s. Beginning with the air engagements of 13 May 1967, a number of the 366th TFW's F-4s were fitted with external M61 20-mm cannon pods. Because the VNPAF pilots failed to quickly grasp the new tactics being used by the USAF, they were slow to change tactics and were too eager to engage in turning dogfights in designated areas. Therefore, in a number of engagements MiG-17s suffered losses. In some engagements the VNPAF lost two or three pilots, including very experienced pilots.[52]

Of particular significance, during the last part of May and the first days of June, MiG-17s fought eight battles in which seven U.S. aircraft were shot down, but the VNPAF suffered losses in six of those battles and nine pilots were killed. During this period, the Americans stepped up their attacks on the airfields to destroy aircraft parked at the airfield, but the aircraft on the ground had not properly dispersed. In three attacks the United States was able to destroy MiGs on the ground, including aircraft belonging to the North Korean unit; on 24 April 1967 fourteen MiG-17s were destroyed; on 1 May 1967 three aircraft parked at an airfield were destroyed; and on 19 May nearly ten MiG-17s were completely knocked out of operating status by American bombs.[53]

3 June 1967: A Hard Day for MiG-17s

The period between late May and early June 1967 was a time of fierce aerial struggle. At that time a number of the USAF's 8th TFW were equipped with AIM-4D Falcon missiles. The AIM-4D was a 1963 version of an old air-to-air missile that had been used to equip fighter aircraft in the U.S. and the West German air forces during the 1950s. The AIM-4D missile had now been improved with a heat-seeker that was superior in many ways to the AIM-9B. It was hoped that this type of missile could replace the AIM-9 missile, which many U.S. pilots did not think was very effective. But actually, the realities of combat over North Vietnam revealed that the AIM-4D was clearly not as effective as the USAF had hoped.

Having intelligence reports that the United States would send in a large strike force to attack targets along Route 1 North, the AF HQ decided to use one flight of MiG-17s taking off from Gia Lâm airfield to intercept American aircraft there. The 923rd FR decided to use two flights in this battle. The first flight consisted of Ngô Đức Mai, Phan Tấn Duân, Trương Văn Cung, and Hà Đình Bôn. The second flight was flown by Phan Văn Túc, Lê Văn Phong, Hoàng Văn Kỷ, and Bùi Văn Sưu.

The first flight took off at 1540 hours and flew toward Lục Nam in Bắc Giang Province. A few minutes later, after spotting two F-105s flying in from the sea, the MiG-17 flight swept in to attack. The two F-105s descended to a low altitude, increased speed, and turned to flee back out to sea. At this time a flight of four F-4 escort fighters flying at an altitude of 6,500 feet dove in, firing missiles at the MiGs. Despite this threat, Phan Tấn Duân closed in and fired two bursts at the trailing F-105. The F-105s jettisoned all their bombs and began firing air-to-air missiles at the MiG-17s. The MiG pilots looked around and saw that the F-105D flying in the No. 3 position (this may have been the F-105D flown by Capt. Larry D. Wiggins) had gotten behind the MiG-17s and fired a Sidewinder missile down from above, at a firing angle of 15 degrees and a range of two miles. The missile exploded beneath the tail of the MiG-17 No. 2 and seriously damaged it. The F-105 continued to chase the MiG and when it was in range, the F-105 used its M-61A1 gun to fire 376 20-mm shells, which hit the MiG-17 No. 2, flown by Phan Tấn Duân.

Knowing that the enemy aircraft greatly outnumbered the MiGs and that his flight was in an unfavorable position, Ngô Đức Mai aggressively maneuvered his aircraft and tried to break away. However, there were too many U.S. aircraft and too many missiles were launched. MiG No. 1 was hit and Ngô Đức Mai was killed. Seeing that the situation was unfavorable, the command post ordered No. 3 and No. 4 to break off and return to land.

In the air battle on 3 June 1967, the MiG-17 flight had accomplished its assigned mission of disrupting the USAF strike group. However, the MiG-17 flight had lost two experienced pilots, Captain Ngô Đức Mai and Senior Lieutenant Phan Tấn Duân. Prior to this battle, Ngô Đức Mai had shot down three American aircraft, including the aircraft of Col. Norman Gaddis (in the air battle of 12 May 1967).

5 June 1967: MiG-17s Suffer Losses

During the afternoon, several groups of U.S. aircraft flew in to bomb targets in the Sơn Dương, Vạn Yên, Phú Thọ, and Việt Trì areas, while the fighters flew air suppression operations over Nội Bài and Kép airfields. Four pilots from the 923rd FR, Trần Huyền, Nguyễn Đình Phúc, Trương Văn Cung, and Nguyễn Quang Sinh, were ordered to take off at 1527 hours and then were directed to the designated battle area over Đại Từ in Thái Nguyên. Two minutes later the second flight, piloted by Hồ Văn Qùy, Lê Văn Phong, Hoàng Văn Kỷ, and Hà Đình Bôn, took off and flew to their designated battle area over Đa Phúc airfield and Vĩnh Yên.

When the first flight was approaching Đại Từ, Nguyễn Quang Sinh reported that he had spotted four F-105s and four F-4s off to the right at an altitude of 6,500 feet to 7,500 feet. Trần Huyền ordered the flight to drop external fuel tanks and make a hard turn to intercept the enemy attack bombers. Trương Văn Cung pursued an F-105 and fired his guns, hitting the fuselage of the F-105. At this time, the F-105s had certainly reported the presence of the MiGs and called for the fighters to support them. The fighters, F-4Ds of the 555th TFS/8th TFW led by Colonel Olds, commander of the 8th TFW, turned back to rescue the F-105s.

The dogfight between the MiGs and the F-4s was ferocious. When the F-4s fired missiles, the MiG-17 lead Trần Huyền immediately pulled up in a climb to evade the missile, but the F-4 launched a second Sidewinder that hit the MiG No. 1's tail. Captain Trần Huyền was killed. It is most likely that the F-4 that hit Trần Huyền's aircraft was flown by Maj. Richard M. Pascoe and Capt. Norman E. Wells.[54] As for MiG No. 4 Nguyễn Quang Sinh, although this was the first time that he actually encountered enemy aircraft, he fought bravely and shot down one F-105. The MiG pilots were ordered to break off the engagement and return to the airfield. MiG No. 3, flown by Trương Văn Cung, was covering the rear of the MiG formation. Trương Văn Cung turned back to mount a counterattack, but his aircraft was hit by a missile. He ejected at an altitude of 320–650 feet, but his ejection was unsuccessful and he was killed.

At the same time, after taking off, the second MiG-17 flight was continuing to circle over Đa Phúc airfield. When he spotted the target, MiG No. 4 requested permission to attack, but No. 1 decided to continue their left-hand turn with the intention of blocking the enemy's flight path and meeting them head-on. The F-4s immediately turned, and, exploiting their superior firepower, fired a large number of missiles at the MiG-17 formation. MiG-17 No. 3 was hit and Lieutenant Hoàng Văn Kỷ was killed.

Although in this battle the marksmanship of the MiG-17 pilots had improved (they shot down one enemy aircraft and damaged another), MiG pilots suffered heavy losses: three pilots were killed (Trần Huyền, Trương Văn Cung, and Hoàng Văn Kỷ). The primary reason for these losses was that they had failed to firmly grasp the formula of attacking quickly and withdrawing quickly. After they had shattered the formation of F-105s, the MiG-17s had allowed themselves to be drawn into a dogfight against a very powerful force of USAF escort fighters, and the MiG pilots had not properly implemented the formula of using both an attack element and a covering element, and instead had allowed their flight formation to be split up.

11 July 1967s: MiGs Fight against USN Aircraft

After more than a month, during which the air-to-air encounters slowed, the MiG pilots had spent time reviewing battle experiences, regrouping and consolidating personnel, and conducting supplementary training. The VNPAF FRs entered the month of July with a strengthened resolve and determination.

With information that USN aircraft would attack the Hải Dương area, VNPAF commander Senior Colonel Nguyễn Văn Tiên ordered the 923rd FR to use four MiG-17s (which had moved down to Kiến An airfield the previous afternoon) to conduct an ambush by preparing to intercept the incoming USN attack groups. The AF commander also ordered several flights of MiG-21s to take off from Đa Phúc airfield to fly a diversionary and support mission for the MiG-17s, which would intercept twelve USN F-8s and A-4s flying in to attack two important bridges along Route 5: Lai Vu and Phú Lương Bridges.

Two flights of MiG-21s, one consisting of Lê Trọng Huyên and Đồng Văn Song and the other piloted by Trần Ngọc Síu and Mai Văn Cương, took off at 0724 hours from Đa Phúc airfield. The first flight was vectored to Đông Triều, Hải Phòng City, at medium altitudes, to be prepared to support the MiG-17s. The second flight was navigated to fly along Route 1 to Ân Thi in Hải Dương as a diversion. A few minutes later, the AF command post ordered a flight of four MiG-17s piloted by Lưu Huy Chao, Lê Hải, Bùi Văn Sưu, and Nguyễn Đình Phúc to take off and fly to the Phủ Cừ–Thanh Miện–Hưng Yên area and wait there to intercept the group of twelve USN aircraft. As the situation developed and seeing that the two MiG-21s were in a good position from which to make an attack, the command post agreed to allow the MiG-21s to shift from a support role to a fighter role.

Within minutes, Lê Trọng Huyên and Đồng Văn Song were ordered to drop their auxiliary fuel tanks and intercept the group of U.S. aircraft. At that moment, MiG No. 1 spotted a formation of A-4s at a range of 7.5 miles. After seeing one A-4 flying alone at a range of three miles, Lê Trọng Huyên switched to full afterburner and quickly turned in to get on the tail of the A-4. When the range was down to 0.9–1.2 miles, he launched a missile that sped straight to the A-4, causing it to dive and flee the area. Lê Trọng Huyên then broke away, returned to the airfield, and landed.

Even though the MiG-17s failed to shoot down any enemy aircraft, the two MiG-21 flights successfully accomplished their mission, especially the flight consisting of Lê Trọng Huyên and Đồng Văn Song, which shifted to the role of attacking and shooting down U.S. aircraft. The important thing was that the MiG-17s and MiG-21s had disrupted a USN strike group that had planned to bomb important bridges along Route 5. With this battle, the MiG-17s returned to the fight after more than a month of a reduced level of combat operations following the heavy losses they suffered in late May through early June 1967.

Air Engagement on 20 July 1967

Three days before, on 17 July, the USN again sent a group of A-4s with fighter escort F-8s to attack the targets around Kép airfield. On that day two MiG-21s, with Nguyễn Nhật Chiêu and Nguyễn Văn Lý, took off to intercept the strike group. During this battle, pilot Nguyễn Văn Lý shot down one F-8 over Lang Chánh, Thanh Hóa.

Between 1200 and 1500 hours on 20 July, the radar net picked up numerous flights of U.S. aircraft flying along the coast east of Phát Diệm and also picked up many F-105s escorted by F-4s approaching to attack the Nho Quan area in Ninh Bình. Knowing that USN aircraft usually made rapid attacks and then left Vietnamese airspace very quickly, the 921st FR's deputy commander Trần Hanh recommended that the combat alert flight be directed to take off and fly to Vụ Bản to intercept the attackers at long range (beyond the range of the AAAs and SAMs) in order to prevent these American aircraft from bombing Hanoi.

Two MiG-21 pilots, Nguyễn Ngọc Độ and Phạm Thanh Ngân, were ordered to take off at 1528 hours then were directed to fly on a heading of 200 degrees at an altitude of 6,500 feet. Five minutes later the command post informed the pilots that the U.S. aircraft were to the right front and below the MiGs at a range of seven to nine miles. The MiG lead issued the order to drop auxiliary fuel tanks and intended to attack the F-4 No. 4, but when he saw the F-4 No. 4 was continuously turning and maneuvering, he decided to target the F-4 No. 3. When the range to the target was one mile and he had a stable sight picture and a good audio tone from the missile's heat-seeker, Nguyễn Ngọc Độ fired the missile then pulled up his aircraft into a climb. Only then did the two lead F-4s realize that there were MiGs behind them. These two F-4s made a tight left-hand turn to reverse course and make a counterattack. However, Nguyễn Ngọc Độ used his MiG's great speed to climb quickly up in the direction of the sun, so the two F-4s were not able to catch him. Both MiG pilots then departed at high speed, returned to the air base, and landed safely.

21 July 1967: Whose MiGs Did the USN Aircraft Encounter?

The famed Navy F-8 pilots, who had excellent air combat skills, did not agree with a number of USAF pilots, who said that it was not possible to conduct a turning dogfight against MiG-17s. The F-8 pilots argued that because their aircraft were armed with both missiles and cannon and because they had good horizontal maneuverability, they could dogfight just as well as the MiG-17s.

Even though for two consecutive months it had suffered many losses inflicted by MiG-21s, on 21 July the USN again launched attacks against targets in the Hanoi area. On that day, USN A-4 and F-8 aircraft flew in to attack the Tạ Xá fuel storage depot located thirty-two miles southwest of Hanoi. The F-8s fought an aerial battle against the MiG-17s. The F-8 pilots claimed that they shot down four MiG-17s. Three F-8s were damaged, but all were able to return and land safely.[55] Ironically, the VNPAF has no record of any combat by either MiG-17s or MiG-21s on 21 July.[56] So what unit did this group of MiG-17s, which the USN described as being rather large, belong to? Could they have been MiG-17 fighters from the North Korean AF unit?

On 21 July 1967 three MiG-17 pilots of the North Korean unit were killed. These pilots were Major Ly Don Il, Major Ly Don Shu, and Captain Xa Xuan He. Major Ly Don Shu was credited with shooting down one F-105. But there is an element of uncertainty to the North Korean pilot's claim, because the U.S. side stated that the forces that encountered MiG-17s that day were the USN F-8s and A-4s from squadrons on board USS *Bonhomme Richard*. The remains of these three pilots, as well as of the other North Korean pilots killed during the war, were buried at the Tân Dĩnh Cemetery in Lạng Giang District, Bắc Giang Province.[57] The remains of the North Korean pilots have now been taken back to North Korea for burial there.

Air Engagement on 10 August 1967

On 9 August 1967, after a two-month suspension of attacks deep into the area around Hanoi, Adm. Grant Sharp, the commander in chief, U.S. Pacific Command (CINCPAC), approved the plan for Operation Rolling Thunder 57 and ordered the Seventh AF and Navy Task Force 77 to attack sixteen more targets from the list of ninety-four targets drawn up by General LeMay in 1965.

On the morning of 10 August two MiG-21s from the 921st FR, flown by Bùi Đình Kình and Đồng Văn Song, were ordered to take off to intercept a Navy strike formation consisting of F-4B aircraft, which were taking off from the aircraft carrier USS *Constellation* to support attackers assigned to attack targets in Phủ Lý. When the MiG-21s climbed out above the clouds, they did not see their target. At that moment, the F-4s detected that two MiG-21s were in the area and headed for them to attack. An F-4B flown by Lt. Cdr. Robert C. Davis and Lt. Cdr. Gayle O. Elie from VF-142, USS *Constellation*, locked onto the MiG-21 flown by Bùi Đình Kình and fired an AIM-9D missile at it.[58] Captain Bùi Đình Kình, one of the most experienced pilots, ejected, but his ejection was unsuccessful, and he was killed.

During that battle, Đồng Văn Song's MiG-21 made a series of evasive maneuvers but because he was in a defensive posture and all alone, and because there were too many U.S. aircraft, the MiG-21 may have been hit by a missile fired by an F-4B from VF-24, USS *Constellation*. Đồng Văn Song ejected and parachuted safely back to the ground.

Air Engagement on 12 August 1967

On 12 August (some documents give the date as 11 August), a group of twenty-six F-105Ds escorted by eight F-4s flew in from Laos, crossed over Tuyên Quang and Thái Nguyên Provinces, then headed straight for Yên Viên, Đuống, and Long Biên Bridges. The USAF planned to conduct three waves of attacks on these targets. It should be noted that there were additional aircraft assigned to the "Wild Weasel" mission, responsible for suppressing North Vietnam's SAM sites. Predicting that the U.S. strike formation flying toward Yên Viên would fly down past the Tam Đảo mountains to attack targets in the Hanoi area, the 923rd FR command post requested that AF HQ (where the commanding officer on duty was AF deputy commander Đào Đình Luyện) grant the regiment permission to launch MiG-17s.

When the F-105s and F-4s had reached a point thirty-five miles from Yên Bái, the 923rd FR ordered a flight of four MiG-17s, piloted by Nguyễn Hữu Tào, Nguyễn Phi Hùng, Vũ Thế Xuân, and Phan Trọng Vân, to take off from Gia Lâm airfield at 1512 hours to intercept the enemy aircraft heading in to attack Đuống and Long Biên Bridges, the Yên Viên railroad yard, and the capital city of Hanoi.

About two minutes later the command post ordered the pilots to turn left to close with the target. Realizing that the American aircraft were too close for the MiGs to be able to get into attack position, the command post ordered the flight to climb to an altitude of 13,000 feet. Immediately thereafter, the flight saw the target twelve miles to their right front. Having seen that the target was a formation of F-105s, the MiG lead Nguyễn Hữu Tào ordered the pilots to drop their auxiliary fuel tanks and head in to attack. The F-105s hastily jettisoned their bombs and turned toward Đuống Bridge to escape. Nguyễn Hữu Tào decided to make a hard turn toward the formation of F-4s and got on the tail of the trailing enemy aircraft. When the range was down to 0.1 miles Nguyễn Hữu Tào fired one burst from his guns. He saw his shells hit the F-4's left wing and the F-4 began trailing smoke. When the order to break off the engagement was given, the MiG-17s returned to Kép airfield and landed safely.

During the battle the pilots exhibited tremendous resolve and a resolute attacking spirit. All four pilots fired their guns and pilot Nguyễn Hữu Tào was credited with shooting down one F-4C in the area of Đuống Bridge. Although the flight shot down only one F-4, it successfully disrupted the USAF strike formation and forced the F-105 aircraft to jettison their bombs and flee before they reached their target.

This battle created a new vigor among the MiG pilots after many months of suffering losses and unsuccessful attacks.

23 August 1967: MiG-21 Tactic for Simultaneous Attacks

Dubbed "Black Wednesday," 23 August 1967 was similar to "Black Friday," 2 December 1966, when six USAF and one USN aircraft were shot down.[59] Of these, the 555th TFS/8th TFW alone lost four F-4Ds. For the VNPAF, the battle of 23 August 1967 signaled the beginning of a new era of progress in formulating tactics for MiG-21s, when MiG aircraft from three different regiments coordinated their combat efforts under the command and direction of the AF HQ command post.

During the three preceding days from 21 to 23 August 1967, the USAF and USN conducted a series of attacks against targets on the outskirts of Hanoi involving large strike groups, with each strike group consisting of more than thirty aircraft. Each day three separate strikes were conducted. Tactically, although the U.S. side knew that during this period there were few MiGs able to be sent up to engage them, the percentage of USAF aircraft assigned to the fighter escort mission remained high.

On 23 August, Lieutenant Colonel Trần Mạnh, the 921st FR's commander, personally commanded the battle at the regimental command post. In the afternoon the USAF sent in a large strike group with more than sixty aircraft, consisting of nine flights of F-105s and four flights of F-4s (including one flight assigned to MiG suppression). This strike group, led by World War II ace Col. Robin Olds, who had led Operation Bolo on 2 January 1967, flew in from Sam Neua (Laos). The flight flew over Yên Bái and then turned toward Tuyên Quang before flying down the northeastern slopes of the Tam Đảo mountain range to attack Hanoi. In order to make things difficult for the Vietnamese ground-based AD forces and MiGs, the USAF employed intense electronic jamming that made it very difficult for Vietnamese SAMs and AAAs to be effective.

The AF command post planned for a coordinated battle involving both MiG-21s and MiG-17s to protect the capital city. The combat intent and guidance formula for this battle was: "Attack from many different directions, split and divide the enemy's flight formations, and amass forces to destroy the enemy in one sector." A flight of two MiG-21s was assigned to attack the enemy strike formation at long range, from Thành Sơn across Route 2 to Đa Phúc airfield. A flight of four MiG-17s was assigned to engage enemy aircraft from Yên Viên–Bắc Ninh to Đa Phúc–Trung Giã. While the VNPAF fighters were in the air, the SAM and AAA units in the air engagement battle area were under instructions not to open fire.

At 1440 hours the long-range radar net picked up a target group forty miles south of Sam Neua. Five minutes later, when the U.S. formation had crossed the border, two MiG-21s flown by Nguyễn Nhật Chiêu and Nguyễn Văn Cốc took off from Đa Phúc airfield at 1458 hours to intercept and attack the enemy strike formation at long range. After taking off, the pilots were navigated to fly west on a heading of 250 degrees, staying at low altitudes. They were then ordered to switch on afterburners, climb to an altitude of 17,500 feet, and then turn left to head north to close the U.S. formation at an intercept angle of 60 degrees, and a detection range of nine miles. At 1508 hours and 30 seconds, Nguyễn Nhật Chiêu reported that he had spotted the target as a formation of forty aircraft, including both F-105s and F-4s flying on a straight, steady course at an altitude below the MiGs.

In that period of time the USAF was using EC-121K airborne early warning and control aircraft carrying QRC-248 electronic modules capable of penetrating the Vietnamese Identification Friend or Foe (IFF) system (the SRO-1 and SRZO-2 systems). The electronic equipment on the EC-121K might have detected MiGs and informed the MiGCAP flight, but for some unknown reason, on that day the commander of the strike formation, commander of the 8th TFW Col. Robin Olds, did not react to the warning. Judging that the F-4 formation did not know that MiG-21s were approaching, the MiG lead Nguyễn Nhật Chiêu gave the order to drop auxiliary fuel tanks and attack. Knowing very well that this was an excellent opportunity, Nguyễn Nhật Chiêu ordered Nguyễn Văn Cốc to be ready to attack using the "tactic method" of both pilots attacking simultaneously in order to create the element of surprise and enhance combat effectiveness.

At the moment when MiG No. 1 was preparing to pull his stick over to turn and get on the tail of the third flight of the enemy aircraft, Nguyễn Văn Cốc suddenly informed his lead, "There are more aircraft to the rear." Nguyễn Nhật Chiêu banked his aircraft to look and saw eight more enemy aircraft flying behind the third enemy flight. Nguyễn Nhật Chiêu told his wingman to attack the trailing enemy flight and told him not to switch on his afterburner too soon in order not to leave a smoke trail (vapor trail) that could cause the MiGs to lose the element of surprise. The flight swept in to attack, Nguyễn Nhật Chiêu controlled his aircraft with quick, precise movements, increased speed and got on the tail of the F-4 No. 4. Having a stable sight picture and at a range of 0.9–1.1 miles and a speed of 680 mph, he pressed the button to fire one R-3S missile. The missile shot down one F-4D (at that time VNPAF had just received the new series of R-3S missile from the Soviet Union and it was in very good condition). The F-4D that Nguyễn Nhật Chiêu shot down crashed in a ravine on Thud Ridge forty-eight miles northwest of Hanoi and most probably was flown by Maj. Charles Robert Tyler and Capt. Ronald Nichalis Sittner of the 555th TFS/8th TFW.[60] Major Tyler ejected and was captured, but the back-seater, Captain Sittner, was listed as killed.

At almost the same moment, Nguyễn Nhật Chiêu saw a missile flashing past him and heading for an F-4 out ahead of him. This was a missile fired by Nguyễn Văn Cốc, who had moved up from his supporting wingman position. After carefully checking to make sure that there were no U.S. aircraft behind him, Nguyễn Văn Cốc moved up almost even with Nguyễn Nhật Chiêu's aircraft in order to target the F-4 flying on the right. When he had a stable sight picture, Nguyễn Văn Cốc fired a missile at a range of approximately 0.5 miles. The missile shot down F-4 No. 3, which was flying off to the right. Since he had fired his missile at a very close range, pieces of the American aircraft were ingested into his engine's air intake, making it impossible for him to increase his speed any further (after he landed the mechanics counted fifty-one pieces of the broken American aircraft stuck in the engine's variable air intake cone). Just a moment after launching his missile, Nguyễn Văn Cốc immediately pulled his stick over hard to break away. When he saw a ball of fire right in front of him and pieces of metal flying past him, Nguyễn Văn Cốc realized that he had begun his breakaway maneuver when he was too close to the enemy aircraft. He quickly pulled his aircraft into a combat spiraling climb up to an altitude of 32,000 feet.

The F-4 that was shot down by Nguyễn Văn Cốc most likely was flown by Capt. Larry Edward Carrigan and 1st Lt. Charles Lane of the 555th TFS/ 8th TFW.[61] Captain Carrigan ejected and was immediately captured, but First Lieutenant Lane was listed as killed in action. Employing the MiG's intercept tactic of attacking quickly and withdrawing quickly, Lieutenant

Colonel Trần Mạnh ordered the flight to break off the engagement and return to Kép airfield to land. On the way back to the air base, when he heard that No. 2's aircraft was damaged, Nguyễn Nhật Chiêu turned back to support and cover his wingman. As he was turning back, Nguyễn Nhật Chiêu suddenly saw a formation of U.S. aircraft flying straight past his MiG's nose. The F-4s continued to fly straight ahead, not realizing that there was a MiG-21 in the area. Realizing that this was an excellent opportunity and knowing that No. 2 was not being chased by F-4s, Nguyễn Nhật Chiêu decided to push his throttle forward and get on the tail of the F-4 No. 2 that was flying on the outside of the formation. At a range of 0.9 miles and with a good audio tone from his missile's heat-seeker, he fired his second R-3S missile at the F-4, which then shuddered and burst into flames. The intercept action was over in seconds, so at that moment Nguyễn Nhật Chiêu did not see the warhead explode but he heard Nguyễn Văn Cốc shout, "Hooray! You got him!" This most probably was an F-4D flown by Maj. Robert Ralston Sawhill and 1st Lt. Gerald Lee Gerndt from the 555th TFS/8th TFW.[62] Both pilots ejected and both were captured.

Only then did the American F-4s see the MiGs. They turned back to surround it. Recognizing the situation and thinking fast, Nguyễn Nhật Chiêu flew into a cloud and escaped from the battle area. After making his breakaway climb to an altitude of 32,000 feet, Nguyễn Văn Cốc rolled his aircraft over and saw three fires burning from the three U.S. aircraft. Two of the fires were close to one another and the third and larger fire was about twelve miles away from the first two. Nguyễn Văn Cốc quickly broke away and returned to the air base. When recalling that moment, the lead of the USAF formation wrote,

> On August 23 I led a MiGCAP from Ubon as part of the overall force hitting the Yên Viên railroad and Doumer bridge in Hanoi. . . . Suddenly, two MiG-21s came screaming supersonic at six o'clock and knocked two of my guys down with Atoll air-to-air missiles before we knew where they were coming from . . . another F-4 was lost just as we got there . . . six of my guys were gone. I learned that three had bailed out, one was dead, and two remained unknown until the POWs were released in 1973.[63]

This was one of the most effective new MiG-21 battle tactics. The two-air-craft flight shot down three F-4s, without any loss to themselves, both pilots scored victories, and the U.S. strike group had jettisoned its bombs. The result of the battle highlighted the advances in the MiG-21's new intercept tactic.

Nguyễn Nhật Chiêu reminisces:

In my entire combat career, I have never seen a case in which the pilot owed his commander such a debt of gratitude as we owed to our com-manders for their contribution to the 23 August 1967 battle. This battle demonstrated regiment commander Trần Mạnh's skill at assessing the situation and at employing his forces, and the ground control skill with which the command and ground control team resulted in my flight being placed in an incredibly favorable position, better even than in a practice flight exercise. We had a whole crowd of American aircraft in front of us and we could choose which ones we wanted to shoot down.

At the end of the battle, however, a very strange thing happened, and it was a most impressive sight. At that time the situation was very complicated and difficult, because the sky over the airfield was filled with American aircraft who were suppressing all air operations at the field and just waiting for MiGs to return low on fuel so that they could attack us. Ironically, Nguyễn Văn Cốc's MiG-21 had been damaged, was almost out of fuel, and his MiG-21 was so close to the American aircraft that they were virtually flying in formation with each other. He could see the faces of the American pilots in their cockpits wearing white helmets. Everyone watching from the airfield down below held their breath, but without precedent, for some unknown reason, as if by a miracle, after circling over the airfield several times the American F-4s and F-105s turned and flew away without attacking. What had just happened? Were the American pilots afraid that the MiGs had "set a trap" for them? Or did the American pilots know that this MiG was being flown by a future VNPAF ace and so were avoiding an encounter with him? [By the end of the war Nguyễn Văn Cốc was the top cred-ited ace with nine victories.]

This was a strange story but a true incident that took place in the skies over Đa Phúc airfield at the end of the 23 August 1967 air battle.[64]

The day of 23 August saw more action for the MiGs when, at 1500 hours (two minutes after the MiG-21s took off), a flight of MiG-17s, flown by Cao Thanh Tịnh, Lê Văn Phong, Nguyễn Văn Thọ, and Lê Hồng Điệp was ordered to take off and then fly at an altitude of 10,000 feet to the designated battle area over Đa Phúc–Phúc Yên. When the flight was circling in the holding area and the radar net picked up the target, the command post directed the MiGs to pursue the target with a small intercept angle of about 20 to 30 degrees. Without hesitation, as he was spotting the enemy aircraft at a range of five miles, No. 1 ordered his pilots to drop their auxiliary fuel tanks and head in to engage, and at the same time he pulled his aircraft into a tight turn. Exactly according to plan, two MiGs of the second section engaged the flight of F-4s in a circular dogfight in order to enable the two lead MiGs to attack the F-105 bombers. Almost at that moment, Cao Thanh Tịnh saw a flight of F-105s in front of him and requested permission to attack. As he was turning inside, intending to attack the aircraft No. 4 in the enemy formation, he saw another aircraft in front of him in a more favorable position to attack. He immediately changed his mind and decided to attack this new target. He fired his guns at a range of 0.17 miles, the F-105 caught fire and dove into the ground in Đông Anh District, Hanoi City. The pilot ejected and was captured.

Meanwhile Lê Văn Phong quickly began to chase an F-4 assigned as a fighter escort when the F-4s turned and began a dogfight with the MiGs. Lê Văn Phong turned his aircraft, got on the F-4's tail, and opened fire, shooting down the F-4. After his victory, however, Lê Văn Phong's MiG was hit by a missile fired by an F-105 and was killed. It is most likely that the aircraft that shot down Lê Văn Phong's MiG was an F-105D flown by 1st Lt. David B. Waldrop III of 34th TFS /388th TFW.[65] The three other MiG-17 pilots broke off the engagement and landed safely.

This was a typical coordinated battle involving three AF FRs and ground-based AD forces under the centralized command of the AF HQ command post (the MiGs of the three FRs all took off within five minutes). The two FRs won a significant victory. The six MiGs shot down five U.S. aircraft, disrupted two large USAF attack waves, and forced the U.S. aircraft to abandon their plan to bomb the Hanoi area.

The victory of the MiG-21s in this battle, as well as many other victories of MiG-21s during the war, had the very important contribution of Lieutenant Colonel Trần Mạnh, the commander of the 921st FR. Many MiG-21 pilots named him "the chief architect" of the MiG-21's intercept tactic. In the postwar period, Trần Mạnh was promoted to the rank of major general, and was appointed vice commander in chief of the VNPAF. In 1976, he was appointed as general director of the Civil Aviation Administration of Vietnam (CAAV), where he made a great contribution to the initial development of Vietnam's civil aviation.

In October 2018, Col. David B. Waldrop, who engaged with Lê Văn Phong in this air engagement, came to Hanoi to attend the VN/U.S. veteran pilot meeting and heard the information about the MiG pilot that he had engaged more than forty years earlier. He brought with him a tribute in the form of a photo of his F-105 pilot badge from 23 August 1967, on which he wrote, "I want you to know that I was after the MiG, not the pilot. . . . [A]lthough we were on different sides during that war, we respected our enemy as fellow fighter pilots flying for their country as we were doing for ours." Colonel Waldrop asked VNPAF veteran pilots to pass this picture to pilot Lê Văn Phong's family.

Air Engagement on 31 August 1967

By the end of August 1967, MiG-21s had fought a number of successful battles. Despite this, the VNPAF HQ continued its policy and general plan to strengthen and improve the combat capabilities, and to test and confirm the proper intercept tactics to be used by MiG-21s, including the plan to attack reconnaissance and EW aircraft. Therefore it is not surprising that during this period MiG-21s concentrated on maintaining and improving the forces and did not fight any big battles. The AD and AF Command predicted that, from the early morning of 31 August, U.S. aircraft would conduct operations in the Thái Nguyên and Hải Phòng areas. However, the AF command post decided to hold off on engaging the enemy. The AF Command anticipated that the enemy reconnaissance aircraft would fly in shortly after 0900 hours, so it ordered the combat alert flight to stand by. As had been predicted, at 0907 hours the long-range radar net picked up a target 110 miles south of Sam Neua. At 0937 hours the two MiG-21s flown by Nguyễn Hồng Nhị and Nguyễn Đăng Kính were ordered to take off to intercept a flight of RF-4s.

At that moment the two MiG pilots saw the target at a range of six miles. Nguyễn Hồng Nhị gave the order to drop auxiliary fuel tanks and ordered Nguyễn Đăng Kính to attack the right-hand aircraft while he attacked the aircraft on the left. Nguyễn Hồng Nhị got on the target's tail and when he got into the firing range he fired his first R-3S missile. He saw that the missile warhead exploded a bit below the target. When the two RF-4s rolled upside down, dove, and split up, Nguyễn Hồng Nhị decided to pursue the aircraft on the left. Getting close to the range of 0.8 miles, he fired his second missile that hit the RF-4, causing it to shudder, catch fire, and then dive toward the ground. Immediately, Nguyễn Hồng Nhị pulled up to an altitude of 29,000 feet to break away then both MiGs departed at high speed, since they had been ordered by GCI to turn back, and landed at the airfield safely.

MiG-21 ACTIVITIES TO DESTROY RECONNAISSANCE AND EB-66 EW AIRCRAFT

From the realities of combat the VNPAF pilots realized that reconnaissance aircraft, air command and control aircraft (EC-121s), and EB-66 EW aircraft played very important roles in conducting air command and control, providing an important link between the enemy bombers and the enemy fighters, performing electronic jamming and reconnaissance, determining the location of MiGs when they were in the air, and determining the location of SAM launch sites.

Very soon after the MiG-21s arrived in the combat fleet, in late 1966 the AD and AF Service Command ordered the AF fighters to draw up plans to locate and destroy these types of U.S. aircraft. However, up to that time the attacks on these types of aircraft were not successful. The VNPAF studied the standard operating procedures used by the reconnaissance aircraft and decided to attack these aircraft after they took photographs and climbed to higher altitudes to exit NVN and escape.[66] The AF HQ ordered the pilots to focus on attacking and destroying enemy reconnaissance and EW aircraft. The MiG-21 flights were provided with very detailed attack plans. Between late August and 3 October 1967 the AF made four attacks on RF reconnaissance aircraft and destroyed five of them (four RF-101s and one RF-4). However, the pilots were still unable to approach and directly attack the enemy's EB-66 EW aircraft.

10 September 1967: Destroying
U.S. Reconnaissance Aircraft

From early morning a number of flights of U.S. aircraft flew in to attack targets in the Vĩnh Yên area. A flight of two MiG-21s, consisting of Nguyễn Hồng Nhị and Nguyễn Đăng Kính, was scheduled to carry out the combat mission of day.

Guessing that a target that was picked up fifty miles south of Sam Neua was a flight of reconnaissance aircraft, the AF Command ordered the flight of two MiGs to take off and then fly toward a point south of Việt Trì. At this time the two U.S. aircraft decreased altitude to 13,000 feet and headed toward the area of the airfield. The command post ordered the flight to go to full afterburner and follow the target down to an altitude of 13,000 feet. When the two RF-101s climbed to an altitude of 19,000 feet, Nguyễn Hồng Nhị quickly pulled up into a climb to follow them, and when the range was six miles he pushed the button to lock onto the target. Even though the RF-101 made hard evasive maneuvers, Nguyễn Hồng Nhị was able to get it into his sights and when the range was 1.2 miles, he fired one missile that hit the RF-101 and it caught fire. Because his speed was so great, Nguyễn Hồng Nhị had to pull up immediately and so was not able to see the missile's warhead explode. Nguyễn Hồng Nhị broke away to the left and climbed to an altitude of 29,000 feet. At this time he had only 220 liters of fuel left. He decided to head straight for Đa Phúc airfield and make a direct landing approach.

Ending the battle of 10 September 1967, Nguyễn Hồng Nhị shot down one RF-101C with one R-3S missile. This meant that in just ten days of the campaign to destroy enemy armed reconnaissance aircraft, Nguyễn Hồng Nhị shot down two reconnaissance aircraft.

16 September 1967: MiG-21 Type FL
(Fishbed-C) in Action

On 16 September, the commanding officer on duty in the AF command post was deputy AF commander Đào Đình Luyện and the GCI officer was Nguyễn Văn Chuyên. The CO on duty at the 921st FR command post was Lieutenant Colonel Trần Mạnh (the GCI officers were Tạ Quốc Hưng and Trần Đức Tụ). During the morning hours, the USAF attacked targets in the area of the Đa Phúc railroad yard, Trung Giã, and areas north and northeast of Thái Nguyên. Guessing that the USAF would send in armed reconnaissance aircraft to assess the results of this attack in preparation for another round of attacks in the afternoon, the AF HQ directed the 921st FR to place a pair of MiG-21s on combat alert to be ready to take off to intercept the enemy reconnaissance aircraft. In this engagement the pilots would be flying MiG-21 F-13s (FL, Fishbed-C).

After receiving information from the radar net about a target approaching from the direction of Sam Neua, the AF command post ordered the flight of Nguyễn Ngọc Độ and Phạm Thanh Ngân to start their engines and wait for the order to taxi out and take off. However, at 1059 hours, the command post ordered them to stop because it had concluded that it was now too late for the pilots to take off. Within minutes, when the radar again picked up two RF-101s making a left-hand turn to a heading of 360 degrees, the command post ordered the pilots to start their engines again and take off. Because it had a firm grasp on the standard procedure activities of the reconnaissance team and the plans and intentions of the USAF, the AF command post was able to accurately predict the flight path that the two RF-101s would follow. This enabled the command post to direct the two MiG-21s into a favorable tactical position (on the inside of the flight path the two RF-101s would follow during their exit after taking their photographs) in the Thành Sơn–Nghĩa Lộ area.

A few minutes later, the MiGs were flying past Nghĩa Lộ when the pilots saw two RF-101s at a range of five miles. These were two RF-101s from the 20th TRS (Tactical Reconnaissance Squadron)/432nd TRW (Tactical Reconnaissance Wing) that had been sent in to reconnoiter and photograph a section of the northwestern railroad line. The two RF-101s were flying in stair-step formation, 1,000 feet apart at an angle of 45 degrees. After finishing their photographs, the two RF-101s began to exit and climbed to an altitude of 26,000 feet. Apparently, the U.S. reconnaissance aircraft did not know that the MiGs were at their six o'clock. The flight of two MiG-21s above them had secretly crept up on the two RF-101s.

One lesson learned from the experience of the 10 September battle was: if the MiG-21 lead fired at and hit the enemy's aircraft No. 1, as soon as the enemy No. 2 pilot saw this he would speed up and escape. So the MiG-21s would not be able to catch him and would not be able to destroy the entire enemy reconnaissance flight. Therefore, this time the MiG lead Nguyễn Ngọc

Độ, decided that he would fire at the enemy aircraft No. 2, thereby giving his wingman Phạm Thanh Ngân an opportunity to accelerate ahead and fire at the enemy aircraft No. 1. Nguyễn Ngọc Độ got into the attack position, closed with the RF-101, stabilized his target designator on the target, and fired a missile at a range of 0.9 miles. The RF-101C was hit by the missile and burst into flames. The pilot flying this RF-101C ejected and was rescued.

Having closed in on the tail of the lead RF-101, Phạm Thanh Ngân brought the target into his sight and when the range was right he fired a missile that sped straight into the RF-101C, causing it to crash on the spot. Immediately after firing, he flew into the slipstream of the enemy aircraft. He instantly pulled his stick back to turn away, and then quickly rolled his aircraft over to observe the results of his attack. The RF-101C that Phạm Thanh Ngân had hit had already gone down. The pilot of this RF-101C was Maj. Bobby Ray Bagley of the 20th TRS/432nd TRW, who ejected at sixty-two miles southwest of Yên Bái and was quickly captured. Phạm Thanh Ngân sharply turned left 90 degrees, flew back to the airfield, and landed. This was the first time that a flight of two MiG-21s shot down and destroyed an entire RF-101C flight, and it was also the first engagement with the use of MiG-21 F-13s, which were each armed with R-3S missiles and an HP-30 gun.[67]

So 16 September 1967 was a bad day for the USAF's armed reconnaissance aircraft because on this day they lost two RF-101s and one RF-4. During this period of time the information provided by the radar net and the VNPAF HQ's situation assessments were very accurate, because they had gained a firm understanding of the pattern of operations of the enemy's armed reconnaissance aircraft. Because of this, and because they had employed the most outstanding MiG-21 pilots in this campaign to destroy armed reconnaissance aircraft, in a short period of twenty-one days, from 31 August to 21 September, the MiGs were able to shoot down seven U.S. armed reconnaissance aircraft.

During the war Phạm Thanh Ngân was credited with eight victories and was awarded the honorable title VNP Armed Forces Hero. In the postwar period he was promoted to the rank of three-star general and was appointed commander in chief of the AD and AF Service and then head of the Political General Department of the VNPA.

MiG-21 F-13S (FL, FISHBED-C) ENTER THE CONFLICT

Based on the results of high-level discussions between North Vietnam and the Soviet Union, in order to quickly replace combat losses and at the request of the first-generation pilots, those who had previously flown MiG-17s in battle, the Soviet Union provided Vietnam with a shipment of MiG-21 F-13 aircraft (the older model of the MiG-21). In addition to two R-3S missiles, this model of the MiG-21 was also armed with an HP-30 gun. However, it had only a semi-active radar (not a fully capable radar such as that installed in the MiG-21 F-94). This meant that in addition to the two missiles, the pilots could also use cannon to engage in air combat against the enemy.

In July 1967 the MiG-21 F-13s (FL) began to be placed on combat alert duty status. Vietnamese pilots felt that the MiG-21 F-13 had relatively superior maneuverability at altitudes of between 6,500 and 19,000 feet, had a tight turning circle, and had a high rate of climb. However, the aircraft also had weaknesses: its fuel capacity was small and it had inadequate navigational/ targeting capabilities (because it had only a semi-active radar).

21 September 1967: MiG-17 Ambush Tactic

On 21 September, VNPAF chief of staff Hoàng Ngọc Diêu was the AF commanding officer on duty. After finishing another mission, the VNPAF command decided to send a flight of MiG-17s from Gia Lâm down to Kiến An airfield to ambush USN aircraft flying in from the east to make attacks.

The MiG-17 flight piloted by Hồ Văn Qùy, Nguyễn Đình Phúc, Bùi Văn Sưu, and Lê Sỹ Diệp secretly landed at Kiến An airfield at 1515 hours and was immediately prepared to carry out the combat mission. When the flight was ordered to take off at 1635 hours, however, the pilot of aircraft No. 2 was unable to start his engine, so the command post ordered the No. 4 pilot to move up to replace No. 2 and the flight took off as a three-aircraft flight. The flight was directed to fly on a heading of 230 degrees and at an altitude of 3,200 feet. Hồ Văn Qùy spotted the enemy aircraft at a range of four miles, and he saw that the enemy formation included both F-4Bs and A-4s. It should be remarked that the auxiliary (visual) ground control station at the airfield helped very much to direct the pilots during the air battle. When Hồ Văn Qùy saw that his target enemy aircraft had turned left but its dive angle was too shallow, he quickly turned and got behind the trailing aircraft. When the range was right, he opened fire from his three cannon, hitting the F-4B. When Bùi Văn Sưu heard someone report that there were two aircraft to his left, he turned left and got on the tail of the aircraft No. 2 in the flight of F-4s. When the range was down to 0.18 miles he opened fire, hitting this F-4.

The circle dogfight lasted for almost four minutes. When they received the order to break off the engagement, all three MiG-17s returned and landed safely. In this battle the command post had correctly predicted the USN's intentions and because of that it secretly sent the flight of MiG-17s down to Kiến An to wait in ambush. The pilots demonstrated high resolve: during the air battle they attacked aggressively and shot down two F-4Bs that were armed as strike bombers. However, the MiGs also displayed a number of mistakes and shortcomings in this battle: the pilots mistakenly thought that the F-4s were assigned to the fighter role, and because of that they did not attack the enemy aggressively right from the start.

Air Engagement on 26 September 1967

In the morning of 26 September the USAF sent a formation of sixteen F-4Ds as part of a large wave of U.S. attacks on Hanoi. In order to accomplish their combat missions, the AF Command ordered the 921st FR to launch a flight of two MiG-21s to intercept the USAF strike group on the outer perimeter.

The flight of MiG-21s flown by Nguyễn Hồng Nhị and Đồng Văn Song was ordered to take off at 0734 hours and fly on a heading of 250 degrees to a point beyond the range of the ground-based air defense umbrella. When the MiG pilots saw that the target consisted of four flights of F-4s flying in an A-shaped formation six miles to their right front, they immediately switched on their afterburners. It appeared that the U.S. pilots did not know that there were MiGs behind them. Determining that the left-hand flight of the F-4s was in a better position for him to attack, Nguyễn Hồng Nhị chose this target to pursue, moved in close, and when the range was right he fired a missile at the F-4 No. 2 in the flight. After launching his Atoll missile, Nguyễn Hồng Nhị then turned hard to pursue the F-4 No. 1, which was flying in front of his MiG's nose. When the range was down to 0.8 miles he fired his second missile. He then pulled into a climb to an altitude of 29,000 feet to break off the engagement, flew back to the airfield, and landed safely.

Air Engagement on 27 September 1967

On 27 September, based on intelligence reports and intuitively observing strong electronic jamming on their radar's screens (both active and passive) in the northeastern region, the AF HQ came to the conclusion that the USAF's attack would come primarily from the northeast, and therefore resolved to intercept the enemy attack in this sector.

The flight of Nguyễn Ngọc Độ and Nguyễn Văn Lý took off at 1453 hours and turned to fly out on a heading of 90 degrees. A few minutes later when the 921st FR's radar picked up a flight of four enemy aircraft crossing Route 1 and heading toward Thái Nguyên, the flight was ordered to turn right and pursue a group of F-105s. When Nguyễn Văn Lý reported that he saw the target 120 degrees to the right, Nguyễn Ngọc Độ gave the order to drop auxiliary fuel tanks, switch to full afterburner power, and chase the F-105s. Realizing that MiGs were chasing them, the F-105s began making violent maneuvers to try to escape. Nguyễn Ngọc Độ resolutely stuck on his target's tail, kept his target designator stabilized on the target, and when the range was 0.9–1.1 miles, he pressed his missile-firing button, then pulled up into a climb to break away. Rolling his aircraft over to observe the results of his missile attack, he saw that the F-105 had been hit by his missile. This was the fifth American aircraft that Nguyễn Ngọc Độ shot down. Nguyễn Ngọc Độ then made a hard left climb and turned to an altitude of 32,000 feet, returned to the airfield, and landed.

Air Engagement on 30 September 1967

Around 1200 hours on 30 September, while anticipating that U.S. aircraft would fly across the border in the northeastern sector and that it was most likely that they would attack Kép airfield, the AF HQ decided to use four MiG-17s of the North Korean FR and two MiG-21s of the 921st FR to intercept the USAF strike group. The MiG-21 flight, with Trần Ngọc Síu flying lead and Mai Văn Cương flying as wingman, took off from Đa Phúc airfield at 1508 hours and headed toward an area north of Kép airfield. When the pilots reached an altitude of 19,000 feet, Mai Văn Cương saw four flights of enemy aircraft nine miles to the left. Since Trần Ngọc Síu had already pulled up even with the trailing enemy flight formation, he told his wingman to make the attack. Mai Văn Cương chose the trailing enemy flight as his target and quickly got on the tail of the F-105. Closing on the target at high speed, he fired a missile at the F-105 and then quickly turned away. When he saw many missiles headed toward him, Mai Văn Cương called Trần Ngọc Síu on the radio, but he got no response.

In summary, during the battle on 30 September 1967, Mai Văn Cương shot down one F-105, but Captain Trần Ngọc Síu, an experienced pilot who had shot down two U.S. aircraft, was killed when his aircraft was hit by a missile. We cannot find any documents or reports from the American side that mention any MiGs being shot down by U.S. aircraft during the battle on 30 September 1967.

Pilot Mai Văn Cương ended the war with eight victories and was given the honorable title of VNP Armed Forces Hero. In the postwar period he was promoted to the rank of major general and became vice chief of staff of the VNPAF (now retired).

3 October 1967: Thwarting a U.S. plan to Attack Airfields

The month of October heralded the beginning of large-scale air operations, with new waves of U.S. bombings over NVN. Analyzing reports from the B-1 net and following the recent air activities of the USAF, the AF HQ anticipated that it was likely that, in addition to road and transportation targets, the USAF would attack the Hanoi area by striking Đa Phúc and Hòa Lạc airfields. The 921st FR was ordered to carry out the pre-arranged plan for attacking a U.S. bomber strike group but to also be prepared to attack small, isolated enemy aircraft and enemy armed reconnaissance aircraft.

The combat mission was given to a flight of two MiG-21s, consisting of Phạm Thanh Ngân and Nguyễn Văn Lý. The flight was ordered to take off to intercept a flight of F-4s at 1349 hours (two F-4Ds escorting two RF-4Cs flying a reconnaissance mission). After lifting off the runway the pilots turned to a heading of 270 degrees, and climbed to an altitude of 19,000 feet. A couple of minutes later pilots Phạm Thanh Ngân and Nguyễn Văn Lý spotted the target. The American aircraft were flying in a parallel line, with each aircraft separated from the next by a distance of 0.9 miles. The MiG lead immediately gave the order to drop auxiliary fuel tanks and chase to attack the target. Seeing that the U.S. aircraft were flying in a line parallel with one another, Phạm Thanh Ngân decided to have his No. 2 move up so that both pilots could make simultaneous attacks. Even though the F-4s realized that there were MiGs in the area and were making evasive maneuvers, Phạm Thanh Ngân took advantage of an opportunity, when the F-4 No. 3 had just leveled out and was preparing to turn to the left, to make his attack. At a range of 0.9 miles and with his target designator stabilized on the target, Phạm Thanh Ngân fired an Atoll missile that flew straight into the left side of the U.S. aircraft's fuselage. The U.S. plane began trailing black smoke and then burst into flames. At this time No. 2 shouted, "He's burning! You got him!" Phạm Thanh Ngân quickly pulled his aircraft into a climb and ordered his wingman to break off and turn to a 360-degree heading. The two pilots flew back to the airfield and landed safely.

In the 3 October 1967 air battle, a USAF F-4D was also lost. This F-4D, flown by Maj. Joseph D. Moore and 1st Lt. S. B. Gulbrandson from the 435th TFS/8th TFW, was shot down by a MiG-21 about fifty miles southwest of Hanoi.[68] The two pilots tried to make it to the border but they were finally forced to eject. Both pilots were rescued.

Based on the details of the air battle we can conclude that in fact pilot Phạm Thanh Ngân shot down the F-4D flown by Major Moore, which was escorting an RF-4, instead of the RF-4 itself.

5 October 1967: MiG-17 Ambush Tactic over the Skies of Kiến An

Early in the morning the AF HQ received information reports stating that USN aircraft would conduct three waves of air strikes against targets in the Hải Phòng area. The first wave, at 0730 hours, would consist of forty-two aircraft divided into four aircraft groups. The second wave, at 1135 hours, would consist of a total of twenty aircraft (fourteen A-4s, four F-4s, and two F-8s). The third wave, at 1550 hours, would consist of forty-seven aircraft (thirty-two A-4s, six F-4s, two F-8s, six A-6s, and one RA-5C). As part of the routine, after the end of the strike waves, the RA-5C aircraft would fly in on a reconnaissance mission to photograph the results of the bombing attacks.

Quickly analyzing the USN's attack intentions, the AF Command ordered a flight of four MiG-17s, piloted by Dương Trung Tân, Lê Hồng Điệp, Lê

Xuân Dỵ, and Nguyễn Đình Phúc, to fly down secretly to Kiến An airfield, where they would wait and be ready to take off to attack enemy bombers at low altitudes in the designated battle area of Quý Cao–Kiến Thụy. In order to accomplish the mission that was given in the battle plan, an auxiliary visual ground control station was set up at the designated battle area. A flight of MiG-21s would take off from Đa Phúc airfield and fly to the battle area at an altitude of 13,000 feet in order to cover and support the MiG-17s, to attract the American fighters, and also to threaten the bombers. The MiG-17 attack flight landed secretly at Kiến An at 1040 hours. As soon as they landed, the flight began preparing for the upcoming battle.

The MiG-17 flight was ordered to take off at 1127 hours and directed to fly on a heading of 230 degrees and then to circle in a holding pattern. A little more than one minute later, the pilots spotted a group of A-4 bombers escorted by F-4s flying over an area near Elephant Mountain (Voi Mountain). Almost immediately, Dương Trung Tân ordered his wingmen to drop their auxiliary fuel tanks, push their throttles forward, and split into two sections to attack the target. The two MiGs of the first section intercepted the A-4s directly over the airfield. Dương Trung Tân rolled his aircraft and dove, got on the tail of the target, and fired his guns at a range of 0.20–0.25 miles, but he missed. At same time the two MiG-17s of the second section fought a swirling and fierce dogfight against the A-4s in the skies southeast of Kiến An airfield. During this ferocious air battle pilots Lê Xuân Dỵ and Nguyễn Đình Phúc each shot down one A-4.

It should be remarked that, for some unknown reasons, the USN did not provide a large number of escort fighters, but MiG-17s did not take full advantage of this opportunity to attack and destroy the A-4s that were approaching and burdened with heavy bomb loads.

7 October 1967: This Was Obviously a MiG Day

The USAF was busy the whole day, starting from its first wave with a large number of aircraft approaching to attack the area west of Hanoi. In fact, the U.S. attack formations consisted of eight F-105s and ten F-4s approaching from both the west and the south, and when they reached the target, all of these aircraft dove to bomb Hòa Lạc airfield.

Being ready to fight against the U.S. attack, the 923rd and 921st FRs placed a flight of four MiG-17s and two flights of two MiG-21s on combat alert duty. Accurately assessing the situation, the AF HQ decided to send two MiG-21s to intercept the enemy aircraft over Thành Sơn (outside Hanoi's ground-based air defense umbrella) and to engage the F-4s assigned to support the F-105s, enabling the MiG-17s to attack the F-105 bombers in the Hòa Lạc area (within Hanoi's air defense umbrella).

Two MiG-21s piloted by Phạm Thanh Ngân and Mai Văn Cương took off from Đa Phúc airfield at 0734 hours and were then navigated under the GCI on a path that led them to Sơn Tây and out toward Thành Sơn. Within seconds the pilots spotted F-4s at a range of nine miles and an intercept angle of 70 degrees. The order was given to drop auxiliary fuel tanks, accelerate, and get into an attack position to attack one at a time, according to the prearranged plan. The MiG lead Phạm Thanh Ngân maneuvered and positioned his aircraft on the tail of an F-4. Suddenly, he heard from his wingman shouting, "You have F-4s behind you!" However, Phạm Thanh Ngân continued determinedly to pursue the F-4 in front of him. Accurately carrying out the firing procedures with great precision, Phạm Thanh Ngân shot down an F-4D. The F-4D tried to make it to the Laotian border, but because its hydraulic system had been damaged the aircraft crashed thirty-five miles southwest of Hanoi. Meanwhile, the command post ordered the MiG pilots to break off the attack immediately to avoid flying into the range of the ground-based air defenses.

Immediately after the first F-4 was shot down, Mai Văn Cương shot down another F-4D in the skies over Ba Vì–Sơn Tây. With just two R-3S missiles, pilots Phạm Thanh Ngân and Mai Văn Cương had each shot down one F-4, then they quickly broke off the engagement, returned to Đa Phúc airfield, and landed safely.

Eight minutes after the MiG-21s took off, the MiG-17 flight consisting of Nguyễn Hữu Tào, Nguyễn Phú Ninh, Lê Sỹ Diệp, and Nguyễn Phi Hùng was ordered to take off from Gia Lâm airfield and directed to turn left to a heading of 270 degrees, then increase speed, cross the Red River, and fly up to the designated battle area of Sơn Tây–Ba Vì–Hòa Lạc at an altitude of 3,200 feet. As the flight was approaching Hòa Lạc airfield the pilots were informed that the target was now only nine miles away. Having spotted two F-4s dropping chaff, Nguyễn Hữu Tào also saw four F-105s making their bombing runs. He gave the order to drop auxiliary fuel tanks and turn in to intercept the F-105s, but when the American bomber pilots spotted the approaching MiGs, they jettisoned their bombs, accelerated away, and escaped.

Spotting a flight of four F-4s that were in the process of splitting into two sections, the MiG-17s also split into two sections in accordance with the pre-arranged plan. The lead two MiGs headed for the F-4 section on the right and pursued these two enemy aircraft as far as Viên Nam Mountain. Flying past Viên Nam Mountain and realizing that they were beyond the point they were allowed to go that was specified in the coordination arrangement with the ground-based AD units, No. 2 shouted over the radio, warning the flight to turn back. At the same time, two MiG-17s of the second section, which were chasing the two left-hand F-4s, were also flying toward Viên Nam Mountain. Anticipating that the two enemy fighters that had just launched missiles would turn away, MiG No. 4 Nguyễn Phi Hùng made an inside turn and closed the range to the enemy fighters. Even though the F-4 pilot saw the MiG and made a hard turn, Nguyễn Phi Hùng doggedly pursued him to the foot of Ba Vì Mountain. Just as the F-4 leveled out after rolling upside down and diving, Nguyễn Phi Hùng quickly fired his guns at a range of 0.08 miles. He saw his shells hit the F-4, which nosed over and dove toward the ground. Nguyễn Phi Hùng made a hard turn, returned to the airfield, and landed.

The VNPAF HQ assessed information input and concluded that in this battle the ratio of American escort fighters to the bombers was one to one. This was a rather high ratio. When the MiG-17s flew into the battle area, they ran into a large number of escort fighters. The F-4s followed their standard tactic of splitting their four-aircraft flights into two sections when they encountered MiGs. If MiGs had chased one section and had not been vigilant, the other section would have turned back to get behind the MiGs and fire their missiles at them. In spite of this, on this day MiG-17s successfully accomplished their mission of disrupting the U.S. strike group. Eventually MiG-17 pilots shot down one F-4 and all four pilots returned and landed safely.

About two hours later another group of USAF aircraft flew in to attack the Quảng Ninh area. A flight of two MiG-21s, flown by Nguyễn Nhật Chiêu and Nguyễn Văn Cốc, was scrambled to intercept a flight of four F-105s. The

MiG-21 flight was vectored to the Quảng Ninh area. Soon after turning to their vector, Nguyễn Nhật Chiêu saw four F-105s 60 degrees to his left, he then gave the order to drop auxiliary fuel tanks and switch on afterburners, and engaged the target. Realizing that MiGs were chasing them, the F-105 pilots jettisoned their bombs, turned, and headed back out to sea. Aggressively moving forward, Nguyễn Nhật Chiêu continued to pursue the F-105. When the range was right he fired an Atoll R-3S missile that hit the F-105F, causing it to burst into flames. Nguyễn Nhật Chiêu quickly pulled his stick over to the left to break away and climbed to an altitude of 19,000 feet.

The F-105F that was hit by Nguyễn Nhật Chiêu's missile was most probably flown by Capt. Joseph D. Howard and Capt. George L. Shamblee from the 13th TFS/388th TFW. The two pilots tried to make it out to the sea but were forced to eject, and both of them were rescued. A short time later Nguyễn Văn Cốc also shot down an F-105D. Based on the records, this F-105D was flown by Maj. Wayne Eugene Fullam from 34th TFS/388th TFW,[69] who was listed as killed in action.

Air Engagement on 9 October 1967

The AF HQ received the information that at about 1500 to 1600 hours a wave of USAF aircraft would fly in from the northwest to conduct air attacks. The 921st FR command post assigned its second company to intercept a USAF strike group approaching from Route 6 to Route 2 to attack the Hanoi area.

The two MiG-21 pilots Nguyễn Hồng Nhị and Đồng Văn Song took off from Đa Phúc airfield at 1528 hours and headed toward the area west of Thành Sơn. Just as they were flying past Thành Sơn, Nguyễn Hồng Nhị spotted a group of F-105s at a range of twelve miles flying in an A-shaped formation at an altitude of 16,000 feet, with each individual flight flying in a spread-finger formation. The command post had accurately directed the two MiG-21s flying in to the intercept point in the rear hemisphere of the enemy bomber formation. Judging that the F-105s still had no idea that MiGs were there, Nguyễn Hồng Nhị and Đồng Văn Song dropped their auxiliary fuel tanks, switched on their afterburners, and closed in on their targets. When the range was right, Nguyễn Hồng Nhị fired his first missile and then pulled into a climb to target the left-hand flight in front of him. To make sure the target was hit, he then fired his second missile and pulled up into a climb to an altitude of 25,000 feet. The F-105D that was shot down by Nguyễn Hồng Nhị probably was flown by Maj. James Arlen Clements from the 388th TFW.[70] The F-105D crashed twenty-five miles northwest of Thái Nguyên and the pilot was captured.

After covering Nguyễn Hồng Nhị during his attack, Đồng Văn Song also spotted another flight of F-105s. He quickly moved into an attack position and fired a missile at an F-105D flying at the rear end of the enemy formation. After launching the missile, he immediately pulled up into a climb to an altitude of 25,000 feet to break off then turned and flew back to the airfield, where he landed safely.

24 October 1967: Reprisal Attack on Đa Phúc Airfield

After a series of air engagements in which U.S. aircraft suffered defeats inflicted by MiG-21s, on 11 October 1967 the forces of the USAF and USN were approved to attack Đa Phúc airfield with the goal of completely destroying the main base of operations of MiG-21s. The VNPAF HQ assessed the situation and anticipated that, following the small exploratory morning attacks, it was likely that during the afternoon the USAF would conduct large attacks against Hanoi and Đa Phúc airfield.

Exactly as predicted, on that afternoon, a large U.S. aircraft formation flew in, signaling the beginning of a wave of attacks against Hanoi City and Đa Phúc airfield. The USAF's biggest concern was still how to deal with the new MiG-21 attack tactics. To resolve the problem and to prepare for this attack, the USAF carried out a large number of new tactical schemes. Especially worthy of attention among these schemes was their use of the array of electronic systems on board their EC-121D/K aircraft, including their QRC-248 device that was able to penetrate the IFF and MiG air-to-air and air-to-ground communications channel and provide early warning on the location of MiGs to American fighters. Additionally, in order to ensure success, one day before the attack the USAF even sent two experienced pilots from the 8th TFW to the airfield where the EC-121Ds were based, to familiarize themselves with the aircraft's capabilities and to develop procedures for communications between the fighters and the EC-121Ds. During the 24 October attack, one of these two pilots was assigned to fly with the MiGCAP attack formation while the other pilot rode in the EC-121D. They communicated by radio to rapidly provide U.S. pilots with the locations of MiG-21s so they could intercept them.[71]

A flight of two MiG-21s piloted by Nguyễn Đăng Kính and Đồng Văn Song took off at 1510 hours to intercept the enemy bombers beyond the outer perimeter of the ground-based air defense umbrella. When they reached Yên Châu–Phú Thọ the flight encountered a large USAF strike formation consisting of F-105s and escorted F-4s. Almost immediately upon seeing the U.S. aircraft, the two MiG-21s dropped their auxiliary fuel tanks, made a hard turn, and headed for the attack. The two MiG-21s fought a ferocious dogfight with the large formation of USAF F-105s and F-4s.

Apparently because they had received a warning from the EC-121D's electronic systems that there were MiGs at their six o'clock, the F-4s immediately made a 180-degree turn and flew head-on toward the MiGs. After several swirling, circling turns, Maj. William L. Kirk, flying the F-4 No. 1, made a sharp turn to get into a good attack position. Even though the MiG-21 turned and maneuvered continuously to avoid missiles and to get the F-4s off his tail, the four F-4s kept flying after him, waiting for an opportunity to fire missiles at him at an altitude of 19,000 feet. Realizing that to continue the fight would not be a good idea, the command post ordered the two MiG-21s to break off the engagement and fly to Gia Lâm airfield to land. The F-4s continued to chase the MiGs, and even though Đồng Văn Song strove to turn as hard as he could, there were too many F-4s and Đồng Văn Song's MiG was hit by a missile. Đồng Văn Song ejected and parachuted safely to the ground. By analyzing the combat's records, the F-4 that shot down Đồng Văn Song's MiG was most probably the F-4 No. 1 flown by Major Kirk and 1st Lt. Theodore R. Bongartz from the 433th TFS/8th TFW.[72]

At the same time, USN aircraft from the aircraft carrier USS *Coral Sea* were approaching from the east to attack Đa Phúc airfield. The Navy attack bombers dropped bombs along the length of the runway and bombed the taxiway, the aircraft parking area, the airfield control tower, the hangars and repair shops, and even the aircraft revetments and antiaircraft gun positions around Đa Phúc airfield. For almost one hour a total of 136 USAF and USN aircraft attacked the airfield in four separate waves. Thirty-two bombs hit the runway, taxiway, and aircraft parking area. Many aircraft parked on the ground suffered major damage, many AAA positions were hit, and there were several personnel casualties.

25 October 1967: New Wave of U.S. Air Attacks on Hanoi

Remarkably, after the savage U.S. attack on the VNPAF's primary air base, Đa Phúc airfield, on 24 October 1967, the soldiers and civilians of Đa Phúc and Kim Anh Districts were mobilized to work overnight with engineer troops to repair the airfield. On the night of 24 October, after a review of the daylight battle, the VNPAF Command HQ anticipated that the next day the United States would again attack targets around Hanoi and Đa Phúc airfield, and it decided to repair the airfields as soon as possible and at all costs, so that MiGs could take off the next morning to engage the enemy.

Between 0700 hours and 1600 hours on 25 October, the USAF and U.S. Navy used more than one hundred aircraft in seven separate waves of attacks against the runway, the aircraft parking area, the aircraft revetments, and the antiaircraft firing positions around Đa Phúc airfield. Other USAF aircraft attacked Đuống and Long Biên Bridges and a number of other targets in the Hanoi area. Having suffered heavy losses on 24 October, on 25 October the USAF and USN made a number of adjustments in their tactics, with the addition of EB-66 and EC-121 aircraft to conduct long-range electronic jamming to suppress the AAA and SAM radars. At 1600 hours, while USN aircraft were conducting brutal bombing attacks against Đa Phúc airfield, USAF aircraft flew in to attack Long Biên Bridge in two separate waves, with a total of fifty-six aircraft. The second wave of attacks on the bridge knocked the bridge's fifth and ninth spans into the water. But very soon after that the engineer troops repaired these two spans, making the bridge available once again for the transportation of trains and cars across it.

After a day of major attacks without encountering VNPAF fighters, the Americans might have dropped their guard. Taking advantage of a pause in between two waves of attacks on Đa Phúc airfield, the AF HQ decided to use a flight of four MiG-17s flown by Nguyễn Hữu Tào, Nguyễn Phú Ninh, Nguyễn Văn Thọ, and Nguyễn Phi Hùng to attack the enemy bombers. The flight was ordered to take off at 1550 hours for the third time. After taking off and climbing to an altitude of 10,000 feet, the flight turned up toward the Tam Đảo mountains. The pilots spotted four F-4s to their right at an altitude of 6,500–7,500 feet and a range of approximately 3.5 miles. Exactly as anticipated, the USAF pilots proceeded on the assumption that, since the airfields had been so heavily damaged, MiGs could not take off. So when they reached this area the American pilots reduced their speed and altitude to prepare to bomb the airfield. At that point the MiGs launched their attack, the U.S. attackers' formation was thrown into confusion, and the fighter escorts had to turn back to engage the MiGs.

When the F-4s turned back and fired missiles repeatedly at the MiGs, the MiGs quickly maneuvered to evade the missiles and then made a sharp turn to attack the F-4s. Nguyễn Phú Ninh chased one F-4 and opened fire at a range of 0.20–0.23 miles that hit the fuselage of the F-4. In this battle the MiG-17s appeared unexpectedly and disrupted the American strike formation, but they did not attack their assigned target, the attack bombers. The MiGs fought a close-quarters dogfight against enemy fighters. In spite of facing many difficulties, because the F-4s had split up and were firing at two different altitudes to suppress the MiGs, the flight was able to shoot down one enemy aircraft and disrupt the USAF strike formation.

26 October 1967: An Unsuccessful Day for MiG-17s

On the two previous days the USAF and USN conducted coordinated attacks on North Vietnamese airfields, which damaged or destroyed twelve MiGs that were parked at the airfield. Analyzing the American air activities, the AF command post concluded that these were indications that the enemy was preparing to mount a large attack against Hanoi.

Exactly as predicted, at 1130 hours a USN strike group consisting of fifty-six aircraft, both A-4s and F-4s, flew in from the direction of Hà Trung–Vụ Bản–Lương Sơn to attack Hanoi. At 1415 hours EB-66s appeared and began transmitting electronic jamming signals from bearings 230 to 290 degrees. More than an hour later, a total of thirty-two USAF F-105s and F-4s flew in from Laos and over Nghĩa Lộ, Tuyên Quang, and Đại Từ–Thái Nguyên, and headed toward Hanoi.

The MiG-17 flight flown by Dương Trung Tân, Nguyễn Hồng Thái, Bùi Văn Sưu, and Lê Sỹ Diệp took off at 1547 hours to intercept and attack the American bombers as they were preparing to make their bombing runs against the area of Đa Phúc airfield. Within minutes, as the flight was making a left-hand turn, the pilots spotted the target. The MiG lead ordered his pilots to drop their auxiliary fuel tanks and split into two sections to make the attack. Just at that moment, having felt his aircraft shudder and finding that his controls would not work, Dương Trung Tân decided to eject while still above the clouds. At that same moment, because he had made too sharp a turn, Lê Sỹ Diệp's MiG stalled, and the pilot was also forced to eject. Concluding that the situation was unfavorable for the MiGs, the command post ordered No. 2 and No. 3 to return to base.

While heading back to the airfield, because he did not keep looking for enemy aircraft and because his turns were too shallow, MiG No. 2's aircraft was shot down by a pursuing enemy aircraft and the pilot was forced to eject. The F-4 that shot down Nguyễn Hồng Thái's MiG with an AIM-4D missile was flown by Capt. Larry D. Cobb and Capt. Alan A. Lavoy from the 555th TFS/8th TFW.[73] In this battle, although the VNPAF helped to successfully disrupt the enemy attack and forced the bombers to jettison their bomb loads before reaching the target, the MiG-17s suffered significant losses. Three MiG-17s were lost but all three pilots were able to eject and parachute safely to the ground.

Obviously, on this day the F-4s had clearly changed their tactics. When they encountered the MiGs they split into two two-aircraft sections, one of which would wait outside the battle area and use EC-121 support to locate targets and wait for the MiGs to make a mistake or to turn back to return to land, dropping their guard. Only then would this section sweep in to attack.

A 921st FR flight of two MiG-21s piloted by Mai Văn Cương and Nguyễn Văn Cốc was scrambled to intercept a group of F-4s over the Nho Quan–Ninh Bình area. After shooting down one F-4, Mai Văn Cương's MiG-21 was shot down by an AIM-7 missile fired by an F-4B, which was flown by Lt. (jg) Robert P. Hickey and Lt. (jg) Jeremy G. Morris from VF-143 off the USS *Constellation*.[74]

Air Engagement on 29 October 1967

The day of 29 October was a Sunday, during the new step of escalation of the war, when the United States repeatedly conducted a series of attacks against targets in the Hanoi area. In order to accomplish the coordinated mission to defend the capital city of Hanoi a flight of MiG-21s piloted by Nguyễn Nhật Chiêu and Đặng Ngọc Ngự from the 921st FR was assigned the combat alert mission to intercept and attack U.S. aircraft over the Nam

Định–Ninh Bình area. After taking off at 1528 hours the flight flew on a heading of 160 degrees toward Phủ Lý. As soon as they made their turn, the pilots saw F-4s approaching them very fast from the rear, repeatedly firing missiles at the MiGs. Nguyễn Nhật Chiêu turned hard and then dove to an altitude of 11,000 feet and got on the tail of an F-4. When the range was down to an altitude of 6,000 feet, Nguyễn Nhật Chiêu stabilized his target designator on the target and launched a missile. Nguyễn Nhật Chiêu saw the F-4 begin to smoke as it dove toward the ground. He then pulled up to an altitude of 25,000 feet, turned to a heading of 330 degrees, returned to Kép airfield, and landed.

With the victory of shooting down an F-4 on this day, Nguyễn Nhật Chiêu had a total of six victories. Senior Colonel Nguyễn Nhật Chiêu was awarded the honorable title VNP Armed Forces Hero and later he was appointed inspector general of the VNPAF.

30 October 1967: Another Wave of Attacks against Hanoi

To continue waves of air attacks against the Hanoi area and VNPAF air bases, at 0803 hours, twelve U.S. aircraft, including both F-105s and F-4s, flew in to attack Kép airfield then at 0900 hours two RF-4s flew over at an altitude of 22,000 feet to photograph the results of the attack on Kép airfield. Based on these indications, the AF HQ anticipated that the Americans were preparing to make a large attack on the Hanoi area.

Exactly as expected, at 1132 hours a large formation of twenty-four aircraft (A-4s, A-6s, and F-4s) flew over Hà Trung, preparing to attack the targets around Hanoi City and Kép airfield. A flight of MiG-17s of the 923rd FR, piloted by Cao Thanh Tịnh, Trần Sâm Kỳ, Nguyễn Văn Thọ, and Nguyễn Quang Sinh, was assigned to take off at 1142 hours. They did not initially intend to attack enemy aircraft but instead to get the aircraft into the air so they wouldn't be damaged during the attack on the airfield. Apparently, because their communications with the command post were being disrupted, the pilots were not able to receive reports on the enemy situation.

Four minutes later, when the MiG-17 pilots saw F-4s very close to their left and began to turn in to engage the F-4s, the F-4s fired a large number of missiles at them. One missile hit MiG No. 2, forcing the MiG pilot to eject, but he died. The F-4B that shot down Trần Sâm Kỳ's MiG was flown by Lt. Cdr. Eugene P. Lund and Lt. (jg) James R. Borst from Squadron VF-152 off the USS *Constellation*. The F-4 that fired on Trần Sâm Kỳ then chased another MiG and fired another AIM-7E, but instead of flying toward the target the missile exploded right in front of the F-4B's nose, seriously damaging the aircraft. Even though the pilots tried to fly the aircraft back to the base, they were forced to eject because the aircraft's landing gear system had been damaged.[75]

After suffering a withering American bombing attack and heavy damage on Đa Phúc and other airfields, MiG-21s were in trouble because they could not take off from their primary air base. Consequently, during the period from 23 to 30 October the VNPAF air combat missions were flown primarily by MiG-17s. However, none of the battles fought by MiG-17s in late October were successful. Five of them were lost and no enemy aircraft were shot down during that period. Faced with a very hard situation, and to the surprise of the USAF, the VNPAF HQ and the 921st FR decided to have MiG-21s use Đa Phúc airfield taxiways to take off and land. The 921st FR's most outstanding pilots rolled up their sleeves and went to work to prepare for the first combat mission using this new plan.

6 November 1967: A Difficult Day for MiG-17s

Vietnam is a country with four distinct seasons, of which autumn is the most pleasant one with the average temperature of about 18–20 degrees Celsius (64–68 degrees Fahrenheit). The morning of 6 November 1967 was a pleasant autumn morning with bright sun, good weather, and visibility of more than twelve miles. Seeing such weather conditions, the duty officers at the command posts and the pilots who were to carry out the missions understood that they would face a day of fierce air battles. Just as anticipated, early that morning the USAF aircraft took advantage of the good weather to send in a large strike force to attack targets in the Hanoi area. In the early morning (0746 hours) a formation of twelve American aircraft (F-105s and F-4s) flew in from Thành Sơn-Hòa Lạc to attack Đông Anh. A few minutes later twelve more F-105s and F-4s flew in to attack Đuống Bridge.

A flight of four MiG-17s flown by Bùi Văn Sưu, Nguyễn Duy Tuân, Lê Xuân Dỵ, and Nguyễn Đình Phúc took off at 0748 hours from Kép airfield, then turned right to a 340-degree heading. When the command post informed the pilots that the target group was flying at an altitude of 1,600 feet, the lead MiG ordered the flight to switch on afterburners. Climbing and turning back to look for the target, the pilots spotted a flight of F-105s. Bùi Văn Sửu ordered the pilots to drop their auxiliary fuel tanks and split up into two sections to make their attacks. Immediately afterward, when spotting one F-105 approaching from the rear, Nguyễn Đình Phúc turned quickly and got on the tail of the F-105. When the range was 0.31 miles he fired his guns. He saw his shells hitting the fuselage of the F-105, and then he made a hard turn to break away and return to Gia Lâm airfield to land.

After landing at Kiến An airfield that morning, the flight of Nguyễn Hữu Tào, Phan Trong Vân, Nguyễn Văn Thọ, and Nguyễn Phi Hùng flew back to Gia Lâm and waited on combat alert there. At 1541 hours the flight took off and flew down to the Thanh Miện area, on a heading of 270 degrees. At 3,200 feet, No. 3 reported that he saw a flight of F-4s coming down from above and two more F-4s heading straight at the MiG formation. The MiG lead ordered his pilots to take evasive action. When the F-4 escort fighters swept in at the MiGs, the MiG-17s turned and maneuvered at low altitudes, drawing the F-4s down to engage them in dogfights. However, the F-4s had learned their lesson about dogfighting with MiG-17s so they stayed at higher altitudes and kept firing missiles at the MiGs.

Seeing an F-105D flying in front of his MiG, Phan Trọng Vân turned inside it, got on its tail, and fired his guns at a range of 0.3 miles. Phan Trọng Vân received the order to break off the engagement before he had a chance to observe the results of his attack. During the return flight, one F-4D approached from behind and fired a 20-mm cannon that hit Phan Trọng Vân's MiG. The pilot ejected and parachuted to earth safely.

In the meantime, Nguyễn Phi Hùng closed in to attack the enemy strike force. He got on the tail of one F-105D and when the range was right he fired a burst. Pulling into a climb after this attack, Nguyễn Phi Hùng encountered another F-105. He pushed his throttle forward, got on the F-105's tail, and fired two more bursts then turned away to break off the engagement.

In summary, during the air battle of 6 November 1967, two flights of MiG-17s took off and attacked USAF bomber aircraft over two different areas. During these engagements MiG pilots Nguyễn Đình Phúc and Nguyễn Phi

Hùng shot down two F-105s but two MiGs were lost and one pilot, Senior Lieutenant Nguyễn Hữu Tào, was killed.

During the post-mission conference to review the battle, the pilots pointed out that the command post had ordered the MiGs to take off too late. Because of that, the F-105s had already dropped their bombs so they were able to accelerate quickly and flee so fast that MiG-17s could not catch them. Furthermore, communication problems had hindered information reports from the command post to the MiGs, so the combat efficiency was not high.

ARRIVAL OF THE MiG-21 PFM (F-94)

There were five main series of MiG-21, built by the Mikoyan-Gurevich aircraft production company. The first in service was the MiG-21FL (Fishbed-C). The second was the MiG-21 PF, including the PFS and the PRM (Fishbed-D). The third in service was the MiG-21 PFM (Fishbed-F), MF/MT/SMT/ST. The fourth was the MiG-21MF (Fishbed-H/J). The fifth and final type in service was MiG-21bis (Fishbed-L/N). All five series of MiG-21s were flown in Vietnam. The MiG-21 PFM officially entered service with the Soviet AF in 1964. It was equipped with an all-weather radar and armed with two R-3S heat-seeking missiles or two radar-guided RS-2US missiles.

In October 1967 the Soviet Union agreed to provide the VNPAF with the new model of MiG-21, called the MiG-21 PFM (which NATO called the Fishbed F-94). The first MiG-21 PFMs arrived at Hải Phòng harbor in late 1967. From mid-1968, MiG-21 PFMs were placed on combat alert duty status. Later, the MiG-21 F-94 became the VNPAF's primary fighter aircraft.

7 November 1967: MiG-21s Take Off from Taxiways

The post-mission analysis of the battles showed that from late October to early November 1967 MiG-17s fought unsuccessful air engagements, shooting down three U.S. aircraft but losing six MiG-17s (with two pilots killed). The AF HQ decided to give MiG-21s more responsibility. During this period, because Đa Phúc airfield was so heavily damaged, the 921st FR moved its combat alert duty aircraft down to Gia Lâm airfield. After realizing that Gia Lâm airfield did not have sufficient support facilities for its operations, the regiment command group decided to move its combat alert forces back to Đa Phúc airfield. The combat alert MiG pilots would take off from a fifty-foot-wide taxiway.

Early in the morning of 7 November 1967, Nguyễn Hồng Nhị and Nguyễn Đăng Kính were picked up by a Mi-4 helicopter from Gia Lâm airfield and flown to Đa Phúc airfield, where Lieutenant Colonel Trần Mạnh personally issued the mission order to the pilots.

During the early afternoon hours of 7 November, the AF HQ informed the 921st FR that at sometime after 1500 hours USAF aircraft would approach from the west to conduct operations, while USN aircraft would come in from the east to make their attacks. The 921st FR was tasked with using a flight of MiG-21s to intercept a USAF strike group approaching from the west.

Based on intelligence reports and on the USAF's electronic jamming activities, at 1509 hours the command post ordered the two MiG-21s to take off from the taxiway and fly in a holding pattern directly above the airfield. The command post informed the pilots that the target was 45 degrees to the flight's right front at a range of ten miles. When MiG pilots spotted the enemy aircraft, Nguyễn Hồng Nhị gave the order to drop auxiliary fuel tanks, switch on afterburners, and attack. The U.S. aircraft were flying in an extended trail formation, with flights of F-4 escort fighters leading the formation and covering the rear, and with the bomb-laden F-105s in the middle.

Following the combat plan to focus on attacking the bombers, Nguyễn Hồng Nhị decided to attack the left flank of the F-105 formation. Quickly getting an F-105 into his sights, at a range of 0.9 miles he pressed his missile-firing button. The missile flew right past the tail of the F-105 (one document says that a piece of Nguyễn Hồng Nhị's missile was found stuck in the tail of the F-105 when it landed). The terrified F-105 pilots turned hard and flew right under the belly of Nguyễn Hồng Nhị's MiG. Nguyễn Hồng Nhị flashed past this flight of F-105s and turned left to get in position behind the next flight of F-105s, which was flying ahead. When he had a stable sight picture and a good audio tone from his missile's heat-seeker, Nguyễn Hồng Nhị fired his second missile, which hit the F-105 flying on the outside of the formation and caused it to catch fire and burn, then it crashed twenty-five miles southwest of Kép airfield. The other F-105 pilots jettisoned their bomb loads and fled. Nguyễn Hồng Nhị and Nguyễn Đăng Kính both landed safely at Kiến An airfield.

Air Engagement on 8 November 1967

On that day two MiG-21s piloted by Đặng Ngọc Ngự and Nguyễn Văn Lý were scheduled to take off from the Đa Phúc airfield taxiway to carry out a combat mission. After taking off, the flight was navigated to intercept a flight of F-4s flying at an altitude of 18,000 feet some twenty-four miles northeast of Yên Bái. The command post concluded that this was a flight of F-4Ds from the 555th TFS/8th TFW that was assigned to fly a MiGCAP mission. When they discovered that MiGs were chasing them, the F-4 pilots followed the old, routine tactic of splitting into two sections. Đặng Ngọc Ngự ordered to drop auxiliary fuel tanks, then swept forward to attack the lead F-4 and ordered his wingman to attack the F-4 No. 2, which was then in a dive. Even though the F-4 No. 1 made violent evasive maneuvers to try to escape, Đặng Ngọc Ngự kept on his tail. When the moment was right, Đặng Ngọc Ngự fired a missile that hit the F-4, causing it to begin to burn. Even though the pilot tried to make it to the Laos–Vietnam border, the crew was forced to eject thirty miles from the Laotian border. Maj. William S. Gordon, the command pilot, was rescued, but the back-seater, 1st Lt. Richard Charles Brenneman, was captured.[76]

Meanwhile Nguyễn Văn Lý was chasing the F-4 No. 2 when he heard his No. 1 shout, "Drink beer!" (VNPAF code for "fired a missile"). A moment later he heard No. 1 shout, "Hit one and set it on fire!" Nguyễn Văn Lý quickly stabilized his sight picture and fired a missile. An instant later he saw the F-4 No. 2 begin to burn and dive toward the ground at a very rapid rate. The command post ordered the pilots to break off the engagement, and both MiGs departed at high speed, returned, and landed safely at Gia Lâm airfield.

A number of analysts state that the reason the MiG-21s won a series of victories in early November (the score was six to zero in favor of the MiGs) was in part because during that time period the Rivet Top program EC-121s, which used electronic warfare devices that could penetrate the MiGs' IFF system, had to temporarily suspend operations to make technical upgrades.[77] This meant that the U.S. pilots did not receive the kind of airborne warning and control assistance that they had during the battles of late October 1967.

18 November 1967: An Active Day for MiG-21s

On 18 November, in spite of the bad weather, sixteen F-105s from the 388th TFW based at Korat, along with F-4 fighter escorts, flew in to attack SAM sites and AAA positions. This was in advance of a second wave of bombers that would attack targets in the Hanoi area and Đa Phúc airfield.

During the last months of 1967, USAF aircraft flying in to bomb targets in North Vietnam were provided with navigational support by a TSQ-81 position-finding radar located atop Pa Thi Mountain in Laos. In addition, based on information regarding the activities of EB-66s and the strength of the enemy's electronic jamming activities, the AF HQ concluded with certainty that the USAF would be more aggressive in its use of EB-66s to provide jamming and EC-121s to provide information to their pilots about the MiGs. After carefully assessing the situation, the AF Command ordered the 921st FR to place a flight of MiG-21s on combat alert duty to intercept U.S. bomber groups. As for tactics, the flight was prepared to use the tactic of "fast attack, deep penetration" and would try to create conditions that would enable both pilots to attack simultaneously.

Two of the regiment's most outstanding pilots, Phạm Thanh Ngân and Nguyễn Văn Cốc, took off at 0748 hours and flew out on a heading of 265 degrees for the holding area over Thành Sơn. A few minutes later the radar picked up a flight of four aircraft flying from Yên Châu to Hạ Hòa. At 0757 hours, following the instructions received from the command post, the two MiG-21 pilots spotted a target 15 degrees to the right front at a range of five miles. In that instant the two MiG-21 pilots had clearly identified all four F-105s flying in a spread-finger formation. The two MiG-21s switched to full afterburner, accelerated, and climbed to gain an altitude advantage of 4,500 to 6,500 feet over the enemy, and got on the tails of the four F-105s. Continually checking behind to ensure that there were no enemy aircraft chasing them, the MiG lead requested permission to attack. The formation of four F-105s was transmitting electronic jamming signals as they flew, but the MiG lead calmly centered the F-105 No. 4 in his sights, enabling his wingman to make a simultaneous attack. When the range to the target was down to eleven miles, Phạm Thanh Ngân pushed his missile-firing button. He saw the F-105 No. 4 burst into flames, drop into a right-hand spin, and dive toward the earth. Based on an analysis of the documents of the two sides, Phạm Thanh Ngân shot down an F-105F flown by Maj. Oscar Moise Dardeau and Capt. Edward William Lehnhoff from the 34th TFS/388th TFW.[78] The U.S. pilots were warned about the presence of MiGs, but for some unknown reason none of the four F-105s heard the warning and did not know that MiG-21s were pursuing them to attack using the "fast attack, fast withdrawal" tactic. The F-105F shot down by Phạm Thanh Ngân burst into flames and crashed in Vân Du hamlet, along the banks of the historic Lô River. Both U.S. pilots were listed as missing in action.

After launching his missile, Phạm Thanh Ngân pulled his aircraft into a climb and then rolled it over to observe the results of his attack. Suddenly, he saw the F-105 No. 3 flying right in front of him at an appropriate firing range. He quickly rolled to his right and placed the F-105 No. 3 in the center of his sights. After firing his second missile, and realizing that his MiG was too close to his target, Phạm Thanh Ngân pulled into a sharp climb to break away, so he was not able to observe the results of his second attack. However, his wingman, Nguyễn Văn Cốc, saw the F-105 No. 3 being hit by Phạm Thanh Ngân's missile and saw pieces of the aircraft breaking off. (It is likely that the F-105 hit by Phạm Thanh Ngân's second missile was severely damaged.) Phạm Thanh Ngân quickly climbed to an altitude of 23,000 feet. Seeing the American aircraft behind him, Phạm Thanh Ngân switched to full afterburner to accelerate, then he descended to an altitude of 16,000 feet to return to land.

After switching to full afterburner to close with the target, Nguyễn Văn Cốc pursued the F-105D No. 1, flown by Lt. Col. William N. Reed, the deputy commander of the 388th TFW who was leading the F-105 formation. At a range of 0.8 miles and a speed of 745 mph, with the target centered in his sights Nguyễn Văn Cốc pressed his missile-firing button. The R-3S missile sped straight into the target, and the F-105 burst into flames. Lieutenant Colonel Reed strove to fly his damaged aircraft out to the Laotian border but was forced to eject when he was still twelve miles from the border. Lieutenant Colonel Reed was then rescued.

In less than one minute, a flight of two MiG-21s shot down two F-105s from the 388th TFW. The two MiG pilots broke off the engagement, then departed at high speed and flew toward the Nan Ning airfield in China to land, but because the weather was bad at that airfield, the pilots decided to return and land at Kép airfield. After the F-105Ds (from a composite flight that included F-105Fs assigned to suppress surface-to-air missiles and to transmit electronic jamming signals) were shot down, the surviving aircraft fled. This cleared the way for the SAM sites to more easily fire at the formation of bombers flying in tight, concentrated formations. Consequently, two more F-105Ds were shot down by SAM-2 missiles.

To the results of that day should be added that one of the two F-105Ds shot down by SAM missiles on 18 November 1967 was an F-105D flown by Col. Edward Burke Burdett, the commander of the fabled USAF 388th TFW. His F-105D was hit while it was flying at an altitude of 17,000 feet. He ejected but died.

In a single day of violent battles the air wing commander, Colonel Burdett, was killed by a SAM and the deputy air wing commander, Lieutenant Colonel Reed, was shot down by a MiG-21 flown by Lieutenant Nguyễn Văn Cốc. These were heavy losses for the 388th TFW, one of the USAF's regular fighter wings based in Thailand.

At the end of the war Nguyễn Văn Cốc became the top-scoring ace of the VNPAF, with nine victories. He was awarded the honorable title VNP Armed Forces Hero. In the postwar period he was promoted to the rank of lieutenant general and acting commander in chief of the VNP AD and AF Service, and then appointed general inspector of VNPA.

19 November 1967: MiG-21s Shoot Down an EB-66

Having fully understood the importance of the EB-66 EW's aircraft to the effectiveness of U.S. bombing campaigns against North Vietnam, the AD and AF Service, soon after MiG-21s began participating in combat operations (1966), started to study the technical characteristics and capabilities along with the pattern of operations of the EB-66s so that MiGs could find ways to hunt down and destroy them. The EB-66 was an EW aircraft that emitted various types of jamming signals to blind North Vietnam's AD and MiG radars. The EB-66 had an important link to the American bombers and fighters whereby it provided information about MiG activities for American pilots during their flights. On 2, 3, and 5 November 1966, as it did later during early November 1967, the 921st FR made a number of attempts to intercept and attack EB-66s, but none of these efforts was successful. The reason for this was that the GCI controllers lacked experience, so not only were MiGs not able to reach the EB-66s, they were also intercepted by enemy F-4s, and on at least one occasion a MiG was lost, forcing the pilot to eject and parachute back to the ground. However, the regiment's command-level officers, GCI officers, and pilots remained determined and continued to prepare plans to hunt down and destroy the EB-66s in order to enable the radars, missiles, and MiGs to operate effectively.

Veteran pilots recalled Sunday, 19 November 1967, as a day of great victories for the VNPAF. On that day, pilots of both fighter regiments, the 921st and 923rd, took off and participated in two large air battles, shooting down four American aircraft, with all returning and landing safely. Based on strategic intelligence reports and the various possible USAF operations that might be conducted on that day, the AF Command (under commanding officer on duty Nguyễn Văn Tiên, the AF commander, and on-duty GCI officers Nguyễn Văn Chuyên and Lê Thành Chơn) laid out a combat plan. This plan prepared for a primary attack force against U.S. bomber strike groups while simultaneously having a number of skilled pilots ready to hunt down and destroy EB-66s if the opportunity presented itself. During the previous several days the Americans had used a number of EB-66s, and in one air strike they had used a total of six EB-66s. On 19 November the responsibility for hunting down the EB-66s was entrusted to a flight made up of Vũ Ngọc Đỉnh and Nguyễn Đăng Kính.

From early morning the radar net closely monitored the activities of EB-66s that were operating in the southwestern sector, with particular attention devoted to tracking two EB-66 formations that were operating west of Route 15. At 0659 hours the radar companies C-43 and C-45's radar sites picked up one target on a bearing of 240 degrees. After discussing the developing situation, the VNPAF command post concluded that this was probably an EB-66 formation, and it was believed likely that the target would fly in the Sam Neua–Lang Chánh–Hồi Xuân corridor, flying along a flight path of 140–320 degrees. The MiG-21 flight took off from Đa Phúc airfield at 0713 hours, turned up to Phúc Yên, and then flew at an altitude of 1,000 to 1,600 feet south along Route 1A. When the pilots reached the designated holding area, they climbed to an altitude of 2,100 feet. As the flight was flying past Thạch Thành in western Thanh Hóa Province, the command post ordered the pilots to climb to 32,000 feet and turn to a heading of 210 degrees, then they were ordered to drop their auxiliary fuel tanks. Within minutes, Nguyễn Đăng Kính and Vũ Ngọc Đỉnh spotted one EB-66 15 degrees to the left front at a range of seven to eight miles. As a result of extensive studies and learning from the experiences of previous unsuccessful attempts, the command post had been able to determine the flight paths and operation patterns of the EB-66s and their F-4 escort fighters. Because of this, the AF command post had directed the flight to intercept the enemy aircraft at the least expected intercept angle, where the F-4 escort fighters would not spot them and where they could quickly get into a favorable attack position.

The MiG lead Vũ Ngọc Đỉnh decided to head straight at an aircraft he saw on the left, but when the range was about 2.5 miles he realized that the closing rate with the target was very fast. Because the closing speed was too great, Vũ Ngọc Đỉnh was not able to make an attack and was forced to turn away. In the meantime, Nguyễn Đăng Kính saw one aircraft 15 degrees to the right at a range of seven to eight miles. He radioed to his lead to "make your approach." He heard Vũ Ngọc Đỉnh respond, "I already did," but he still could not see Vũ Ngọc Đỉnh approaching the target on the left (it is probable that Vũ Ngọc Đỉnh was closing in on another aircraft target). Nguyễn Đăng Kính immediately turned to get on the tail of the second target, the one flying on the right. Nguyễn Đăng Kính calmly and quickly got the target into his sights as he continued to close the range to the target. Obviously, the closer he got the bigger the target looked. When the range to the target was 3.5 miles Nguyễn Đăng Kính even was able to see two big engines and a fuselage that looked as big as that of a Soviet Union-made AN-24 aircraft.

Determining positively that this was an EB-66, Nguyễn Đăng Kính continued to close on the target. When the range was approximately 1.5 miles and he could hear a good tone from the missile's heat-seeker, he fired his first missile. It sped straight toward the EB-66 and he saw the warhead explode on the right side of the target. Nguyễn Đăng Kính decided to move in closer, and when the range to the target was 0.7 miles he fired his second missile. This missile flew straight into the EB-66. He quickly broke away by climbing sharply to an altitude of 40,000 feet and then turned to a heading of 30 degrees to fly over Hòa Bình and Thái Nguyên.

Only at that time did the F-4 escort fighters realize that a MiG-21 had shot down the EB-66. The F-4s turned back to engage the MiG-21s. As MiG

No. 2 had fired both of his missiles already, Vũ Ngọc Đỉnh turned back to cover and support him. After making several tight circles, the F-4s realized that it would be difficult for them to be able to get on the tails of the MiG-21s so they broke off the attack. The two MiGs returned and landed safely at Kép airfield.

After many previous unsuccessful efforts to attack EB-66 EW aircraft, in this battle the flight of two MiG-21s successfully accomplished their mission by shooting down an EB-66 for the first time in the history of the Vietnam War. Although they shot down only one aircraft, this battle was very significant from a tactical standpoint. The VNPAF could now find a suitable method to attack and destroy this type of aircraft that was very heavily defended.[79] At the same time this successful attack meant that from now on the USAF no longer dared to send EB-66s deep into North Vietnamese airspace, and it was also forced to increase the size of the fighter escort force assigned to protect the EB-66s.

In the postwar period, with six victories credited, Major General Nguyễn Đăng Kính was given the honorable title VNP Armed Forces Hero. Nguyễn Đăng Kính became head prosecutor of the VNPA and then was appointed vice general prosecutor of Vietnam.

DESCRIPTION BY NGUYỄN VĂN CHUYÊN, A GCI OFFICER

After studying dozens of engagements during which EB-66s had entered our airspace and after examining hundreds of maps, our team concluded that we had to direct our MiGs in from the most unexpected sector, and then, when the F-4 escort fighters were the farthest away from the EB-66s, we would bring our MiGs in to the most favorable point. We could not be off by more than 30 seconds of one degree. During the battle of 19 November 1967 pilot Nguyễn Đăng Kính shot down one EB-66, signaling that we now had the ability to destroy this EW aircraft, causing the EB-66s from then on to be afraid to fly deep into Vietnamese airspace. This was a combat achievement of our MiG-21 pilots, but it was also evidence of a victory in the battle of wits against the sophisticated tricks and schemes of the EB-66s.[80]

In the eastern front, the AF command post changed their pattern of sending the fighters down to Kiến An in the early morning, which the Americans might now have known. This time, on the morning of 19 November 1967, the MiGs waited until the U.S. aircraft had completed their morning air strikes and until after the post-strike reconnaissance aircraft completed their photographic missions. A flight of MiG-17s piloted by Hồ Văn Qùy, Lê Hải, Nguyễn Đình Phúc, and Nguyễn Phi Hùng was ordered to secretly fly down to land at Kiến An airfield in the afternoon and wait in ambush there. If the American strike groups flew in from the ocean, the MiG flight would attack them, taking them by surprise, in order to help to protect Hanoi and Hải Phòng. Just as predicted, the USN overconfidently believed that Kiến An airfield had been destroyed and that MiGs could not take off from it.

Facing the situation that the USN would send a large strike force to attack Hải Phòng, at 1102 hours the flight was ordered to take off earlier than planned and then navigated to fly on a heading of 220 degrees toward Ninh Giang, rather than circling over Kiến An as it had done in the previous battles. As the MiG flight was flying past Ninh Giang, the pilots saw American aircraft flying in from the sea. The pilots dropped their auxiliary fuel tanks and intercepted the U.S. strike formation over the south end of Kiến An airfield, approaching the Americans out of the sun where they had a favorable attack position. When the A-4 pilots heard that there were MiGs in the area, they hastily jettisoned their bombs and turned to escape out to sea. Meanwhile, the flight of F-4s in the lead accelerated and turned out toward the coast to try to lure the MiGs away from the bombers, then a second flight of F-4s swept in to intercept the MiGs.

Lê Hải quickly pursued to get on the tail of the closest U.S. aircraft. With three quick bursts from his guns he shot down an F-4B that crashed on the spot. Since the range that he had fired at the target was so close, he pushed his stick forward so that his aircraft flew right under the belly of the F-4 that he had just hit. The F-4B that Lê Hải shot down was probably flown by Lt. (jg) James Erlan Teague and Lt. (jg) Theodore Gerhard Stier from VF-151 of the USS *Coral Sea*. James Teague was killed but the rear-seater, Lieutenant Stier, a veteran of 155 combat missions, was able to eject and was captured. A few moments later Nguyễn Phi Hùng also shot down another F-4 with three very accurate bursts from his guns. As he turned away, Nguyễn Phi Hùng saw that the F-4 had been hit and he watched as it broke in two halves and two parachutes blossomed in the air. The F-4B that was shot down by

Nguyễn Phi Hùng most likely was flown by Lt. Cdr. Claude Douglas Clower and Lt. (jg)Walter O. Estes from VF-151 of the USS *Coral Sea*.[81] Lieutenant Commander Clower ejected and was captured but the attempt by the rear-seater, Lieutenant Estes, was unsuccessful and he was listed as killed in action (KIA). At that time, Hồ Văn Qùy had dropped back to cover and support Nguyễn Đình Phúc while he shot down another F-4. The surviving U.S. aircraft were so frightened that they jettisoned their bombs and fled back out over the sea. The large U.S. air strike aimed at Hải Phòng was completely disrupted.

The battle of 19 November 1967 was a successful battle for both MiG-21s and MiG-17s. The VNPAF shot down four American aircraft, including one EB-66, and all of the MiG-17 and MiG-21 pilots returned and landed safely. The 923rd FR fought only one battle during November 1967, but that battle was a glorious victory.

Reminiscence by Senior Colonel Lê Hải:

During the air battle on 19 November I got in very close before firing my guns. I was so close that I decided to dive my aircraft right under the belly of the F-4 that I had just hit. When I turned back I saw another F-4 and chased it. Farther away I saw a MiG-17 flown by Nguyễn Phi Hùng. Hùng and I understood each other very well, so I decided that I would make myself a "bait" to get the F-4 to chase me in order to give Hùng an opportunity to get on his tail and fire at him. This was a very anxious moment and I had to be very precise. When I saw the F-4 launch a missile, meaning when I saw a puff of black smoke, I immediately made a sharp turn (if I had waited to see white smoke, it would have been too late). At that moment the F-4 was following my maneuver, and that gave Phi Hùng his opportunity to open fire. The F-4 that Phi Hùng fired at was hit and caught fire.

Air combat is a battle of wits as well as a test of strength. You always have to remember that there is an enemy aircraft right behind you [at six o'clock], you have to have firm, solid knowledge of the capabilities and characteristics of the enemy aircraft, and you have to understand your opponent's psychology, his thinking. Creating the element of surprise is really an attack on your opponent's psychology.[82]

20 November 1967: Foiling the Sixth Wave of U.S. Air Attacks

Between early October and 20 November 1967 the USAF and USN conducted five waves of fierce attacks against targets in North Vietnam. Most damaging was the fifth wave of attacks, which consisted of brutal attacks against the Hanoi area and Đa Phúc airfield. In late November 1967 the Americans launched their sixth wave of attacks. During this wave of attacks, the USAF and USN flew a total of almost three hundred attack sorties in seven large attacks against key, vital targets in Hanoi and direct attacks against the airfields, in an effort to destroy the combat strength of the VNPAF.

In the early morning, a group of U.S. aircraft southwest of Mộc Châu was picked up by the radar net. Analyzing the developing situation, the AF HQ surmised that the Americans might be sending in an attack from the west. The AF command post recommended a battle plan employing a flight of MiG-21s to cooperate with the MiG-17s in a coordinated attack against a large U.S. strike group approaching from the west. The flight of MiG-21s, flown by Phạm Thanh Ngân and Nguyễn Văn Cốc, took off at 0733 hours to intercept an EB-66 EW aircraft that was approaching Nghĩa Lộ–Yên Bái at a speed of 560 mph. Then something unexpected happened: the target that they spotted was not an EB-66. Instead, it was two F-4s flying in a tight formation 15 degrees to their left front at a range of four to six miles. With the target identified, Phạm Thanh Ngân decided to attack the F-4 formation. Regrettably, at this time the two F-4s had also spotted the MiGs; they dove to reduce altitudes and gain speed. The two MiG-21s returned and landed at Kép airfield. By the afternoon, after seeing that an EB-66 had begun transmitting jamming signals from southeast of Sam Neua, Colonel Đào Đình Luyện talked to the 921st FR commander, Trần Mạnh, and decided to have the MiG-21s fight an independent battle. They were ordered to intercept and disrupt a large enemy strike formation consisting of twelve F-105s and four F-4s flying in to attack a target southeast of Yên Bái.

The 921st FR's flight, piloted byPhạm Thanh Ngân and Nguyễn Văn Cốc, took off at 1550 hours (this was their third combat sortie of the day). At 1601 hours, when the pilots had seen the target 45 degrees to the left at a range of six miles, Phạm Thanh Ngân gave the order to drop auxiliary fuel tanks and decided to attack a flight of F-105s on the left side of the formation. Perhaps the Red Crown air early warning system was not functioning properly on 20 November 1967 and as a result the F-105s did not hear the warning that there were MiGs chasing them. Having targeted the F-105 No. 3, at a range of 0.9 miles, Phạm Thanh Ngân fired his missile, which hit the F-105 and caused it burst into flames. The F-105D hit by Phạm Thanh Ngân's missile was probably flown by Capt. William Wallace Butler from the 469th TFS/ 388th TFW.[83] Captain Butler ejected and was captured. When he was turning away, Phạm Thanh Ngân saw an F-105 right in front of him. He decided to target that aircraft and fired his second missile, and then immediately pulled up to break away, so he was not able to see the missile explode. He returned to the airfield and landed.

When he spotted two F-105s climbing in front of him, Nguyễn Văn Cốc quickly got on the tail of the F-105 No. 1 and, when the range was 0.5 miles, he fired his Atoll missile, which sped straight into the F-105 and caused it to burst into flames. Nguyễn Văn Cốc then quickly broke off the engagement and flew back to Đa Phúc airfield, where he landed.

After Phạm Thanh Ngân and Nguyễn Văn Cốc shot down two F-105s, the other F-105s jettisoned their bombs and abandoned their planned attack on the target.

Air Engagement on 12 December 1967

The weather in the first half of December 1967 was not good, with the northeast monsoon wind blowing earlier than usual, resulting in overcast sky, drizzle, and low visibility. By mid-month, the sky was better. Taking advantage of the good weather, the USAF launched a massive attack against targets in the Hanoi area.

On 12 December, a U.S. attack formation consisting of twelve F-105s and four F-4s flew in to attack targets in the Hanoi area. The 921st FR assigned a flight of two MiG-21s, flown by Nguyễn Văn Cốc and Nguyễn Văn Lý, to carry out the combat mission. Nguyễn Văn Cốc had been given the nickname "Super Wingman" because he had flown many missions as No. 2, during which he had not only supported and covered his lead but had also seized opportunities to attack and destroy enemy aircraft himself. In this battle he would be flying in the No. 1 position as the flight lead. At 0720 an EB-66 electronic jamming signal appeared from the west, but the 921st

FR command post still believed that the enemy aircraft would most likely be coming from the east, so they focused the radar net to the east. At 0740 the flight of two MiG-21s took off and was directed on a heading to the battle area over Lục Ngạn–Sơn Động. At 0745, when the U.S. strike formation was flying deep into Vietnamese airspace, the 921st FR HQ ordered the flight of MiG-21s to change its course and fly between Hải Dương and Hải Phòng to intercept the flight path of the U.S. formation.

When he spotted the target to the right about 40 degrees, Nguyễn Văn Cốc ordered his wingman to drop auxiliary fuel tanks, switch on afterburners, and begin to attack. Nguyễn Văn Cốc ordered No. 2 to attack the rear flight, while he would attack the F-105 No. 3 of the flight in the front of the formation. At a distance of about 0.9 to 1.1 miles, he launched an Atoll missile, then turned sharply to break away. When he rolled his aircraft back to observe the results of his attack, he saw distinctly that the F-105 was burning. This was Nguyễn Văn Cốc's sixth victory. After shooting down an F-105, the two MiG-21s turned back to land at their base.

14 December 1967: Defending the Capital City of Hanoi

Early on the first day of the seventh wave of American air attacks on targets in the Hanoi area, thirty F-105s and F-4s flew across the border and headed for Hanoi, where they would attacked Long Biên Bridge and the Yên Phụ electrical power plant. An F-105D flown by Capt. James Eldon Sehorn was hit by AAA fire. Captain Sehorn ejected and was captured.

During the afternoon the USN put together a large strike force, made up of F-8Es from squadrons VF-111 and VF-162 and A-4s from VA-163 and VA-164 0f the USS *Oriskany*, to attack targets in the Red River delta. At 1614 hours the AF HQ ordered a flight of MiG-17s (pilots Lưu Huy Chao, Lê Hải, Bùi Văn Sưu, and Nguyễn Đình Phúc) to take off, and it flew on a heading of 180 degrees while climbing to an altitude of 6,500 feet. At 1626 hours MiG No. 4 spotted a formation of USN aircraft at a range of twelve miles. When the A-4s reported that there were MiGs in the area, the F-8E fighter escorts swept forward to engage the MiG-17s. The MiG-17 flight split into two sections and closed with their target, with one section fighting at an altitude of 11,000 feet to 13,000 feet and the second fighting at an altitude of 4,500 feet to 6,500 feet.

More than ten USN F-8s fought the four MiG-17s in a swirling battle to the death, with the aircraft intermingled as they chased one another. When the F-8E No. 2 got on the tail of a MiG-17 and was preparing to fire a missile, he was warned that another MiG-17 was on his tail. The MiG-17 behind him had another F-8E on its tail and ready to fire a missile.

The air battle ranged from an altitude of 16,000 feet all the way down to an extremely low altitude (below 1,500 feet). The MiGs would get on an opponent's tail and prepare to attack but the F-8s were constantly making hard, sharp turns and the MiGs were not able to cut inside the turns to get into a position to fire their guns. The USN F-8Es were quite maneuverable, they were armed with both missiles and 20-mm guns, and they flew in an extended, loose formation. So when a MiG would engage in a turning dogfight with one F-8, other F-8s would move away and wait for a favorable opportunity to push their throttles forward and charge in to fire missiles. The two opposing sides engaged in a swirling fight, with the F-8s repeatedly firing missiles and the MiGs taking evasive maneuvers. The F-8s tried to draw the MiGs out toward the sea, but the MiG-17s kept circling and would not move far away from their original position.

The second MiG-17 section, made up of Bùi Văn Sưu and Nguyễn Đình Phúc, was engaged in a separate ferocious dogfight against three F-8Es. During a battle that lasted for seven minutes, all four MiG-17s fired their guns and Lưu Huy Chao shot down one F-8E. At 1630 hours the AF command post ordered the pilots to break off the engagement. Lưu Huy Chao led his pilots up along the course of the Red River at an extremely low altitude to return to base to land.[84] (Lưu Huy Chao always broke off air engagements this way.) When the pilots broke off and were headed back to the airfield, No. 1, No. 2, and No. 4 turned back to counterattack when they discovered F-8s chasing them. The flight lead called each of his pilots to check on them and then the flight formed up to fly back to the airfield. Nguyễn Đình Phúc was trailing about 3.5 or 4 miles behind the rest of the flight. At that moment a formation of six F-8s swept in from the direction of Hải Dương and No. 4 turned back to drive them away. A missile struck the left side of the fuselage of Nguyễn Đình Phúc's MiG-17. The MiG crashed and the pilot was killed. The F-8E that shot down Nguyễn Đình Phúc's MiG with an AIM-9D missile was flown by Lt. Richard E. Wyman of VF-162-USS *Oriskany*.[85]

During that day's battle, the USN pilots changed their tactics. Rather than striving to dogfight with the MiG-17s, they strove to fly away quickly to lure the MiGs to follow them. When the MiGs refused to chase them, the U.S. aircraft waited for the flight of MiGs to form up together to return to the airfield. They then split up into small sections and snuck up, taking advantage of times when MiG pilots dropped their guard to make surprise attacks when the MiGs were low on fuel and when the pilots were tired. Lieutenant Nguyễn Đình Phúc was killed while he was making his second counterattack. This experience taught MiG pilots lessons in timing, formation, and support tactics when breaking off engagements to return to base when MiGs were heavily outnumbered.

The air engagement on 14 December 1967 was ferocious, and the pilots from both sides demonstrated their combat skills. The Vietnamese pilots fought with great determination, and Lưu Huy Chao was able to shoot down one F-8E, resulting in a one-to-one exchange ratio in this battle.

Later, Senior Colonel Lưu Huy Chao became a MiG-17 ace with six victories (he was never forced to parachute) and was given the honorable title VNP Armed Forces Hero. He was appointed vice director of the AF Academy. Lưu Huy Chao is the author of a book in Vietnamese: *The MiG-17 and Us*.

17 December 1967: A New MiG-21 Combat Formation

Continuing the seventh wave of attacks on targets around Hanoi, on 17 December a large formation of USAF F-105s and F-4s flew in again to attack targets in the Hanoi area. The flight of 921st FR MiG-21s was ordered by the AF Command to cooperate with MiG-17s to conduct a coordinated attack against a USAF strike formation flying in from the northwest to attack Hanoi. To carry out the mission, the 921st FR decided to test a new combat formation consisting of three aircraft. The three experienced pilots assigned to this combat mission were Vũ Ngọc Đỉnh, Nguyễn Đăng Kính, and Nguyễn Hồng Nhị.

The early warning radar informed the AF Command that the Americans would approach from two different directions, perhaps employing a "pincer tactic" to attack Hanoi. However, the bad weather might cause problems for the USAF strike formations. Two large U.S. strike groups approaching from two directions were encountering some confusion in figuring out how to avoid running into each other when MiGs suddenly appeared.

When the radars picked up electronic jamming signals along the flight path approaching from the west, the AF command post ordered Vũ Ngọc Đỉnh, Nguyễn Đăng Kính to take off at 1513 hours (earlier than planned), then they were vectored toward Hòa Bình and climbed to an altitude of 20,000 feet. As the pilots were flying past Đoan Hùng–Phú Thọ, they saw six flights of U.S. aircraft, both F-105s and F-4s. Vũ Ngọc Đỉnh decided to bypass the flight of F-4s and turn in to attack the F-105s out in front. When the formation of F-105s realized that they were being chased by MiGs they immediately pulled up into a climb, and then pushed over into a dive. Vũ Ngọc Đỉnh calmly centered an F-105 in his sights and when the range was 1.1 miles he fired his first missile, which hit the F-105 and caused it to dive toward the ground in the Thái Nguyên area. Vũ Ngọc Đỉnh broke away by turning to the right and then he continued to target a flight of F-105s that he had seen flying in the direction of Hanoi. He quickly stabilized his target designator on the trailing F-105 and fired a second missile. The missile dropped from the missile pylon and sped forward, hitting the F-105 and setting it ablaze. Vũ Ngọc Đỉnh quickly broke off by pulling into a climb to an altitude of 32,000 feet. He then flew to Gia Lâm airfield and landed there.

While the U.S. strike formation was still reeling from surprise and seeking to escape, the AF command post directed Nguyễn Hồng Nhị (who had taken off a few minutes after Vũ Ngọc Đỉnh and Nguyễn Đăng Kính) to make a follow-up attack on the formation of F-105s, which was still in a state of confusion. While flying past Thành Sơn, Nguyễn Hồng Nhị spotted eight aircraft below him. He put his aircraft into a dive and closed in on a target, and when he had a stable sight picture, Nguyễn Hồng Nhị fired an R-3S missile that flew directly into the target. Nguyễn Hồng Nhị pulled into a turning climb to break away. When he turned back to look he saw that the F-105 was consumed by flames and that the F-105 formation had been shattered. At that moment, when he spotted a group of sixteen F-105s headed toward Hanoi, Nguyễn Hồng Nhị switched to full afterburner power and got on the tail of the formation of F-105s flying in front of him. When the range was right and he had a stable sight picture, Nguyễn Hồng Nhị pressed the button to fire his second missile. Regrettably, there was a technical problem and the missile failed to launch. Nguyễn Hồng Nhị then pulled up his stick and climbed to 25,000 feet to break off the engagement, returned to Đa Phúc airfield, and landed there.

In this air battle, the flight of three MiG-21s coordinated with one another well, determined the correct targets to attack (they bypassed the F-4s to attack the bombers), swept in on the F-105s from out of the sun, and fired accurately, shooting down three F-105s. Vũ Ngọc Đỉnh alone shot down two of the F-105s.

At 1517 hours the 923rd FR's flight, flown by Lưu Huy Chao, Nguyễn Hồng Thái, Bùi Văn Sưu, and Lê Hải, was ordered to take off and fly toward Hòa Lạc to intercept a group of U.S. aircraft flying in to attack Hanoi. A few minutes later, the MiG pilots spotted four F-4s flying in front of them and in the process of dropping their external fuel tanks before turning to bomb targets in the area of Yên Bái airfield. The MiG lead gave the order to drop auxiliary fuel tanks, increase speed, and attack this target. At the same time, the two MiGs of the second section swept in to attack two F-4s flying at the back of the flight. No. 3 Bùi Văn Sưu aimed at an F-4 and fired three bursts. The F-4 dove down to the ground. Meanwhile, Lê Hải also got on the tail of an F-4 and fired three bursts that hit the fuselage and the right wing of the enemy plane. The F-4 shuddered and then went into a dive. The flight of F-4s, taken by surprise and in a defensive posture, was forced into a dogfight at a low altitude. During the air engagement Bùi Văn Sưu and Lê Hải each shot down one F-4D. The MiG No. 2, flown by Nguyễn Hồng Thái, was hit by an F-4's missile and Nguyễn Hồng Thái was listed as KIA. The F-4D that shot down Nguyễn Hồng Thái was flown by Capt. Doyle D. Baker and 1st Lt. John D. Ryan Jr. from the 13th TFS/432nd TFW.[86]

On 17 December 1967, the VNPAF's MiG-17s and MiG-21s fought a coordinated battle and won a clear victory. Five U.S. aircraft, both bombers and fighters, were shot down, and the other U.S. aircraft were forced to jettison their bombs and turn away to escape, thereby shattering the U.S. plan to bomb Hanoi.

During the war, Vũ Ngọc Đỉnh was credited with six victories and was given the honorable title VNP Armed Forces Hero. Senior Colonel Vũ Ngọc Đỉnh later worked in civil aviation and was appointed general director of the Vietnam Air Service Company (VASCO), a subsidiary of Vietnam Airlines Corporation.

19 December 1967: Quite a Day for MiGs

Guessing that the weather might soon turn bad again, on 19 December the Americans sent in a large number of aircraft from two directions, down from the northwest and up from the southeast, to attack targets in the Hanoi area. In order to fight off the USAF and USN attack waves, the VNPAF HQ decided to implement a plan to coordinate the operations of MiGs with the ground-based AD forces. The SAM and AAA forces would engage the enemy strike groups approaching from the southeast, the MiG-17s and MiG-21s of the North Korean AF unit would intercept strike groups approaching from the east and the northeast, and the VNPAF's FRs would engage strike groups approaching from the northwest.

During the early morning hours when the B1 net detected enemy aircraft approaching from the west, the 921st FR decided to send two MiG-21s (piloted by Nguyễn Đăng Kính and Bùi Đức Nhu) to intercept this target between Tuyên Quang and Sơn Dương. When the flight was passing Thành Sơn, the pilots were directed to turn left and fly on a heading of 80 degrees in order to intercept the enemy bombers. Seeing the target, a formation of both F-4s and F-105s at a range of seven miles, Nguyễn Đăng Kính immediately accelerated and got on the tail of an aircraft on the right-hand edge of the enemy formation. When the range was right, he fired a missile that hit an F-4, setting it on fire. The AF command post ordered the flight to break off the engagement and return to land at Nội Bài.

At 0706 hours a flight piloted by Vũ Thế Xuân, Nguyễn Quang Sinh, Lê Hồng Điệp, and Nguyễn Phi Hùng from the 923rd FR was ordered to take off from Gia Lâm airfield and fly toward Hòa Lạc while climbing to an altitude of 6,500 feet. A few moments later the flight was directed to move toward Phú Thọ when the flight spotted F-4s and a large number of F-105s at a range of six miles and an intercept angle of 90 degrees. Vũ Thế Xuân ordered his pilots to drop their auxiliary fuel tanks and engage the enemy. MiG No. 1 turned in and dove on the lead enemy aircraft, which was flying at a lower altitude. At a range of 0.28 miles Vũ Thế Xuân fired a burst of cannon shells. The F-105D was hit by the shells, rolled over, and dove toward the ground. While chasing an F-105D, Nguyễn Phi Hùng fired a long burst at an F-105 that hit the fuselage of the enemy aircraft. When Nguyễn

Phi Hùng turned away he saw another enemy plane and fired at it continuously until he ran out of ammunition. By the end of the battle pilots Nguyễn Phi Hùng and Vũ Thế Xuân each had shot down one F-105D. All MiG pilots returned and landed at Đa Phúc airfield at 0744 hours. It was quite a day for the two types of MiGs. They fought a total of four air engagements against USAF strike formations. VNPAF MiG-17s shot down two F-105Ds and MiG-21s shot down one F-4, thereby helping to disrupt a large wave of USAF attacks aimed against targets in Hanoi.

After 19 December 1967, the USAF and USN were forced to end the seventh wave of attacks against Hanoi City. Based on the air engagements against the USAF on 19 December 1967, the MiG pilots and the AF command post concluded that the U.S. pilots had learned lessons from the air battles in early December and had changed their tactics by having their individual flights split into two-aircraft sections in order to counter both MiG-17s and MiG-21s. On 19 December 1967 an F-105F flown by Capt. Phillip M. Drew and Maj. William H. Wheeler, the No. 3 aircraft in an Iron Hand formation from the 357th TFS/355th TFW, fired several rounds of 20-mm shells into the fuselage and right wing of a MiG-17. In addition, while flying in the F-105F No. 2 slot in another Iron Hand flight, Maj. William M. Dalton and Maj. James L. Graham from the 333rd TFS/355th TFW claimed half-credit for shooting down a MiG-17 (this MiG-17 had previously been damaged by fire from an F-4D crewed by Maj. Joseph D. Moore and 1st Lt. George H. McKinney Jr. of the 8th TFW).[87] However, according to the combat log of the 923rd FR, during the battles on 19 December 1967 all four MiG-17s that flew two separate combat engagements returned and landed safely. It might have been that the U.S. aircraft engaged with North Korean AF MiGs.

Some Assessments of the Year 1967

The year 1967 was the year of the most intense air battles in the Vietnam air war. Starting with the 2 January battle—Operation Bolo, whose purpose was to kill MiGs—there were continual changes in tactics from both sides. Some authors have assessed that in 1967, the balance of power over the skies of North Vietnam had shifted. If the first half was in favor of the United States, then the second half was in favor of the VNPAF.[88]

In 1967, the VNPAF strengthened its organizational and battle effectiveness. In this year, the VNPAF flew more than a thousand air combat sorties (1,284 air combat sorties), fought 101 air engagements, and shot down 96 USAF and USN aircraft,[89] but two FRs lost 39 MiGs (22 MiG-17s and 17 MiG-21s) and 21 pilots were killed.

There are various statistics mentioned in U.S. documents on the number of MiGs shot down by U.S. pilots in 1967, but Donald McCarthy gives the figure of seventy-seven MiGs shot down during air battles in North Vietnam (including MiG-17s and MiG-21s).[90] It is clear the appearance of the electronic modules QRC-248 in the EC-121 aircraft helped the U.S. side understand more in depth how the flights of MiGs would take off and fly toward the waiting areas, and how GCI units directed the MiG flights to approach the targets.

The year 1967 also witnessed the creation and confirmation of new intercept tactics for MiG-21s. Now the MiG-21 pilots were confident when using the tactic of striking deep into the center of a large USAF strike formation and using R-3S missiles to attack quickly and then depart quickly, surprising the enemy pilots. This fighting method was also of great tactical significance because it disrupted the U.S. attack formations at long range, while the American pilots were in the process of deploying into attack formation, and it forced the enemy attackers to jettison their bombs and abandon their planned missions against ground targets.

But as a survival rule of war, tactics are flexible and are meant to be applied in specific battle situations. More than that, during the air war in Vietnam, the U.S. pilots themselves also discovered the intercept tactics of the MiG-21 and changed several elements of their tactics and weapons to adapt. Therefore, MiG pilots had to carefully analyze every success or failure in battle in order to deal with the opponent's every new tactic and new weapons.[91]

President Hồ Chí Minh visiting the VNPAF's 921st FR at Đa Phúc airport in early 1967. *Reproduced with permission from Vietnam News Agency*

Minister of National Defense General Võ Nguyên Giáp at the AD and AF Service Command on 28 December 1972. *From left*: Senior Colonel Hoàng Phương, Colonel Trần Hanh, General Võ Nguyên Giáp, Senior Colonel Lê Văn Tri, and unknown man. *Photographer: Xuân Át; reproduced with permission from Nguyễn Anh Xuân*

Minister of National Defense General Võ Nguyên Giáp visiting the AF Corps after the "Điện Biên Phủ in the Air" campaign (1973). *From left*: VNP Army Vice Chief of the General Staff Senior Colonel Phùng Thế Tài, Commander in Chief of the AD and AF Service Senior Colonel Lê Văn Tri, General Võ Nguyên Giáp, Lieutenant Colonel Nguyễn Thành Ut, and six MiG-21 pilots: Nguyễn Hồng Nhị, Ngô Duy Thư, Đỗ Văn Lanh, Nguyễn Đức Soát, Phạm Tuân, and Dương Bá Kháng. *Photographer: Xuân Át; reproduced with permission from Nguyễn Anh Xuân*

Chief of the VNPA General Staff General Văn Tiến Dzũng (*center left*) and Hanoi mayor Dr. Trần Duy Hưng (*left, wearing glasses*) visiting the 921st FR at Đa Phúc airport (1973). *Photographer: Xuân Át; reproduced with permission from Nguyễn Anh Xuân*

Lieutenant Colonel Đào Đình Luyện, first commander of the 921st FR. He later became a three-star general and the chief of the VNPA General Staff. *Photographer: Xuân Át; reproduced with permission from Nguyễn Anh Xuân*

Senior Colonel Phùng Thế Tài, commander in chief, and all high-ranking officers of the AD and AF Service were present at its command post to lead and instruct the pilots during the first air battle on 3 April 1965. *Standing, from right*: Colonel Hoàng Ngọc Diêu, Senior Colonel Lê Văn Tri, Senior Colonel Phùng Thế Tài, Senior Colonel Đặng Tính, Senior Colonel Nguyễn Xuân Mậu, and unknown man. *Photographer: Xuân Át; reproduced with permission from Nguyễn Anh Xuân*

MiG-17 pilots. *From left*: Phạm Ngọc Lan, Phan Văn Túc, Hồ Văn Qùy, and Trần Minh Phương, all of whom successfully opened up the air front on 3 April 1965. *Photographer: Xuân Át; reproduced with permission from Nguyễn Anh Xuân*

A MiG-17 flight of the 923rd FR returning to Kép airfield after a victorious air battle, 1967. *From left*: Lưu Huy Chao, Lê Hải, Lê Xuân Dy, and Hoàng Văn Kỷ. *Photographer: Xuân Át; reproduced with permission from Nguyễn Anh Xuân*

Two MiG-17 pilots, Trần Hanh (*left*) and Phạm Ngọc Lan, checking their gun camera film after the first two air battles on 3–4 April 1965 opened up the air front. *Reproduced with permission from Vietnam News Agency*

A MiG-17 flight of the 923rd FR. *From left*: Hồ Văn Qùy, Đỗ Huy Hoàng, Võ Văn Mẫn, and Nguyễn Văn Bảy (A). *Photographer: Xuân Át; reproduced with permission from Nguyễn Anh Xuân*

Two MiG-17 pilots, Lê Hải (*right*), six victories, and Nguyễn Đình Phúc at Kép airfield, 1967. *Photographer Xuân Át; reproduced with permission from Nguyễn Anh Xuân*

Two MiG-21 aces, Phạm Thanh Ngân (*left*), eight victories, and Nguyễn Văn Cốc, nine victories, at Đa Phúc airport, 1968. *Photographer: Xuân Át; reproduced with permission from Nguyễn Anh Xuân*

Two MiG-21 aces, Nguyễn Hồng Nhị (*right*), eight victories, and Nguyễn Đăng Kính, six victories, at Đa Phúc airport, 1967. *Photographer: Xuân Át; reproduced with permission from Nguyễn Anh Xuân*

MiG-21 pilots of the 921st FR at Đa Phúc airport, 1968. Behind them are the pilots' hidden bunkers under Hàm Lợn Mountain. *From right*: Nguyễn Đăng Kính, Lê Trọng Huyên, Bùi Đức Nhu, Đồng Văn Song, Nguyễn Văn Thuận, and Nguyễn Văn Lung. *Photographer: Xuân Át; reproduced with permission from Nguyễn Anh Xuân*

Two MiG-21 pilots, Vũ Ngọc Đỉnh (*right*), and his wingman, Nghiêm Đình Hiếu, after a combat mission. Đa Phúc airport, December 1966. *Reproduced with permission from Vũ Danh Cường, director of the VNP AD and AF Service Museum*

MiG-21 ace Nguyễn Đức Soát, six victories, and his wingmen exchanging experiences after a successful air battle, Đa Phúc airport, December 1972. *From left*: Ngô Duy Thư, Nguyễn Đức Soát, Trần Việt, and Nguyễn Thanh Qúy. *Photographer: Xuân Át; reproduced with permission from Nguyễn Anh Xuân*

MiG-21 pilots of the 921st FR running to their aircraft on the order of Combat Alert Duty Level 1, Đa Phúc airport, 1971. *Reproduced with permission from Vietnam News Agency*

MiG-21 pilots after victorious air battles on 27 June 1972, in which they shot down four F-4s. *From left*: Phạm Phú Thái, Bùi Thanh Liêm, Nguyễn Đức Soát, and Ngô Duy Thư. *Reproduced with permission from Vũ Danh Cương, director of the VNP AD and AF Service Museum*

MiG-19 pilots of the 925th FR exchanging combat experiences after combat missions, Yên Bái airport, 1971. *From left*: Trần Trọng Vượng, Bùi Phúc Chỉnh, Trần Văn Chiến, Vũ Viết Tần, Mai Chí Lưu, Nguyễn Văn Thục, Lê Thanh Qúy, Vũ Công Thuyết, Nguyễn Thế Ngữ, and Nguyễn Văn Tập. *Reproduced with permission from Vũ Danh Cương, director of the VNP AD and AF Service Museum*

Douglas Brian "Pete" Peterson, U.S. ambassador to Vietnam, with a group of VNPAF veteran pilots at the meeting of Vietnamese and American veteran pilots in Hanoi, 13 April 2016. *From left*: Lieutenant General Phạm Phú Thái, Pete Peterson, Dr. Nguyễn Sỹ Hưng (author), and Lieutenant General Nguyễn Đức Soát. *Photographer: Vũ Anh Tuấn; reproduced with permission*

A group of VNPAF and U.S. veteran pilots attending their first meeting in Hanoi, 13 April 2016. *First row, from left:* Senior Colonel Từ Đễ, Kent Ewing, Senior Colonel Nguyễn Công Huy, Dave Skinling, Lieutenant General Phạm Phú Thái, Senior Colonel Đồng Văn Song, Lieutenant General Nguyễn Đức Soát, Senior Colonel Mai Đức Toại, Charles Tutt, Senior Colonel Nguyễn Văn Lâm, Senior Colonel Nguyễn Văn Nghĩa, Lieutenant Colonel Vũ Phi Hùng, and Senior Colonel Lê Thanh Đạo. *Second row:* Rick Hartnack, Senior Colonel Nguyễn Kim Khôi, John Kerr, Senior Colonel Nguyễn Thanh Quý, Senior Colonel Nguyễn Văn Bảy (A), Jack Ensch, Senior Colonel Hà Quang Hưng, and Lieutenant Colonel Nguyễn Sỹ Hưng (author). *Third row:* Curt Dose, Clint Johnson, Pete Pettigrew, Doug Little, and Jim Hoogerwerf. *Photographer: Vũ Anh Tuấn; reproduced with permission*

A group of Vietnamese and American veteran pilots posing for a photo on the USS *Midway* in San Diego, September 2017. *First row, from left:* two unknown U.S. veteran pilots, Hà Quang Hưng, unknown U.S. veteran pilot, Phạm Phú Thái, Nguyễn Đức Soát, Lê Thanh Đạo, Phùng Văn Quảng, Nguyễn Văn Bảy (A), Lữ Thông, Vũ Phi Hùng, Từ Đễ, Nguyễn Thanh Quý, Nguyễn Sỹ Hưng, Nguyễn Kim Cách, and Nguyễn Nam Liên. *Second row:* Three unknown U.S. veteran pilots, Charles Tutt, Pete Pettigrew. *Photographer: Vũ Anh Tuấn; reproduced with permission*

Vietnamese and American veteran pilots (with family members) posing for a photo, October 2018, in Tam Đảo township near Thud Ridge. This used to be the landmark USAF F-105 pilots used to mark where they would turn around to bomb Hanoi during the war. It is now a famous tourist destination. *Photographer: Vũ Anh Tuấn; reproduced with permission*

Vietnamese and American veteran pilots (with family members) posing together for a photo at Yên Viên railway station, October 2018. This used to be one of the locations most frequently bombed by U.S. strikes during the war.

Photographer Vũ Anh Tuấn; reproduced with permission

Vietnamese and American veteran pilots posing together for a photo at the Bay Việt Pilot Training School (Vietnam Airlines) in Hồ Chí Minh City, October 2018. *Photographer: Vũ Anh Tuấn; reproduced with permission*

5

1968–1971
CLASHES WITH THE
USN OVER THE SKIES OF
MILITARY ZONE 4

After the Tet Offensive, in which the Liberation Army of South Vietnam (which belonged to the National Liberation Front of South Vietnam, also known as an organization that gathered forces from southern Vietnam against the Saigon government and foreign interference) simultaneously attacked larger cities under the rule of the Republic of South Vietnam, the Johnson administration had to seriously reconsider its plans and calculations. By 31 March 1968, President Lyndon Johnson was forced into the position of announcing the policy of limited bombing north of the twentieth parallel, concentrating a large number of aircraft to bomb targets along Strategic Transportation Road 559. In addition, by 30 October 1968 President Johnson was compelled to announce the end of Operation Rolling Thunder, the longest air campaign in the history of U.S. warfare. However, in the next three years, from late 1968 to early 1972, the USAF and USN stepped up their military operations, and in particular they increased the reconnaissance flights they directed against North Vietnam's seaports and its main transport routes and lines of communication. They did this using high-altitude SR-71 reconnaissance aircraft and unmanned reconnaissance drones to closely monitor and undermine the amount of military assistance the socialist countries were providing to Vietnam.

Also in 1968, many changes occurred in the highest level of senior personnel of the U.S. war machine, including the USAF headquarters. In August 1968, Gen. George S. Brown replaced Gen. W. W. Momyer as the new commander of the Seventh AF. In 1969, the USN started the Strike Fighter Tactics Instructor Program, known as Top Gun, at Naval Air Station (NAS) Miramar in California, with the purpose of training their aircrews in new tactics and methods, and in the employment of improved weapons. Fleets of fighter aircraft were significantly upgraded, with several technical improvements for the aircraft and armaments.

Responding to this situation, the VNP AD and AF Service Command decided to send some SAM regiments and AF units to Military Zone Four's (MZ4) area and airfields. Several experienced fighter pilots were assigned to operate in MZ4's airfields, ready for air combat alert duties.[1] The main opponent of the MiGs in the MZ4 theater were the USN aircraft, with their highly skilled pilots and direct support from U.S. warships off the east coast of North Vietnam. With all of these new factors in place, air engagements over the skies of MZ4 in 1968 would become very fierce.

At the same time, the VNPAF was strengthening its own organization and consolidating its forces in preparation for future air combat battles. In late 1969, Colonel Đào Đình Luyện was appointed the VNPAF commander, Lieutenant Colonel Trần Mạnh was appointed deputy commander, and Lieutenant Colonel Nguyễn Phúc Trạch was appointed chief of staff. According to the AD and AF Service's approvement, the 921st FR was based at Đa Phúc airfield, the 925th FR was based at Yên Bái airfield, and the 923rd FR was based at Kép airfield. Vinh, Đồng Hới, Thọ Xuân, and Anh Sơn airfields were repaired and expanded to be able to accept MiGs when necessary.

This meant that by early 1969 the VNPAF had three AF FRs with hundreds of MiGs and hundreds of combat pilots. During this period when the United States restricted its bombing of North Vietnam, the VNPAF stepped up its training of a number of new pilots who had just finished flight training in the Soviet Union and China. Since 1968 there had been improvement both in the quantity and the quality of VNPAF fighter pilots. In 1969 a total of more than 13,000 training flights were conducted for MiG pilots, resulting in a 30 percent increase in the number of pilots who were qualified and ready to stand combat alert duty.[2] Assessing the improvements of VNPAF at that time, one U.S. author described: "During three and one-half years in which U.S. activities over North Vietnam were restricted, the VNPAF steadily increased and improved its MiG force. At the end of 1970, total MiGs had risen from 149 aircraft to 265 aircraft (140 MiG15/17s; 31 MiG-19s; 94 MiG-21s). These MiGs were a significant equipment upgrade for the VNPAF."[3]

3 January 1968: A MiG Master Pilot:
One against Thirty-Six

Due to the fact that the air battle fought on 3 January was the first battle of the savage year of 1968, and also a very important battle, the VNPAF's command decided to use aircraft from both the 921st and 923rd FRs. From early morning the USAF sent a large number of aircraft, approximately eighty F-105s and F-4s, to attack Hanoi. The on-duty commanding officer of the 921st FR, deputy regiment commander Trần Hanh, ordered a flight of two MiG-21s piloted by Nguyễn Đăng Kính and Bùi Đức Nhu to take off from Đa Phúc airfield at 0733 hours, and then directed the pilots to fly toward Thành Sơn.

The two MiG-21 pilots soon spotted a flight of F-4s flying in a spread-finger formation. At that moment, the MiG lead Nguyễn Đăng Kính saw that there was a group of F-105s in front of the F-4s. He decided to fly past the F-4 fighters and engage the bomb-laden F-105s. Nguyễn Đăng Kính quickly got on the tail of the F-105 No. 2 in the middle of the flight, placed his target in the center of his sight, and launched a missile that hit the F-105. The F-105 formation began to jettison their bombs and to turn away to escape.

A few minutes later a flight of four MiG-17s flown by Lưu Huy Chao, Lê Sỹ Diệp, Bùi Văn Sưu, and Lê Hải took off from Gia Lâm airfield and were directed to fly up toward Thái Nguyên. Lưu Huy Chao saw eight F-4s at a bearing of 45 degrees and a range of 3.5 to 4.5 miles. This was a flight of F-4Ds carrying gun pods that was part of the morning strike formation. At that moment, the MiG No. 2 aircraft, flown by Lê Sỹ Diệp, was hit by a missile. Lê Sỹ Diệp was able to eject successfully. The F-4D that shot down Lê Sỹ Diệp's MiG was the lead F-4 aircraft flown by Maj. Bernard J. Bogoslofski and Capt. Richard L. Huskey of the 433rd TFS/8th TFW. A few moments later, MiG-17 No. 1 was also hit by a piece of missile shrapnel that penetrated the right wing. The U.S. aircraft that fired the AIM-4D missile that hit Lưu Huy Chao's MiG-17 was an F-4D flown by Lt. Col. Clayton K. Squier and 1st Lt. Michael D. Muldoon of the 435th TFS/8th TFW.[4] However, Lưu Huy Chao's MiG was only slightly damaged and he was able to continue the battle and later returned to the airfield and landed safely.[5]

While turning to the left, the two MiGs of the second section saw a flight of F-4s flash past them. Bùi Văn Sưu turned in to chase them, then when he had closed the range to 0.3 miles he opened fire. His shells missed, passing behind his target, so he flew up and fired another burst that hit an F-4D and caught it fire. MiG No. 3 descended, turned back, and landed at Đa Phúc airfield at 0815 hours.

At the beginning of 1968, VNPAF units were facing the grim reality of lacking both combat aircraft and experienced MiG pilots for combat duty. In early January 1968 there were times when there were only two MiG-21s able to fly combat missions. After the morning battle on 3 January 1968, because one of the aircraft ran off the end of the runway when it landed, there was only one MiG-21 left able to fly combat missions. Undaunted by this situation, the 921st FR command post decided to place this single aircraft on combat alert duty in accordance with the spirit of the slogan, "As long as we have even just one pilot and one aircraft, we will still fight!"

During that afternoon, a large USAF strike formation with a total of thirty-six aircraft, including both F-105s and F-4s, flew in from the direction of Yên Châu to attack Hanoi. The 921st FR command post ordered the only aircraft left, MiG-21 flown by pilot Hà Văn Chúc, to take off earlier than originally planned and then fly out on a heading of 240 degrees toward the designated battle area over Yên Châu. Hà Văn Chúc spotted three formations of American aircraft flying in an extended trail formation, with a flight of F-4s flying behind them to cover their rear. These were a group of F-105s carrying bombs, with F-4 fighter escorts, assigned to bomb Kinh Nỗ railroad line. Suddenly the F-4 fighters flying rear cover spotted the MiG and began to turn to the right. Even though the 921st FR command post had intended to direct Hà Văn Chúc to turn to the right, the AF HQ command post intervened by ordering him to continue to fly on a heading of 40 degrees and to head straight for the thirty-six enemy aircraft out in front. Because Hà Văn Chúc's MiG had taken off earlier than originally planned, he had accumulated speed so that he was flying a great deal faster than the F-105s. He quickly bypassed the two trailing formations, got in behind the lead formation of F-105s, and placed his target designator on the F-105 No. 1 in the formation. When the range was down to 0.6 miles, he pressed his missile-firing button. The F-105 leading the formation was hit by Hà Văn Chúc's R-3S missile, causing it to burst into flames and crash on the spot. The other F-105s were forced to jettison their bomb loads in order to turn to engage the MiG.

The F-105D that Hà Văn Chúc shot down was flown by Col. James Ellis Bean from the 469th TFS/388th TFW.[6] Colonel Bean ejected and was captured. Colonel Bean was the 388th TFW's deputy commander of wing for combat operations. As the F-105 formation dispersed, Hà Văn Chúc switched his afterburner to full power, pulled up into a climb to an altitude of 32,000 feet, and then switched off his afterburner (at this point in time he had only four hundred liters of fuel left) and quickly turned away, then landed safely at base. Immediately after Hà Văn Chúc made his attack, the SAM forces shot down two more F-105s.

Hà Văn Chúc's victory was extremely significant. In spite of the difficult conditions, with only one MiG able to take off, he still accumulated a speed advantage, got into the proper attack position, flew over the top of the entire USAF extended trail strike formation, and then nosed his aircraft over and shot down the lead aircraft of the formation, causing the enemy's attack to disband. Later the MiGs veteran pilots and the media called Hà Văn Chúc "a master pilot: one against thirty-six."

14 January 1968: The Second EB-66 Downed by MiG-21s

On the engagement of 5 January 1968, a number of U.S. documents stated that a flight of F-105s clashed with MiG-17s, and one F-105 assigned to suppress SAMs was shot down by a MiG-17. However, VNPAF has no record of any engagement on that day. On Sunday, 14 January 1968, the VNPAF was informed that on that day the USAF would send a large strike formation of between thirty and forty aircraft, mostly F-105s, in from the west to attack targets along Route 2. Gradually, from the early hours, the radar net reported that EB-66s were detected conducting jamming from a bearing of 230 to 265 degrees. At the same moment many flights of U.S. aircraft were detected. The 921st FR asked the AF Command for permission to launch aircraft.

A flight of two MiGs with Hà Văn Chúc and Nguyễn Văn Thuận took off at 0745 hours and flew out on a heading of 290 degrees. It was then that Hà Văn Chúc spotted four enemy aircraft headed in the opposite direction from the two MiG-21s and at a lower altitude. At the same time, he spotted four more enemy aircraft off to the left front of the MiGs; these were F-105s that had conducted a bombing attack in the area of Yên Bái airfield.

After giving the order to pursue the F-105s, the MiG lead swept in to attack aircraft No. 2 in the flight of F-105s, which was then 2 to 2.5 miles ahead of the MiGs. When fixing the F-105 in the center of his sight and after getting a good audible signal from the missile's heat-seeker, Hà Văn Chúc fired an R-3S Atoll missile. Unfortunately, the missile did not leave the pylon. Hà Văn Chúc immediately lowered a wing and pressed the firing button again. This time the missile left the pylon, dropped for a moment, and then headed straight for the F-105, setting the enemy aircraft on fire, and it went down east of Yên Bái, right next to the Red River. Hà Văn Chúc quickly pulled into a right-hand turn, climbed to an altitude of 28,000 feet, and then flew back to the airfield. The F-105D that Hà Văn Chúc shot down was flown by Maj. Stanley Henry Horne from the 469th TFS/388th TFW; the pilot was listed as KIA. The other F-105Ds jettisoned their bombs so that they could engage the MiG, but the MiG had already accelerated away and escaped in accordance with the tactic of "fast attack, fast withdrawal."

When they received information indicating that an EB-66 EW aircraft would fly into the territory of North Vietnam with twenty-four F-4s in company, AF HQ approved the recommendation from 921st FR command and ordered its pilots to shoot down and destroy the EB-66. A flight of two MiG-21s flown by Nguyễn Đăng Kính and Đồng Văn Song was ordered to get ready to take off.

After taking off at 1527 hours, the flight was directed to fly on a heading of 180 degrees and then ordered to switch on afterburners and climb to an altitude of 26,400 feet. When the pilots were informed that the target was 10 degrees to their right front at a range of ten miles, Nguyễn Đăng Kính almost instantly spotted the EB-66. However, he was surprised that he did not see any F-4 fighter escorts as usual. Nguyễn Đăng Kính ordered his wingman to stick close and cover him. Perhaps at this time the EB-66 still did not know that there were MiGs chasing it. When the range was down to less than 2.5 miles, MiG No. 1 targeted the aircraft and fired a missile. Unfortunately, the missile did not launch. Nguyễn Đăng Kính continued to close in on the target and pressed his firing button a second time at a range of less than two miles. The R-3S missile exploded off to the right of the EB-66. Nguyễn Đăng Kính wasted no time and immediately ordered his wingman to attack the target. After seeing No. 1 launch his missile, Đồng

Văn Song turned his aircraft to the right and chased another EB-66 that was in front of him. MiG No. 2 quickly closed in on the EB-66. To make sure that his attack would be successful, Đồng Văn Song closed in to a range of 0.9 miles before firing his missile. The missile hit the engine under the EB-66's right wing. When he saw the EB-66 begin to emit a trail of black smoke, Đồng Văn Song decided to flip his switch to fire a second missile, but at that moment he saw the EB-66 suddenly erupt into a big ball of flames.[7] Đồng Văn Song quickly pulled his stick over to one side to turn and pushed his throttle forward to break off the engagement by climbing to an altitude of 32,000 feet, then descended to an altitude of 10,000 feet and returned to the airfield to land. As he was making his own breakaway maneuver and flying past the EB-66, Nguyễn Đăng Kính saw the second EB-66 burning fiercely and diving toward the ground. He then pulled up to an altitude of 32,000 feet to break off the engagement, returned to the airfield, and landed.

The EB-66 that was shot down by Đồng Văn Song's MiG-21 missile crashed thirty-five miles west of Thanh Hóa. It was flown by Maj. Pollard Hugh Mercer and a crew of six from the 41st TEWS (Tactical Electronic Warfare Squadron)/355th TFW.[8] On 15 January 1968 rescue aircraft finally reached the area where the aircraft had crashed. However, three rescue helicopters were shot down or damaged. It was not until midday on 17 January that a helicopter, Jolly Green 71, arrived to rescue the crew of the helicopter that had been shot down by ground fire. Of the seven members of the EB-66 crew Major Mercer, First Lieutenant Thompson, and 1st Lt. Pete Pedroli were rescued by an HH-3E helicopter. However, Mercer later died of his injuries at the Clark Air Force Base (AFB) hospital. The other four members of the flight crew were captured and became prisoners of war.

The EB-66 that was shot down in this engagement was the second EB-66 that was shot down by MiGs in less than two months. After this second EB-66 was shot down, the USAF ordered the EB-66 crews not to fly deep into North Vietnamese airspace.[9]

With regard to the death of Pilot Hà Văn Chúc, some Vietnamese historians wrote that he was severely injured in the battle on 14 January 1968 and died at Military Hospital 108 on 19 January 1968. We cannot find any American record or documents that stated that a MiG was shot down by a U.S. fighter on 14 January 1968.[10]

3 February 1968: An F-102 Is Killed by a MiG

In late 1967 and early 1968, the USAF faced many losses to MiG-21s. Their leadership analyzed the situation and changed a number of elements of the tactics they used against MiG-21s. In the second half of January 1968, MiG-21s flew many combat missions but did not achieve significant results. After carefully analyzing the changes in tactics made by the USAF, the MiG-21 pilots discussed the situation, came up with lessons learned, and agreed to employ new tactics aimed at achieving secrecy and surprise in order to ensure victory.

The 921st FR command post earnestly studied reports received from the intelligence net and anticipated that on 3 February the USAF would send in a large strike formation that would approach from the west and fly in along Routes 2 and 3 to attack Hanoi. Because the regiment was short of both pilots and aircraft, the 921st FR command post decided to use a "2+1 formation" made up of three very experienced pilots: Phạm Thanh Ngân, Nguyễn Văn Cốc, and Mai Văn Cương.

Early in the morning hours, Phạm Thanh Ngân and Nguyễn Văn Cốc took off twice and flew to Tuyên Quang to try to find and destroy EB-66 planes. While closing on an EB-66 flying along the border, the MiGs clashed with F-4 escort fighters. Both sides fought each other furiously, but neither side was able to get into firing position. The two MiG-21s decided to break off the engagement and return to land.

At 1545 hours Phạm Thanh Ngân and Nguyễn Văn Cốc took off a third time and then flew on a heading of 290 degrees toward Hòa Bình. A few minutes later the pilots spotted the target at an altitude of 30,000 feet near the Hồi Xuân area of Thanh Hóa Province. When the MiGs were in the right position, the command post ordered the pilots to switch on afterburners and make a hard left turn to get in behind the target. Phạm Thanh Ngân radioed to his wingman, "Keep your eyes peeled and cover me. I will attack the enemy aircraft No. 2, the one on the right." With this order Phạm Thanh Ngân enabled his wingman to attack the U.S. aircraft No. 1, the one on the left. As the range closed, Phạm Thanh Ngân saw that the targets were not EB-66s but instead were F-102A Delta Daggers. When the two F-102As encountered the MiG-21s at an altitude of 36,000 feet, the F-102A No. 1, flown by Major A. L. Lomax, turned to counterattack the MiGs. He fired three AIM-4D Falcon missiles but all three missiles missed. Meanwhile, Phạm Thanh Ngân had gotten into a position behind the F-102 No. 2 to prepare to make his attack.

When the range was down to 1.2 miles and he had a stable sight picture, Phạm Thanh Ngân pressed his firing button, but unfortunately the missile failed to fire. He immediately pressed the button to fire his second missile. The R-3S missile left the missile pylon and sped straight into the tail of the F-102, causing it to burst into flames.[11] This F-102A was hit by the missile at an altitude of 35,000 feet and was flown by 1st Lt. Wallace Luttrell Wiggins of the 509th FIS (Fighter Interceptor Squadron)/405th FW (Fighter Wing).[12] Lieutenant Wiggins was listed as KIA. The AF Command ordered the pilots to break off the engagement and fly back to land at Đa Phúc.

Air Engagement on 5 February 1968

Early in the morning the USAF sent a large force of F-105s escorted by three flights of F-4 fighters to attack targets in the Sơn Dương, Tuyên Quang, and Thái Nguyên areas. After taking off at 0739 hours, a flight flown by Nguyễn Ngọc Độ and Hoàng Biểu climbed to an altitude of 13,000 feet and flew on a heading of 310 degrees to the designated battle area over Sơn Dương and Hòa Bình. Seeing the target to the left and below, the pilots made a hard turn to chase the target. The target they saw was a formation of F-105s escorted by F-4s. When the enemy formation flew across the border, the QRC-248 system on the EC-121 early warning aircraft almost certainly reported that MiGs had taken off from Đa Phúc airfield. For some unknown reason, however, the F-4s assigned to MiGCAP duty failed to spot the MiGs. Following the tactic of "deep penetration," the two MiG-21s flew right over the top of the enemy fighters and closed with the F-105D very rapidly.

The MiG lead Nguyễn Ngọc Độ took a quick look at the American formation and decided to fire one missile at the F-4s in order to force them to break their formation. Just as judged, when they saw the MiG-21 fire a missile, the F-4 pilots immediately split up and broke their formation. Nguyễn Ngọc Độ quickly flew right past the F-4s and closed on the flight of F-105s flying out in front. Nguyễn Ngọc Độ got on the tail of the trailing F-105 (aircraft No. 4), brought his target into the center of his sight, and when the range was right he fired his R-3S missile, which flew straight into the F-105, making it burn fiercely. The F-105 that he shot down was probably flown by Capt. Carl William Lasiter of 34th TFS/388th TFW.[13] The pilot ejected and was taken prisoner. (Perhaps because of the difference in time zones, the date that the Vietnamese records show that Nguyễn Ngọc Độ shot down Captain Lasiter is off by one day from the date that American records say Lasiter was shot down.) The other F-4s turned back to attack the MiGs. F-4 No. 1 fired two AIM-7 missiles at the MiG but both missiles missed. Nguyễn Ngọc Độ climbed to an altitude of 32,000 feet, turned back toward his base, and landed at the airfield.

DESCRIPTION BY PILOT NGUYỄN NGỌC ĐỘ

I decided to fire one missile into the enemy formation to force them to take evasive action and disrupt their combat formation. Two F-4s split up and headed in different directions. At that time I accelerated, flashed right past the two F-4s, and got on the tail of a flight of F-105s flying in front of the F-4s. I quickly placed my target designator on the trailing aircraft that was level at a speed of 900 kmph. When the range was down to 0.9 miles I fired my missile and it dropped from the pylon and then headed straight at the enemy aircraft, which turned into a ball of fire. I took maximum advantage of the MiG-21's ability to make sharp turns at high speed and I pulled into a climb up to 32,000 feet and returned to base and land.

This battle was over very quickly and it was the most intense and ferocious of all the battles I fought.[14]

DEPLOYMENT OF AF AND SAMS UNITS IN MZ4

Under the direction of the AD and AF Service, the VNPAF command post aggressively prepared to conduct air operations and participate in the defense of the Strategic Transportation Road 559, especially in the Panhandle area. AF commander Nguyễn Văn Tiên, AF political commissar Phan Khắc Hy, 921st FR commander Trần Mạnh, and his deputy Trần Hanh personally moved down to MZ4 to command this air campaign. After a period of study and preparation, the 921st FR completed its battle plan and selected the pilots who would fight the first battle. In early May 1968, three MiG-21s were secretly flown from Nội Bài down to Thọ Xuân airfield in Thanh Hóa.

As there was a shortage of MiG-21 pilots, the AF HQ decided to convert a number of MiG-17 pilots over to fly the MiG-21, and to shift a number of nighttime fighter pilots over to fly daylight missions. During this same period of time, one group of MiG-21 pilot trainees and two groups of MiG-17 pilot trainees who had completed their training returned to Vietnam, increasing the number of pilots available for combat alert duty. Of the more than seventy young pilots who graduated from training courses and returned to Vietnam in 1968, dozens of them later shot down American aircraft and more than ten of them were awarded the honorable title Vietnamese People's Armed Forces Hero.

As for the combat aircraft, during this period the Soviet Union provided thirty-six MiG-21 PFMs (F-94s) to the VNPAF.[15]

7 May 1968: The First MiG-21 Victory over MZ4

Nearly three months earlier, on 23 February 1968, during an air battle with an F-4 flight on the MiGCAP mission over Sơn Động–Lục Ngạn, pilot Hoàng Biểu from 921st FR shot down one F-4D crewed by Maj. Laird Guttersen and 1st Lt. Myron L. Donald from the 477th TFS/8th TFW. Both pilots ejected and were captured.

In the first week of May, the VNPAF command posts all came to the conclusion that the USAF and USN would probably conduct intense, large attacks against ground traffic targets along Route 7 in MZ4. The ground command posts at Thọ Xuân (X-1), Vinh (X-2), Đô Lương (X-3), and others monitored the situation closely. The VNPAF command post tasked the 921st FR with using MiG-21s to intercept the U.S. bombers and protect the targets. This combat mission was assigned to a flight consisting of Đặng Ngọc Ngự and Nguyễn Văn Cốc, waiting at Thọ Xuân airfield, to serve as the primary attack element. Another flight, flown by Nguyễn Đăng Kính and Nguyễn Văn Lung, was assigned to take off from Nội Bài to serve as a diversion.

The primary attack flight was ordered to take off from Thọ Xuân airfield at 0823 hours, then the pilots were directed to fly at low altitude on a heading of 190 degrees. Just as they reached Đô Lương, and anticipating that they were about to encounter the enemy, the MiG lead gave the order to drop auxiliary fuel tanks. As the flight flew over Vinh airfield, Đặng Ngọc Ngự saw two F-4Bs to the right and below the MiGs at a range of 2.5 miles. The weather was bad with thick clouds so the U.S. strike formation was falling apart. Although the formation included an EKA-3B assigned to jam North Vietnam's communications, perhaps the jamming device had broken down and the air control system was not working properly, because the American pilots did not know that MiGs were approaching them. Meanwhile, the VNPAF's auxiliary ground control station network was working properly and it provided timely and accurate commands to the MiG pilots.

Nguyễn Văn Cốc lost sight of his flight lead because of the bad weather. After making a hard right turn to look for the target, he saw one F-4B at an altitude of 3,000 to 4,500 feet. The pilot of the F-4B also spotted Nguyễn Văn Cốc's MiG and the two aircraft engaged in a dogfight, making sharp turns and weaving back and forth to try to get into a favorable attack position. After making two circles, the F-4 suddenly leveled out and accelerated in a straight line headed straight out toward the sea. Nguyễn Văn Cốc quickly switched to full afterburner to pursue him.

At that moment, in order to give the pilot greater confidence, Trần Hanh, who was in the X-1 command post, gave this firm command over the radio: "I think this looks good for you. Continue your attack. Destroy the enemy aircraft!" At this time the F-4B was over the sea at an altitude of 8,000 feet. Nguyễn Văn Cốc calmly closed in on his target and when the range was down to 0.9 miles and he heard a good audible signal from the missile's heat-seeker, he pressed his missile-firing button. He then quickly threw the switch that allowed him to fire his second missile. Both of the R-3S missiles flew straight into the fuselage of the F-4B, causing it to burst into flames and to dive nose-first into the sea. Both of the American pilots ejected and were rescued. Nguyễn Văn Cốc quickly pulled his stick over to break off the engagement, and returned to Thọ Xuân to land.

The F-4B that was shot down by Nguyễn Văn Cốc was from Squadron VF-92 of the USS *Enterprise* and was flown by Lt. Cdr. E. S. Christensen and Lt. (jg) W. A. Kramer.[16]

14 June 1968: The First MiG-17 Victory over MZ4

By the middle of 1968 the USAF had learned that MiG-21s were now aggressively operating over MZ4, and so it realigned the attack formations it sent to attack targets in MZ4 by increasing the number of fighters assigned to

MiGCAP and the number of fighter escorts flying in trail formation, in two- or four-aircraft sections, to be able to react when MiGs were encountered.

On 14 June, Lieutenant Colonel Đào Đình Luyện decided to use both MiG-17s and MiG-21s to intercept the American strike formations. Two MiG-17 pilots, Lưu Huy Chao and Lê Hải, took off at 0815 hours and flew from Gia Lâm airfield down to Thọ Xuân. After being briefed on their mission by the regiment's on-duty commanding officer at Thọ Xuân airfield, Nguyễn Văn Bảy (A), the pilots went on combat alert at the airfield. At 1432 hours the flight of MiG-17s took off, then the pilots were directed to fly along Route 15 to the holding area at Tân Kỳ to prepare to fight the enemy in the area over Đô Lương–Diễn Châu. The mobile ground control station at Quảng Bình (X-3) closely monitored the movements of the USN aircraft and selected just the right moment for the MiG-17s to make a sharp left turn. Flying at a speed of 465 mph and an altitude of 6,500 feet, the MiG-17s intercepted the target at an intercept angle of 90 degrees. Lưu Huy Chao ordered the flight to drop auxiliary fuel tanks and swept in to engage six F-4Bs in the skies over Đô Lương and Thanh Chương in Nghệ An Province. Both Lưu Huy Chao and Lê Hải fired accurately and each pilot shot down one F-4B. The pilots then returned and landed safely at Thọ Xuân airfield.

16 June 1968: MiG-21 versus USN F-4J over MZ4

After learning lessons from their previous losses, in this period of time, the USAF usually sent in two or three waves of air strikes each day, using strike formations of eight to twelve aircraft and with an operation time of thirty minutes to one hour for each. The ratio of fighter escorts in each strike group increased from the previous level, with one fighter for each attack bomber. Responding to the situation, the AF Command decided to order the 921st FR to send MiG-21s down to Thọ Xuân airfield and launch the MiGs from there to intercept a USAF air strike over the Đô Lương area in Nghệ An. Two new MiG-21 flight school graduates who had just returned from training in the Soviet Union were given this combat assignment. The pilots were Đinh Tôn and Nguyễn Tiến Sâm, two excellent pilots capable of fighting independently and who handled tactical situations properly. This was the first combat mission for young pilot Nguyễn Tiến Sâm, who formerly had been a student at Chu Văn An High School and Hanoi Polytechnic University.

In accordance with forecasts, the weather was bad that day, with low clouds and rain, but by 1400 hours the clouds had dissipated and after the rain ended visibility had increased to more than six miles. Đinh Tôn and Nguyễn Tiến Sâm were ordered to take off at 1430 hours and fly from Nội Bài down to Thọ Xuân airfield. At 1600 hours the flight took off, then flew on a heading of 200 degrees and at an altitude of 1,000 feet toward Nghĩa Đàn. Both pilots increased their visual scans of the sky and spotted four F-4Js flying in a spread-finger formation. Based on reports received, this was a flight of F-4Js from VF-102 of the USS *America* and assigned to fly a MiGCAP mission for bombers that were attacking targets located northwest of Vinh City.

At that time the U.S. Navy air war commander (AWC) was on board USS *Jouett*, a PIRAZ (positive identification radar advisory zone) ship in the Gulf of Tonkin. When he heard that the F-4Js from VF-102 were inbound, he decided to clear the fighters from the area so that he could attempt to shoot down MiGs with Talos surface-to-air missiles, as had been done on 23 May 1968. Even though they were already engaging in their MiGCAP mission, the AWC ordered the flight lead, Cdr. Walter Eugene Wilber with back-seater Lt. (jg) Bernard Francis Rupinski, to abort the mission and turn his formation of four F-4Js to the south.[17] The F-4Js turned back to the south of the nineteenth parallel, but the two MiG-21s stayed right with them. As soon as he saw the retreating F-4Js, Đinh Tôn gave the order to drop auxiliary fuel tanks and to switch on afterburners. While turning to the north and then continuing to the east and returning to the ship, the F-4J No. 2, piloted by Lt. Emory Brown with radar intercept officer Lt. (jg) Don Manlove, picked up MiGs to the north on his radar, and within seconds they were passing under Đinh Tôn's MiG.

As the MiGs and the F-4J approached each other head-on, Đinh Tôn saw three of the U.S. aircraft turn away to flee while the fourth F-4 had turned to pass under the belly of his MiG. Đinh Tôn pulled his aircraft into a left-hand turn and dove to pursue the fourth U.S. aircraft. Manlove tried to warn Wilber and Rupinski, not knowing that they had lost communications due to the high G turn they had executed.

Seizing his speed advantage, Đinh Tôn closed the range, brought his target into his sight circle, and waited for the target to level out so that he could fire a missile. Manlove kept calling out the range of Đinh Tôn's MiG behind

Wilber, but his warnings fell on deaf ears. When the F-4 suddenly leveled its wings, Đinh Tôn pressed his missile-firing button at a range of 0.9 miles. He saw the R-3S warhead explode and the explosion seemed to envelope the tail of the F-4J. Đinh Tôn pulled into a climb and rolled his aircraft to the left to see the results of his attack, then turned away to break off the engagement and returned to Thọ Xuân to land. The aircraft experienced an ejection system failure and only the pilot, Commander Wilber, was able to eject manually seconds before the plane hit the ground. Lieutenant Rupinski died in the crash. It wasn't until years after returning to the United States in 1973 that Wilber found out his plane had been hit by Đinh Tôn's missile.

After he saw No. 1 fire his missile and the missile hit the tail of the U.S. aircraft, Nguyễn Tiến Sâm saw the F-4 begin to trail black smoke and flames began shooting from the aircraft's rear section. Thinking that the F-4J that was hit by Đinh Tôn's missile was switching on his afterburners to escape, Nguyễn Tiến Sâm flicked his ordnance switch and adjusted his weapons sight to prepare to fire a missile. As he was moving into range and preparing to fire a missile, he saw a yellow flame shoot out from the tail of the F-4, and saw the pilot eject. Nguyễn Tiến Sâm made a sharp turn to a heading of 330 degrees and landed at Thọ Xuân airfield at 1620 hours.

During the war, Đinh Tôn was credited with four victories and was given the honorable title of VNP Armed Forces Hero. In the postwar period he was promoted to the rank of senior colonel and was appointed commander of one of the VNPAF's divisions.

9 July 1968: Dealing with the USN's New Tactical Scheme

Since the VNPAF first deployed forces to the MZ4 battle area, the pilots of the 921st and 923rd FRs had fought a number of engagements, during which they won three battles. The USAF and USN, which were initially surprised by the appearance of MiGs in MZ4, so far from their bases, became concerned and worried, and sought new methods and tactics to deal with this new threat. A larger number of the U.S. Navy F-8s were assigned to carry out fighter missions and deception operations designed to lure MiGs into taking off to intercept. Usually the F-8s flew in stair-step formation with extended separation between aircraft in order to be able to split up to engage in combat against MiGs. In particular, the F-8s also tried to draw MiG-17s to fly out to sea, where their warships could fire sea-to-air missiles at the MiGs.

Responding to the new U.S. schemes, the AF HQ ordered the 923rd FR to fight another battle on 9 July 1968 in order to crush the new U.S. air tactics. To be able to support MiG flights, the 923rd FR established a number of visual observation posts in the area of Cầu Cấm (Forbidden Bridge) and Vinh airfield. A flight consisting of Nguyễn Phi Hùng and Nguyễn Phú Ninh was assigned to this frontline combat mission. According to the battle plan, on the afternoon of 6 July 1968 the flight was ordered to secretly take off and fly down to Thọ Xuân airfield in order to ambush and be ready to take off, and their target would be A-4 attack bombers.

Two MiG-17s took off at 0734 hours and were directed to fly on a heading of 170 degrees, then to fly east of a parallel to Route 15 at an altitude of 350 feet. The flight maintained total radio silence. Just at the moment that the MiGs passed Nghĩa Đàn, the auxiliary ground control station informed the pilots that there were two F-4s flying over the area of Cầu Cấm. Since the pilots had not yet spotted the target, the pilots continued to maintain their heading toward Thanh Chương, then Nguyễn Phú Ninh spotted the target and radioed: "Two F-8s, 45 degrees to the right front!" The target was a flight of F-8Es flying as fighter escorts to an RF-8 photo-reconnaissance aircraft. Hearing the attack order from his lead, Nguyễn Phú Ninh immediately switched on his afterburner and turned in hard to pursue the enemy aircraft. The two F-8s also switched on their afterburners, leaving a trail of black smoke behind them, then the two F-8s made a shallow turn toward the mountains. Following the tactic for dealing with MiG-17s, the two F-8s split up, with one aircraft continuing to fly straight and level while the other aircraft turned to the left. Without hesitation, No. 2 chased the F-8 turning left and increased speed to close in on his target. When the range was right he squeezed his trigger, firing three bursts from his guns and seeing his shells hit the top of the F-8's fuselage. He then made a hard turn to the left to break away. When he rolled his aircraft back he saw that his lead was pursuing the F-8 No. 2 out toward the sea.

Nguyễn Phú Ninh heard the command post order the pilots to turn back to the coast but he heard no response from his lead. At that time Nguyễn Phi Hùng was diving to continue chasing the F-8, and when the range was right he fired a burst that hit the F-8's fuselage. Continually looking around to find the F-8 No. 1, Nguyễn Phú Ninh spotted another F-8 flashing in and firing a missile at MiG No. 1. Nguyễn Phú Ninh shouted, "They're firing missiles! 89, turn hard!" After flying one complete circle looking for No. 1 but not seeing him, he decided to descend to a lower altitude and then returned and landed at Thọ Xuân airfield.

While escorting an RF-8G reconnaissance aircraft near Vinh City, an F-8E from VF-191 of the USS *Ticonderoga* encountered and fired three AIM-9 missiles at a MiG-17. His third missile hit the MiG. When Nguyễn Phi Hùng realized that his aircraft had been hit, he quickly turned back toward the coast in order to be able to eject. However, he was too low so his ejection attempt was unsuccessful. Lieutenant Nguyễn Phi Hùng died a heroic death. With five victories, as a Vietnam air war ace, he was posthumously awarded the honorable title of VNP Armed Forces Hero.

Air Battle on 10 July 1968

As U.S. aircraft attackers with fighter escorts again flew in to attack targets along Strategic Transportation Road 559 (Ho Chi Minh Trail) in the MZ4 area, the VNPAF command post gave the combat assignment to a flight of three MiG-21s flown by Phạm Thanh Ngân, Phạm Phú Thái, and Đặng Ngọc Ngự of the 921st FR. The MiG-17s and MiG-21s had used the three-aircraft formation in previous battles. In the afternoon the flight was ordered to secretly fly from Nội Bài down to Thọ Xuân airfield and was then immediately placed on combat alert duty.

According to information from the intelligence net, on that day Navy F-4J aircraft (from VF-33 of the USS *America*) would carry out a MiGCAP mission to support a formation of attack bombers flying in to prosecute traffic and transportation targets in the MZ4 area. When the MiGs appeared and intercepted the U.S. formation, the bombers quickly turned away and withdrew to allow the F-4J fighters to fire missiles at long range, to threaten the MiGs and frighten them away. As the two MiG-21 pilots intensified their scan of the sky and looked for the target, Đặng Ngọc Ngự, the MiG No. 3, suddenly shouted, "The enemy is firing missiles!" Hearing the warning, because they did not know that the enemy was firing missiles from the forward hemisphere (from ahead of them), MiGs No. 1 and No. 2 immediately made a sharp turn. Unfortunately, because the F-4J's missiles were fired at the MiGs from the front, their turn placed them in an unfavorable position.

No. 2, who was flying in the rear, ended up in the sights of the F-4Js. The F-4J flown by Lt. Roy Cash and Lt. Joseph E. Kain Jr. targeted the MiG No. 2 and fired two AIM-7 guided missiles. Both of the AIM-7 missiles missed so the F-4 fired an AIM-9D missile, which hit the MiG No. 2.

The VNPAF reports acknowledge that one MiG-21 was shot down during the battle of 10 July 1968. Pilot Phạm Phú Thái ejected and parachuted safely back to the ground.

In September 2017, pilot Phạm Phú Thái and USN pilot Roy Cash Jr. met each other in the VN/U.S. veteran pilots meeting at San Diego. They spent time recalling what they saw and did when they engaged in the sky of North Vietnam more than forty years earlier. That was an amazing meeting between two former enemies who were now friends. Pilot Roy Cash said that after he shot down the MiG, he wondered whether the MiG's pilot could parachute or not. Lieutenant General Thái responded: "Your victory to shoot me down was not so vigorous because at that time I was only 18 years old and that was my first air battle." Roy Cash then said: "If I had known that inside the MiG was a young pilot, I would not have decided to launch the missile, because that would have been against the law relating to juveniles." All the people at the meeting let out a rejoicing laugh as the two former enemies but now friends were in a good humor.[18]

29 July 1968: MiG-17s versus F-8s over MZ4

On that day, the CO on duty at at the 921st FR command post was Lieutenant Colonel Trần Mạnh, while at the 923rd FR the CO on duty was the regiment commander, Nguyễn Phúc Trạch. At the auxiliary ground control station on Trọc Mountain (Bald Mountain), the CO on duty was pilot Lâm Văn Lích.

Early in the morning, a large formation of USN strike aircraft supported by fighter escorts began attacking transportation traffic targets and a number of other targets in Thanh Chương, Vinh, and Nghệ An. In carrying out the missions, the USN pilots used the tactic whereby when they encountered the MiGs, they would try to draw the MiGs out over the sea where another flight of F-8s would be waiting to attack the MiGs. The VNPAF decided to continue to fight air battles over MZ4 to protect Route 7, the Đức

Thọ ferry crossing in Hà Tĩnh, and the Gianh ferry crossing in Quảng Bình. According to the coordination plan, a flight of MiG-17s would fight at low altitudes while two MiG-21s would engage the enemy at high altitudes.

At 1016 hours Colonel Đào Đình Luyện ordered the primary attack flight, piloted by Lưu Huy Chao, Hoàng Ích, Lê Hải, and Lê Sỹ Diệp, to take off. Then the Đô Lương (X-3) ground control station directed the flight to fly on a heading of 180 degrees toward Nghĩa Đàn, Nghệ An Province. Less than one minute later, at an intercept angle of 140 degrees, No. 1 spotted F-8s at a range of 2.4 miles. The MiGs dropped their auxiliary fuel tanks and engaged in a dogfight against eight USN F-8s. While chasing one F-8, the MiG lead Lưu Huy Chao spotted another aircraft flying across his nose from left to right. He immediately turned in and waited for an opportunity to fire his guns. At a range of 0.23 miles No. 1 squeezed his trigger. Seeing his shells hit the nose of the F-8, he held his trigger down until he had fired all of his ammunition. Seeing that the F-8 was now trailing smoke, he immediately broke off the engagement by making a hard turn.

Seeing that an F-8 was turning left, Lê Hải quickly turned inside the F-8's turn, and at the right range he squeezed his trigger, but his first burst of shells missed, exploding behind the enemy plane's tail. Immediately, Lê Hải adjusted his sight and fired a second burst. He saw the shells hit the enemy plane, which rolled completely upside-down. Seeing that the F-8 was going to crash, he made his break-off maneuver, pulling over into a climbing turn to gain altitude. On his way back to base, Lê Hải flew on a heading of 360 degrees low along the flanks of the mountains until he landed at the airfield.

Lê Sỹ Diệp's MiG-17 was hit by a missile fired by an F-8. He tried to level his wings and climb but could not, and his aircraft crashed northwest of Tân Kỳ in Nghệ An. Lê Sỹ Diệp ejected but his ejection was unsuccessful and he was killed.

The AF Command ordered the MiG-17s to break off the engagement. At the same time, at 1042 hours, ground control station X-1 directed the MiG-21s into the battle area in order to cover the MiG-17s as they landed at Thọ Xuân. During this savage battle between MiG-17s and F-8s, pilots Lưu Huy Chao and Lê Hải each shot down one F-8.

Although MiGs suffered a loss during this battle with Lieutenant Lê Sỹ Diệp listed as killed, the MiG pilots did successfully disrupt the USN strike formation. However, the VNPAF learned many lessons from this battle about fighting air battles over MZ4, especially under conditions in which the USAF and USN were conducting powerful electronic jamming using their EB-66 and EC-121 EW aircraft.

MiG pilot Lê Hải described the battle as follows:

> I took aim quickly with super-range setting, turned the sight circle up to maximum brightness, used the center of the sight as the mark from which I made my firing bearing and lead calculations, and fired a first burst at a range of 0.2 miles. The enemy aircraft was hit by the shells and burst into flames. I hastily kicked my left rudder pedal hard and yanked up on my stick. This control maneuver caused the aircraft to go into a high-speed stall. Naturally, my aircraft dropped like a rock, pointing its nose down at the mountains. I pulled my aircraft out of this dangerous situation while at the same time I was watching out for the two F-8s. . . .
>
> In the skies over MZ4, whenever we encountered F-8s our battles were always very intense and ferocious. The F-8s had good horizontal maneuverability, and the American carrier pilots had excellent technical skills. It took experience to be able to fight F-8s, and you had to maneuver and dogfight well to be able to shoot down your opponent.[19]

During the war, pilot Lê Hải was credited with six victories. He was never hit by enemy aircraft and was never forced to parachute. He was given the honorable title of VNP Armed Forces Hero. In the postwar period Senior Colonel Lê Hải was appointed commander of the 370th Fighter Division of the VNPAF.

1 August 1968: The MiGs' Three-Aircraft Combat Formation

Analyzing the recent air engagements over MZ4 and the special characteristics of this battlefield that was far from the main air bases, the AF HQ and the 921st FR HQ decided to change some elements of tactics, including redesigning the MiG-21s' formation to increase their attack power, as well as their ability to scan the skies and provide early warning, and to enable the pilots to attack and support one another during the actual attack, the break-ing off of the engagement, and the return to air bases. On 1 August 1968 the 921st FR command post decided to again use a three-aircraft flight for-mation, this time consisting of pilots Nguyên Đăng Kính, Phạm Văn Mạo, and Nguyên Hồng Nhị. The two lead MiGs would be responsible for attack-ing the enemy attack bombers while MiG No. 3 would provide support and would command the flight's attack when the pilots closed with and inter-cepted the target.

Early in the morning, the weather was bad: cloudy with a ceiling of only 600 to 900 feet. However, after 1000 hours the weather improved and the cloud ceiling lifted to a higher altitude. The flight was ordered to take off at 1237 hours and fly on a heading of 190 degrees at an altitude of 4,500 feet. A few minutes later, when the MiGs were east of Đô Lương, the pilots were informed by the X-3 ground control station: "The target is 50 degrees to your left at a range of twenty-five miles." Just a moment later the ground con-trol station X-3 ordered the pilots to turn left to intercept the target group, which was then flying south of Route 7. The MiG lead Nguyên Đăng Kính immediately gave the order, "Switch on afterburners!" While the two lead MiGs were turning left, No. 3 radioed, "There are two aircraft 120 degrees to your left rear, range 7 to 8 miles." It is most likely that these were two F-8Gs conducting a reconnaissance mission. Scanning the sky in the left rear, they spotted the target at an altitude of 4,500 feet and turning toward the MiGs. Nguyễn Đăng Kính shouted, "Drop auxiliary fuel tanks!" Then he tightened his turn to get in behind the F-8s. However, the F-8s, following their instructions to avoid a dogfight against MiGs, accelerated and headed straight out to sea. Nguyên Đăng Kính ordered his wingman to break off the engagement and return to Thọ Xuân.

During the engagement, Nguyễn Hồng Nhị carried out his support and observation mission, spotting targets and quickly and precisely inform-ing the two lead MiGs so that they could maneuver quickly and attack. As he was flying at an altitude of 11,000 feet and a speed of 560 mph, Nguyễn Hồng Nhị saw a target group in front of and below him. He turned toward this target to chase it. At that moment the two F-8s split up, with one aircraft turning left and the other turning right. Quickly assessing the situation, Nguyễn Hồng Nhị pulled his stick over to chase the aircraft turning left and headed out toward the sea in order to be able to exploit his superior turning ability. If the second aircraft turned back toward him it would have to make a 180-degree turn, costing time. In addition, the F-8 pilot would be surprised by this action because he would not think that the MiG would head out over the sea. After reaching a range of 1.1 miles from the F-8 and with his target designator placed solidly on the nose of the F-8, MiG No. 3 fired one R-3S missile that flew straight toward the F-8. Without waiting to see the results of his attack, Nguyễn Hồng Nhị switched on his afterburner and pulled into a hard turn because he had seen another F-8 headed toward him at only 1.5 miles away.

However at that very moment, Nguyễn Hồng Nhị discovered that his afterburner was not functioning. He wisely dove into a cloud at an altitude of 6,000 feet, with his speed down to only 460 mph. At that moment, Nguyễn Hồng Nhị spotted two missiles headed for his MiG. He made a shallow turn to evade the missiles (he could only make a shallow turn because his speed was so low) and the two missiles exploded very close to his aircraft. The aircraft was damaged and rapidly began to lose altitude. Nguyễn Hồng Nhị decided to eject over the Thanh Chương State Forestry Enterprise.

In the post-mission review the VNPAF commanders and pilots discussed the tactical assessments used in this engagement and learned many lessons from these air battles against F-8s over MZ4. In the battles fought on 10 July and 1 August 1968, the results of the battle plan of using a three-aircraft flight formation were not especially great and the MiGs suffered some losses. However, from a tactical standpoint this was a flight formation suited for the number of aircraft available and the battle area; further studies were needed to supplement the battle plan to increase its effectiveness.

17 August 1968: Dealing with USN Fighter Tactics

Between mid-June and mid-August 1968, the 921st FR experienced many problems, both because of the very fierce and difficult combat conditions in the MZ4 area and because the USAF and USN were constantly changing their tactics. For these reasons MiG-21s scored few successes in these air battles. They fought seven separate air battles, shooting down only two U.S. aircraft and losing three MiGs.

The information received by the AF HQ revealed that during this period the USN was aggressively using F-8s, which analysts said was the most effective counterbalance to the MiG-21's tactic of "quick attack, quick withdrawal." The F-8s had good low-speed horizontal maneuverability, so of course their ability to maneuver and see their target was better, and they were also heavily armed with both missiles and guns. The F-8 pilots were considered the United States' best air combat pilots. After studying the tactics used by MiG-21s, the F-8 pilots usually tried to lure MiG-21s into a turning dogfight in order to prevent them from being able to make use of their speed and altitude superiority. This F-8 tactic caused MiG-21s considerable problems.

In order to deal with this F-8 tactic scheme, the AF HQ decided to employ a combination of forces: MiG-17s, which were superior at turning dogfights, and MiG-21s, which had speed and altitude superiority, to intercept the USN F-4Bs and F-8s, especially when the enemy used his tactic of accelerating and fleeing out to the sea. With these detailed tactical assessments, the VNPAF ordered the 921st FR to have a flight of two MiG-21s take off secretly and unexpectedly from Thọ Xuân airfield to cooperate with a flight of MiG-17s in intercepting and attacking a USN attack bomber formation. The pilots were directed to use their MiG-21s to make a surprise attack on the F-8s but not to be drawn into a dogfight. Instead the pilots were to utilize their speed and altitude superiority to follow the tactic of "fast attack and fast withdrawal." After receiving the forecast that the weather would improve, in the morning the AF HQ decided to carry out the battle plan involving coordination between MiG-17s, MiG-21s, and the AAA units. According to reports from the B-1 net, many flights of U.S. aircraft were active off the coast in the area of Diễn Châu–Cửa Lò in Nghệ An. AF Commander Colonel Nguyễn Văn Tiên concluded that the USN would conduct another round of attacks and it was likely that U.S. aircraft would fly into the assigned battle area, so the MiGs could carry out their prepared plan.

Two MiG-21s piloted by Đinh Tôn and Nguyễn Văn Minh were ordered to take off at 1556 hours and directed to fly on a heading of 200 degrees at an altitude of 4,500 feet. Colonel Trần Mạnh (commander of the X-3 command post) ordered the two aircraft to increase speed to 600 mph and intercept a flight of reconnaissance aircraft that was approaching Nam Đàn–Thanh Chương and Nghệ An. When the enemy reconnaissance flight spotted the

MiGs, they turned around and headed out over the sea. The X-3 ground control station ordered the MiG-21 pilots to turn left up to Quỳ Hợp and wait there to attack another target. Minutes later the X-3 station directed the flight to turn right to a heading of 180 degrees and informed the pilots, "The target is 100 degrees to your right, range 9.3 miles, altitude 13,000 feet." The target was a flight of four F-4s approaching over Cửa Sót. Đinh Tôn and Nguyễn Văn Minh decided to drop their auxiliary fuel tanks and switch on afterburners to climb to an altitude of 16,000 feet.

Nguyễn Văn Minh spotted four F-4s behind them at a range of about four miles. This was a flight of F-4Bs from VF-142 of the USS *Constellation*, which had been assigned to cover and support attack bombers that were about twenty miles northwest of Vinh. The two MiG-21 pilots decided to use the same tactic that the F-4s usually used, which was to split up, turning in opposite directions in order to turn back to meet the F-4Bs head-on. When they saw the MiGs split up and use their own tactics against them, the F-4s turned to flee. One F-4 was pursuing Nguyễn Văn Minh but then, afraid that the second MiG would turn back and get on his tail, the F-4 pilot decided to level his wings, reduce altitude, and make an S-turn in order to turn away and escape.

Taking advantage of this opportunity, Nguyễn Văn Minh quickly switched on his afterburner and closed in on his target. He brought the F-4 into the center of his missile sight then launched his R-3S missile straight at the F-4, causing it burst into flames. Nguyễn Văn Minh pulled his stick back into a turning climb, saw the F-4 burning, and quickly broke off the engagement, flew back and landed at Thọ Xuân at 1625 hours. This F-4B was flown by Lt. (jg) Markham Ligon Gartley and Lt. William John Mayhew from VF-142 of the USS *Constellation*.[20] Both airmen ejected and both were captured.

17 September 1968: A Violent Dogfight with F-8s

On 17 September a large number of USN attackers escorted by F-8s flew in to bomb targets in MZ4. The assigned targets of MiG pilots were the enemy's attack bombers, but the pilots were instructed to be ready to engage in air combat against F-8 fighters.

The 921st FR's flight, consisting of Nguyễn Văn Cốc and Phạm Phú Thái, took off at 1117 hours and flew out on a heading of 200 degrees at an altitude of 3,000 feet. After the flight switched on afterburners and made a climbing left turn, the pilots spotted two F-8s 90 degrees to their left at a range of 4 miles and an altitude of 16,000 feet. Nguyễn Văn Cốc shouted, "Drop auxiliary fuel tanks and attack!" He then turned sharply to the left to head toward the two F-8s. Nguyễn Văn Cốc made five or six complete circles in his dogfight with the F-8 but was not able to get into position to make an attack. The two F-8s were still behind him at an angle of 70 to 80 degrees, and fired four missiles at him but the missiles missed. Nguyễn Văn Cốc decided that continuing the dogfight would not be a good idea and, since his fuel was running low, he made his break-off maneuver by using his afterburner to make a spiraling combat climb from his altitude of 6,500 feet up to 16,000 feet. Seeing that he was not being pursued, he switched off his afterburner and returned to land. While checking his aircraft, the mechanics found many pieces of missile shrapnel embedded in his aircraft's tail and flaps.

While sticking with his lead, Phạm Phú Thái had spotted two other F-8s at an angle of 60 degrees, and he decided to engage in a dogfight against them. These were two F-8s, flown by Lt. Cdr. Red Isaacks and Lt. (jg) Paul Eugene Swigart from VF-24 of the USS *Hancock*, which were flying a fight cover mission. The F-8s took turns firing missiles at MiG No. 2 but the MiG pilot was able to evade all of the missiles and turn back hard to counterattack, forcing the F-8s to push their throttles forward to turn away and out to sea. The two F-8Hs decided to withdraw from the battle since their fuel was running low. Both aircraft flew out to the coast to refuel in the air before returning to land. Just a few minutes later, however, the engine of Swigart's F-8H shut down. He ejected and was rescued.

Although the MiG-21 flight of Nguyễn Văn Cốc and Phạm Phú Thái did not directly shoot down any F-8Hs, because of the ferocious dogfight against the two MiG-21s, Lieutenant Swigart's F-8H was not able to break off in time to refuel, so it ran out of fuel and crashed into the ocean.[21]

Air Engagement on 26 October 1968

On 26 October, the USN sent in a deep penetration air strike to attack chokepoint targets along the transportation routes in the MZ4 area. The AF HQ decided to use a flight of four MiG-17s and a flight of two MiG-21s to fight a coordinated battle to protect the traffic choke-points. The MiG-17s were ordered to attack the outer perimeter of the enemy strike group as a diversion.

Meanwhile, the MiG-21s were directed to attack F-4s loaded with bombs and assigned to carry out a bombing mission. The 921st FR assigned the task of conducting this coordinated battle to pilots Nguyễn Đăng Kính and Vũ Xuân Thiều; this would be Vũ Xuân Thiều's first combat mission. The MiG-21 flight took off at 0817 hours and flew out on a heading of 190 degrees at an altitude of 1,000 to 1,600 feet. At 0828 hours, Nguyễn Đăng Kính reported that he had spotted the target to his left front at a range of ten miles. Closing the range to 1.5 miles, he saw that the target was two F-4s splitting up. Kính decided to pursue the enemy aircraft No. 2. When the range was down to 0.7 miles, he pressed his missile-firing button. Without waiting to see the results of his attack, Nguyễn Đăng Kính pulled up on his stick and the MiG flashed right over the top of the F-4's fuselage. As soon as he began to turn right Nguyễn Đăng Kính spotted the F-4 No. 1. He decided to chase this aircraft and adjusted his sight picture. The range closed to 1.1 miles, then 0.9 miles. At 0.7 miles Nguyễn Đăng Kính pressed his missile-firing button. Just as he had with his first missile, he did not wait to see the results of his attack but instead pulled the stick back to break off the engagement. He landed safely at Thọ Xuân at 0854 hours.

By the end of the campaign to send MiGs down into MZ4 (which began on 14 June 1968), the VNPAF had fought a total of twenty air battles and had shot down eleven USN aircraft. During this same period, the VNPAF had lost seven aircraft, including two that were shot down by Talos missiles fired by U.S. warships.

THE FORMATION OF THE 925TH FR:
THE MiG-19 ENTERS THE CONFLICT

In late 1968 the AD and AF Service decided to bring the group of pilots trained to fly MiG-19s back home from China to form the 925th FR at a location on the outskirts of Hanoi. A number of the key officers of the 925th FR were on hand to receive the official order forming the regiment. Major Lê Quang Trung was appointed the commander of the new regiment. Major Hồ Vinh was appointed the regiment political commissar. MiG-17 pilots Mai Đức Toại and Hồ Văn Qùy were appointed deputy regiment commanders. The 925th FR was initially based at Kép, but it later moved and its primary base of operations became Yên Bái airfield, in order to cover the northwestern sector.

The regiment's aircraft consisted of thirty-six MiG-19s and four UMiG-15s that Vietnam received from the Chinese AF in March 1969. During the fighting against the USAF and USN, the 925th FR was assigned to intercept and attack American aircraft approaching from the northwest. During more than three years of fighting, the regiment fought many battles, shot down nine American aircraft, and together with the other fighter regiments and the ground-based air defense forces won victories over the American Linebacker I and Linebacker II operations in 1972. Many of the regiment's cadres and pilots were awarded medals of various types.

28 January 1970: First Air Battle of the Year

The weather was rainy in the early morning, but at 1000 hours the radar net detected many flights of U.S. aircraft conducting air operations. Guessing that the USAF would attack SAM sites and supply stockpiles, the AF Command ordered the combat alert flights to prepare for action. Early in the afternoon one F-105 was shot down by the 230th AAA Regiment/367th AD Division north of the Mụ Giạ Pass. This was an F-105G from the 44th TFS/355th TFW. This aircraft, which was a modification of the F-105F (Wild Weasel), was assigned to carry out air defense suppression missions. The two F-105 crewmen were seen to have ejected and parachuted to the ground, and the downed pilots had established radio communications with airborne EW aircraft. The USAF immediately implemented a RESCAP plan using four HH-53 helicopters from the 40th ARRS (Air Rescue and Recovery Squadron), one flight of A-1Hs, and one HC-130P aircraft. After collating and analyzing the reports from radar stations C-45 and C-41, Lieutenant Colonel Trần Mạnh at the X-3 command post in Đô Lương ordered the 921st FR's forces to be deployed immediately in accordance with the coordinated plan that had been worked out. Two MiG-21 pilots, Vũ Ngọc Đỉnh and Phạm Đình Tuân, were given the order to take off at 1435 hours and then fly on a heading of 150 degrees to a holding area west of Bến Thủy. After receiving a report from radar station C-41 that a flight of enemy aircraft was circling in the area of the Khe Ve Bridge, GCI officer Lê Thành Chơn recommended that the attack sector be changed. He directed the flight to fly up Route 15 while maneuvering at altitudes of between 3,200 feet and 4,000 feet. A few minutes later, the command post ordered the pilots to switch on their SOD-57 module. This was a device that amplified the aircraft's radar return signal in order to improve the ground radar's ability to detect and track the aircraft, and to avoid shooting at its own aircraft.

Just a few minutes later the X-3 command post informed the pilots that the target was 30 degrees to their right front at a range of twelve miles. Lieutenant Colonel Trần Mạnh ordered the pilots, "Hit fast and finish the target off fast." Just as the MiG pilots were given information that the target was 60 degrees to the right front, range six miles, Vũ Ngọc Đỉnh saw two F-4s flying below the MiGs, and he swept in to attack. The two F-4s turned and headed straight out toward the sea. While he was making a turn to the left, Vũ Ngọc Đỉnh spotted two aircraft flying in the opposite direction and one aircraft flying in the same direction as his aircraft. This aircraft, flying at an altitude of 10,000 feet, was flying very slowly. He decided to attack the aircraft flying in the same direction.

Vũ Ngọc Đỉnh quickly turned his aircraft behind the target. When the range was less than 1.25 miles, he brought the target into the center of his sights and fired a missile. The R-3S missile hit the helicopter's fuselage, causing it to explode and break into fragments. The air-to-ground radio channel echoed with Vũ Ngọc Đỉnh's shout of, "I hit him!" Vũ Ngọc Đỉnh rolled onto his left side and pulled into a climb to avoid the ball of flames from the exploding helicopter, then rolled back upright and saw a huge fireball. The helicopter he hit was one of two HH-53 Jolly Greens that had just finished refueling and had begun to circle over the area where the F-105G was believed to have crashed. Even though there had been a warning that MiGs had taken off, the warning did not provide the location of the MiGs (perhaps the altitude was too low for the warning signal to be received). While the HC-130P was refueling one helicopter, the crews of HH-53 Jolly Green 71 and Jolly Green 72 suddenly spotted a MiG-21 flying out at a low altitude through a gap in the mountain peaks, firing missiles. HH-53 Jolly Green 71 burst into flames and crashed. All members of the crew, including the pilot, Maj. Holly Gene Bell, were killed. American documents acknowledge that this HH-53 helicopter was shot down by Senior Captain Vũ Ngọc Đỉnh, a young pilot assigned to the 921st FR.[22]

After having ordered his wingman to break off the engagement, Vũ Ngọc Đỉnh heard his No. 2 reply, "Roger." When his aircraft was flying past Hương

Sơn, he radioed No. 2 again but got no reply. However, when he landed the ground technicians discovered that four of his engine turbine blades and the inlet cone (shock cone) were cracked and that there was a hole in his flaps from a missile fragment because his closing speed when he launched his missile had been so great.

After Vũ Ngọc Đình shot down the HH-53, command post X-3 transmitted the order to break off the engagement three different times. However, No. 2 reported that he was making a counterattack against enemy aircraft. Just before his aircraft reached a mountain peak 7,000 feet high, the SOD-57 signal from No. 2's aircraft suddenly was lost. Because of this, it was determined that Lieutenant Phạm Đình Tuân had probably flown into a mountain while counterattacking U.S. fighters at a low altitude during his return flight. In 2011 a group of people looking for scrap metal found a jet engine on Mountain 2235. This jet engine was determined to be a MiG-21 engine. It was determined that this must have been the engine of Phạm Đình Tuân's MiG-21.

Air Engagement on 28 March 1970

Early in the afternoon a large USAF strike force, including twenty-four F-4s, twelve F-105s, and ten OV-10s, attacked an area that the Americans suspected of being the rear area (logistics support area) of the Pathet Lao Campaign at Mường Xén–Nọng Rẻ. The combat plans prepared by the 921st FR on 28 March 1970 were that the flights on combat alert duty would take off from either Thọ Xuân airfield or Kiến An airfield to intercept and attack the USAF strike formations. The two flights of MiG-21s to be used in this effort consisted of one flight flown by Phạm Phú Thái and Phạm Thành Nam and another flight flown by Bùi Văn Long and Hoàng Quốc Dũng, based at Kiến An airfield. Since the weather over Thọ Xuân airfield was bad, the command post ordered the two flights on combat alert duty at Kiến An airfield to take off and decided not to use the MiG-21s on combat alert duty at Thọ Xuân airfield (pilots Nguyễn Đức Soát and Trần Việt).

The first flight flown by Bùi Văn Long and Hoàng Quốc Dũng took off at 1230 hours and flew to the Vụ Bản–Lang Chánh area as a diversion flight. Six minutes later, the second flight with Phạm Phú Thái and Phạm Thành Nam took off then flew to Vụ Bản–Lang Chánh and circled there twice.

Because of poor coordination between the AF Command and the Thọ Xuân command post, the flight was directed straight into a formation of enemy fighters. These were a flight of three F-4Js led by the executive officer of VF-142 of the USS *Constellation*. The flight of F-4Js was being directed by the radars and electronic equipment mounted on a U.S. warship off the coast (they were probably listening to the MiGs' radio communications). While flying at an altitude of 12,500 feet, the F-4J No. 2 spotted the flight of MiGs at two o'clock (a bearing of 30 degrees) to the front and at higher altitude.

Although Phạm Phú Thái's flight was caught in a bad position, the MiG pilots still decided to attack the F-4s head-on. MiG lead Phạm Phú Thái decided to split up his flight, with one turning right and the other turning left. He pursued the F-4J No. 1 ferociously and decided to fire one missile. Just at the moment when he was making a right-climbing turn, he spotted an aircraft to his right front flying in the same direction. He quickly charged in and launched his second missile, but the missile missed. Meanwhile the F-4J No. 2 had chased and fired two AIM-9 missiles at the MiG No. 2, flown by Phạm Thành Nam. When Phạm Phú Thái saw the trail of a missile headed toward the MiGs, he shouted to his wingman to turn sharply but then he saw the MiG No. 2 being hit by the missile, which caused it to burst into flames. He immediately shouted to No. 2 to eject, but he never saw a parachute open. Lieutenant Phạm Thành Nam was killed. Based on some U.S. reports, probably the F-4J that shot down the MiG No. 2 was flown by Lt. Jerome E. Beaulier and Lt. Steven J. Barkley of VF-142 from the USS *Constellation*.[23] Phạm Phú Thái flew on a heading of 360 degrees, then turned down to the airfield and landed.

13 April 1971: Air Battle at Sunset

After studying the operational pattern of various types of U.S. aircraft operating over the transportation corridor (the Ho Chi Minh Trail), the intelligence officers and command level officers of Vietnamese frontline GCI were able to determine the characteristics and operational patterns of enemy OV-10 and O-2A reconnaissance aircraft. These reconnaissance aircraft were very effective at spotting the targets for the attack bomber aircraft. They were slow flying but very maneuverable, which made hitting them difficult for the air defense forces. The AF HQ ordered the 921st FR to draft a plan and conduct an attack against OV-10 aircraft at dusk on 13 April 1971. MiG-21 pilot Đinh Tôn was assigned to carry out this attack mission, taking off from Thọ Xuân airfield.

At 1700 hours the command post ordered radar station C-41 to switch on its radar transmitter. At 1724 hours the radar picked up a target flying at an altitude of 11,000 feet. One minute later a second target was picked up at an altitude of 24,000 feet. Đinh Tôn was ordered to take off at 1759 hours and fly at low altitudes along Route 12 (Anh Sơn–Hương Khê–Tân Ấp). By this time the sun had set behind the mountains in the distance and the sky was clothed in a dry mist, making it difficult to spot the target. A few minutes later the command post ordered the pilot to turn to a heading of 270 degrees. At 1816 hours Đinh Tôn reported that he had spotted two O-2A aircraft 30 degrees to the left at a range of five miles and an altitude of 8,000 feet.

Đinh Tôn descended to a low altitude, reduced his speed, and turned on his aircraft's onboard radar, but after a short time the radar lost the target. He then decided to look for the target with his naked eyes and then immediately spotted an O-2A. When the range was 0.7 miles, his speed was 460 mph, and as he had his target designator centered between the target aircraft's two engines, he fired a missile from under his left wing, then he pulled his aircraft into a left-turning climb to look back. He saw the missile explode right under the belly of the O-2A. Just to make sure, Đinh Tôn fired the second missile. However, his second missile refused to fire. Looking at the target, he saw that the O-2A was flying very unsteadily and that it was gradually losing altitude.

Đinh Tôn decided to switch on his afterburner and leave the area, then he landed safely at Anh Sơn airfield at 1838 hours. Based on information provided by local forces, the AD and AF Service confirmed this victory and credited Đinh Tôn with shooting down one O-2A. Between March and September 1971 more than ten OV-10 and O-2A reconnaissance aircraft were shot down by the AD forces and MiGs.

20 November 1971: A MiG-21 First Fires at a B-52

After accurately learning lessons from Đinh Tôn's unsuccessful attack on B-52s on the night of 4 October 1971, the B-8 command post concluded that the USAF knew about the plan for MiG-21s to intercept B-52s on the night of 4 October 1971 and that the Americans would increase their vigilance, the number of fighter escorts, and their use of jamming of all kinds.

The VNPAF, therefore, had to concentrate its efforts to develop a new plan that would give MiGs the best chance of intercepting and shooting down a B-52. Technically, there had to be effective ways to eliminate the jamming signals and coordinate the signal returns from R-35 (air search) radars and PRV-11 (height-finding) radars in order to precisely determine the location of the B-52s in an environment of very powerful enemy jamming. With regard to the pilot's intercept technique, the AF Command would require the pilot to fly all alone at low altitudes (below 4,500 feet) with no radio contact with the command post for a distance of seventy-five miles in the black of night while flying between two mountain ranges, the Đại Huệ mountains and the Annamite (Trường Son) mountains. This would be a tremendous challenge that would require the pilot to make careful preparations and to accept considerable risks. In order to ensure absolute secrecy, the entire communications network changed its codes. In addition, in order to trick the USAF command network, the B-8 command post deployed one MiG-21 into position to fly a diversionary mission in order to make the Americans believe that the VNPAF had only one MiG active over the MZ4 area.

After a period of time when MiG-21s temporarily did not appear over the skies of MZ4, and after all preparations were complete, the B-8 command post (where deputy AF commander Trần Mạnh and 921st FR commander Trần Hanh were the COs on duty; the GCI officers were Nguyễn Văn Chuyên, Tạ Quốc Hưng, and Trần Hồng Hà; and the radar ground control officers were Lê Thiết Hùng and Lê Kiểu) recommended that the attack on the B-52s should be made on the night of 20 November 1971. At the time, GCI officer Nguyễn Văn Chuyên said this would be the MiG-21's only chance to destroy a B-52, that there would never be another.

The AD and AF Service Command and the AF HQ (under Commander Đào Đình Luyện) agreed, and they directed the 921st FR to send two more MiG-21s down to MZ4 (one to Vinh airfield and one to Anh Sơn airfield) and stand by for take off to attack the B-52s. In preparation for the attacks in late November 1971, on 19 November an An-2 aircraft flew pilots Hoàng Biểu and Nguyễn Ngọc Thiên to B-2 (Vinh airfield) and pilots Trần Cung and Vũ Đình Rạng to B-4 (Anh Sơn airfield). In the early morning of 20 November, highly skilled pilots Đặng Ngọc Ngự and Lương Thế Phúc flew two MiG-21s down to MZ4, one landing at B-2 (Vinh) and one at B-4 (Anh Sơn).

After the air battle on the night of 4 October 1971, the B-52s temporarily pulled back and only operated in areas where the MiG-21s did not have enough range to reach. Approximately one month later, after there were no more appearances of MiG-21s, the B-52s began to give indications that they were resuming their normal operations. After a period of the B-52s' absence in the area, the B-3 and B-8 command posts both agreed that on the night of 20 November it was likely that B-52s would fly in to bomb targets along Route 12 and Route 20. The AF command posts decided to place pilot Hoàng Biểu on combat alert duty at Vinh airfield (B-2) and that pilot Vũ Đình Rạng would stand combat alert duty at Anh Sơn airfield (B-4). After a lengthy period drafting the plan and conducting preparatory training, the 921st FR's night fighter pilots were determined to find and destroy B-52s. The destruction of a B-52 would not only be of great military significance at both the tactical and the campaign level; it would also be of tremendous political significance for the entire Vietnam War because up to this point in time no B-52 had ever been shot down.

As had been predicted, at 1930 hours B-52s were detected flying east of Savannakhet-Laos. Hoàng Biểu was ordered to take off from Vinh airfield and fly up to the Tân Ấp–Mụ Giạ Pass area at an altitude of between 25,000 and 32,000 feet to divert the enemy's attention. Hoàng Biểu then flew back to Nội Bài and landed there. It is likely that U.S. intelligence detected this flight and believed that after the departure of this MiG there were no other MiGs operating in the MZ4 area.

At 2000 hours AF commander Đào Đình Luyện forwarded to the B-8 command post the following strategic intelligence report from the AD and AF Service Command: "At 2045 hours B-52s will conduct a bombing mission forty miles north of Tchepone-Laos." Lieutenant Colonel Trần Mạnh ordered the B-8 command post to go to combat alert condition Level 1 and ordered three ground control radar stations (C-41, C-37, and C-45) to switch on their radar transmitters. Even though radar station C-41 experienced problems with the screen of its radar's round view indicator (IKO) when the radar was switched on, the B-8 command post ordered C-41 to switch the transmitter on and make immediate repairs to the radar's IKO equipment. By 2025 hours all three radar stations were operating properly.

Vũ Đình Rạng took off at 2040 hours and flew alone from the airfield up to the Tân Ấp area following the pre-arranged flight plan. At 2045 hours, based on the calculated positions of Vũ Đình Rạng's MiG-21 and the B-52 cell, the B-8 command post's ground control team determined that it would be possible to direct Vũ Đình Rạng in to intercept and attack the B-52s before the B-52 cell reached Route 20 to carry out its bombing mission. Four minutes later the command post transmitted its first radio message to the pilot and told him to turn sharply to a heading of 230 degrees and to maintain a speed of 560 mph and an altitude of 10,000 feet. Three minutes later the B-8 ground control station ordered the pilot to drop his auxiliary fuel tank, increase speed to 595 mph, and to turn to a flight heading of 160 degrees. The pilot was informed that the target was thirty-five miles in front of him, then he was ordered to switch on his afterburner and climb to an altitude of 32,000 feet. At this time the command post switched to the radar guidance system and continuously informed the pilot of the target's position, speed, altitude, and heading. At 2055 hours the command post informed the pilot that the target was 30 degrees to his right front at a range of sixteen miles and ordered the pilot to turn left to a heading of 90 degrees. When the range was eight miles, the command post told the pilot to turn on his aircraft's onboard radar.

As soon as he switched on his radar, Vũ Đình Rạng detected three B-52s flying in a right-hand stair-step formation, range 6.8 miles. This began a period during which the entire command post waited anxiously for Vũ Đình Rạng to score a victory. When the range was down to five miles, the command post ordered the pilot to accelerate to a speed of Mach 1.3 (more than 870 mph) and to target the first (leading) B-52. At this time Vũ Đình Rạng heard the voice of the 921st FR's commander Trần Hanh over his earphones telling him, "Stay calm as you make the attack." Vũ Đình Rạng got in behind the B-52, placed the center of his sighting circle directly on the target, and fired the missile under his left wing when the range was 1.5 miles. After firing this missile, the pilot pulled into a hard right-climbing turn. When he rolled his aircraft back level he saw another aircraft with two lights on its wingtips. He checked his radar and saw that the range to the target was two miles. When he had a stable sight picture he pressed the button to fire his second missile. He then immediately pulled up into a right-climbing turn and reported to the command post that he was breaking off the engagement. The B-8 command post ordered him to fly on a heading of 330 degrees, then descend to an altitude of 13,000 feet. The pilot landed safely at B-4 (Anh Sơn) airfield at 2115 hours.

In the VN/U.S. veteran pilots meeting in Hanoi, in October 2018, Colonel Vũ Đình Rạng, MiG-21 pilot, and Col. David Volker, co-pilot of the B-52, who participated in the air engagement on the night of 20 November 1971, met each other. Recalling what had happened, Colonel Vũ Đình Rạng said that on that night the weather was very good, and when he switched on his onboard radar at a distance about five miles, he could see very clearly all three B-52s in front of his MiG. He didn't know why the B-52s did not launch jamming and he did not see any F-4 escorts around the B-52s as usual. Colonel Nguyễn Văn Chuyên, the GCI officer, said that on that day he believed that the air battle would take place as planned and that Colonel Vũ Đình Rạng would shoot down the B-52, because every element of victory had been well predicted. Meanwhile, Col. David Volker said that on that night the B-52s had a very good jamming system and a formation of fighters to escort them, but he didn't know why the system did not operate, and he didn't know that a MiG-21 was approaching. Later on he heard the Red Crown system informing him that the MiG had appeared . . . and through his window he saw a MiG—Vũ Đình Rạng's MiG.

In a talk show on Vietnamese television, the three main persons involved in that engagement were together and for the first time talking about what had happened on that night from their own viewpoints. This talk show received a large number of likes and visits, and perhaps it impressed viewers as an image of the reconciliation process of VN-U.S. veteran pilots.[24]

ENTER THE MiG-21 MF (F-96)

The MiG-21 MF type 96 (NATO called it the Fishbed-H/J) was the next version of the MiG-21 PFM (F-94). The first flight of this type of fighter was in 1970. A MiG-21 MF has one Tumansky R-13–300 jet engine, with four pylons to carry four R-3S air-to-air/surface missiles. The MiG-21 MF can carry one gun with two hundred 23-mm shells (GHS-23). By the end of 1971, the Soviet Union had sent to Vietnam a number of MiG-21 MFs to replace the old types of MiG-21 and also the MiGs lost during the war. In fact, although a MiG-21MF carried the GHS-23 gun, most Vietnamese pilots did not like to use that gun.

18 December 1971: An Active Day for MiG-21s and MiG-19s

After a number of MiG-21 night attacks that threatened the B-52s, the USAF increased its fighter operations aimed at countering MiG operations in the direction from which the American bombers frequently crossed the Vietnamese border. The AF Command concluded that the United States might violate the order to end the bombing north of the twentieth parallel and resume large-scale air attacks against targets deep inside North Viet-namese territory, including against the airfields in MZ4. To respond to the U.S. attack operations, on 18 December 1971 the entire VNPAF was placed on a high level of combat readiness and increased the number of fighters assigned to combat alert duty at the airfields. The VNPAF HQ decided to fight a coordinated battle, including coordination between MiG-21s and MiG-19s and between the AF fighters and the SAMs. The designated battle area was the area along the Vietnam–Laos border.

When the radar picked up three groups of F-4s operating over Mường Lát and Lang Chánh–Hồi Xuân, the AF Command decided to launch MiGs. A flight of two MiG-19s (Bùi Văn Sưu and Phạm Cao Hà) took off at 1312 hours and flew up to Vạn Yên. A few minutes later a flight of two MiG-21s (Lê Thanh Đạo and Võ Sỹ Giáp) took off and flew up to Suối Rút. At 1322 hours when radar picked up a group of F-4s flying from Sam Neua toward Thọ Xuân airfield, the AF Command directed MiG-21s to intercept the attack bombers and prevent them from attacking Thọ Xuân airfield. The MiG-21s were informed that the target was 15 degrees to their right front at a range of ten miles.

When MiG No. 2 announced that he had spotted a single F-4 flying in front of him, the MiG lead Lê Thanh Đạo increased speed and took his position behind this target. At a range of 0.7 miles and with a good sight pic-ture, he calmly pressed the button to fire an R-3S missile. After seeing that the missile was speeding straight at the F-4, he quickly pulled his aircraft into a climb to break away. As he did so, he yelled to his wingman to make a follow-up attack. Võ Sỹ Giáp turned his aircraft and headed toward the tar-get, but then he saw that the F-4 had been hit by Lê Thanh Đạo's missile and was on fire, so he decided not to pursue the target any further. It was most likely that the F-4 that Lê Thanh Đạo shot down was flown by Maj. Kenneth

R. Johnson and 1st Lt. Samuel R. Vaughan of the 555th TFS/432nd TRW. Both pilots ejected and were captured.[25] This was the first U.S. F-4 that Lê Thanh Đạo shot down during the course of the war.

In summary, on 18 December 1971 the 921st and 925th FRs flew three different waves (twenty-four sorties) designed to threaten U.S. aircraft flights and prevent them from carrying out their plan to attack ground targets. MiG-21 pilots shot down one F-4. In this engagement the U.S. side proved to be passive and reactive, and they failed to shoot down any MiGs.

After Major Johnson's F-4 was shot down at 1330 hours by Lê Thanh Đạo's MiG, as described above, U.S. documents state that two other F-4s were shot down by MiGs more than three hours later while they were trying to find and rescue the downed pilot.[26] This means that the pilots who might have scored these victories were the pilots of the MiG flights that took off in the late afternoon, MiG-21 pilots Hoàng Quốc Dũng, Lê Khương, Mai Văn Cương, and Trần Sang and MiG-19 pilots Hoàng Cao Bổng, Nguyễn Hồng Sơn (A), Bùi Văn Sửu, and Phạm Cao Hà. MiG-21 pilots Nguyễn Ngọc Hưng and Đỗ Văn Lanh and MiG-19 pilots Nguyễn Văn Cương and Vũ Viết Tản took off later and did not encounter the enemy aircraft.

More than forty years have passed and a number of the pilots who participated in the air battle of 18 December 1971 have died, making it impossible to find evidence to determine which of these MiG pilots was responsible for shooting down the two other F-4Ds on 18 December 1971. This was the last air-to-air claim made by both sides in the intermission period (1968–1971).

During the period from 1968 to the end of 1971, the VNPAF flew hundreds of combat sorties, fought forty-three battles, and shot down a total of twenty-two U.S. aircraft and twenty-five unmanned reconnaissance drones, and during this same period the VNPAF lost eleven MiGs. With regard to the fleet of fighter aircraft, also during that period of time, the VNPAF received an additional 156 MiG fighter aircraft. It should be specially noted that in early 1969, the VNPAF fighter force was strengthened by the addition of a MiG-19 FR that included thirty-six combat aircraft, and in 1971, the addition of a group of new series MiG-21 MF (F-96) aircraft. As such, between 1968 and 1971, both the quantity and the quality of the VNPAF's fleet of combat aircraft were considerably enhanced.

6

1972
TACKLING LINEBACKER I

After several air strikes on targets inside North Vietnam were attempted on 16 April 1972, but were not successful, at 9:00 p.m. on 8 May 1972 President Richard Nixon went on television to deliver an important speech to the nation on the developments of the conflict in Southeast Asia. After reviewing the situation, he announced a U.S. plan to mine all entrances to North Vietnamese ports, and promised that air and naval strikes against military targets in NVN would continue. Forty-seven minutes after his speech, the Pentagon issued its executive order to launch the first phase of Operation Linebacker.[1] Linebacker I and II would be the last strategic air campaigns in the air war in Vietnam to use B-52 bombers to conduct strategic strikes on targets deep inside NVN, including Hanoi, Hải Phòng, and other big cities. Operation Linebacker I began on 10 May 1972 with a coordinated USAF and USN interdiction campaign against the logistics network throughout NVN, beginning the full-scale reaction period in the Vietnam air war.

Taking advantage of the three-and-a-half-year bombing halt period, the USAF and USN took a series of measures to improve the operational capability of combat units that participated in the second phase of the Vietnam air war. First and foremost was the USN's Top Gun pilot training program (at NAS Miramar) for its fighter pilots, with many lessons on tactics and strategies to improve air maneuverability. Separately, with regard to combat aircraft technical characteristics and weapons, the F-4s were improved with the addition of leading-edge slats on the wings that enhanced the aircraft's horizontal maneuverability. Meanwhile, besides the GCI agencies of Disco and Red Crown, in order to improve the effectiveness of the U.S. fighters against the MiGs, the United States used an electronic system code named Teaball, which began operations in July 1972. Air-to-air missiles (AIM-7 and AIM-9) also were improved with the latest versions. In terms of changes to the high-ranking staff of the USAF Command HQ, in April 1972 Gen. John Vogt was appointed commander of the Seventh AF during the most critical time of the war.[2]

Predicting the strategic intent of the United States, the Vietnamese side initiated several activities to steadily strengthen VNPAF forces, improve its tactical and operational capacity, and enhance its readiness to carry out air combat missions in order to win this strategic campaign. To begin, the AD and AF units completed the general plan against the U.S. strategic air campaign and it was approved by the VNPA General Staff. On 3 February 1972, the 927th FR was established, thus strengthening the VNPAF's forces to a total of four FRs with roughly two hundred MiGs ready to fight against the strategic attack campaign of the USAF and USN.

The year 1972 would be a long year with many challenges for the VNPAF. Ahead lay fierce air battles in strategically significant campaigns.

19 January 1972: The First Air Battle of the Year

At the beginning of 1972, the USAF constantly conducted reconnaissance to closely monitor the activities of the VNPAF. On 19 January 1972, when the Vietnamese radar network picked up a group of U.S. aircraft flying over the Mai Châu area, the VNPAF HQ concluded that it was very likely that the U.S. aircraft would attack the Hòa Bình–Suối Rút area and targets along Route 3. The 921st and 925th FRs received the order from AF HQ to coordinate their operations to intercept the U.S. aircraft in the area west of Hòa Bình–Suối Rút.

The MiG-21 flight of Nguyễn Hồng Mỹ and Lê Minh Dương was ordered to take off at 1418 hours, then was directed to fly at 240 degrees at an altitude of 6,500 feet. At 1430 hours the pilots were ordered to drop their external fuel tanks, switch on their afterburners, and climb to 25,000 feet. After continuing their climb up to 30,000 feet, the pilots received a radio report stating that their target (U.S. RF-4s) was 45 degrees to their right at a range of twelve miles. When Nguyễn Hồng Mỹ spotted the target, he ordered his No. 2 to keep a sharp eye out to cover them while he prepared to make his attack. Nguyễn Hồng Mỹ immediately pushed his throttle forward and switched on his targeting radar. When the range was down to 1.2 miles he flipped the cover over the firing switch up, and when the range was 0.5 miles and his speed was Mach 1.4 he fired his missile and saw its warhead explode about 0.3 miles in front of the target. The target aircraft continued to fly straight ahead. Nguyễn Hồng Mỹ decided to get on the RF-4's tail again to pursue him, but because the weather was bad, he shouted for his wingman to waggle his wings to ensure that he was not firing at the wrong target.

At that moment the frontline command post at Thọ Xuân airfield radioed to inform him, "The target is right in front of you!" When the range was about 2.4 miles he got a good radar lock. Nguyễn Hồng Mỹ continued to close the range, and when the range was down to 1.1–1.2 miles, speed Mach 1.4, and altitude over 40,000 feet, he stabilized his sight of the target and fired his second missile. This one flew straight into the contrail behind the American aircraft's tail. He quickly broke off by turning to the right and then rolled his aircraft upside down to watch the missile warhead explode. He saw the F-4 explode, break in half, and fall straight down toward the ground.

At that very moment, he discovered that his engine rpm (revolutions per minute) was at only 22 percent and that his airspeed was down to 200 mph. He realized that, because he had fired at too close a range and he had flown into the slipstream of the U.S. aircraft at such a high altitude, his engine had stopped. He calmly descended to below 19,000 feet and then successfully restarted his engine. The command post directed him back to Thọ Xuân airfield, where he landed safely.

Also on 19 January 1972, during a MiGCAP mission for a reconnaissance flight in the Quảng Lãng area, Lt. Randall H. Cunningham and Lt. (jg) William P. Driscoll, flying an F-4J from VF-96 of the USS *Constellation*, reported that they had engaged two MiG-21s. Cunningham got on the tail of one MiG-21 and launched a Sidewinder missile at a range of about 0.7 miles. The missile hit the MiG-21, causing the tail section of the MiG to explode and the MiG crashed.[3] However, according to the records and combat logs of the 921st, 923rd, and 925th FRs, all MiG-21 and MiG-19 aircraft that took off that day returned to base and landed safely.[4] This means that the above report that one F-4J from VF-96 of the USS *Constellation* shot down a MiG-21 is incorrect.

The U.S. documents do not record any losses on 19 January 1972, but on 20 January 1972 the United States acknowledged the loss of an RF-4 flown by Maj. R. K. Mock and 1st Lt. J. L. Stiles of 14th TRS/432nd TRW, which was shot down while conducting a reconnaissance mission.[5] The two pilots ejected and were rescued. It is possible that because of the time zone differences the records maintained by the two sides give different days for the date of this air battle.

ESTABLISHMENT OF THE 927TH FR

On 3 February 1972, a second fighter regiment equipped with MiG-21 fighter jets was established. This regiment was designated as the 927th FR and was directly subordinate to the 371st AF Division. The first commander of this regiment was the ace pilot Major Nguyễn Hồng Nhị. Major Trần Ưng was the first regiment political commissar. The deputy regiment commanders were ace pilot Major Nguyễn Nhật Chiêu, ace pilot Capt. Nguyễn Đăng Kính, and Captain Nguyễn Văn Nhiên. Captain Mai Bá Quát was the regiment's chief of technical affairs.

When it was first formed, the regiment had two flight squadrons and was stationed at Đa Phúc airfield. Its assigned mission was to use MiG-21 PFM (F-94) aircraft to fight enemy aircraft from the twentieth parallel northward, and to be ready to provide support and assistance to the 921st and 923rd FRs. During just eight months of combat operations in 1972, the pilots of the 927th FR shot down forty-four U.S. aircraft, representing more than 50 percent of the U.S. aircraft shot down by the VNPAF during the second American war of destruction against North Vietnam (during the Linebacker I and II campaigns in 1972).

Air Engagements on 6 March 1972

On the previous day, 5 March, Vietnamese radar systems detected a great deal of U.S. air activity. This activity, together with strategic intelligence reports, revealed the possibility that the next day, 6 March 1972, several large U.S. aircraft would conduct operations against targets in the MZ4 area.

The VNPAF HQ decided to conduct a coordinated combat operation involving MiG-17s and MiG-21s (with different aircraft types fighting at different altitudes) in the area south of the Lam River, near Anh Sơn and Thọ Xuân airfields. A flight of MiG-21s, piloted by Bùi Đức Nhu and Nguyễn Văn Nghĩa, flew to Anh Sơn airfield on the afternoon of 5 March 1972, and another flight of MiG-21s, flown by Trần Việt and Nguyễn Công Huy, would stand combat alert at Thọ Xuân airfield. The 923rd FR would use a flight of MiG-17s to stand combat alert duty at Thọ Xuân airfield.

The MiG-17 flight, with Lê Hải and Hoàng Ích, took off at 1215 hours, then flew along Route 15 at a low altitude. When the flight reached the western end of the Anh Sơn runway, Lê Hải saw columns of smoke rising from the end of the runway. He concluded that it was very likely that the first wave of enemy attack bombers had already dropped their bombs. Guessing that the next attack groups would soon be coming in to drop their bombs, Lê Hải decided to begin a left-hand circle, maintaining an altitude of 0.7 to 0.9 miles and a speed of 460 mph, and circle above the airfield to wait for the attackers.

After completing the third complete circuit, Lê Hải suddenly saw two missiles streaking toward the MiG formation. He shouted for Hoàng Ích to drop his external fuel tank and to turn back to attack two F-4s that were flying in front of the MiGs. Lê Hải chased the enemy aircraft, at a range of 0.45–0.50 miles, a dive angle of 30 degrees, speed of 460 mph, and an altitude of 3,200 feet; he attacked the enemy aircraft by using the "super-range" method. The F-4 dove nose-first toward the ground west of the airfield. Lê Hải reported that he had hit one F-4. He then turned left, descended, and flew back to the airfield. While flying back to the airfield he spotted some F-4s chasing him, so Lê Hải turned back and fought a turning dogfight with them. After running out of ammunition and deciding that it would not be a good idea to continue this circling dogfight, he turned, broke away from the battle area, flew back to the airfield, and landed at Anh Sơn airfield at 1244 hours.

Having seen two F-4s flying overhead, Hoàng Ích had to turn and break away from his lead to chase the F-4s. He fired at one of them and set it on fire. MiG No. 1 ordered his wingman to break off the engagement and reminded him to descend to low altitudes and make sure that he constantly turned and kept a watch to his rear. At that point he heard No. 2 reply,

"Roger." However, as he was flying past Nghĩa Đàn, Lê Hải found that he was unable to contact his wingman. During his return flight to the airfield he continued to try to reach his No. 2 by radio, but Hoàng Ích did not reply.

In fact, while flying back to the airfield and realizing that these were two F-4Bs chasing him from behind, Hoàng Ích decided to turn back to make a counterattack. The two F-4Bs split up, so that while Hoàng Ích was chasing one of the enemy aircraft the other one got behind him and fired a missile that hit Hoàng Ích's aircraft. As he was flying so low, he was unable to eject and was killed. Later, when the search and rescue team arrived, the local residents said that Hoàng Ích was flying very low when he was chased by two F-4s that began firing missiles at him. He was able to avoid the first missile but the second missile hit him. First Lieutenant Hoàng Ích was killed in the area of the Qùy Hợp District, Nghệ An Province. Vietnamese records show that during the 6 March 1972 air engagement the MiG-17s flown by Lê Hải and Hoàng Ích shot down two F-4s.

To carry out the plan to coordinate combat operations with the MiG-17s, a flight of MiG-21s piloted by Bùi Đức Nhu and Nguyễn Văn Nghĩa was ordered to take off at 1225 hours from Anh Sơn airfield. Because the pierced-steel runway was only 69 feet wide and 1.1 miles long, the flight had to take off one at a time. After lifting off the runway, the pilots kept their afterburners on and turned right to a heading of 360 degrees, to head for Thanh Chương. Just for a moment, they spotted a formation of USN aircraft, four F-8s and a number of A-4/A-7 attack bombers making diving bombing runs to bomb the airfield. Both MiG-21s kept their afterburners on as they made a hard combat turn to pursue the four F-8s flying up above them. The aircraft of the two sides ended in a position in which they were meeting each other head-on. When the command post ordered the pilots to break off the engagement, Bùi Đức Nhu decided to turn to break off and fly back to Thọ Xuân to land. However, Nguyễn Văn Nghĩa decided to continue to chase and dogfight against the F-8s. After making three or four circles without any success, Nguyễn Văn Nghĩa decided to launch one missile at the F-8 formation to make it break and enable the MiG to get into an attack position, but the F-8s continued to make very tight turns, leaving the MiG turning on the outside. Nguyễn Văn Nghĩa decided to switch on his afterburner and break off the engagement, then flew back to Thọ Xuân airfield and landed there.

16 April 1972 : An Unsuccessful Day for MiGs

The month of April heralded the beginning of large-scale air strikes over NVN. At 0300 hours on 16 April, the USAF and USN used a total of 270 combat sorties (including a number of B-52s) to attack the city of Hải Phòng. At the same time, the USN warships off the coast fired hundreds of rounds of sea-to-ground artillery into the Đồ Sơn area. That same day, from 0915 to 1000 hours, the USAF sent sixty combat aircraft from Thailand to mount a ferocious attack on the Đức Giang fuel storage depot located northeast of Hanoi.

Implementing a combat plan that had been prepared beforehand, the VNPAF HQ ordered aircraft of all four FRs to take off to intercept the USAF and USN attack bombers in order to protect the targets. A total of thirty combat sorties (ten MiG-21 sorties, fourteen MiG-17 sorties, and six MiG-19 sorties) was launched. The 921st FR flight, piloted by Nguyễn Hồng Mỹ and Lê Khương, and the 927th FR flight, piloted by Nguyễn Ngọc Hưng and Dương Đình Nghi, took off and flew toward the designated battle area. However, they did not encounter the attackers that were their intended targets. Instead, they ran into F-4 fighters at an altitude of 32,000 feet, flying in formation and using electronic jamming devices to make them appear to be B-52s. As a result, the MiG pilots were placed in the defensive position in which the F-4s had the upper hand. After analyzing the situation the command post concluded that the F-4s that clashed with MiGs were a flight of four F-4Ds that were originally assigned to escort the bombers but, probably because the attackers crossed the Vietnamese border later than had been planned, they were ordered to shift to carrying out a MiGCAP mission.

The flight of four F-4s used equipment that allowed them to infiltrate the Vietnamese Identification Friend or Foe (IFF) network to detect and identify MiGs at a range of twenty miles. The F-4s split into two two-aircraft sections to attack the MiGs. An F-4 flown by Maj. Edward D. Cherry and Capt. Jeffrey S. Feinstein from the 13th TFS/ 432nd TRW targeted and fired two AIM-7E-2 missiles at Nguyễn Hồng Mỹ's MiG, which was flying in the No. 1 position.[6] When he realized that his aircraft had been hit by a missile, becoming uncontrollable and beginning to fall toward the earth, Nguyễn Hồng Mỹ decided to eject. At the same time, the MiG-21 flown by Lê Khương had made a tight turn and gotten on the tail of the F-4 No. 1. This

F-4 turned back and counterattacked, firing three missiles at the MiG-21. Lê Khương was forced to eject, and he landed safely.

Two MiG-21s flown by Nguyễn Ngọc Hưng and Dương Đình Nghi from the 927th FR took off from Đa Phúc airfield to intercept U.S. aircraft approaching from Thailand. The MiG-21s were directed to the Vạn Yên area where they encountered a flight of F-4Ds. The MiG-21s fought a ferocious dogfight against the F-4s. The F-4s fired six AIM-7E-2 missiles at the MiGs and one of them hit Dương Đình Nghi's aircraft. The MiG pilot, however, ejected and landed safely.

Ending an unsuccessful day, the MiGs did not claim to have shot down any enemy aircraft, while three MiG-21s were lost.

27 April 1972: MiG-21s Fight against USN F-4Bs

The weather at Đa Phúc airfield on 27 April was 70 percent cumulus cloud cover with a visibility of 4.5 to 6.5 miles. However, the weather in the battle area was good.

Radar station C-26 detected a group of eight aircraft coming in from the sea forty-five miles southeast of Thanh Hóa and headed toward the Lạch Trường Inlet. This was a formation of USN attack bombers and fighters. The command post ordered a MiG-21 flight, flown by Hoàng Quốc Dũng and Cao Sơn Khảo from the 921st FR, to take off at 1623 hours and fly to the Hòa Bình–Vụ Bản area to protect Hàm Rồng (Dragon's Jaw) Bridge and Thọ Xuân airfield. At 1636 hours, when the MiGs were eighteen miles from the target, the pilots were ordered to drop their external fuel tanks and switch on their afterburners. Thirty seconds later, MiG No. 1 spotted two F-4s flying at a lower altitude 30 degrees to his right front and at a range of 3.5 miles. These were two F-4Bs being directed by radar controllers on board a USN warship off the coast and that were assigned to intercept the MiGs. As they flew past Bái Thượng dam, even though the radar warning system (Red Crown) in an EC-121 aircraft informed them that MiGs were very close, the F-4 pilots failed to spot the MiGs.

After quickly assessing the situation, Hoàng Quốc Dũng decided to attack the F-4 No. 1 on the right and ordered his No. 2 to attack the F-4 on the left. Hoàng Quốc Dũng quickly rolled his aircraft upside down and, with an extremely precise swoop, he got on the tail of the F-4 No. 1. When the range was down to 0.9–1.1 miles, at a speed of 620 to 680 mph and with the aircraft in a slight, 5-degree turn, he calmly centered the target in his sight and pressed the missile-firing button. The missile dropped from the pylon and then sped forward. After initially corkscrewing, the missile straightened out and sped straight to the target. Hoàng Quốc Dũng pulled into a climb and turned back to check on the target. Since the target was not yet burning, he decided to level out and get on the target's tail again to fire another missile. At that moment, however, he saw the F-4 burst into flames. He quickly turned away to break off the engagement, flew back to Đa Phúc airfield, and landed at 1648 hours.

Based on the records from VNPAF and some U.S. authors, the F-4B that Lieutenant Hoàng Quốc Dũng shot down was flown by Lt. Albert R. Molinare and Lt. Cdr. James Burton Souder from VF-51 of the USS *Coral Sea*. The two U.S. pilots bailed out thirty miles northwest of Thanh Hóa and both were quickly captured.[7] Lieutenant Commander Souder had completed 325 combat missions during the war in Southeast Asia.

During this air battle the young pilot, Lieutenant Hoàng Quốc Dũng demonstrated his ability to assess the situation and make very precise maneuvers in order to get into a favorable position above the target. Firing from a range of a little over 0.6 miles, with just one single missile he shot down an F-4. The air action of Hoàng Quốc Dũng was remarkable not only because he killed an F-4 skillfully, but also this was the first USN F-4B that was shot down by MiG-21s during the second phase of the U.S. air war against North Vietnam.

Air Battles on 6 May 1972

On this day a flight of two MiG-17s, flown by Nguyễn Văn Lục and Nguyễn Văn Bảy (B) from the 923rd FR, took off to intercept a USN formation of A-6s and A-7s that was sent to attack targets in Vinh and Đồng Hới. After several circles of fierce dogfighting in which the USAF aircraft outnumbered him, Nguyễn Văn Bảy (B)'s MiG-17 was hit by a missile fired from an F-4. He was killed just seventeen days after the victory of his attack on the Navy Task Force 77 destroyer USS *Oklahoma City*. The F-4B that pursued and attacked Nguyễn Văn Bảy (B)'s MiG-17 may have been the one flown by Lt. Cdr. Jerry B. Houston and Lt. Kevin T. Moore from VF-51 of the USS *Coral Sea*.[8]

In order to carry out the combat plan entrusted by the AF HQ, the 927th FR assigned a flight of four MiG-21s to stand combat alert duty at Đa Phúc airfield and placed two more MiG-21s on reserve (standby) alert at Kép airfield. The four pilots of the combat alert flight were Nguyễn Tiến Sâm, Nguyễn Thế Đức, Nguyễn Văn Nghĩa, and Lê Văn Lập. The flight was ordered to take off at 1731 hours. The battle plan was for the flight to concentrate its attack on the enemy attack bombers in order to disrupt a USAF strike group.

The MiG-21 flight was directed to a "battle waiting" area south of Miếu Môn airfield, where it began flying in circles while waiting to engage a formation of attack bombers flying in to attack Nam Định. A few minutes later the flight spotted the target in the Đồng Giao–Vụ Bản area. The flight lead gave the order to drop external fuel tanks and attack. After dogfighting with the F-4s for a few minutes and seeing that the situation was not to the MiGs' advantage because the pilots had in fact encountered U.S. fighters, the GCI post ordered the flight to break off the engagement and return to land at Nội Bài. As he was about to break away, MiG No. 4, flown by Lê Văn Lập, was hit by a missile. The pilot ejected and landed safely on the ground.

On 6 May, two fighter aircrews, one consisting of Lt. Cdr. Kenneth W. Pettigrew and Lt. (jg) Michael J. McCabe and the other consisting of Lt. (jg) Robert G. Hughes and Lt. (jg) Adolph J. Cruz from VF-114 of the USS *Kitty Hawk*, reported shooting down two MiG-21s with AIM-9G missiles.

However, the combat log of the 927th FR states that only one MiG-21, the one flown by Lê Văn Lập, was shot down and that the other three aircraft returned and landed safely. In the meeting between Vietnamese and American veteran pilots in Hanoi on 13 April 2016, Rear Adm. Kenneth Pettigrew and Senior Colonel Nguyễn Văn Nghĩa, two pilots who fought in that engagement, met each other and recalled what had happened. It can be confirmed that Lê Văn Lập's MiG was hit by the missile of the F-4 flown by Kenneth Pettigrew.

Although this was the 927th FR's second combat mission, the regiment still had not scored any victories and instead had suffered losses. After this engagement the commanders and pilots of the 927th FR reviewed its combat experiences, identified continuing tactical issues such as engaging the wrong opponent (fighters instead of attackers), not gaining the advantage in the attack because the pilots spotted their opponent when the opposing aircraft were very close, and the regiment's decision to utilize a four-aircraft flight formation, which was not suited to the strengths and capabilities of the MiG-21. The regiment also developed new combat battle plans and resolved to score the first success for the newly established 927th FR.

8 May 1972: First Victories for MiG-19s

During the last days of April and the first days of May 1972 the USAF used a large number of aircraft (including B-52s) to attack targets on the outskirts of Hanoi, Thanh Hóa, Hải Phòng, Hòn Gai, and along lines of communications. The AF HQ concluded that on 8 May 1972, the USAF would again fly in from the west to conduct their bombing attacks, and their fighters would provide cover for tactical attack bomber formations sent to bomb Yên Bái and the Bái Thượng dam. The AF HQ ordered the 925th FR to use its MiG-19s to intercept the enemy's first attack, in order to protect Yên Bái airfield and the Thác Bà electrical power plant and to block the American strike groups approaching from the west.

Because it was the first air battle of the 925th FR, the AF HQ decided to use a flight of MiG-21s from the 921st FR to support the flights of MiG-19s by carrying out a mission designed to divert the attention of the U.S. fighter aircraft. Meanwhile the 925th FR used two flights of MiG-19s on combat alert duty. The first flight was assigned to wait at the north end of the runway and the second flight was waiting at the south end of the runway.

The MiG-21s flight flown by Phạm Phú Thái and Võ Sỹ Giáp took off at 0840 hours, then were directed to fly to the Tuyên Quang area to provide air cover and to attract the attention of the American fighter aircraft. While the savage battle between MiG-19s and the U.S. F-4s was raging in the skies over Yên Bái airfield, in the Tuyên Quang area the MiG-21 flight spotted four F-4s. This flight of F-4Ds was probably being directed by the radar controller on the Navy's air direction ship, and that was why it was able to close with the MiG-21s so quickly. The two sides swept in and engaged each other, but because the mission of the MiG-21s was to attract and divert the American fighters, the MiG lead decided to draw the F-4s away from the area where the MiG-19s were fighting. The MiGs and the F-4s turned and maneuvered, striving to get into position to make an attack, but neither side got an opportunity to fire. Finally, seeing that his fuel was running low, Phạm Phú Thái requested permission to break off the engagement.

Seeing that two MiGs were breaking off the engagement and turning to fly back northward, the four F-4s repeatedly turned hard, chasing and firing missiles at them. The flight made a steep dive to accumulate airspeed and then pulled up into a steep climb and turned away to fly back to Nội Bài. At that time No. 2 reported that his aircraft seemed to have been damaged. He said that his fuel level was dropping very rapidly and that he did not have enough fuel to make it back to the airfield. When No. 2 requested permission to make a forced landing, both the GCI post and MiG lead strongly ordered him to eject, but they did not hear any response from No. 2.

Võ Sỹ Giáp requested permission to make a forced landing in a field in Vĩnh Tường District, Vĩnh Phú Province. However, just before the aircraft was about to touch the ground the pilot saw that if he continued straight ahead his aircraft would hit a school filled with children, so he courageously pushed his rudder pedal to turn the aircraft into a nearby water-filled ditch. Võ Sỹ Giáp suffered serious injuries and was quickly transported to Military Hospital 108 in Hanoi for emergency treatment, but his injuries were too severe and he died on 11 May 1972. Phạm Phú Thái returned to base and landed safely.

The flight of MiG-19s standing combat alert duty at the northern end of the runway (Yên Bái airfield) was ordered to take off at 0851 hours, climb through the cloud layer, and circle directly over the southern end of the airfield. A few minutes later, the pilots spotted the target. Just to make sure, Nguyễn Hồng Sơn (A) asked for and received confirmation from the GCI that these were enemy aircraft. At this time two flights of the enemy aircraft were heading into the area of Yên Bái airfield. When the MiG-19s reached an altitude of 13,000 feet, two MiG pilots, No. 1 and No. 3, reported that they could see the target at a range of four miles. The MiG lead ordered his wingmen to drop their external fuel tanks and pursue the enemy aircraft.

At the same time, the F-4s had spotted the formation of MiG-19s, then flying in extended fingertip formation. The F-4s immediately shifted to an extended trail formation in order to be able to cover each other and then made a hard turn to get behind the MiGs. Seeing that the four MiGs had begun to turn in toward them, the F-4 pilots decided to change tactics and split up. Nguyễn Ngọc Tiếp ordered Nguyễn Hồng Sơn (A) and Nguyễn Hùng Sơn (B) to pursue the two enemy aircraft on the right and to the rear while he and No. 2 attacked the two aircraft in front and to the left. When he turned to the right to look around, Nguyễn Ngọc Tiếp saw two more F-4s at an altitude of 6,500 feet and immediately turned to pursue them. The two F-4s began a combat weave maneuver to counter his attack, but MiG No. 1 pushed his stick over in a determined effort to get in close to the F-4 No. 1. When the range was right, he fired his guns. The F-4 was hit by his shells and went down, crashing on the spot. Nguyễn Ngọc Tiếp then quickly turned to break off the engagement, and with No. 2 both returned to the airfield and landed safely.

Seeing that the two F-4s on the right made a hard diving turn, Nguyễn Hồng Sơn (A) got on one F-4's tail and fired two bursts from his guns, but he missed. Meanwhile, during the fighting with the other F-4s, MiG No. 4 fired a second burst, which hit the tail of the F-4. He then noticed that there was a mountain peak right in front of him, so he pulled up into a climb, turned to break off the engagement, and flew back to land at his base.

This was the first time that MiG-19s encountered USAF F-4Ds over Yên Bái. When the MiG-19 lead Nguyễn Ngọc Tiếp ordered his flight to drop their external fuel tanks, Nguyễn Hùng Sơn (B) mistakenly pushed the button to deploy his landing drogue chute. The drogue chute popped out and hung there, swinging back and forth in the sky. This perhaps made the American pilots think that one of the MiG-19s had stalled when making a maneuver that was too extreme, causing the pilot to decide to eject. The U.S. pilots who were credited with "shooting down" this MiG-19 were Maj. Barton P. Crews and Capt. Keith W. Jones Jr. from the 13th TFS/432nd TRW.

In reality, according to the records of the 925th FR, all four MiG-19 pilots returned and landed safely. This means that the report that the F-4 shot down one MiG-19 was inaccurate. Meanwhile, pilots Nguyễn Ngọc Tiếp and Nguyễn Hùng Sơn (B) were each credited with shooting down one F-4.[9]

At 0900 hours, a group of A-7s and A-6s from the USS *Coral Sea* flew in and dropped thirty-six 1,000-pound Mark-52 and Mark-55 mines into Hải Phòng Harbor. Two USN F-4Js assigned to a MiGCAP mission were directed in by a radar controller on a Navy warship to intercept a flight of four MiG-17s. While the F-4s were looking to spot their target, suddenly one MiG-17 popped up from the clouds, turned in, and attacked the F-4 No. 2, but his cannon shells missed. The F-4 No. 1 was heading toward the

MiG at a 60-degree encounter angle when it saw two more MiG-17s at a higher altitude, so it fired two missiles in an attempt to help the F-4 No. 2 get rid of the MiGs chasing it. At that moment, the two MiG-17s suddenly turned to attack the F-4 No. 1 and began firing their guns. The F-4 No. 1 took evasive action to avoid their cannon shells and made an inside turn in order to fire missiles, then he was forced to make an extremely high-G turn to the left, and quickly flew into the clouds to escape.

In total, during the air battles on 8 May 1972 the VNPAF's FRs flew twenty-four sorties (including twelve combat sorties of MiG-17s). Two of the combat flights encountered enemy aircraft and engaged in air battles, but only MiG-19s from the 925th FR shot down two F-4s. Some U.S. documents state that a USN F-4J flown by Lt. R. Cunningham and Lt. (jg) William P. Driscoll shot down a MiG-17, but in fact all the MiG-19s and all twelve MiG-17s from the 923rd and 925th FRs that took off that day returned safely without any losses. This shows that the U.S. record that says a USN F-4J shot down a MiG-17 on this day is incorrect.[10]

10 May 1972: The Longest and Most Ferocious Battle Day

The United States simultaneously launched two large-scale air campaigns on 10 May 1972, involving a total of 414 combat sorties flown by tactical aircraft of the Seventh AF and the USN's Task Force 77. A large number of A-6 Intruders, A-7 Corsairs, and F-4 Phantoms from U.S. aircraft carriers flew in to attack targets in the Hải Phòng area and southeast of Hanoi. At 0800 hours, the first attack groups took off from the USS *Constellation*, then, with those from the USS *Coral Sea* and the USS *Kitty Hawk* following at ten-minute intervals, all attack formations headed for Hải Phòng.[11] In this attack mission the U.S. aircraft carried cluster bomb unit (CBU) bombs to bomb Kiến An airfield and SAM sites.

Meanwhile, early in the morning the USAF tactical squadrons based in Thailand began preparing to use a total of 120 aircraft to attack targets deep inside North Vietnamese territory. This formation of aircrafts included sixteen F-4s and five F-105s that were sent in first to suppress the ground-based AD positions and MiG fighters. Forty-four F-4s and ten more F-105s were assigned to attack the Long Biên Bridge and Yên Viên railroad yard.

Additionally, eighty-eight more aircraft were assigned to fly support missions. One of the top priority missions given to the USAF and USN was to destroy the Long Biên Bridge across the Red River. This was a bridge that the USAF had attacked several times over the previous seven years, managing to damage some of its spans and causing it to become temporarily unusable. But each time it was damaged, it was quickly repaired and made reusable by the engineering troops and the people of Hanoi, and transportation between the two sides of the Red River continued.

At 0400 hours on 10 May, a group of international journalists staying at the Metropole Hotel in Hanoi was woken up early for a trip to Hải Phòng, where they hoped to photograph the attacks by the USN aircraft and to take part in a press conference that was to be held to denounce the United States for the mining of Hải Phòng Harbor. Among the international journalists were two French reporters, Theodore Ronco and Claude Julien from the newspapers *L'Humanité* and *Le Monde*.[12] These reporters would become witnesses to the American bombing of civilian targets.

On that day, AF commander Đào Đình Luyện was the officer in charge of the command duty section at the AF HQ, assisted by deputy AF commanders Trần Mạnh and Trần Hanh. Facing the very aggressive plans of the USAF and USN, the AD and AF Command decided to coordinate the efforts of all three types of MiGs and all four FRs with the SAM and AAA units. The AD and AF Command's combat intent was to engage the USAF and USN attack aircraft in all three sectors: the eastern sector, to protect Hải Phòng; the northeastern sector, to protect the Hanoi area, including the Long Biên Bridge and targets along Route 1 North; and the western sector, to protect the Bái Thượng dam and Yên Bái airfield.

Three two-aircraft flights of MiG-21s from the 921st and 927th FRs would be used to accomplish the combat missions. Two more MiG-21 flights stood on combat alert duty at Đa Phúc airfield. The 923rd FR would use three four-aircraft flights and two two-aircraft flights of MiG-17s, which were placed on combat alert duty at Kép airfield. The 925th FR placed two four-aircraft flights of MiG-19s on combat alert duty. At 0753 hours the AF command post ordered radar station C-53 to switch on its radar transmitters. Once the radar station picked up U.S. aircraft operating in the Hải Phòng area, a flight of MiG-17s flown by Vũ Văn Đang, Nguyễn Công Ngũ, Trịnh

Văn Quy, and Nguyễn Văn Lâm took off at 0840 hours from Kép airfield and flew to a holding area over Phả Lại. No enemy aircraft was encountered, so the flight flew back to the airfield and landed safely. Then, from 0905 hours to 1708 hours, ten more flights of MiG-17s (a total of thirty-two sorties) of the 923rd FR took off to fly operational missions.

The flight of MiG-21s flown by Đặng Ngọc Ngự and Nguyễn Văn Ngãi was ordered to take off at 0852 hours from Kép airfield. Just as the flight lifted off the runway and retracted its landing gear, the MiGs were spotted and attacked by a flight of two F-4Js. These two F-4Js were led by Lt. Austin Hawkins of VF-92 of the USS *Constellation*, who was conducting a patrol at an altitude of 10,000 feet. While flying past Kép airfield, the two F-4s saw the MiGs as they were taking off. The F-4 No. 2, flown by Lt. Curt Dose and Lt. Cdr. James McDevitt, swept in at them and fired two AIM-9G missiles. The second missile hit the MiG No. 2, flown by Nguyễn Văn Ngãi, who had just reached an altitude of 450–600 feet. First Lieutenant Nguyễn Văn Ngãi did not have time to eject and was killed.

When the MiG lead Đặng Ngọc Ngự had reached an altitude of 2,000 feet and a speed of 460–490 mph, he saw two F-4s behind him, firing missiles. He took a violent series of evasive maneuvers to escape the missiles, executing several tight turns close to the ground. By doing so Đặng Ngọc Ngự managed to keep his MiG out of reach of the Sidewinder (AIM-9).[13] In fact, he was able to evade five attempted Sidewinder shots, and made a skilled maneuver to escape. A few moments later he spotted two more F-4s heading straight at him at a range of 2.5 to 3.5 miles. He quickly switched on his afterburner, accelerated to 560 mph, and turned hard. The two F-4s spotted Đặng Ngọc Ngự's MiG-21 and made a hard turn to the left to chase him. The two F-4s maneuvered, using the old, familiar tactic of splitting up and conducting a combat weave, with one aircraft above and the other flying below.

When the F-4 at a higher altitude turned to chase him, Đặng Ngọc Ngự made a move in such a way as if he intended to chase the higher-altitude F-4. As he predicted, the F-4 below immediately turned back to chase him. Waiting for this action, Đặng Ngọc Ngự immediately made a hard turn to completely change direction, quickly got on the tail of the lower-altitude F-4, and brought the target into the center of his sight. When the range was 0.54

miles, speed 700 mph, and altitude 4,500 feet, he fired the R-3S missile under his left wing. As he did not have enough time to see the result of his first missile, he then quickly broke off the attack by turning to chase the other F-4. At a range of 0.54 miles he fired a second missile, but fortunately for the F-4 pilot the missile under Đặng Ngọc Ngự's right wing failed to fire. Đặng Ngọc Ngự quickly broke off the engagement, flew to Đa Phúc airfield, and landed safely.

So, during an air engagement on 10 May 1972, a flight of MiG-21s flown by Đặng Ngọc Ngự and Nguyễn Văn Ngãi from the 921st FR shot down one F-4. Meanwhile, MiG No. 2 pilot First Lieutenant Nguyễn Văn Ngãi was killed. Later, in the emails exchanged between the former pilot of the F-4 No. 2 and some VNPAF veteran pilots discussing what had happened in that engagement, he said that he had seen the MiGs lift off the ground and drop their external fuel tanks right after takeoff, and that his flight lead, Lt. Austin Hawkins was not shot down.

> During the meeting between Vietnamese and U.S. veteran pilots in Hanoi in April 2016, Curt Dose and members of the U.S. delegation asked to visit the place where he encountered two MiG-21s on 10 May 1972, as well as pilot Nguyễn Văn Ngãi's family. With the help of the Vietnamese veteran pilots, pilot Nguyễn Văn Ngãi's family agreed to welcome the Americans to their house and they all prayed at Nguyễn Văn Ngãi's tombstone. The scene was captured in a VTV talk show video clip in April 2016; the cameraman filmed USN pilot Curt Dose hand-in-hand with Nguyễn Văn Ngãi's sister walking to Nguyễn Văn Ngãi's tombstone.[14]

Less than one hour later, in the northwestern sector, eighty-four F-4s and five F-105s flew over northern Laos and entered the airspace of North Vietnam. They were in a strike formation that included aircraft loaded with bombs, aircraft assigned to serve as escort fighters, aircraft assigned to MiGCAP missions, reconnaissance aircraft, SAR mission aircraft, and helicopters. Having received the intelligence information in advance that the American plan was to attack the Bái Thượng dam and Yên Bái airfield, the

AF Command had already prepared a plan against this attack. It decided to send a flight of two MiG-21s to fly a diversionary mission and to support the MiG-19s fighting to protect targets in the Yên Bái–Tuyên Quang area.

Two MiG-21s flown by Nguyễn Công Huy and Cao Sơn Khảo took off at 0939 hours from Đa Phúc airfield and headed for Tuyên Quang (according to the statements of U.S. pilots there were four MiG-21s). At this time a flight of four F-4Ds led by Maj. Robert A. Lodge and Capt. Roger C. Locher was assigned to MiG-CAP duty in the skies over Tuyên Quang, to support the attack bombers attacking Long Biên Bridge in Hanoi and Yên Viên railroad yard. According to the information from the intelligence networks these F-4Ds were a newer generation of the F-4 that had been improved with the addition of leading-edge slats, and were the first to be equipped with the Combat Tree IFF Interrogator. This enabled the F-4s to close in on the MiGs without Vietnamese forces being aware of their presence.

While continually searching the skies for the target, Nguyễn Công Huy saw two missiles heading at them from the left rear. He shouted an order to make a hard turn to the right. However, he did not hear a reply from his wingman. The F-4D that launched the missile at MiG No. 2 was most likely one of two F-4Ds of the 555th TFS/432nd TRW, flown by Capt. Richard S. Ritchie and Capt. Charles B. DeBellevue (these two pilots would later become the USAF's first and second aces of the Vietnam War), or it may have been the F-4 flown by 1st Lt. John D. Markle and Capt. Steven D. Eaves.[15] When he heard the ground control command post issue a warning "Keep an eye out to your right," Nguyễn Công Huy spotted two F-4s about 2.5 miles to his right rear and saw that the F-4s were firing missiles at him. He quickly rolled his aircraft, broke off the engagement, descended to a low altitude, and navigated his aircraft down along the Tam Đảo mountain range, which he knew very well, back to Kép airfield where he landed at 1028 hours.

From the moment (at 0957 hours) when Nguyễn Công Huy shouted to make a hard right turn, there was no radio contact with Cao Sơn Khảo. According to local residents who witnessed No. 2's actions during this engagement, and as later confirmed by the AD and AF Service, during this battle Cao Sơn Khảo shot down one F-4 before he was hit by an enemy missile. First Lieutenant Cao Sơn Khảo ejected, but his ejection was unsuccessful and he died.

MiG-19s VERSUS F-4Ds

The 925th FR's deputy commander, Hồ Văn Qùy, ordered a flight piloted by Phạm Ngọc Tâm, Phạm Hùng Sơn, Nguyễn Văn Phúc, and Lê Đức Oánh to take off at 0944 hours, then fly in circles waiting above the airfield. The flight flew three complete circles above the airfield and during their third circuit the MiG pilots spotted U.S. aircraft approaching from the southwest. This was a formation of thirty-two F-4s from the 432nd TFW that was flying in to attack Long Biên Bridge and Yên Viên railroad yard. The USAF flight assigned to the MiG suppression mission was led by Maj. Robert Alfred Lodge and Capt. Roger C. Locher. As the F-4s had been warned by the Navy's Red Crown radar system of the presence of MiGs in the area, they were looking for two MiG-21s (flown by Nguyễn Công Huy and Cao Sơn Khảo) that were flying the diversionary mission at an altitude of 15,000 feet.

While two F-4s were focused on chasing the MiG-21s, they failed to see that two MiG-19s (No. 3 and No. 4) were heading toward them at high speed. Even when they shot up even with the F-4s, the U.S. pilots did not see them. The two F-4s were continuing to chase the MiG-21 in front of them when MiG-19 No. 3 got in close behind the two F-4Ds and fired two bursts of cannon shells at Major Lodge's F-4.

Despite his No. 2 calling out a warning, Lodge did not have time to dodge Nguyễn Văn Phúc's cannon shells. The F-4D No. 1 was hit, shuddered, and then went into a flat spin. The MiG-19 No. 3 swept in again and fired a third burst of cannon shells. The F-4D broke in half and burst into flames. The air crew of the F-4 that was shot down consisted of the pilot Maj. Robert A. Lodge, the chief of weapons and tactics of the 432nd TRW, an experienced pilot who had great prospects of becoming the first USAF ace (because he had already been credited with shooting down three MiGs), and the backseater, Capt. Roger C. Locher. Major Lodge was listed as KIA. However, Capt. Roger C. Locher ejected, parachuted to the ground, and wandered in the jungle for twenty-three days before he was rescued. Locher became the pilot who spent the longest time on the ground before being rescued, in the longest rescue operation in the history of the air war.

The MiG-19 No. 3 piloted by Nguyễn Văn Phúc landed safely at Yên Bái airfield at 1019 hours. Meanwhile, when No. 4 Lê Đức Oánh spotted a flight of aircraft behind him, he decided to turn back to counterattack. He fired almost his entire load of ammunition but failed to obtain any hits. At that moment two F-4s behind him fired a missile at his aircraft, forcing him to eject from his aircraft. For some unknown reason, however, his ejection was unsuccessful and Lieutenant Lê Đức Oánh was killed.

As the engagement had lasted so long, the MiG-19s were running low on fuel, but more American aircraft kept flying into the area. At this time the command post ordered the second flight, waiting at the north end of the runway, to take off to provide cover for the aircraft of the first flight when they came back in to land safely at Yên Bái airfield.

The second flight of MiG-19s, composed of Hoàng Cao Bổng, Phạm Cao Hà, Nguyễn Văn Cương, and Lê Văn Tưởng, took off at 1002 hours and then encountered a flight of USAF F-4s. This was a flight of F-4Es assigned to escort a flight of attack bombers armed with laser-guided bombs. The four MiG-19s closed with their opponents at an intercept angle of almost 90 degrees. The entire MiG flight made a tight turn to cut in behind the formation of F-4s. As MiG-19 No. 4 was very far from the rear, its pilot made an incredibly tight turn and got on the tail of the F-4E No. 4. He quickly got the enemy aircraft in his gunsight and fired two bursts that hit the F-4E's right wing. The F-4E crashed southwest of the airfield. The crew of this F-4E, Capt. Jeffrey Lyndol Harris and Capt. Dennis Edward Wilkinson, were not able to eject and were listed as killed in action.[16]

The command post ordered the flight to return to Yên Bái airfield, where it landed safely at 1047 hours.

COLONEL NGUYỄN TOON OR 1ST LT. TRÀ VĂN KIẾM

From early afternoon on 10 May the USN sent in a large number of aircraft (approximately sixty-six), including F-4Bs, A-6s, and A-7s to conduct several waves of air strikes (Alpha Strike) against targets in the Hải Phòng and Hải Dương areas, and especially against Lai Vu and Phú Lương Bridges along Route 5. The USN aircraft were equipped with new electronic jamming devices to suppress Vietnam's ground-based radars, which made it very difficult for the ground control command system to help MiG pilots. During this same period of time the Combat Tree system was still able to infiltrate the IFF system used by the MiGs, and this system alerted the F-4 pilots to the presence of MiGs in the air.

Responding to that situation, a flight of four MiG-17s, piloted by Nguyễn Văn Thọ, Tạ Đông Trung, Đỗ Hạng, and Trà Văn Kiếm, was ordered to take off from Kép airfield at 1256 hours then was instructed to turn left to a heading of 160 degrees while flying at an altitude of 1,600 feet to the Bắc Giang area. The command post constantly provided the flight with information about the enemy aircraft and reminded the pilots to operate only at low altitudes (as part of the coordination arrangements with the MiG-21 flight). When the flight was approaching Phả Lại, the command post informed them of U.S. aircraft over southern Hải Dương, at a range of twelve miles, and warned the pilots to keep their eyes peeled for the enemy aircraft. A few moments later, after the flight had switched on afterburners to climb to an altitude of 3,200 feet, Nguyễn Văn Thọ spotted four American aircraft approaching from the southeast. He ordered his wingmen to drop their external fuel tanks, accelerate to a speed of 520–560 mph, and climb to 4,500 feet.

When Nguyễn Văn Thọ turned back, he saw four other F-4s chasing a flight of two MiG-17s flown by Đỗ Hạng and Trà Văn Kiếm. When the F-4s fired missiles, he shouted loudly, "Take evasive action!" However, only MiG No. 4 reacted in time. Before No. 3 had a chance to turn, his MiG-17 was hit by a missile. Đỗ Hạng ejected and his parachute opened properly, but the parachute landing was not successful and Lieutenant Đỗ Hạng died.

Meanwhile Tạ Đông Trung decided to sweep to the front to attack the aircraft No. 3 in the flight of A-7s, when it descended to a low altitude and flew straight out toward the sea. Tạ Đông Trung tried chasing and firing at this A-7 aircraft. When he reached the coastline, however, he decided to turn back and fly above the Thái Bình River and back to Kép airfield, landing at 1323 hours. Nguyễn Văn Thọ decided to turn back to support No. 4 Trà Văn Kiếm. During the circling dogfight, MiG No. 1 got on the tail of one F-4. As the range was so close he decided to set his gunsight on superrange with a lead angle of 66 seconds. He squeezed his trigger but his shells missed, exploding in front of the enemy aircraft.

A few moments later when Nguyễn Văn Thọ felt his aircraft shake very hard and he could no longer control it, he decided to eject at an altitude of 3,200 feet. While he swung under his parachute he saw his wingman Trà Văn Kiếm still fighting against the F-4s. Nguyễn Văn Thọ touched the ground safely. At the same time the young pilot Trà Văn Kiếm was continuing to dogfight against the USN fighters. As there were so many U.S. aircraft against Trà Văn Kiếm's MiG, in this battle, he constantly had to evade the missiles being fired by the U.S. F-4s.

According to some American publications, one F-4J with the call-sign Showtime 100, which was assigned to MiGCAP duty and was flown by Lt. Randall H. Cunningham and Lt. (jg) William P. Driscoll of VF-96 of the USS *Constellation*, was credited with shooting down three MiG-17s. In addition, three more USAF F-4 crews were also credited with shooting down four more MiG-17s.[17]

After breaking off an engagement, Lieutenant Cunningham's F-4J was heading back to his aircraft carrier when he had a head-on encounter with a single MiG-17 flying all alone (the MiG may have been the one flown by First Lieutenant Trà Văn Kiếm). Lieutenant Cunningham closed with the MiG-17 and intended to fire at it to scare the pilot, but the MiG-17 opened fire first. The surprised pilot pulled his F-4 into a vertical climb, hoping that the MiG-17 would not be able to keep up with him. However, Trà Văn Kiếm demonstrated very solid air combat skills by sticking with him and making maneuvers in the vertical plane to keep up with the F-4. There were times when the two canopies of the two aircraft were virtually right next to each other and each pilot could clearly see the face of his opponent at a very close distance. When assessing this engagement and his opponent, Lieutenant Cunningham even said that no enemy pilot he encountered previously had been so aggressive.[18]

The two aircraft twisted and turned in the vertical plane. Trà Văn Kiếm repeatedly got on the tail of the F-4 and fired his guns ferociously at the American aircraft. Lieutenant Cunningham utilized the "Feather Duster" technique of making a vertical climb and then suddenly reducing speed to make the MiG shoot past him. The F-4 immediately took aim and fired an AIM-9G missile. The MiG-17 was slightly damaged, but because it had stalled it began diving toward the ground. First Lieutenant Trà Văn Kiếm was not able to bail out and he died.

There was a period when the American media mentioned that this was a MiG flown by Colonel Nguyễn Toon, a legendary pilot who reportedly had shot down thirteen American aircraft.[19] In reality, however, the pilot that engaged Cunningham so aggressively remains unidentified.[20] In its entire history the VNPAF has never had a "Colonel Nguyễn Toon," and no Vietnamese pilot shot down thirteen U.S. aircraft. The young pilot Trà Văn Kiếm had had only a little over two hundred hours of flight time and this was his very first air combat mission, but he was able to carry out combat maneuvers so skillfully that Cunningham thought he was fighting against the legendary Colonel Nguyễn Toon. After his air battles against MiG-17s, as he was flying back to his aircraft carrier Cunningham's F-4J was shot down by a SAM. Both crewmen ejected and both were rescued.[21]

In the VN-U.S. veteran pilot meeting in San Diego in September 2017, while discussing the 10 May 1972 engagements, the VNPAF delegation detailed all the information about the legendary but unreal Colonel Nguyễn Toon and the last combat of First Lieutenant Trà Văn Kiếm.

On October 2018, while he was discussing that air engagement in the VN-U.S. meeting in Hanoi and Ho Chi Minh City, Randall Cunningham remembered that he had engaged many Vietnamese MiG pilots but he had never before encountered such a matchless and staunch opponent as First Lieutenant Trà Văn Kiếm. The air combat of 10 May 1972 lasted nearly three minutes, during which the MiG pilot had twice won the favorable position to fire at him. Lieutenant Cunningham had to dodge Trà Văn Kiếm's bursts before he could regain his mindfulness to use all his flying experience, training, and skills for his victory.[22]

In October 2018, with the assistance of Vietnamese veteran pilots and Trà Văn Kiếm's family, Randall Cunningham realized his wish. He visited pilot Trà Văn Kiếm's family to whom he offered a banner tribute: "Trà Văn Kiếm fought for his country with honor and skill. I honor him as I do friends I lost." A lot of Vietnamese and U.S. media coverage considered the visit by Cunningham to Trà Văn Kiếm's tombstone in Khánh Hòa Province as a manifestation of the policy to "put aside the past and together build the future" for Vietnam–U.S. relations.

IN THE NORTHEAST SECTOR

On 10 May, the commanding officer on duty at the 927th FR's command post was regiment commander Nguyễn Hồng Nhị. At 0953 hours, the 927th FR had ordered a flight consisting of Nguyễn Đức Soát, Ngô Duy Thư, Nguyễn Văn Nghĩa, and Hạ Vĩnh Thành to take off from Nội Bài and fly up to Đại Từ to protect the airfield, but the flight did not encounter any enemy aircraft so the flight turned back and landed safely.

When the radar network picked up a group of twenty-four aircraft that was approaching from east of Thanh Hóa, the MiG-21 flight flown by Lê Thanh Đạo and Vũ Văn Hợp was ordered to take off at 1257 hours and flew on a heading of 360 degrees at an altitude of 6,500 feet. When they were informed that an enemy target was heading toward them at a range of twenty miles and 30 degrees to their left front, Lê Thanh Đạo gave the order to drop external fuel tanks and to visually look for the enemy. Right after this order was given, both MiG pilots spotted the target heading straight toward them at an altitude of 16,000 feet. The pilots had studied and had a firm grasp of the new tactic being used by the F-4s, which was that the enemy's two-aircraft section would split up, with one aircraft going high and the other going low. The two aircraft would fly in a weave, back and forth, to force the MiGs to split up also. With a firm understanding of the enemy's trick, Lê Thanh Đạo still decided to seize this opportunity to pursue the F-4 No. 1 and ordered his wingman to attack the F-4 No. 2. Vũ Văn Hợp turned hard and got on the tail of the F-4 No. 2. When the range to the target was 1.1 miles, his speed was 745 mph, and when he had a good audible signal from the missile's heat-seeker, he fired an R-3S missile. He saw that the missile seemed to be heading a bit off to the right of the target, so he again stabilized his sight to fire a second missile. However, at that instant he saw that the F-4 No. 2 was on fire. He shouted loudly, "He's burning!" He then broke off by making a turn to the left and landed safely at Kép airfield at 1318 hours.

Hearing his No. 2 shout, "He's burning," Lê Thanh Đạo looked over and saw that the F-4 No. 2 had indeed been hit by his wingman's missile. He immediately increased speed to pursue the F-4 No. 1. Just after the F-4 had leveled his wings, he quickly stabilized his sight picture and fired his first missile at a speed of 680–745 mph, and a range of 0.9 miles. Just as what had happened with his wingman, when he saw that his first missile seemed to be heading slightly off course to the right, he decided to again get a stable sight picture on the target to fire his second missile. However, he then saw that the F-4 No. 1 was on fire. Lê Thanh Đạo reported, "He's burning" and quickly dove to a low altitude, then flew back and landed safely at Kép airfield at 1318 hours.

In summary, during the ferocious air engagements fought on 10 May 1972, the VNPAF shot down a total of six U.S. aircraft (MiG-21s shot down four U.S. aircrafts and MiG-19s shot down two more). Meanwhile, the VNPAF lost six aircraft: two MiG-21s (flown by Nguyễn Văn Ngãi and Cao Sơn Khảo), three MiG-17s (flown by Nguyễn Văn Thọ, Đỗ Hạng, and Trà Văn Kiếm), and one MiG-19 (flown by Lê Đức Oánh), and five VNPAF pilots were killed.[23]

On the night of 10 May 1972 Minister of National Defense General Võ Nguyên Giáp was personally briefed by the AF commander Đào Đình Luyện on the long, savage air battles fought on 10 May 1972. General Võ Nguyên Giáp praised the courage and intelligence of MiG pilots and provided the following words of guidance: "Our Air Force personnel should continue to attack aggressively, using secrecy and surprise to fight battles in which victory is certain, and we must counter the incorrect new concept of 'one for one' exchanges, a concept that needs to be immediately rejected."[24]

This was the end of a day that U.S. publications called "one day in a long war." In addition, in December 2007 the History Channel on U.S. television broadcast an episode on the air battles of 10 May 1972 as part of the *Dogfights* documentary that was entitled "The Bloodiest Day".

ASSESSMENTS AND ANALYSIS

The date of 10 May 1972 went down in the history of the Vietnam air war as the day when, according to Vietnamese statistics, MiGs flew the greatest number of sorties. There was a total of twenty-two separate flights including sixty-four MiG sorties, with six of the flights engaging in combat against U.S. aircraft. The Vietnamese aircraft involved included three different types of fighters from four FRs (thirty-eight MiG-17 sorties, eight MiG-19 sorties, and eighteen MiG-21 sorties). From the USAF and USN records, more than 414 air combat sorties were recorded. This was the day with the greatest number of air engagements over the skies of North Vietnam. That day also recorded the greatest number of downed and damaged aircraft from both sides. MiG-17 pilots ran into trouble, failed to shoot down any American aircraft, and suffered heavy losses.

Meanwhile, a number of American authors state that on 10 May 1972, U.S. pilots shot down eleven MiGs (seven MiG-17s and four MiG-21s). The

American side acknowledges that ten aircraft were hit on 10 May (seven F-4s, one A-6, one RA-5C, and one RF-4C), but they said only four of these aircraft crashed and that the other aircraft were only damaged.[25]

After reviewing archived Vietnamese documents and interviewing VNPAF pilots who personally participated in the battles on that day, it turns out that in actuality only four MiG-17s actually fought against American aircraft. None of the thirty-four other MiG-17 sorties flown that day encountered American aircraft and all of these aircraft returned and landed safely. The Vietnamese side acknowledges that three MiG-17s were shot down and the other MiG-17 involved (pilot Tạ Đông Trung, No. 2) returned and landed safely. Therefore there is no basis for the U.S. pilots to claim to have shot down a total of seven MiG-17s. The American pilots also claimed to have shot down four MiG-21s, but on that day four of the six MiG-21s that took off and engaged in combat returned and landed safely. On the other hand, the Americans do not list any MiG-19s shot down, but the 925th FR's records acknowledge that one MiG-19 (flown by Lê Đức Oánh) was shot down.

As mentioned above, three MiG-17s were shot down, but beside Lieutenant Cunningham's claims, in this engagement three more U.S. F-4 crews claimed to have downed MiG-17s. On this list, Lt. Matthew J. Connelly and Lt. Thomas J. J. Blonski claimed to have shot down two MiG-17s, and two other F-4 crews (Lt. Steven S. Shoemaker and Lt. (jg) Keith V. Crenshaw, of VF-96 from the USS *Constellation*, and Lt. Kenneth L. Cannon and Lt. Roy A. Morris, of VF-51 from the USS *Coral Sea*) each reported shooting down one MiG-17.[26]

If Lieutenant Cunningham had shot down three MiG-17s, then no more MiG-17s would have been shot down by any other F-4 crews. Conversely, if one or two MiG-17s were shot down on 10 May 1972 by other F-4 crews, his score of shooting down three MiGs on that day would be called into question.

11 May 1972: Who Shot Down Gopher 01?

After the most savage and longest battle in the history of the air war over North Vietnam, in which both sides had flown a very large number of sorties, the AF HQ predicted that on 11 May 1972 the USAF might again continue to attack important targets deep inside North Vietnam, including the possibility of using B-52s to bomb targets in the southern part of Nghệ An

Province. Although on that morning the skies over North Vietnam were very quiet, during the afternoon something changed. While scanning the skies at 1437 hours, the 26th Radar Company picked up a large number of enemy aircraft approaching from the direction of Sầm Tơ. The group of U.S. aircraft included twenty-six attackers assigned to attack Bạch Mai airfield, four fighters assigned to escort the strike formation, and eight aircraft assigned to suppress VNPAF air operations at Đa Phúc and Hòa Lạc airfields. Having analyzed the situation, Lieutenant Colonel Đào Đình Luyện decided to order two flights of MiG-21s (a total of four aircraft) to take off, and ordered the pilots to use the tactic of "flying out at a low altitude, then climbing high and attacking" to intercept the enemy formation.

The 927th FR's first MiG-21 flight would fly at a low altitude toward the area south of Hanoi to intercept U.S. aircraft approaching from the south. The second flight would take off and fly toward Tuyên Quang–Vạn Yên, both as a diversion and to be ready to intercept and attack enemy strike aircraft attacking Hòa Lạc airfield. The first flight, piloted by Ngô Văn Phú and Ngô Duy Thư, was ordered to take off from Đa Phúc airfield at 1446 hours and then make a right turn to fly south of Hanoi at an altitude of 1,600 feet. Under the direction of GCI, the two MiG-21s were flying on a heading of 210 degrees at an altitude of 25,000 feet and had increased speed to 560 mph to pursue a group of F-4s flying toward Mai Châu–Hòa Bình. When the F-4s were flying over Route 15, the MiG flight changed course 30 degrees to close on the target. At 1457 hours Ngô Duy Thư spotted the target and requested permission to attack. No. 1 shouted, "Attack. It looks good." MiG No. 2 decided to attack the aircraft on the right-hand side.

At the same time, the MiG lead Ngô Văn Phú called out, "You attack the aircraft on the right and I will attack the aircraft on the left." In fact, however, the two pilots were attacking two different enemy flights. Ngô Duy Thư made a hard turn to chase one F-105. When he had closed in on the target, had a stable sight picture, and a good audible sound from his missile's heat-seeker, he fired his R-3S missile at a range of 0.54 miles and it flew straight into the tail of the F-105. Ngô Duy Thư shouted that he had hit the target. The F-105G that was hit by Ngô Duy Thư was flying in the No. 4 position in a flight of four aircraft from the USAF 17th TFS/388th TFW. The flight was assigned to suppress SAMs. The crew of this aircraft, Maj. William Hansen

Talley and Maj. James Phillip Padgett, both ejected and were captured. Because the four F-105s were concentrating on SAM sites, they did not realize that they were being attacked by MiGs.

Meanwhile Ngô Văn Phú turned left to sweep and attack the aircraft on the left. When he got closer, however, he saw that in fact what he was attacking was a flight of F-4 escort fighters flying right behind the formation of F-105 bombers. He was preparing to pursue the F-4s when he saw a single F-4 in front of him; he then quickly got on its tail. As he was chasing the target and had closed to a range of 1.2 miles, he heard his No. 2 Ngô Duy Thư shout that he had hit a U.S. aircraft. Ngô Văn Phú quickly stabilized his sight picture and fired a missile. When he saw that the missile had exploded to the left of the F-4, he continued to stick with the target and fired a second missile. Because he was so close to the target, he was not able to watch as the warhead detonated. The F-4D that his missile hit was being flown by Lt. Col. Joseph W. Kittinger and 1st Lt. William J. Reich of the 555th TFS/432nd TRW, based at Udorn, Thailand, and assigned to escort the strike group. The aircraft was shot down ten miles from Thái Nguyên. Both pilots ejected and were captured.[27]

Only a few seconds after making his breaking-off maneuver, Ngô Văn Phú felt his aircraft shake hard and become uncontrollable. He decided to eject. In fact, what had happened with the MiG and F-4 pilots at that moment was a very special and unusual situation. While the flight of F-4Ds (call sign Gopher) was performing the MiGCAP mission, the No. 1 and No. 2 pilots of this F-4 flight spotted a single MiG-21. The F-4 No. 1 immediately increased speed in order to make a visual identification. He then shouted for the F-4 No. 2 to attack. Because the F-4 No. 1 was flying so fast, it shot out in front of the MiG. Ngô Văn Phú wasted no time and seized the opportunity by getting on the F-4's tail, quickly centering his sight on the F-4, and firing the missile that shot down the Gopher 01's aircraft. Meanwhile, the F-4 No. 2 had locked his radar on the MiG No. 1 and fired an AIM-7 missile at Ngô Văn Phú's MiG. Only a few seconds after the pilot of the F-4D Gopher 02 launched his missile, he saw another missile hit the wing of the F-4 No. 1 (Gopher 01), which then went down and crashed on the spot. The scene of Gopher 01 being shot down upset the pilot of Gopher 02 so much that he did not think to check the results of his own attack.

Initially, perhaps the 555th TFS thought that it was very possible that Gopher 01 had been shot down by an AIM-7 fired by another F-4. However, some years later, based on information from both sides and on the statements made by U.S. POW pilots after they were released, they were able to reconstruct the entire sequence of this air battle and assumed that Lieutenant Colonel Kittinger's F-4 No. 1 was shot down by MiG No. 1 Ngô Văn Phú, after which the MiG was hit by a missile fired by the F-4 No. 2, which was flown by Capt. S. E. Nichols and 1st Lt. James R. Bell. Ngô Văn Phú ejected and landed safely back on the ground. Lt. Col. Joseph Kittinger was already a living legend of the USAF. He had served three tours in the Vietnam War and had flown a total of 485 missions before he was shot down. The details of the reconstructed picture of engagement match the description given in the combat log of the 927th FR and in the books of some U.S. authors.[28]

18 May 1972: An Active MiG Day

After the savage attack by the USAF aircraft on Việt Trì Bridge and targets along Route 2, the AF HQ predicted that on 18 May 1972 it was likely that the Americans would continue their attacks by bombing targets along Route 1 North and attacking Kép airfield in order to suppress the air operations of MiGs. The AF HQ issued an air combat plan to use three different types of fighter aircraft assigned to three FRs to intercept and attack the large U.S. strike groups. The 925th FR would fly a total of ten MiG-19 sorties, the 923rd FR would fly twelve MiG-17 sorties, and the 927th FR would fly four MiG-21 sorties. The weather in the battle area was good, with 30 percent cumulus cloud cover at an altitude of 1,600 feet. Visibility was more than 32,000 feet.

After receiving reports from the B-1 network that, sometime around noon, the U.S. aircraft would fly in from the direction of Mường Xén, the AF Command ordered radar stations (of the 26th, 42nd, and 53rd Radar Companies) to switch on their radar transmitters. At 1139 hours radar station C-42 picked up many aircraft six miles east of Uông Bí. Five minutes later the radar network picked up many more U.S. aircraft approaching from southeast of Thái Bình and headed toward Hòn Gai–Cẩm Phả.

MiG-17 ACTIONS

Soon after detecting the U.S. aircraft flying from the direction of Long Châu Island toward Cẩm Phả and by Yên Tử Mountain, the AF command post

ordered the flights of MiG-17s and MiG-19s to take off. At 1152 hours a
two-aircraft section of MiG-17s flown by Hán Vĩnh Tưởng and Nguyễn Văn
Điển took off. A few minutes later, Hán Vĩnh Tưởng saw two pairs of F-4s 80
degrees to his left. One pair of F-4s was out ahead and at a lower altitude
while the second pair maintained a higher altitude behind the first pair. When
Hán Vĩnh Tưởng saw the two leading F-4s begin a dive, he decided to drop
external fuel tanks and chase this pair of enemy aircraft. When the two F-4s
suddenly pulled up into a climb, he decided that he would aim at the F-4
No. 2 and told Nguyễn Văn Điển to aim at the F-4 No. 1. Hán Vĩnh Tưởng
made a tight turn and accelerated to pursue the F-4. At a firing angle of about
30 degrees he squeezed his trigger, but his shells missed, falling behind the
tail of the enemy aircraft. He continued his pursuit and fired a second burst,
but his shells again missed to the rear. He then decided to increase the lead
angle on his sight and then fired a third burst. Seeing that his shells hit the
nose of the F-4, he quickly broke off. The alternate ground control command station saw the F-4 crash right near the western end of the airfield.
Hán Vĩnh Tưởng then flew back and landed safely at Đa Phúc airfield.

A HARD DAY FOR MiG-19s

The flight of four MiG-19s with Phạm Ngọc Tâm, Nguyễn Thăng Long,
Nguyễn Hồng Sơn (A), and Vũ Viết Tản was ordered to take off from Đa
Phúc airfield at 1155 hours, flew one complete circuit over the airfield, and
then flew to the battle area in the Phả Lại–Lục Nam area. Immediately afterward, MiG No. 3 and No. 4 spotted two F-4s flying from Hanoi up toward
the Tam Đảo mountains. The pilots decided not to engage these aircraft and
continued on their way. When they reached Bắc Giang they spotted two
F-4s on a bearing of 20 degrees, range three miles. The MiG flight dropped
their external fuel tanks, switched on afterburners, and charged forward to
attack. At 1203 hours Phạm Ngọc Tâm, covered by his wingman, turned inside
and got on the tail of the F-4 No. 2, then fired two bursts from his guns at
a range of 0.3–0.4 miles, but he missed. He then continued to close the range,
and at a range of 0.3 miles he fired a third burst that hit the top of the F-4's
fuselage. The other pilots in the MiG-19 flight all saw the U.S. aircrew's parachutes open when they ejected. The F-4D that Phạm Ngọc Tâm shot down
was flown by 1st Lt. Wesley Dallas Ratzel and 1st Lt. Jonathan Bruce Bed-
narek of the 421st TFS/366th TFW.[29] The four MiG-19s then flew to Đa Phúc
airfield and landed there safely.

By 1630 hours, when two F-4Bs assigned to MiGCAP duty were approaching Kép airfield, they spotted two MiG-19s (Phạm Ngọc Tâm and Nguyễn Thăng Long) flying toward the airfield. The two F-4s split up. One of the F-4s swept in to attack the two MiG-19s while the other F-4 stayed back at a higher altitude to maintain an altitude advantage. The two MiG-19s immediately turned back to counterattack. The two sides turned and fought but neither side was able to get into position to make an attack. After a few circles and maneuvers, the two MiG-19s gradually gained superiority in maneuvers on the horizontal plane. Seeing this, the F-4 No. 2, still waiting at a higher altitude, jumped into the fray. A ferocious air battle was fought in the skies over Kép airfield. Realizing that to continue the dogfight would not be to their advantage, the two MiG-19s leveled off and flew straight. The two F-4s immediately fired AIM-9G missiles at the two MiG-19s. Both MiG-19s were hit and both pilots ejected and parachuted safely to the ground. The two F-4Bs that attacked the MiG-19s most likely were from VF-161 of USS *Midway*.

WITH THE 927TH FR

The flight of MiG-21s flown by Nguyễn Ngọc Hưng and Mai Văn Tuế was ordered to take off from Đa Phúc airfield at 1212 hours and flew out to circle over Kép airfield. When the MiG-21s reached north of Thái Nguyên the GCI informed them that there was an enemy target in front of them and directed them to change course to a heading of 60 degrees. A few minutes later, when both MiG pilots spotted two F-4s to their left and below them, the MiG lead gave the order to drop their external fuel tanks and switch on afterburners in order to attack. At that moment, however, he spotted two more F-4s behind them. Not wanting to miss an opportunity to attack, he ordered his No. 2 to attack the two aircraft in front of them while he turned back to counterattack the two enemy aircraft behind them. When the F-4s saw the MiGs, they used the routine tactic of splitting up. Seeing that the F-4 No. 4 was continuing to turn to the right, the MiG lead quickly rolled his aircraft over, made a hard right turn, and pursued the F-4 No. 4. After he had closed in and had a stable sight picture, he pressed the button to fire his R-3S missile, which flew straight into the F-4 and exploded. Nguyễn Ngọc Hưng made a hard turn to the right to break away then landed safely at Đa Phúc at 1235 hours.

On 18 May 1972, the VNPAF flew twenty-six sorties and fought eight separate air engagements. All three types of fighters shot down enemy aircraft.

Air Engagements on 20 May 1972

After moving the base of operations from Thọ Xuân airfield back to Đa Phúc airfield, the 921st FR command post reviewed its recent operations and drew up new battle plans. This time they employed the tactic of using flights of MiG-21s to fly out at low altitudes, and when the American aircraft crossed the border, to unexpectedly appear in the area west of Thọ Xuân by suddenly climbing to high altitudes and attacking them.

Around noon, the 921st FR's radar network detected a group of twelve enemy aircraft flying past Vụ Bản. The 921st FR's flight of two MiG-21s, flown by Lương Thế Phúc and Đỗ Văn Lanh, was ordered to take off and then turn left to fly down east of Gia Lâm airfield, and then was directed to follow Route 1 down to a point south of Phủ Lý. As the flight was approaching Phủ Lý, the command post ordered the flight to attack the group of twelve enemy aircraft that was then flying from Suối Rút toward Việt Trì.

At 1157 hours, Lương Thế Phúc spotted two F-4s 60 degrees to the left at a range of nine miles. The two F-4s were flying in an extended formation, one behind the other, and were constantly weaving back and forth. The MiG No. 1 repeatedly tried to close in to attack but was not able to do so because the two F-4s were making such hard turns and violent maneuvers. The command post ordered No. 1 to return, and he landed at 1210 hours.

Seeing two F-4s behind them firing missiles, Đỗ Văn Lanh gave a timely warning to his lead, then he pursued a single F-4 in front of him. By reducing the range to the target to 0.9 miles, at a speed of 680 mph and with a stable sight picture he fired his first missile, then made a hard turn to the left to break away and therefore did not see the missile warhead detonate. All that he saw was the F-4 turning to the right and diving toward the ground very quickly. After breaking off this engagement, he saw two F-4s chasing his lead to try to fire missiles at him. He shouted a warning to No. 1 to take evasive action and then quickly got on the tail of the two F-4s that had just fired missiles at MiG No. 1. At a speed of 680 mph and at a range of 0.9 miles, he fired his second missile. Đỗ Văn Lanh broke off by turning to the left, turned to a heading of 360 degrees, descended to low altitudes, and landed at 1215 hours.

According to some American authors,[30] as well as the 921st FR combat reports, the F-4D that was hit by First Lieutenant Đỗ Văn Lanh's first missile was flown by 1st Lt. John D. Markle and Capt. James W. Williams of the 555th TFS/432nd TRW. Pilot John D. Markle ejected and was rescued but James W. Williams was captured. By the time he was shot down, Captain Williams had flown a total of 228 missions.

In October 2019, Captain Williams visited Hanoi and wished to meet his opponent. But unfortunately, MiG pilot Đỗ Văn Lanh, whom he had encountered more than forty years earlier, had died in a training flight in 1980.

23 May 1972: A Day of Coordinated Battles

When studying the information received from the B-1 networks and on reviewing the activities of the USAF and USN during the early morning hours, the AF command post (headed by deputy AF commander Trần Hanh) anticipated that on 23 May 1972 the USAF would probably mount even larger air strikes against targets along Route 1 North and Route 2, while the USN would continue to attack Hải Phòng, Kiến An, Thái Bình, Nam Định, and Ninh Bình. At 0810 hours twenty USN attackers flew in to attack Uông Bí, Hòn Gai, the Cọc 6 Coal Mine, Nam Định, and Phủ Lý. To support the strike formation, twenty USN fighters flew in to suppress MiG activity by circling in the skies over Phủ Lý, Nho Quan, Vụ Bản, and Ninh Giang in Hưng Yên.

When one group of the U.S. aircraft was detected turning toward the mouth of the Đáy River and flying up to Nho Quan and another group was detected heading for Phủ Lý, the 927th FR command post ordered a flight consisting of Nguyễn Đức Soát and Ngô Duy Thư to take off from Gia Lâm airfield at 1154 hours. The pilots climbed to an altitude of 1,000 feet and flew on a heading of 140 degrees, then the pilots were informed that the target was nine miles in front of them. Nguyễn Đức Soát ordered his flight to drop external fuel tanks, switch to afterburners, and climb to an altitude of 32,000 feet. To deal with U.S. fighters when Vietnamese radars were not able to detect them, the two MiG pilots initiated a weave tactic, a tactic that American fighters very frequently used.

After flying one complete circuit using the weave tactic, Nguyễn Đức Soát spotted a target 30 degrees to the right at a range of four to five miles. He quickly informed his No. 2 and simultaneously turned and got on the target's tail. After adjusting his sight properly, when the range was 1.1 miles he fired his first missile. After pulling up into a climb to watch the results and after failing to see his missile's warhead detonate, he decided to switch on his afterburner and dive back down to attack again. He adjusted his sight and when the range was 1.1 miles he fired his second missile then quickly pulled up into a climb and rolled his aircraft over to watch. He and Ngô Duy Thư both saw the A-7 explode in the bright mid-day May sunshine. The two MiG pilots were ordered to break off the engagement, turn to a heading of 340 degrees, descend to a low altitude of 750 feet, and land at Gia Lâm airfield at 1215 hours.

The A-7 that was shot down by Nguyễn Đức Soát was flown by Cdr. Charles Edward Barnett of VA-93 off the USS *Midway*.[31] This aircraft crashed fifteen miles northeast of Nam Định and the pilot was listed as KIA. Commander Barnett had been shot down once before, on 13 December 1966, but on that occasion he was rescued.

Early in the afternoon, a flight of four MiG-19s flown by Hoàng Cao Bổng, Vũ Chính Nghị, Nguyễn Hồng Sơn (A), and Phạm Hùng Sơn was ordered to take off. After passing Phả Lại the flight split into two two-aircraft sections. When the flight was making its second circuit over the airfield, the two MiGs of the second section spotted two F-4s 60 degrees to their right. The command post ordered the flight to drop external fuel tanks, switch on afterburners, and pursue these aircraft. The F-4s, which were approaching from the east, fired missiles at the MiG formation. Reacting to an order from the alternate command post to take immediate evasive action, No. 1 turned hard to avoid the missiles. At this time the alternate ground control command post shouted to MiG No. 2, "Turn hard!" but no response to this order was heard from MiG No. 2. Realizing that his aircraft had been damaged and that it was no longer controllable, MiG No. 2 requested permission to eject and landed safely on the ground in the west end of Kép airfield.

When he spotted the two F-4s, Nguyễn Hồng Sơn (A) turned hard to attack. He fired his first burst at an altitude of 3,000 feet but he missed. The F-4 dove and Nguyễn Hồng Sơn (A) continued to chase it and fired two more bursts. He saw the F-4 flip over and dive into the ground east of Kép airfield. He pulled his stick hard to break off the engagement, returned to the airfield, and landed.

Meanwhile, MiG No. 4 saw two F-4s flying past, traveling south to north over the airfield, and he also decided to turn in to attack. His first burst missed and he continued to chase the target. After stabilizing his sight, he fired a long burst and saw his shells hitting the fuselage of one F-4, causing it to nose over into a dive, begin trailing smoke, and turn to flee toward the east. He shouted, "He's burning!" The regiment's command post ordered the flight to break off the engagement and return to land at Gia Lâm airfield at 1407 hours.

AN UNSUCCESSFUL DAY FOR THE 923RD FR

During the afternoon, a large number of USN aircraft flew in from the sea to attack targets in the areas of Kiến An, Hải Phòng, and Route 1 North. A 923rd FR flight consisting of Vũ Văn Đang, Nguyễn Văn Điển, Nguyễn Văn Lâm, and Nguyễn Công Ngũ took off from Kép airfield at 1635 hours, turned right, and climbed to an altitude of 1,640 feet. When it was seen that the American aircraft seemed to be targeting the four MiGs, the flight dropped external fuel tanks, switched on afterburners, and turned to counterattack the F-4s. The flight of MiG-17s fought a ferocious dogfight against the USN F-4s. During the air battle, MiG-17s No. 1 and No. 2 each shot down one F-4. MiG-17 No. 2 tried to stay on the tail of another F-4 that was in a vertical climb (apparently the F-4 pilot was using the "Feather Duster" tactic). However, he could not maintain the climb and went into a downward spin. Before he could pull out, because his dive angle was so steep, the aircraft hit the ground and the pilot was killed.

After making many circles and launching many missiles, the pilot of the F-4, who had received Top Gun training, decided to suddenly switch off his afterburner and reduce speed, which caused the MiG-17s to shoot right past him. He seized this opportunity to launch an AIM-9 missile at MiG-17 No. 1, which had just leveled his wings before making a turn in the other direction. The MiG-17 was hit by the missile and its pilot, Vũ Văn Đang ejected, but his attempt to parachute was unsuccessful and he died. The F-4B that pursued and attacked the two MiG-17s was flown by Lt. Cdr. Ronald E. McKeown and Lt. John C. "Jack" Ensch of VF-161, from the USS *Midway*.[32]

In this battle, even though the MiG-17s accomplished their mission of disrupting the attack by the American bombers, the flight suffered heavy losses. The VPNAF's records show that on that day only two MiG-17s and one MiG-19 were lost during the air engagement (the third MiG-17 was a loss by air accident); no MiG-21s were lost.[33]

In the VN-U.S. veteran pilots' meeting in Hanoi on April 2016, Col. Jack Ensch and MiG-17 pilot Nguyễn Văn Lâm met each other and talked about that very ferocious air battle.

Air Engagement on 31 May 1972

After several days of bad weather over North Vietnam, the B-1 network reported that on 31 May 1972 the USAF would probably use forty aircraft to attack road traffic targets along Route 1 North and Route 3. The USN would continue to conduct attacks from Thanh Hóa southward in MZ4. The ratio of fighter cover and escorts would be two-to-one (two fighters for every bomber), and the fighters would establish three holding areas over Sơn Động–Lục Nam, over Bắc Ninh–Phả Lại, and over Thái Nguyên–Nhã Nam.

Responding to this situation, the 927th FR was ordered to prepare to engage the enemy in all three attack sectors. The first 927th FR flight, with Nguyễn Văn Lung and Mai Văn Tuế, was ordered to take off at 1517 hours then was ordered to fly on a heading of 110 degrees to Hải Dương, after which the flight was ordered to climb to 22,000 feet and turn to a 60-degree heading. At that moment No. 2 spotted four F-4s 20 degrees to the right at a range of six to seven miles. Nguyễn Văn Lung was not able to spot the targets so he shouted for No. 2 to make the attack. Mai Văn Tuế saw eight F-4s firing a number of missiles at the MiGs. He shouted a warning to his No. 1, but he heard no reply. When he swept in to make his attack, the flight of twelve F-4s made a hard turn to meet his aircraft head-on. Realizing that the situation was not in his favor, he requested permission to break off the engagement and flew back to land safely at Đa Phúc airfield at 1536 hours.

Realizing that he had an F-4 right on his tail, Nguyễn Văn Lung switched on his afterburner and pulled his stick over into a hard climbing turn, but he was too late. The F-4 had fired a volley of four AIM-7E-2s missiles (during this period, because the AIM-7 missiles were so ineffective, American pilots had to fire four missiles all at once in order to ensure a hit). The first three missiles missed the target, but the fourth missile hit the MiG-21's cockpit, destroying the entire nose section of the aircraft, and pilot Nguyễn Văn Lung was listed as killed in action. Based on the information from the ground control command post and from a number of U.S. documents, it is most likely that the F-4D flown by Capt. Richard S. Ritchie and 1st Lt. Lawrence H. Pettit of the 555th TFS/432nd TRW was the aircraft that was on the tail of the MiG No. 1.[34]

On that same day, 31 May, an F-4 that was flying a MiGCAP mission, piloted by Capt. Bruce G. Leonard and Capt. Jeffrey S. Feinstein of the 13th TFS/432nd TRW, was reported to have fired an AIM-9 missile that hit a MiG. The pilot did not actually see the warhead detonate. However, the success of this flight crew was confirmed by other sources.

However, the combat log of the 927th FR reveals that four MiG-21s took off to fly missions on 31 May 1972 but that Lieutenant Nguyễn Văn Lung was the only one who crashed. The other three MiG pilots returned and landed safely.

Air Engagement on 1 June 1972

On 1 June a flight of two MiG-21 PFM aircraft from the 921st FR was assigned to stand on combat alert duty. The weather that day, both at the airfield and in the battle area, was relatively good.

Two MiG-21s, flown by Phạm Phú Thái and Nguyễn Công Huy, took off at 0930 hours and turned left to a heading of 360 degrees. As they reached Sơn Dương, the command post ordered them to climb to 22,000 feet and turn to a heading of 150 degrees. Just after the pilots had leveled off on their new course and altitude, the MiG lead spotted a flight of four F-4s 40 degrees to his right at a range of eight to nine miles. The F-4s were divided into two two-aircraft sections separated from one another by 2 to 2.5 miles. In addition to the F-4s assigned to attack ground targets, some flights were also assigned to help the search and rescue effort to recover Capt. Roger Locher, who had been shot down by a MiG-19 on 10 May 1972. When the F-4s spotted the MiGs, the two lead aircraft switched on their afterburners and pulled up into a climb while the other two aircraft dove to a lower altitude.

Based on his combat experience and after a quick assessment of the situation, MiG No. 1 decided to pursue the two aircraft that were diving. Two MiG pilots rolled their aircraft upside down and dove from their altitude of

22,000 feet down to an altitude of 6,500 feet. Phạm Phú Thái then selected the F-4 No. 3 as his target. He placed his target designator on the F-4, and at a range of 0.9–1.1 miles he pressed the button to fire the missile under his right wing and then turned immediately to break away. He saw the missile explode close to the tail of the F-4.

Phạm Phú Thái decided to pursue the F-4 to fire a second missile, but then he felt his aircraft shake hard twice. He immediately pulled away. Looking at the front of his aircraft, he saw that his pitot tube had broken into two parts. The pitot tube may have broken because his breakaway maneuver after firing his missile had been too violent (a 9.5 G turn). He decided to break off the engagement, left the battle area, returned to the airfield, and landed safely at Đa Phúc airfield.

Based on the details of the air battle, Phạm Phú Thái's missile hit and brought down the F-4 flown by Capt. G. W. Hawks and Capt. David B. Dingee of the 308th TFS/31st TFW, while it was carrying out a RESCAP mission near Yên Bái airfield. The two U.S. pilots ejected and both were rescued.[35]

Air Engagements on 2 June 1972

On 2 June, the USAF and USN sent a large number of aircraft to attack traffic targets along Route 1 North and to suppress air operations from Kép airfield. The AF HQ issued combat mission orders to the 921st and 925th FRs to conduct coordinated combat operations to intercept the approaching bomber strike groups. The battle plan was either to take off, fly up to Phả Lại, and fight the enemy along the way back to Đáp Cầu, or to fly to Lục Nam and then turn and fight the enemy on the way to Kép airfield.

Two MiG-21s from the 921st FR, flown by Nguyễn Công Huy and Bùi Thanh Liem, took off at 1150 hours and flew toward Nhã Nam. The MiGs encountered a flight of four USN F-4s. However, after making three complete circles in this turning dogfight, Nguyễn Công Huy decided that to continue this engagement would not be to the flight's benefit, and he requested permission to break off the engagement.

After taking off from Yên Bái airfield, the four MiG-19s, flown by Phan Trọng Vân, Phùng Văn Quảng, Nguyễn Hồng Sơn (A), and Phạm Hùng Sơn, flew toward Đông Anh with the assigned mission of defending the Đông Anh electrical transformer station. When flying past Bắc Giang, just as the flight penetrated through the top of the clouds (there was 70 percent cumulus cloud cover) and before the pilots had time to get back into combat formation, two F-4s swept in at them and began firing missiles, one after another. The MiG No. 4 pilot saw a missile fired by the F-4s heading for the MiG-19s and shouted, "Turn left hard!" However, Phan Trọng Vân did not have time to react and his aircraft was hit by the missile. The aircraft crashed four miles west of Kép airfield, and Senior Lieutenant Phan Trọng Vân was killed.

The three remaining MiG-19s stuck together in a ferocious dogfight against the F-4s, after which the three MiGs were ordered to break off the engagement and landed at Gia Lâm airfield.

8 June 1972: Dealing with Reconnaissance Aircraft

After analyzing and studying the operations pattern of the United States' reconnaissance aircraft, the GCI officers of the AF HQ worked out the operational pattern employed by the enemy's RF-4 armed reconnaissance aircraft. After a period of time during which MiGs suspended efforts to hunt down the enemy's reconnaissance aircraft, the Americans may have become careless and overconfident. Operating under that presumption, the AF HQ ordered MiG-21s to prepare plans to attack the enemy armed reconnaissance aircraft in all different sectors.

Following the USAF tactical plan, the reconnaissance aircraft would fly in two hours ahead of the air strikes. Then fighters would come in, flying the same flight path as that used by the attacking aircraft but at low altitudes and seven to ten minutes ahead of the bombers, in order to suppress MiGs. At 1203 hours the 927th FR's commander, Nguyễn Hồng Nhị, ordered Nguyễn Đức Soát and Nguyễn Thanh Xuân to take off and directed them to fly on a heading of 240 degrees, altitude 1,600 feet, speed 560 mph. The pilots were informed that the target was nine miles in front of them. When the MiGs climbed to 6,500 feet, Nguyễn Đức Soát decided to continue their climb up to an altitude of 19,000 feet, higher than the target. Under the instruction of the command post, MiG No. 1 spotted two aircraft 40 degrees to the left at a range of ten miles. He informed his No. 2 and ordered him to attack the F-4 No. 1 while he attacked the F-4 No. 2.

When approaching the range of 0.7 miles, Nguyễn Đức Soát stabilized his target designator and fired the missile under his left wing. He looked out but did not see the missile explode. He pulled up into a climb, looked around, and saw two other F-4s diving. He then decided to attack the F-4 No. 2 in this section. When the range was 0.7 miles and he was preparing to stabilize his target designator to fire a second missile, he saw a missile fired from behind him flashing pass at the American aircraft. The missile exploded to the right and above the enemy aircraft. At that moment he saw his wingman Nguyễn Thanh Xuân flash past him and move out in front of his aircraft. He called No. 2 to tell him to pay attention to his speed, then gave the order to break off the engagement and return to land at Đa Phúc airfield at 1223 hours.

Meanwhile, young pilot Nguyễn Thanh Xuân decided to push ahead to attack the F-4 No. 1, as he had been ordered. At an altitude of 10,000 feet, as the F-4 was in a climb, he stabilized his target designator and pressed his missile-firing button. He then pulled into a climb to break away and was not able to see where the missile detonated. At that moment he saw an enemy aircraft climbing at an appropriate range for an attack. He decided to chase this target. When the range was down to 0.4–0.5 miles, he fired his second missile. After firing this missile, he felt his aircraft shake hard and the aircraft became difficult to control. Realizing that his aircraft was beginning to stall, he quickly rolled over and dove to gain speed. When he was down to an altitude of 600 feet he leveled off and flew back to Nội Bài airfield, where he landed at 1223 hours.

The result of that engagement was that young pilot Nguyễn Thanh Xuân in his first combat mission shot down one RF-4 reconnaissance aircraft.

11 June 1972: A Hard Day for MiG-19s

Information from the B-1 network reported that on 11 June 1972 the USAF strike groups would fly in from the west through the Nghĩa Lộ–Tuyên Quang sector, while the USN would attack from the direction of the Thái Bình rivermouth, and they would attack the Yên Phụ electrical power plant and targets southwest of Hanoi. The AF HQ ordered the 925th FR to have four MiG-19s take off to defend targets in the Hanoi area.

The flight of MiG-19s, consisting of Nguyễn Hồng Sơn (A), Phạm Hùng Sơn, Nguyễn Văn Phúc, and Nguyễn Hùng Sơn (B), took off at 1010 hours and climbed to an altitude of 3,200 feet. When the flight was passing Vân Đình, the pilots were informed that the target was in front of them at a range of eighteen miles. Three minutes later Nguyễn Hồng Sơn (A) spotted a target to the right front. He ordered the flight to make a hard turn to chase the target, but the two U.S. aircraft increased speed and escaped. At that moment, Nguyễn Hồng Sơn (A) spotted a line of smoke heading toward the MiG flight. He called MiG No. 3 and No. 4 but received no reply.

These two USN F-4Bs that had split from an F-4B flight of the USS *Coral Sea* had been launched to carry out a MiGCAP mission. Radar controllers on Navy warships off the coast directed the F-4s in to intercept the four MiG-19s (one U.S. document mistakenly states that these were four MiG-17s). This was a new F-4 tactic, one in which the pilots flew in at very low altitudes following the course of the Red River. When the F-4 pilots spotted MiGs, they would pull up, fire a volley of missiles, and then increase speed and immediately turn and escape (resembling the "Hit and Run" tactic used by MiG-21s). The crews of the two USN F-4Bs that attacked and shot down two MiG-19s (No. 3 and No. 4) were, respectively, Lt. Winston W. Copeland and Lt. Donald R. Bouchoux, and Cdr. Foster S. Teague and Lt. Ralph M. Howell. Both crews were from VF-51, based on the USS *Coral Sea*.[36]

In the battle of 11 June 1972, no MiG-17 was shot down, but instead two MiG-19s from the 925th FR were shot down. Nguyễn Hùng Sơn (B) ejected and parachuted to earth safely, but Lieutenant Nguyễn Văn Phúc did not have a chance to eject and died.

Air Engagement on 12 June 1972

On 12 June, based on analysis of the enemy's activities during the early morning hours, the AF HQ drafted a battle plan that called for the use of MiG-21s to intercept and disrupt the USN strike groups in the Lục Nam area.

The morning began with a wave of attacks by twenty USN aircraft against Đò Lèn Bridge in Thanh Hóa. At 1155 hours, twenty more USN aircraft attacked the Lục Nam area in Bắc Giang. To provide cover for the strike bombers, eight F-4B fighter aircraft were assigned to fly in a holding pattern over Yên Bái airfield while four other USN fighters flew in a holding pattern over the Thành Sơn area in Phú Thọ. At 1158 hours, when the long-range radar network picked up three groups of enemy aircraft approaching from the east, the AF command post concluded that this was probably a strike formation coming in to attack Route 1 North, so they quickly issued orders to attack it. When it was certain that the USN attack groups were heading in to attack Route 1 North, the 927th's command post ordered a MiG-21 flight, with Lê Thanh Đạo and Trương Tôn, to take off at 1202 hours then fly on a heading of 30 degrees toward Nhã Nam–Đồng Mỏ. After a little over one minute, the pilots were ordered to drop their external fuel tanks, switch on their afterburners, and climb to an altitude of 16,000 feet. Lê Thanh Đạo spotted four F-4s that were in the process of splitting up into two sections. Just when he had decided to target the two F-4s that were decreasing altitude, he spotted two more F-4s that were heading straight for the MiGs. Lê Thanh Đạo decided to continue to target the F-4 No. 2 of the section that was decreasing altitude.

Having realized that they were being pursued by MiGs, the two F-4s suddenly made a hard left turn, but MiG No. 1 was able to place his target in the center of his sight. When the range was down to 0.5 miles and he had a good sight picture, he pressed the missile-firing button. The R-3S missile flew straight as an arrow toward the F-4. Because the range was so short, he made a hard right turn to break away and returned to land at Đa Phúc airfield at 1221 hours.

Later, Lê Thanh Đạo, an ace with six victories, was given the honorable title VNP Armed Forces Hero and became the general prosecutor of Vietnam. He was among four VNPAF aces who attended all three Vietnam/U.S. veteran pilot meetings in Hanoi and San Diego.

13 June 1972: An Active Day for MiG-21s

The AF HQ had information from the long-range radar networks about the USAF and USN's operations in the first weeks of June, when the latter focused their attacks on such targets as traffic movement, transportation arteries, and logistic warehouses. The AF HQ concluded that on 13 June the United States would continue attacking the above targets and would use a great number of fighter aircraft to combat the MiGs.

Two flights of two aircraft each from the 921st FR were placed on combat alert duty and stood ready to take off immediately. When a formation of U.S. aircraft was detected, flying by Sam Neua at 0900 hours, the regimental command post ordered the first flight, flown by Lương Thế Phúc and Đỗ Văn Lanh, to take off to attack a group of twelve USAF aircraft flying near Yên Châu.

After taking off from Đa Phúc airfield, the two pilots were ordered to turn to a heading of 260 degrees then were ordered to drop their external fuel tanks. When the MiG lead spotted four F-4s flying in a trail formation, with a two-aircraft section in front followed by a trailing section of two aircraft, he gave the order to switch on afterburners and climb to 10,000 feet, then turned hard to chase the F-4 No. 4. However, the F-4 pilots saw that they were being chased by MiGs, so both F-4s made a hard turn and passed under the belly of the MiG No. 1, making it impossible for him to make an attack. When he spotted four more F-4s 30 degrees to the right at a range of four to five miles, Đỗ Văn Lanh decided to turn inside to pursue these four aircraft. He got on the tail of the closest F-4 on the left, and when the range was 0.9 miles and his speed was 560 mph, Đỗ Văn Lanh fired his R-3S missile, which exploded just above the top of the F-4's fuselage. He quickly pulled his stick over to break away by turning to the right. At that moment he spotted another F-4 at an appropriate firing range and at an angle of 20 to 30 degrees. Deciding to attack this aircraft, he got on the F-4's tail, placed his target designator pointer on the F-4, and when the range was 0.6 miles he fired his second missile, which exploded to the right of the target. As the range was so close, he decided to break off by flying directly under the belly of the F-4, then turned back and landed safely at the Đa Phúc airfield at 0924 hours.

The second flight, with Phạm Phú Thái and Nguyễn Công Huy, was ordered to take off from the west end of the Nội Bài runway, then the two MiGs were ordered to turn to a heading of 360 degrees to fly to the battle area of Sơn Dương–Đại Từ. When the flight climbed to an altitude of 12,000 feet and was flying past Bắc Cạn, the pilots spotted four F-4s 30 degrees to the right at a range of eight miles. Phạm Phú Thái gave the order to drop their external fuel tanks and switch on afterburners. He decided to attack the F-4s No. 3 and No. 4. The two F-4s were performing a snake maneuver, making 30-degree turns to the left and to the right in order to be able to keep an eye on their own tails.

When the F-4 No. 4 leveled out, Phạm Phú Thái immediately placed his target designator in the middle of the target, and when the target was stabilized, at a range of 0.9 miles and a speed of 560 mph, he fired his missile. It sped straight toward the target, but he did not see an explosion. He decided to flip his firing switch in order to fire another missile. When he had a stable firing picture at a very close range (0.49 miles), as he was preparing to press the firing button he saw that the F-4 was on fire.[37] Phạm Phú Thái quickly made a hard turn to the left to break away.

The F-4 No. 4 that was hit by Phạm Phú Thái's missile was flown by 1st Lt. Gregg Omar Hanson and 1st Lt. Richard J. Fulton of the 308th TFS/31st TFW. Their radio communications system must have been experiencing problems because the F-4 crew did not receive the warning that there were MiG-21s in the area. Both U.S. pilots ejected and both were captured. Only at this point did the other three F-4s realize that their No. 4 had been hit. They made a quick, hard turn to pass under MiG No. 1's belly in order to make a counterattack. They fired two missiles at MiG No. 1 but because the range was so great, Phạm Phú Thái had time to dive to a low altitude and return to base to land safely at 0941 hours.

To summarize, during the battle on 13 June 1972, the 921st FR pilots Phạm Phú Thái and Đỗ Văn Lanh each shot down one F-4 in the area of Tuyên Quang Province.

21 June 1972: Dealing with Chaff-Dropping Aircraft

Based on the analysis of the situation, the AF HQ put forward the following combat plan: If we should decide to intercept the USAF strike formations attacking the Route 1 North area, we would use four MiG-21s from two MiG-21 FRs. These four aircraft would take off from Đa Phúc airfield, with the second flight flying nine to twelve miles behind the first flight. Our aircraft would fly in between the Đồng Mỏ and the Lạng Sơn ground-based AD fire umbrellas, fly along the border, and attack the enemy down to the Đình Lập–Chũ area. If we decided to intercept strike groups attacking the Route 2 area, we would use the same four MiG-21s waiting at Đa Phúc airfield. The second flight would follow one minute to one and a half minutes behind the first flight on a flight path out to Hạ Hòa and then attack the enemy from beyond the AD umbrella's outer perimeter to Việt Trì–Thành Sơn. The AF HQ issued the battle mission orders to the 921st and 927th FRs.

During the early morning a formation of sixteen USN aircraft attacked the Tân Đệ ferry crossing and Gia Viễn Bridge in Ninh Bình. A few hours later, a group of twenty USN attack bombers flew in to attack Hòn Gai City. The USN fighters assigned to MiGCAP duties flew in a holding pattern over the Sơn Động area. In the northwest, thirty USAF aircraft attacked Route 2. F-4s assigned to MiGCAP duties flew in a holding pattern over Tam Đảo area, just west of Đa Phúc airfield. The 927th FR's command post ordered a flight, with Lê Thanh Đạo and Mai Văn Tuế, to take off at 1104 hours and then directed them to fly on a heading of 120 degrees. A few moments after the flight flew past Phả Lại, the MiG lead spotted two U.S. aircraft 90 degrees to his right, heading straight for the MiG flight. Lê Thanh Đạo promptly informed his wingman of the approaching aircraft and made a hard turn to meet the F-4s head-on. Right after receiving his No. 1's warning, Mai Văn Tuế spotted two more F-4s to the left (in fact, this had been a flight of four F-4s that had split into two two-aircraft sections in order to attack the MiGs). He informed No. 1 of his new sighting and turned to meet these two enemy aircraft.

Lê Thanh Đạo turned to engage the two F-4s that had been behind them. He fought an extended dogfight against the two F-4s, making a number of complete circles to try to get into attack position. However, because the two aircraft constantly maneuvered to keep on his tail, Lê Thanh Đạo realized that continuing this dogfight would not be a good idea and requested permission to break off the engagement. He landed safely at 1123 hours. At that time Mai Văn Tuế saw the F-4 No. 1 flying in front of him at a range of 1.8 miles and at an upward angle of 15 to 20 degrees. He was preparing to stabilize his targeting designator in order to fire a second missile when he felt his aircraft shake very hard and nose over toward the ground. Realizing that he could no longer control his aircraft, he ejected and landed safely in the Sơn Động area. Although the flight of MiG-21s failed to shoot down any U.S. aircraft in this engagement, the pilots helped to disrupt the USAF attack.

Another flight, with Lương Thế Phúc and Đỗ Văn Lanh flying MiG-21 MFs (F-96s), was ordered to take off at 1341 hours. Seven minutes later the pilots were informed that the target was 30 degrees to their right front at a range of seven miles. At that moment the MiG lead Lương Thế Phúc spotted four F-4s six miles away and headed straight for the MiGs. This was a flight of F-4Es escorting a formation of chaff-dropping aircraft. The American pilots reported that three MiG-21s (in fact there were only two MiG-21s) were attacking the chaff-dropping aircraft. Lương Thế Phúc turned right to close with the enemy aircraft. He then made a hard turn to the left to get behind and attack the F-4 fighter escort flight. Meanwhile, MiG No. 2 turned back to attack the chaff-dropping aircraft.

Lương Thế Phúc got on the tail of the F-4 No. 2. When the range was 0.7 miles and he had a stable sight picture, he fired one missile, but the missile failed to launch. He decided to target the F-4 No. 1. When the range was 0.8 miles, he pressed the button to fire his second missile, but this missile also failed to fire. He quickly broke off by turning to the right and then turned in to use his gun (the MiG-21 F-96 was equipped with a 23-mm gun). However, the F-4 had seen that he had a MiG on his tail so the F-4 increased speed, dove, and escaped.[38] Lương Thế Phúc turned back and landed safely at Đa Phúc airfield at 1401 hours.

Đỗ Văn Lanh spotted four F-4s above his altitude but he also saw that farther away, behind and below him, were six more F-4s. This flight of six aircraft were flying in an extended trail formation, with the two trailing aircraft a long way behind the leading four aircraft. MiG No. 2 decided to attack the four leading aircraft (this was in fact the flight of chaff-dropping aircraft). He placed his target designator on the F-4 aircraft No. 3, and when the range was 1.2 miles, at an altitude of 10,000 feet, he fired the missile under his left wing. However, seeing that the target was continuing to fly straight and level, he decided to flip his firing switch, placed the target designator on the target, and when the range was 0.5 miles he fired his second missile. The second missile had just dropped off his pylon and begun to speed toward the target when Đỗ Văn Lanh immediately pulled into a left turn to break away. He climbed to 16,000 feet and then down to a low altitude to return to base, landing safely at Nội Bài at 1402 hours.

It is likely that the F-4 No. 3 in the chaff-dropping flight had not heard the radio warning about the appearance of MiGs in the area. The aircraft was hit by an Atoll missile that exploded right in the engine exhaust nozzle and shattered into many pieces of shrapnel. The aircraft's tail section broke off and fell toward the ground in the midst of the chaff strips that covered the sky over the Red River, opposite the Phú Thọ area, thirty-five miles northwest of Hanoi. Both pilots ejected and were taken prisoners. This F-4E, flown by Capt. George A. Rose and 1st Lt. Peter A. Callaghan of the 334th TFS/4th TFW, was assigned to drop chaff to protect the strike group bombers.[39]

Also on 21 June an F-4J from VF-31 of the aircraft carrier USS *Saratoga* claimed to have shot down one MiG-21 with an AIM-9G missile. However, the combat logs of the 921st and 927th FRs reveal that on 21 June just four MiG-21s took off. Aside from Mai Văn Tuế's aircraft, which was shot down, the other three aircraft returned and landed safely. This means that the report that U.S. aircraft had shot down two MiG-21s is incorrect.

Air Engagement on 23 June 1972

During the two previous days, the USAF had concentrated its attacks on traffic choke points and logistic warehouses along Route 1 North (the Hóa River Bridge), Route 3 (supply stockpiles in Thái Nguyên), and Route 2 (around Yên Bái airfield). After analyzing the intelligence reports, it was considered likely that on 23 June the USAF and USN would continue to conduct heavy attacks on vital traffic arteries and in the Hanoi area. In terms of their tactics, the USAF strike formations would probably continue to send in fighters seven to ten minutes ahead of the bombers to cover and suppress the airfields, and the fighters would fly at higher altitudes than the bombers. During their approach flight, the USAF strike groups would fly in large formations, but after crossing the border between Laos and Vietnam the strike groups would spread out to fly in separate small groups.

The AF HQ issued the following battle plan: MiG-21s, MiG-19s, and MiG-17s would be used to fight in a coordinated effort based on flying at different altitudes within the AD umbrella, to intercept and disrupt USAF strike groups in order to protect Hanoi and Route 1 North. The weather on that day was good, with 30 percent cumulus cloud cover at an altitude of 1,800 feet and visibility of more than twelve miles. The 927th FR command post decided to use a flight of two aircraft, flown by Nguyễn Văn Nghĩa and Nguyễn Văn Toàn, on combat alert duty at Gia Lâm airfield (these two pilots had flown to Gia Lâm airfield on 22 June 1972).

The MiG flight was ordered to take off at 1030 and then to turn to a heading of 240 degrees and fly toward Hòa Bình. When Nguyễn Văn Nghĩa saw four F-4s 45 degrees to the left at a range of nine miles and twelve more enemy aircraft farther away, he gave the order to drop auxiliary fuel tanks and switch to afterburners to gain altitude. Since the MiGs were four to five miles from the target, the F-4s began their old and familiar tactic of splitting up into two separate groups. The four leading F-4s swept in to attack the two MiGs while the other twelve aircraft provided cover from a distance and waited for an opportunity to join the fight. This meant that the MiGs were in an unfavorable position. Nguyễn Văn Nghĩa quickly assessed the situation and then ordered his wingman to attack two F-4s that were chasing him while he pursued the two lead F-4s. Using carefully practiced air combat techniques, Nguyễn Văn Nghĩa made a hard turn and quickly got behind the two F-4s. After gaining control of the situation, when the range was down to 0.7–0.8 miles and he had a stable sight picture, he fired his first missile and then pulled into a climb to break away. When he quickly rolled over to see his missile detonate, he saw both wings of the F-4 catch fire and then the F-4 dove into the ground, crashing on the spot. This was the first U.S. aircraft that Nguyễn Văn Nghĩa shot down.[40] The crew of the F-4 ejected twenty-five miles west of Hanoi. The front-seater was rescued but the back-seater was captured. After seeing that two F-4s were racing toward his MiG, Nguyễn Văn Nghĩa quickly pulled up into a climb to 13,000–16,000 feet, then rolled upside down and dove steeply down. He leveled off at an altitude of 660 feet and a speed of 800 mph, then headed back for his base, landing at Nội Bài at 1120 hours.

The American pilots concluded that in mid-June 1972 the MiG-21s began using a new tactic, which was to use the cloud cover at 1,650–1,950 feet to hide beneath the clouds. When the auxiliary ground control station network informed the MiGs that they were close to a target the MiGs would pull up into a climb and attack the U.S. aircraft. On 23 June 1972 a flight of F-4s using call sign Barstow, which had been assigned to MiGCAP duty, was attacked by two MiG-21s that used the tactic of "popping up through the clouds to attack" the F-4s.[41] One MiG attacked an F-4 on the left while the other MiG attacked the section on the right.

24 June 1972: A Great Day for MiGs

On 24 June the 927th FR commander, Nguyễn Hồng Nhị, decided to place three flights of two aircraft each on combat alert duty. Even though the weather on that day was bad, the USAF had sent a large force to attack the Thái Nguyên industrial zone and vital transportation arteries around Hanoi and Lạng Sơn. The USAF strike formation consisted of twenty-four attack bombers, twelve chaff-dropping aircraft, eight close escort fighters, and twenty fighters assigned to the MiGCAP mission to cover the areas of Phú Thọ, Yên Bái, Hòa Bình, Chợ Bến, and Sơn Dương.

In order to protect targets in the Hanoi area, the VNPAF planned to coordinate the use of all three fighter types (MiG-21s, MiG-19s, and MiG-17s) to intercept U.S. strike groups approaching the capital city. When radar station C-43 picked up a group of eight aircraft that was flying in from Sam Neua at an altitude of 22,000 feet, pilots Bùi Đức Nhu and Hạ Vĩnh Thành were ordered to take off at 1512 hours to intercept this target. After taking off, when it was determined that this was a group of fighters assigned to MiGCAP duties, the AF HQ decided not to direct the flight into an engagement with the enemy fighters but to instead use the flight as a diversion to attract the attention of the USAF fighters and lure them away. Ten minutes later radar station C-43 picked up another group of eight aircraft approaching west of Phú Thọ, and this group did not have a fighter escort. (When Bùi Đức Nhu and Hạ Vĩnh Thành's MiGs were spotted, the American fighters left the bombers to pursue the MiGs.)

At 1529 hours, the scramble order was given. Nguyễn Đức Soát and his wingman Ngô Duy Thư took off then turned right to a heading of 270 degrees and climbed to an altitude of 6,500 feet. When the flight was passing Việt Trì, the AF command post ordered the flight to turn and make one complete circle, and then continued ahead on a heading of 270 degrees. After crossing through a large bank of clouds, the command post told the pilots that the target was in front of them and to the right at a range of twenty-five miles. A few moments later, two MiG-21 pilots spotted sixteen more aircraft flying in standard formation and with a separation of 1.2–1.8 miles between each four-aircraft flight. Nguyễn Đức Soát gave the order to drop auxiliary fuel tanks, switch on afterburners, and turn right to pursue the USAF strike formation.

When he calmly reviewed the entire sixteen-aircraft formation, Nguyễn Đức Soát saw four aircraft break off from the formation to confront the MiGs. This was in accordance with the new F-4 tactic, which dictated that when MiGs were encountered the F-4s would turn to meet them head-on, to fire missiles at the MiGs to frighten them and to prevent them from getting in behind U.S. aircraft. In an instant, with his keen tactical instincts, Nguyễn Đức Soát determined that the flight of U.S. aircraft coming at him head-on would not be able to turn back in time to get on the tails of the MiGs for attack. Nguyễn Đức Soát decided to immediately pursue and attack the fourth flight in the formation. At that moment, Ngô Duy Thư spotted one more group of enemy aircraft behind them, so the MiGs decided to split up and attack the two tail-end enemy flights. Nguyễn Đức Soát targeted the aircraft No. 4 in the fourth flight, which was a fighter escort flight. When he was close to the correct range and he had a stable sight picture, he fired a missile that sped straight at the F-4, causing it to explode into flames and then dive straight down into the ground. Based on the reported details of the air engagement, it was likely that the F-4E that was hit was flown by Capt. David B. Grant and Capt. William David Beekman of the 421st TFS/366th TFW.[42] The F-4 caught fire and crashed thirty-five miles west of Hanoi. Both pilots ejected and were captured.

After firing his missile, the MiG lead immediately broke away by turning to the left. He intended to pursue and attack the lead aircraft of the F-4 flight, but he was too close and so he decided to fly past the fourth flight and attack the third flight of F-4s. But when the third flight made a hard turn to the right, Nguyễn Đức Soát decided not to pursue this flight and instead to target the lead flight, which was still flying straight and level. This flight of F-4s also realized that there was a MiG at their six o'clock, so they nosed over into a dive, accelerated, and escaped. Continually scanning the area, Nguyễn Đức Soát knew that there was a large number of American aircraft behind him, so he decided to break off the engagement, descended to an altitude of 1,650 feet and then flew back to Đa Phúc airfield, where he landed safely at 1547 hours.

Meanwhile, Ngô Duy Thư decided to attack the flight of four F-4s that were still flying straight and level, apparently unaware that there was a MiG behind them. Ngô Duy Thư decided to target aircraft No. 4 in this flight.

When the range to the target was about 1.2–1.5 miles, and seeing that the F-4 No. 3 was flying straight and level ahead of him, making it easier to stabilize the target designator, he decided to change the target to the F-4 No. 3. At a range of 0.7–0.8 miles he fired his missile, setting the F-4 aflame. After making this attack, he pulled his stick over to the left to break away. Then, because of his great speed, Ngô Duy Thư shot past the fourth and third F-4 flights and decided to attack the lead flight because he saw that this flight was still flying straight and level. He placed his target designator on the lead F-4 and when the range was 0.6–0.7 miles, with a stable sight picture, and a good audible signal from the missile's heat-seeker, he launched a second missile. Because his speed was so great and because he made a hard turn to break away, he was not able to see the missile explode. After looking around and determining that no enemy aircraft were chasing him, he quickly descended to low altitudes and landed at Đa Phúc airfield at 1549 hours.

There was another success for the MiG-21s on 24 June 1972 when another flight, consisting of Nguyễn Văn Nghĩa and Nguyễn Văn Toàn, was credited with shooting down one more F-4. At 1542 hours Nguyễn Văn Nghĩa and his wingman were scrambled to intercept the U.S. formation. After lifting off the runway, the flight was directed to a 360-degree heading. After a few minutes the pilots spotted four F-4s 20 degrees to the left at a range of seven miles. This was a flight of F-4Ds, which was assigned to bomb a target in the Thái Nguyên steel mill complex. When the MiGs were four to five miles from the target, the F-4s split into two sections. The two F-4s of the second section made a right diving turn. After quickly assessing the situation, Nguyễn Văn Nghĩa decided to chase the two lead F-4s, which were making very violent combat weave maneuvers, and ordered his wingman to attack the aircraft on the right.

Nguyễn Văn Nghĩa continued to pursue the left-hand aircraft, which was trying to escape back to the border. At a range of 0.7–0.8 miles and with a stable sight picture, Nguyễn Văn Nghĩa pressed the button to fire a missile. He then pulled up into a vertical climb to break away. When he rolled his aircraft over to see the results of his attack, he saw the F-4 turning right under the right wing of his aircraft. At the same time, Nguyễn Văn Toàn in MiG No. 2 shouted, "He's burning!" The F-4D that was hit by Nguyễn Văn Nghĩa's missile was flown by 1st Lt. James Lon McCarty and 1st Lt. Charles Allen

Jackson.[43] The back-seater, Jackson, was able to eject and was captured, but the pilot, McCarty, did not have time to eject and was listed as killed in action. After checking to make sure that there were no enemy aircraft behind him, Nguyễn Văn Nghĩa descended to an altitude of 660 feet and flew back to Đa Phúc airfield, where he landed safely at 1600 hours.

It should be noted that 24 June 1972 was the twenty-sixth birthday of Nguyễn Đức Soát and he impressively celebrated his birthday with one memorable victory. During the war Nguyễn Đức Soát was credited with six victories, became a VNPAF ace, and was awarded the honorable title VNP Armed Forces Hero. He was later promoted to lieutenant general and was commander in chief of the AD and AF Service, and vice chief of general staff for the VNPA.

Air Engagement on 25 June 1972

Analyzing the operations of the USAF and USN on the preceding days, the AF HQ concluded that the USAF and USN would conduct large strikes against all targets in the Hanoi area on 25 June, including targets deep inside Hanoi. In preparation, the AF HQ issued combat orders to FRs directing them to use all three types of fighters (MiG-17, MiG-19, and MiG-21) to intercept U.S. strike groups.

The 927th FR flight flown by Lê Thanh Đạo and Trương Tôn was ordered to take off at 0654 hours, then fly on a heading of 160 degrees at an altitude of 3,200 feet. A little more than two minutes later the flight was ordered to drop their auxiliary fuel tanks and were informed that the target was then flying across in front of them from left to right at a range of about twelve miles. No. 1 immediately spotted a group of twelve enemy aircraft 40 degrees to the left. This was a formation of A-7 Corsair attack bombers from VA-22 of the USS *Coral Sea*. Lê Thanh Đạo ordered his wingman to chase the four tail-end A-7s. At the same time, when they realized that they were being pursued by MiGs, the A-7s split up, two aircraft turning to the left and two others turning to the right. MiG No. 1 ordered No. 2 to attack the A-7 No. 3, while he would attack the A-7 No. 4.

When he was close to the target at a range of 1.1–1.2 miles, Lê Thanh Đạo pressed the button to fire the first missile at the target, but he was not able to see the warhead explode. He continued the attack in order to fire his second missile, but the A-7 took strong evasive action and, because his air-craft was too close to the enemy aircraft, the missile exploded in front of the target. He then quickly broke off the engagement, flew back, and landed safely at Đa Phúc airfield at 0719 hours.

Meanwhile, Trương Tôn engaged in a dogfight with an A-7. The two aircraft turned and maneuvered, each trying to get into a favorable position behind the enemy aircraft. Trương Tôn was able to stand on the target tail's and, when the range was 1.2 miles, he fired his missile, which sped straight for the A-7. Before he had a chance to see the missile explode, he quickly pulled up to break off the engagement and flew back to land safely at Nội Bài. In the battle on 25 June 1972, pilot Trương Tôn was credited with one victory, having shot down one A-7E.

Air Engagement on 26 June 1972

During the second half of June 1972, the USAF and USN continued their constant series of strikes against targets inside North Vietnam. Faced with the development of the situation, the 921st FR command drafted a plan to deal with the American attacks in three different sectors.

Nguyễn Công Huy and Trần Sang were ordered to take off at 0921 hours, and while flying on a heading of 360 degrees over Quốc Oai District, the AF command post informed the pilots of two F-4s that were flying at an altitude of 22,000 feet. The two MiG pilots were ordered to drop their auxiliary fuel tanks, switch on afterburners, and climb to 22,000 feet. When the flight reached Thành Sơn, MiG No. 1 spotted a formation of eight air-craft 90 degrees to the right. The eight aircraft were flying in extended finger formation and were six miles away. As he passed the first flight of enemy aircraft, the MiG lead decided to make a hard right turn to get on the tails of the last two aircraft in the flight of F-4s. While the four F-4s in the lead continued to fly straight ahead, the four trailing F-4s switched on their after-burners and began to carry out combat weave maneuvers. Nguyễn Công Huy continued to chase the two tail-end aircraft. When the range was 0.17 miles, he decided to fire one missile at the two aircraft that were weaving back and forth. When he saw the two F-4s make a hard diving turn, he decided to dive after them. When the range was down to 0.9 miles he fired a second missile. Without waiting to see the results of his missile attack, he made a very quick turn to the right and returned to base, landing safely at Đa Phúc airfield at 0948 hours. The command post ordered No. 2 to return, and he landed at Nội Bài at 0947 hours.

During the air battle on 26 June 1972, pilot Nguyễn Công Huy was credited with shooting down one F-4.

27 June 1972: A Day of Great Victories for MiG-21s

On 27 June 1972, MiG-21s of both the 921st and 927th FRs took off, fought a coordinated battle, and scored a significant victory by shooting down five U.S. aircraft, disrupting USAF attack waves, and protecting the targets. That day was a day of major victories for the VNPAF.

During the two previous days (25 and 26 June 1972), the USAF had attacked targets in the Việt Trì area, transportation targets along Route 2, and the area of the Bạch Mai airfield, the AD and AF HQ command post in Hanoi. The B-1 network information revealed that, from around 1000 hours to 1100 hours on 27 June, the USAF and USN would send about sixty aircraft to attack targets close to Hanoi and along the coast at Hải Phòng and in Nam Định. Responding to this situation, the AF HQ issued combat plans to its two MiG-21 regiments, directing the regiments to intercept and disrupt the USAF and USN attack groups at long range in two different sectors. The combat plans specified that the primary battle area would be in the west. At the same time, the regiments were ordered to prepare plans to attack U.S. aircraft flying in to perform RESCAP missions for U.S. downed pilots.

On 27 June, the on-duty CO of the 927th FR was Nguyễn Hồng Nhị. Two flights of MiG-21s of the 927th FR were placed on combat alert at Đa Phúc airfield. The 921st FR placed a flight of two MiG-21s on combat alert duty at Yên Bái airfield. Between 0840 hours and 0940 hours, the USAF sent forty-four aircraft (twenty-four attackers and twenty fighter escorts) to attack the Bạch Mai command post complex, the Kim Liên area, and many other civilian targets. The number of American fighter escorts was rather large and they flew in holding patterns over three areas: southeast of Đa Phúc airfield, southeast of Gia Lâm airfield, and over the Nghĩa Lộ–Yên Lập–Thanh Ba area. Of particular note was the reappearance of a rather large number of F-105s (the new F-105G model that had appeared in early 1972) to suppress Vietnam's AD and radar units.

The morning began when one F-4 assigned to chaff-dropping duty was shot down by a SAM, and a flight of F-4s assigned to the MiGCAP mission received a warning signal indicating that a SAM-2 was being fired at them. In reality, however, no SAM was fired; instead, this was a "classic example" of "coordination between MiGs and SAM units." A flight of two MiG-21s flown by Bùi Đức Nhu and Hạ Vĩnh Thành was ordered to take off at 0842 hours, then fly on a heading of 290 degrees and climb to 22,000 feet. When the MiG lead spotted two aircraft 90 degrees to the left at a range of twelve miles and flying in extended finger formation, the 927th's GCI ordered the pilots to drop their auxiliary fuel tanks and asked AF HQ for permission to attack. However, because the target was within the umbrella of the ground-based AD forces, the AF HQ refused to give permission to attack and ordered the MiGs to continue to fly on a heading of 280 degrees to get beyond the perimeter of the ground-based AD umbrella. One minute later, Bùi Đức Nhu spotted three enemy aircraft flying on a heading of 280 degrees at an altitude of 13,000 feet. He also saw a single aircraft flying by itself farther away. When the four F-4s turned left to a heading of 180 degrees, the MiG lead made a diving turn to follow them. He ordered his wingman to keep his eyes peeled for other aircraft.

The MiG lead decided to attack the two rear aircraft. He chased the F-4 No. 4, but when he saw that this aircraft had turned and was too far away, he switched afterburners to chase the F-4 No. 3. When he had a stable firing situation, at a range of 0.8 miles and a speed of 745 mph, he launched his first R-3S missile, which sped straight into the U.S. aircraft. When the smoke of the warhead explosion dissipated, the F-4 exploded into a ball of flames and fell toward the earth. Bùi Đức Nhu quickly pulled his stick over to turn away, then descended to low altitudes, flew back to Đa Phúc airfield, and landed safely at 0902 hours.

More than three hours later, the USAF sent in a number of flights of F-4s to conduct a very aggressive SAR operation to retrieve the downed pilots. Anticipating the U.S. RESCAP operation, the VNPAF HQ implemented a plan to destroy the U.S. aircraft assigned to the SAR mission. (Some U.S. authors have written that "unfortunately, the North Vietnamese were apparently listening to the radio calls starting the rescue attempt and made a full-scale attempt to stop it, turning rescue into a disaster.")[44] In order to carry out this combat plan, after Bùi Đức Nhu and Hạ Vĩnh Thành returned from their victorious mission, the command post decided to send pilots Nguyễn Đức Soát and Ngô Duy Thư out to replace them. At this time, in the area where the early morning air battle was fought, many groups of U.S. aircraft had flown in and were continuously flying back and forth trying to find and rescue the downed pilots. The command post decided that this was an excellent opportunity to attack U.S. aircraft carrying out the RESCAP mission.

At Đa Phúc airfield, the AF HQ ordered the flight of Nguyễn Đức Soát and Ngô Duy Thư to be ready to fly from Vĩnh Phú straight to the western Hòa Bình–Vạn Yên area to attack the American aircraft conducting the RESCAP operation. At the same time, a flight of two aircraft from the 921st FR would be directed in to attack downward from the Yên Bái–western Nghĩa Lộ area, thereby catching the U.S. aircraft conducting the SAR operation in between the two jaws of a pincer.

A flight from the 921st FR, flown by Phạm Phú Thái and Bùi Thanh Liêm, was ordered to take off at 0850 hours and was sent to fly a holding pattern over Vạn Yên, but because the American aircraft were too far away the flight was unable to catch them, so it returned and landed at Yên Bái. At 0918 hours and again at 1002 hours, a flight of four MiG-19s and two MiG-21s took off and flew in holding patterns over Gia Lâm airfield and over Nhã Nam–Tuyên Quang, but they did not encounter any enemy aircraft and returned to land.

A flight from the 927th FR, flown by Nguyễn Đức Soát and Ngô Duy Thư, took off at 1153 hours and was directed to a heading of 210 degrees and to maintain an altitude of 1,500 feet. The command post's radar network picked up one group of enemy aircraft approaching and another group flying into the Suối Rút area. After receiving orders from the command post, the MiG flight turned to intercept the group that was crossing the Vietnam–Laos border, but this group suddenly turned away. Immediately afterward, the command post ordered the flight to climb to an altitude of 15,000 feet and informed the pilots that the target would be 30 degrees to their left at a range of 10–14 miles. The MiG lead spotted two aircraft 30 degrees to the left at a range of twelve miles. This was a group of chaff-dropping aircraft that had supported the strike formation and that had now been assigned to the effort to locate and rescue the downed pilots. Nguyễn Đức Soát gave the order to drop auxiliary fuel tanks, switch on afterburners, and pursue the target. When the F-4s realized that they were being chased, they switched on their afterburners and fled to try to escape across the border. The command post informed the pilots that the targets were leaving the area and said that if the pilots felt conditions were right they could attack, but if not the pilots should break off the engagement and return.

Seeing that the F-4s had crossed the border, the command post ordered the flight to break off the engagement. No. 1 replied, "Roger," but MiG No. 2 saw that the target was in a very tempting position and urged his lead to attack, saying, "This looks good. Go ahead and attack and I will cover you." With his mind now at ease, Nguyễn Đức Soát continued to try to center his target designator on the F-4 No. 2. When the range was 0.9 miles, he pressed the missile-firing button. The missile flew straight as an arrow toward the target. Nguyễn Đức Soát saw the missile explode on the left side of the target. Smoke began streaming from the target's wing, but to ensure the target's destruction, he decided to fire a second missile. The missile flew straight at the U.S. aircraft, making it explode into flames.[45] Nguyễn Đức Soát quickly turned to break off the engagement, returned to Đa Phúc airfield, and landed safely at 1220 hours.

According to a number of documents from both sides and the reported details of the air engagement, the F-4E that was hit by Nguyễn Đức Soát's missiles was flown by Capt. John P. Cerak and Capt. David B. Dingee of the 308th TFS/31st TFW. Both pilots ejected and were captured thirty-five miles west of Hanoi. The pilots were both veteran USAF pilots with a combined total of more than six hundred combat missions.[46]

At almost the same time, Ngô Duy Thư attacked the F-4 No. 1. However, when he was 1.8 miles from his target he saw two more aircraft 45 degrees to the left and in a more favorable position to attack. He decided to attack these two aircraft. When the range was down to 1.2 miles, the two F-4s split up, with one aircraft turned to the right and the other turned to the left. Ngô Duy Thư decided to pursue the F-4 No. 1. When the range was one mile and he had a stable sight picture, he pressed his missile-firing button. As he did not see the missile explode, he readjusted his target designator and launched a second missile at a range of 0.7 miles. The missile sped straight toward the F-4, causing the F-4 to explode into flames, and pieces of the aircraft broke off and floated toward the ground. Ngô Duy Thư quickly turned to break away then landed at Hòa Lạc at 1218 hours. It was most likely that the F-4E that was shot down by MiG No. 2 was flown by Lt. Col. Farell Junior Sullivan and Capt. Richard Logan Francis of the 308th TFS/31st TFW. Lieutenant Colonel Sullivan was listed as killed in action, while Captain Francis was captured.

The VNPAF had more successes on 27 June. At 1159 hours a pair of the 921st FR MiG-21s, flown by Phạm Phú Thái and Bùi Thanh Liêm, took off from Yên Bái airfield and were directed to fly up to the Nghĩa Lộ–Vạn Yên area, climbing to an altitude of 19,000 feet then flying on a heading of 120 degrees. Eight minutes later the pilots spotted a flight of four F-4s flying directly toward them and preparing to hide in a bank of cumulus clouds. Phạm Phú Thái decided that it would not be a good idea to pursue them into the clouds. One minute later, he spotted a flight of F-4s in front of them, 15 degrees off to one side, at a range of nine miles. When the F-4s learned of the presence of the MiGs, the four F-4s immediately split up into two sections. The two lead F-4s turned to the left and disappeared. The MiG pilots decided to chase the F-4s No. 3 and No. 4.

When the MiG flight was 2.4 miles from its targets, the two F-4s began a combat weave maneuver. After ordering his wingman to keep a lookout for the two F-4s that had turned to the left and after being informed by No. 2 that he could not see any other enemy aircraft, the MiG lead ordered his wingman to pull up beside him in order to make simultaneous attacks by both pilots. Phạm Phú Thái ordered his wingman to attack the aircraft on the left while he attacked the aircraft on the right. The two silver MiG-21s with bright red stars painted on their wings switched to full afterburner and sped side by side toward the two F-4s. At this point of time, the roar of their engines echoed throughout the entire Hoàng Liên Sơn mountains. When the range was down to 0.7–0.8 miles, after stabilizing his sight picture, Phạm Phú Thái fired the missile under his left wing at a speed of 745 mph. Immediately after pressing his missile-firing button, he pulled up to break away. When he rolled his aircraft over to observe the results of his attack, he saw that the target F-4 was burning.

The F-4E that was hit by Phạm Phú Thái's missile was flown by Capt. Lynn A. Aikman and Capt. Thomas J. Hanton of the 366th TFW. Both pilots were able to eject safely. Captain Aikman was rescued but the back-seater was captured. Almost at the same time, Bùi Thanh Liêm simultaneously attacked the F-4 on the left. When the range was 0.9 miles and his airspeed was 745 mph, he pressed the button to fire the missile under his left wing. He saw the missile leave the missile pylon and fly straight into the F-4, causing it to burst into flames. It was most likely that this was the F-4E flown by Maj. R. C. Miller and 1st Lt. Richard H. McDow from the 366th TFW. Both pilots were able to eject. The pilot sitting in front was rescued but the navigator who sat in the back seat was captured.

When MiG No. 2 turned to break away and follow No. 1 back to land, he looked back and saw the two F-4s looking like two balls of fire in the blue June sky. Under the wings of the MiGs, in the distance he could see the vast Mộc Châu wilderness stretching all the way to the terraced rice paddies at the foot of the Hoàng Liên Sơn mountains. When he shot down his first F-4E the former Hanoi high school student Bùi Thanh Liêm was not yet twenty-two years old. The two MiG-21 pilots landed safely at Yên Bái airfield at 1238 hours.

This would turn out to be a very special day for the VNPAF, when its MiGs shot down five U.S. aircraft without any loss to themselves. For the U.S. side, this day was later described by some authors as a "worst air-to-air day."[47] Five of the U.S. pilots were captured after ejecting, and one pilot was killed, but they did not shoot down a single MiG. At the same time this was also a day of successful combat coordination in which two MiG-21 FRs had achieved the highest level of combat efficiency by shooting down five F-4Es, the newest and most modern version of the USAF's F-4 series. This victory also demonstrated the VNPAF command post's ability to "read" the situation and to employ the proper tactics. After concluding that the USAF would concentrate on locating and rescuing their pilots and would not be on guard against the surprise appearance of the two flights of MiG-21s, the AF HQ decided that this would be an excellent opportunity to destroy enemy aircraft.[48] The results proved the correctness of the AF's battle plan. Six young MiG-21 pilots (their average age was less than twenty-four and the oldest pilot was only twenty-six years old), with an average of less than 250 flight hours in the MiG-21, fought bravely and used outstanding air combat techniques and marksmanship to shoot down five U.S. aircraft, thereby scoring one of the most wonderful victories for MiG-21s in the Vietnam air war.

Pilot Phạm Phú Thái later became a lieutenant general, and was promoted to the positions of first vice commander in chief, chief of staff of the AD and AF Service, and general inspector of the VNPA. He was also given the honorable title VNP Armed Forces Hero.

Pilot Major Bùi Thanh Liêm later became the second Vietnamese astronaut in 1980, but regretfully, he died on a training flight in a MiG-21 in 1981.

5 July 1972: A MiG Flies through an F-4's Blast

Almost two centuries earlier in 1776, after six days of discussion, John Hancock, the president of the American Continental Congress, signed the U.S. Declaration of Independence that Thomas Jefferson (who later became the third president of the United State of America) had submitted. From that day onward, the Fourth of July every year is celebrated as the Independence Day of the United States of America. The date of 4 July 1972 was just four years before the two-hundredth anniversary of this historic signing. However, that was four years in the future. On 4 July 1972, in the skies over North Vietnam, thousands of miles from the United States, bomb-laden aircraft of the USAF continued to fly in to bomb targets in North Vietnam, and on this day the VNPA AD and AF personnel continued to fight ferociously to defend the freedom and independence of Vietnam that President Hồ Chí Minh declared on 2 September 1945.

After temporarily suspending operations to learn lessons from their experience, during the first days of July the USAF and USN sent in many waves of large strike groups to attack targets deep inside North Vietnam, including a large force to directly attack Hanoi. They attacked the AD and AF HQ command post at Bạch Mai with laser-guided bunker-buster bombs in an effort to paralyze the VNPAF HQ command post. Meanwhile, the USN also mounted attacks against the Xuân Mai area and Kép airfield.

Based on the analysis of information from several reliable sources and from observing American aerial reconnaissance activities on 5 July, deputy AF commander Trần Hanh believed that the USAF would again attack Hanoi and Route 1 North, while the USN would attack the area southwest of Hanoi and the Hải Phòng–Hải Dương area. The AF command post put into effect a plan to fight in three different sectors. At Đa Phúc airfield, Lieutenant Colonel Nguyễn Hồng Nhị placed a flight of two MiG-21s on combat alert duty. The weather at Đa Phúc airfield was 60 percent cumulus cloud cover at an altitude of 3,200 feet. The weather in the battle area was 75 percent cumulus cloud cover at an altitude of 2,500 feet.

In the morning time, the USN aircraft attacked targets in Hải Dương, Hưng Yên, Bắc Giang, and Bắc Ninh. From 1015 hours to 1100 hours, a group of thirty-two USAF aircraft attacked targets in the Thái Nguyên area and attacked Kép airfield. Nguyễn Tiến Sâm (aircraft No. 5020) and Hạ Vĩnh Thành (aircraft No. 5052) from the 927th FR took off at 1023 hours and were then ordered to fly on a 110-degree heading. When the pilots were informed that the target was 40 degrees to the right at a range of thirty miles, they were also ordered to drop their auxiliary fuel tanks, switch on their afterburners, and climb to an altitude of 18,000 feet. A few moments later, Hạ Vĩnh Thành spotted four F-4s 20 degrees to the left at a range of fourteen miles. This was a flight that was escorting a formation of sixteen bombers flying in to attack targets in the Hanoi area. The F-4Es were deployed in the customary tactical formation: divided into two sections flying at two different altitudes and maintaining a separation of 1.2–1.8 miles between the two sections. After assessing the situation, Nguyễn Tiến Sâm decided to attack the leading two aircraft and directed his wingman to attack the two trailing aircraft.

Hạ Vĩnh Thành quickly got on the tail of the trailing section. He targeted the F-4 No. 4, and when the range was 1.1 miles and he had a stable sight picture, he fired his first missile. He saw the missile streak straight at the F-4 and flames began to flicker from the F-4's right wing. To make sure, he decided to fire a second missile that dropped from the pylon and then headed straight for the F-4, causing the F-4 to explode into a ball of flame and then to dive toward the earth. Hạ Vĩnh Thành shouted, "He's burning!" This F-4E was flown by Maj. William J. Elander and 1st Lt. Donald K. Logan of the 34th TFS/388th TFW.[49] Both pilots ejected successfully and both were captured.

Meanwhile, MiG lead Nguyễn Tiến Sâm decided to turn hard to pursue the F-4 No. 2 in the leading section. Because the F-4 was turning so hard, it was very difficult to bring the target into the center of his sight. When he saw one F-4 that had just leveled its wings and with a stable sight picture at a range of 1.2 miles, Nguyễn Tiến Sâm fired a missile. He saw the warhead explode about 180 feet to the right of the target. The F-4 rolled into a right-hand turn. When the F-4 had just leveled its wings, which was the best opportunity for Nguyễn Tiến Sâm, he stabilized his sight picture and pressed the button to fire a second missile at a range of 0.5 miles (later, pilot Nguyễn Tiến Sâm recalled that the range when he fired apparently was only 0.40–0.45 miles). Nguyễn Tiến Sâm saw the missile speed straight at the F-4 right after it left the pylon. The F-4 exploded, its right wing broke off, and the aircraft burst into flames, which reached all the way up to the cockpit. This was an F-4E flown by Capt. William A. Spencer and 1st Lt. Brian J. Seek from the 34th TFS/388th TFW. Both pilots ejected and both pilots were captured.

As the range between the U.S. aircraft and his MiG was so close after firing, Nguyễn Tiến Sâm did not have time to pull up and his aircraft flew straight through the center of the explosion. As it flew right through the ball of flames, his aircraft's engine died at an altitude of 19,000 feet. He calmly maneuvered his aircraft and tried to restart the engine. When his altitude was down to 12,000 feet he was able to successfully restart the engine. He then turned back and landed at Đa Phúc airfield at 1045 hours. This MiG-21 aircraft No. 5020, with thirteen red stars painted on its nose, is the aircraft that is now on display at the AD and AF Museum at Bạch Mai (on Trường Chinh Street) in Hanoi.

For some unknown reason, even though during this battle the EC-121 airborne command post aircraft repeatedly issued warnings about the location of the MiGs as they approached, the flight of F-4s did not hear these radio messages, and as a result Nguyễn Tiến Sâm and Hạ Vĩnh Thành were able to shoot down two of the flight's aircraft.[50]

During the air battle on 5 July 1972 the flight of MiG-21s flown by Nguyễn Tiến Sâm and Hạ Vĩnh Thành from the 927th FR successfully accomplished their mission of disrupting the USAF strike group in the northeastern sector and almost simultaneously shot down two F-4s. Both F-4s crashed on the spot and all four U.S. pilots were captured.[51] This was the first victory for the flight of Nguyễn Tiến Sâm and Hạ Vĩnh Thành, which was one of the 927th FR's most outstanding flight units.

During the war, ace pilot Nguyễn Tiến Sâm was credited with five victories (five F-4s) and was given the honorable title VNP Armed Forces Hero. It should be noted that his five victories were confirmed by both sides. After the war he was promoted to the rank of senior colonel and became chief of staff of the AD and AF Service. He was eventually appointed vice minister of the Ministry of Transport.

8 July 1972: A Difficult Day for MiG-21s

Having suffered heavy losses in air battles with MiG-21s in June and early July, the USAF carefully studied the tactics used by the MiG-21s during the final days of June and then decided to make a number of changes to its own tactics. Special attention was given to increasing the size of the support package by increasing the number of fighter escorts. Even in July, the support-to-strike ratio increased to 5.2 support aircraft for each strike. At the same time increased the number of fighter to the MiGCAP mission in order to deal with the MiG threat. After the loss on 5 July, the USAF also added an additional EC-121 to provide added air search and warnings off the coast of North Vietnam.

Because the weather over North Vietnam at that time was bad, the USAF and USN did not conduct air strike missions on 6 and 7 July 1972, but they did step up their armed reconnaissance activities, including using an SR-71 to reconnoiter important targets in the city of Hanoi and the airfields. After studying the reports received from the intelligence networks and analyzing the enemy's activities during the early morning hours, the AF HQ issued the following combat plan: "The AF would use two-aircraft flights of MiG-21s standing combat alert at Gia Lâm, Nội Bài, and Yên Bái airfields to take off and attack USAF strike groups at long range, beyond the range of the ground-based AD umbrella, in both the northwestern and southeastern sectors, but with special attention to the southwestern sector."

According to the combat plan, in the northwestern sector, the AF Corps would use four MiG-21s from Đa Phúc airfield to attack incoming groups beyond the range of the ground-based AD umbrella. In the southeastern sector, four MiG-21s from Đa Phúc would be sent out to Hòa Bình–Suối Rút to attack incoming strike groups. At 1009 hours, radar station C-43 picked up a group of sixteen aircraft flying north from Hồi Xuân. The GCI officers at the AF command post guessed that this was a formation of attacker aircraft, so they decided to order the primary attack flight to take off. The MiG-21 flight, with Đặng Ngọc Ngự and Trần Việt from the 921st FR, took off from Đa Phúc airfield at 1013 hours and flew out to the Thành Sơn area. At 1025 hours the command post ordered the flight to drop their external fuel tanks, switch on afterburners, climb to an altitude of 16,000 feet, and fly on a heading of 120 degrees to intercept the enemy aircraft in the Suối Rút area. Three minutes later, while flying on a heading of 90 degrees, Đặng Ngọc Ngự spotted four F-4s 30 degrees to the left at a range of nine miles. This was a flight of F-4Es assigned to escort a formation of chaff-dropping aircraft. After completing its mission, this flight was exiting the battle area from left to right at an altitude of 13,000 feet, flying in an extended trail formation of two two-aircraft sections.

The MiG lead Đặng Ngọc Ngự immediately ordered his wingman to make a hard right turn to attack. He ordered his No. 2 to attack the target on the left while he engaged the target on the right. He then turned hard toward the two lead F-4s on the right. While No. 2 was pursuing the target on the left, he informed his lead that there were still two F-4s behind them. At that moment, he could see that No. 1 was chasing the right section of two F-4s, which was conducting a combat weave maneuver. Đặng Ngọc Ngự got on the tail of the F-4 No. 1, brought the F-4E into his sights, and fired a missile at the appropriate range, then he quickly turned to break away without waiting to observe the results of his attack.

According to the description provided by some American authors,[52] after firing his missile, because the speed difference between the MiG and the F-4s was so great, Đặng Ngọc Ngự's aircraft shot out in front of the F-4E No. 3 in the "Brenda" flight. This aircraft was flown by Capt. Richard F. Hardy and Capt. Paul T. Lewinski of the 4th TFS/366th TFW assigned to escort the chaff-dropping flight. It was one of the two F-4s that MiG No. 2 had brought to the attention of his lead. The F-4E quickly jumped onto the MiG's tail and fired four AIM-9 Sidewinder missiles at the MiG. However, all of the missiles missed the target. Captain Hardy then decided to fire two AIM-7E-2 missiles in a volley (the AIM-7E-2 was a new model of the Sparrow missile). One of these two missiles hit Đặng Ngọc Ngự's MiG-21. The American fliers did not see the pilot eject.

According to Vietnamese records, after Đặng Ngọc Ngự completed his attack and broke off by turning to a heading of 360 degrees, radio contact with him was lost. Captain Đặng Ngọc Ngự, a courageous and talented pilot, died heroically after shooting down his seventh U.S. aircraft out of the skies over Suối Rút, Hòa Bình. Captain Đặng Ngọc Ngự was one of a few MiG pilots with the highest number of combat sorties and the most years of continuous combat service (more than six years, from early 1966 to July 1972).

Meanwhile, Trần Việt was turning left to a heading of 330 degrees when he spotted two F-4s conducting a combat weave at a lower altitude four to five miles in front of him. At a range of 1.1 miles and with a good sight picture, he pressed the button to fire the missile under his left wing. When he turned to break away he saw one F-4 crossing from right to left and climbing at a 30-degree angle. Deciding to chase this aircraft, Trần Việt placed the target pointer on his sight on the F-4. When the range was 0.5 miles and he had a good audible signal from the missile's heat-seeker, he fired his second missile, which hit the F-4E, destroying the aircraft's left engine. The crew of this F-4E, Lt. Col. R. E. Ross and Capt. S. M. Imaye of the 4th TFS/366th TFW, ejected and was rescued.[53] After Trần Việt launched his missile and as he was making his breakaway maneuver, because he had fired at such close range he flew past the F-4 and saw that the F-4 had been hit and was shuddering in flight as it passed under his aircraft's belly. The command post ordered No. 2 to break off and return. He landed at Hòa Lạc airfield at 1038 hours.

At 1029 hours the second flight, flown by Nguyễn Ngọc Hưng and Vũ Văn Hợp, was ordered to take off from Gia Lâm airfield. It was ordered to fly to Phủ Lý and then remain in a low-altitude holding pattern over this area. When radar station C-26 picked up a group of eight enemy aircraft at an altitude of 10,000 feet heading toward Vụ Bản, the command post concluded that this was a group of bombers and decided to direct the flight to attack this target. At this time the radar was experiencing difficulties and was not able to track all of the target groups. The command post was forced to direct the flight using calculated map plots. The flight was directed to fly from Hưng Yên across Route 1 to Hòa Bình. At 1048 hours it was calculated that the flight would intercept the target. However, the flight did not see the target. The command post decided to order the flight to break off this intercept and fly back to a holding area over Hưng Yên.

When Vũ Văn Hợp reported that he spotted two aircraft at a lower altitude heading straight toward the MiGs, the MiG lead ordered him to attack these aircraft. At 1052 hours, the AF command post ordered the flight to break off the attack and to turn to a heading of 60 degrees. At 1053 hours the command post began repeated attempts to contact the pilots, but neither pilot responded. All communications with both pilots were lost.

Based on some documents from both sides that described this battle, it is most likely that Nguyễn Ngọc Hưng and Vũ Văn Hợp clashed with a flight of F-4s, led by Capt. Richard S. Ritchie. This F-4E flight was assigned to a MiGCAP mission to support and protect attack bombers as they were exiting after making their attacks. Based on the details of the description, it may be surmised that under the direction of the airborne early warning and control system, Captain Ritchie ordered his flight to maneuver constantly as they approached the MiG area following air control directions. Ritchie's F-4E approached below and to the rear of the MiG No. 2. At a range of 1.2 miles he fired two AIM-7E-2 radar-guided missiles.[54] The MiG-21 was hit and burst into flames. This may have been the moment when, after being directed blindly (without radar tracking) from Hưng Yên to Hòa Bình and failing to spot a target, the flight was directed to turn back and return to Hưng Yên. In fact, this flight of MiGs should not have been asked to fly holding patterns for such a long time.

When the MiG No. 2 was hit, MiG No. 1 turned back to counterattack. He got on the tail of the F-4 No. 4. The lead F-4 had to turn back to rescue his wingman. Nguyễn Ngọc Hưng was fighting all alone against four F-4Es. Because there were so many American aircraft and because his MiG had been caught in an unfavorable position, he was hit by an AIM-7 missile. The crew of the F-4 that attacked him consisted of Capt. Richard S. Ritchie and Capt. Charles B. DeBellevue of the 555th TFS/432nd TRW.[55] Later, Captain Ritchie became the USAF's first ace of this war.

In the battles of 8 July 1972, three MiG-21s were lost and three MiG pilots were killed, including the famed captain Đặng Ngọc Ngự. Later, in a post-battle conference held to review these battles, the GCI officers and pilots concluded that after Đặng Ngọc Ngự was killed, the battle should have been halted in order to learn lessons from the experience. However, the flight consisting of Nguyễn Ngọc Hưng and Vũ Văn Hợp was ordered to take off even though the radars were being so heavily jammed that they were unable to pick up targets. As a result the flight was forced to fly in a holding pattern for an extended period of time, after which it was directed to use only map calculations to the Hòa Bình battle area, where American fighters were waiting. Even though the command post had ordered the flight to return, the flight of MiG-21s still engaged in air combat with F-4s when they were in a passive (defensive) and unfavorable position. This was a day of great losses for MiG-21s after two months of continuous victories.

11 July 1972: The MiG-17s' Last Air-to-Air Victory

The MiG-21s temporarily interrupted their combat sorties to learn lessons from 8 July 1972. On 11 July 1972, two MiG-17 pilots, Hán Vĩnh Tưởng and Hoàng Thế Thắng from the 923rd FR, were conducting a training flight in the skies over Kép airfield when the GCI post alerted them of U.S. fighters over the Phả Lại area, heading toward Kép airfield. The two MiG-17 pilots were ordered to fly to Nội Bài and land there. The two MiGs had just started their turn to head for the airfield when they spotted two F-4s 3.5 miles behind them. These were two USN F-4Js from VF-103 of the USS *Saratoga*, which were assigned to provide air cover for a group of attack bombers near Kép airfield.

Faced with such a situation developing, the command post approved the flight's request to attack the enemy aircraft. The MiGs quickly dropped their auxiliary fuel tanks and switched from a training mission to a combat role. After a few minutes of engaging in a turning dogfight with the F-4s, Hán Vĩnh Tưởng closed to a range of 0.31 miles from one F-4 and, with three quick bursts from his guns, shot down the F-4, which crashed on the spot. The F-4J that was shot down was flown by Lt. Robert Irving Randall and Lt. Frederick J. Masterson of VF-103 of the USS *Saratoga*. Both pilots ejected and both were captured. Together with an F-4 that was shot down by Hoàng Thế Thắng, this was the last F-4 that was shot down by a MiG-17 during the Vietnam War. However, there is a slight difference in timing between the accounts of the two sides. The American records indicate that this battle was fought on 10 July while Vietnamese records indicate that it was fought on 11 July. This may be due to the use of different time zones in the records made by the two sides.[56]

After covering MiG No. 1 during his attack, MiG No. 2 chased another F-4 to the area over Hiệp Hòa. After a few minutes of engaging in a turning dogfight with the F-4, he opened fire and shot down this F-4. Before he could break off the engagement, Hoàng Thế Thắng was hit by a missile fired by an F-4 that was behind him. Lieutenant Hoàng Thế Thắng died. While the Vietnamese side stated that his MiG was hit by a missile fired by an F-4, there are no American reports of shooting down a MiG-17 on 10 or 11 July 1972.

Air Engagement on 18 July 1972

The AF HQ received a report from B-1 networks that on 18 July the USAF would probably send forty-eight aircraft to attack targets along Routes 2 and 3, along with sixteen fighters to provide fighter escort and MiG suppression support by flying over Đa Phúc and Hòa Lạc airfields. The USN would send sixty aircraft to attack targets south of Hanoi and in the Hải Phòng and Route 5 areas. Twelve fighters would be sent in ahead of time to perform the BARCAP mission in Vụ Bản–Bắc Ninh–Bắc Giang area.

At 0909 hours, the 927th FR command post ordered Nguyễn Đức Soát and Nguyễn Thế Đức to take off, then directed them to a heading of 160 degrees. When the two MiG-21s reached the area south of Hanoi, the command post ordered the pilots to drop their auxiliary fuel tanks and climb to an altitude of 16,000 feet. At that moment MiG No. 1 spotted two F-4s coming at the MiGs head-on and saw eight more enemy aircraft in the distance. After quickly assessing the situation, Nguyễn Đức Soát gave the order to turn left and then immediately to turn back to the right to get on the tails of the lead enemy aircraft. By this time the lead F-4 aircraft had realized that they had MiGs on their tails so they turned very rapidly. Knowing that there were many more fighters behind the MiGs and that continuing to chase the target would not be a good idea, Nguyễn Đức Soát requested permission to break off the engagement.

After receiving the order to break off the engagement, No. 2 quickly changed his heading to fly to Kép airfield, but in fact he actually flew to Hòa Lạc airfield. After learning that American fighters were covering Hòa Lạc, the command post ordered No. 2 to turn to a heading of 90 degrees to fly to Gia Lâm airfield, but at that moment two F-4Ds assigned to MiGCAP duties near Đa Phúc airfield, who had been waiting in ambush behind the Ba Vì mountains, got behind Nguyễn Thế Đức's MiG. The F-4D that targeted and attacked MiG No. 2 was most likely flown by Lt. Col. Carl G. Baily and Capt.

Jeffrey S. Feinstein of the 13th TFS/432nd TFW.[57] The F-4D fired a series of four AIM-7E-2 Sparrow missiles from a range of 2.5 miles. Even though the missiles were radar-guided, they failed to hit the MiG. Lieutenant Colonel Baily decided to launch two AIM-9E missiles. One of the missiles hit the MiG's right wing and the MiG caught fire. The MiG No. 2 crashed near Hà Đông. Lieutenant Nguyễn Thế Đức was unable to eject and was listed as killed.

24 July 1972: A Successful Day for MiG-21s

After analyzing the activities of the USAF and USN during the previous two days, the AF HQ leaned toward a conclusion that on 24 July the USAF would continue its attacks against transportation targets along Route 1 North and Route 3, as well as targets in the Thái Nguyên area. The USN would continue to attack targets along the coast and in the Hải Phòng and Quảng Ninh areas.

The 927th FR was given the order to send aircraft to attack USN attack bombers in the southwestern sector, in the Red River delta, and along Route 1 North. After radar stations C-26 and C-43 both had good radar returns from enemy aircraft target groups located twenty-five miles west of Bạch Long Vĩ Island and heading in toward the coast, the AF command post ordered Nguyễn Tiến Sâm and Hạ Vĩnh Thành to take off from Đa Phúc then fly on a heading of 360 degrees, before turning to a heading of 90 degrees. At this time the target aircraft group was directly over the top of Mountain 1068 in the Yên Tử mountain range, then turned toward the Hóa River Bridge. When the MiGs were flying over Route 13B, Hạ Vĩnh Thành reported spotting eight F-4s flying in extended trail formation 20 degrees to the left at a range of nine miles. Nguyễn Tiến Sâm gave the order to drop auxiliary fuel tanks in order to attack. Continually checking the flight's rear to make sure there were no F-4s behind them, he decided to chase the four F-4s on the left and selected the F-4 No. 4, which was some distance to the rear of the rest of the flight, as his target. When he had his target designator stabilized on the target at a range of 0.7 miles and a speed of 800 mph, he fired his missile. It flew straight as an arrow into the tail of the aircraft, where it exploded. This F-4E that Nguyễn Tiến Sâm shot down most likely was flown by Capt. S. A. Hodnett and 1st Lt. D. Fallert of the 421st TFS/366th TFW.[58] Both pilots ejected successfully and were rescued by an HH-3A helicopter.

As there were a number of enemy aircraft over Đa Phúc at that time, the command post ordered Nguyễn Tiến Sâm to land at Gia Lâm. After learning that Đa Phúc was no longer being covered by American aircraft, Nguyễn Tiến Sâm requested permission to land at Nội Bài. He landed safely at 1141 hours.

After spotting three flights (a total of twelve American aircraft) flying to his right front, Hạ Vĩnh Thành requested permission to attack the two tail-end aircraft in the third flight, then he quickly got on the tail of the F-4 No. 4. When the range was down to one mile and his speed was 745 mph, he fired his missile, which exploded to the right of the F-4. Hạ Vĩnh Thành pulled his stick over and targeted the F-4 No. 3. When the range was 0.7 miles and he had a stable sight picture, he fired his second missile, which flashed past the enemy aircraft and exploded out in front of the F-4. When he received an order to break off the engagement, Hạ Vĩnh Thành pulled up into a climb to an altitude of 30,000 feet, and then turned back to Đa Phúc airfield and landed, approaching from the east.

At that moment he heard MiG No. 1 request permission to make a direct landing approach from west to east (Runway 11) because he was completely out of fuel. At this time Hạ Vĩnh Thành was approaching to land from the opposite direction, and he did not have enough fuel left to make a second landing approach. Hạ Vĩnh Thành decided to land on the dirt runway, leaving the main runway to his MiG lead for his landing. Everything was fine when his wheels first touched down, but after rolling a short way down the runway the front wheel strut broke and the nose of the aircraft dropped to the ground. However, he was still able to safely bring his aircraft to a stop at the end of the auxiliary runway. Both aircraft landed safely.

Lê Thanh Đạo and Trương Tôn took off at 1224 hours from Gia Lâm airfield. After flying past Hải Dương, the pilots were ordered to switch on afterburners, climb to 19,000 feet, and fly on a heading of 80 degrees. At 1233 hours, as they were still climbing, MiG No. 1 saw twelve F-4s exiting the area, approximately 30 degrees to the left at a range of nine miles. Lê Thanh Đạo decided to chase this target. When the MiGs had closed to a range of three miles the F-4s were almost to the coast but still did not know that they were being chased by MiGs. This may be an example of the ineffectiveness of the airborne early warning and control system.

Seeing that the MiGs were almost to the coastline, the AF command post ordered the flight to break off the engagement. However, because the MiG pilots saw that the F-4s were still flying straight and level and that they were in a very good position to make an attack, No. 1 requested permission to continue the attack. He decided to target the F-4 No. 4 in the tail-end flight. When the range was down to one mile and he had a stable sight picture, he launched a missile. The R-3S missile dropped for a moment when it left the missile pylon, but then it sped straight into the F-4E, causing the target aircraft to explode. Lê Thanh Đạo quickly turned away and ordered his wingman to make his attack.

Trương Tôn closed in on the F-4E No. 3. When the range was down to one mile and he had placed his target designator firmly on the target, he fired his missile, which sped straight at the F-4, making it explode into a ball of flame. He pulled his stick over to turn away then quickly formed up with No. 1 to return to land. Both pilots dove down under the clouds and the two victorious pilots regrouped and turned toward Kép airfield to land there. In summary, during the air battles on 24 July 1972 two separate flights of MiG-21s from the 927th FR shot down three USAF F-4s by firing a total of six R-3S missiles.

29 July 1972: The Ratio of Battle is One-to-One

On 29 July for the first time the USAF followed a new flight path, flying from the Bà Lạt Inlet over Ninh Giang, Hải Dương, and Lục Nam to attack the Hóa River Bridge. For this attack the USAF also set up three holding areas where fighters would fly in holding patterns to wait to suppress MiGs. The USAF would also send a small diversionary flight of aircraft to the area west of Việt Trì–Sơn Dương, flying at an altitude of 19,000–22,000 feet. When the 927th FR was given the combat mission of intercepting enemy bomber strike groups approaching from the west and southwest in order to protect Hanoi, it placed a flight of two MiG-21s on combat alert. The weather in the battle area was good with visibility more than six miles.

The MiG-21 flight with Nguyễn Tiến Sâm and Nguyễn Thanh Xuân took off at 1312 hours and was directed to fly on a 170-degree heading at an altitude of 1,600 feet. The AF command post had intended to direct the flight to intercept a group of F-4s in the west, but this target was just a small group of four F-4s. The command post decided to instead direct the flight to the east to attack a group of twelve aircraft that radar station C-43 had been able to detect. At this time the pilots were ordered to drop their external fuel tanks, switch on their afterburners, and climb to an altitude of 13,000 feet. After more than two minutes, Nguyễn Thanh Xuân spotted eight F-4s 15 degrees to the right, flying in spread-finger formation at a range of ten miles. This was a group of F-4Es assigned to MiGCAP duties to support a strike formation of F-105s that was attacking the railroad line northeast of Hanoi, near Kép airfield. When the pilots of this flight learned that there were MiGs chasing their four trailing aircraft, the F-4 flight split up. The two lead F-4s turned left while the two aircraft of the second section turned right.

Assessing the situation, Nguyễn Tiến Sâm decided to increase speed to 800 mph and attack the two F-4s that were turning to the left. Despite the fact that the F-4 No. 2 was constantly turning and maneuvering, Nguyễn Tiến Sâm was able to place his sight target designator on the target and when the range was one mile, he pressed the button to fire a missile. At that moment, however, the F-4 pulled up into a climb and the missile warhead exploded underneath the F-4. The AF command post ordered him to break off the engagement, but the pilot decided to continue the attack against the F-4 No. 2. When this F-4 pulled up into a 40-degree climb, at a range of 0.62 miles and with a good sight picture, Nguyễn Tiến Sâm fired his second missile, which flew straight at the F-4. Because he had fired at such close range, after firing the missile he immediately pulled his stick into a turn to break away and did not have a chance to see his missile explode. The command post told him to climb to an altitude of 22,000 feet and return to the airfield to land. The F-4E that was hit by Nguyễn Tiến Sâm's missile near Kép airfield was flown by Capt. James D. Kula and Capt. Melvin K. Matsui of the 4th TFS/366th TFW.[59] Both pilots ejected and were captured.

When Nguyễn Thanh Xuân decided to increase speed to make a simultaneous attack with his lead, he felt his aircraft shake violently and become uncontrollable. He ejected over Hữu Lũng and parachuted safely to the ground. The F-4 that was credited with attacking and shooting down MiG No. 2 with three AIM-7E-2 Sparrow missiles was an F-4D flown by Lt. Col. Carl G. Baily and Capt. Jeffrey S. Feinstein.

Another detail about this engagement has become available, which revealed, that after completing its SAM suppression mission, an F-105G flown by Maj. T. J. Coady and Maj. H. F. Murphy of Squadron Wild Weasel 17, assigned to the 388th TFW, was headed out toward the sea when it encountered a single MiG-21. This was probably the MiG-21 flown by Nguyễn Tiến Sâm that was flying back to land after shooting down an F-4. The F-105G performed a "figure S" maneuver and then launched an AIM-9 Sidewinder missile at the MiG. Unexpectedly, however, the missile exploded as soon as it left the pylon, damaging the F-105G's right wing and the right side of its fuselage. Major Coady tried to fly his aircraft back to his base, but the F-105G became uncontrollable and crashed into the sea. Both pilots were rescued.

Also on 29 July 1972 an F-4E flown by Lt. Col. Gene E. Taft and Capt. Stanley M. Imaye, assigned to escort a group of attackers in strike formation deep inside NVN, encountered MiGs. Lieutenant Colonel Taft reported that he had shot down one MiG-21 with an AIM-7E-2 missile.[60] However, the combat log of the 927th FR and other VNPAF documents state that on 29 July 1972 only two MiG-21s flew a combat mission.[61] The flight lead, Nguyễn Tiến Sâm, landed safely and only one MiG-21, flown by Nguyễn Thanh Xuân, was shot down.

Air Engagement on 12 August 1972

Early in the morning, the B-1 radar net picked up a flight of four U.S. aircraft flying at an altitude of 16,000 feet over Ban Ban (in Laos) and heading toward Yên Châu–Phú Thọ–Tuyên Quang, then it split into two sections, made a turn to the left, and flew out of Vietnamese territory. The AF HQ believed that this was an armed reconnaissance flight sent in to prepare the way for the attack waves that would be sent in later that day.

The radar net was able to plot the flight path of four F-4s from Udorn, which were flying along the Red River and along the northeast railroad line to perform weather reconnaissance and to reconnoiter possible targets. The 921st FR command post ordered Lương Thế Phúc and Nguyễn Công Huy to take off at 0813 hours from Gia Lâm airfield, then the flight was vectored to fly on a heading of 240 degrees. When they were flying past Thành Sơn (at 0823 hours), the pilots were ordered to drop their auxiliary fuel tanks, switch on afterburners, climb to an altitude of 6,500 feet, and keep the direction on a heading of 20 degrees. The pilots were informed that the target would be 30–40 degrees to their left at a range of ten to twelve miles.

At this time, it was most likely that the Teaball system informed the F-4 pilots that two MiGs had taken off from Đa Phúc airfield and were being directed to fly south and then to turn right to get in behind the F-4s. The F-4s dropped their auxiliary fuel tanks, shifted into combat formation, and made a hard turn to meet the two MiG-21s head-on. When they were headed directly at the oncoming MiGs, the four F-4s switched on their afterburners in order to increase speed and also to eliminate the white smoke trails created by the engines of the F-4s (this was one of the weaknesses of the F-4's engines). When the range to the MiGs was down to 2.5 miles, the flight of F-4s split up into two sections. The F-4s No. 1 and No. 2 attacked, launching four AIM-7 missiles. However, MiG No. 1 managed to avoid the missiles.

While he was turning right to a heading of 60 degrees, Lương Thế Phúc saw that the American aircraft had fired two missiles and he heard the MiG No. 2 pilot shout, "They have fired two more missiles!" The flight lead decided that the flight would make a hard climbing turn to gain altitude. After making the climbing turn, No. 1 made radio calls to his wingman but got no response. He decided to climb to an altitude of 30,000 feet and turn back toward Gia Lâm airfield to land at 0838 hours.

Meanwhile, Nguyễn Công Huy had seen that there were two more enemy aircraft closing in on the MiGs from the rear and that these aircraft were firing missiles. As he was looking around, he felt his aircraft shake hard, after which the aircraft became uncontrollable and began diving toward the ground. Realizing that he could no longer control his aircraft, he decided to push his ejection seat button. Nguyễn Công Huy parachuted safely down to the ground in Phù Ninh District, Vĩnh Phú Province.

Based on detailed reports of the engagement, the F-4E that pursued and shot down MiG No. 2 was probably flown by Capt. Lawrence G. Richard and Lt. Cdr. Michael J. Ethel from the 58th TFS/432nd TRW.[62] During the VN/U.S. veteran pilot meeting in Hanoi in October 2018, Capt. Larry G. Richard and the two MiG-21 pilots, Colonels Lương Thế Phúc and Nguyễn Công Huy, met and recalled what had happened forty-six years earlier.

Air Engagement on 19 August 1972

At 1220 hours, the 927th FR command post ordered the on-duty combat flight, consisting of Lê Thanh Đạo and Nguyễn Thắng Được, to take off from Đa Phúc airfield and fly on a heading of 130 degrees. Immediately after takeoff, the pilots were informed that the target would be 30 degrees to the right at a range of fourteen miles. When the MiG lead spotted twelve enemy aircraft turning from left to right, he decided to approach and close in on the formation of F-4s. This was a flight of F-4Es that was flying in from the sea to provide fighter cover for a formation of chaff-dropping aircraft that was approaching the target ahead of the bomber formation.

The four F-4s had certainly been informed of the appearance of MiGs by the Teaball network, so the U.S. pilots were keeping their eyes peeled for MiGs. When the back-seater of the F-4 No. 4 spotted two MiGs following the F-4s, he immediately informed the entire flight, which turned back to make a counterattack. While Lê Thanh Đạo chased the F-4s No. 1 and No. 2 in order to get into position to attack, the F-4s No. 3 and No. 4, now at a higher altitude, rolled upside down and dove down to get on the tail of Lê Thanh Đạo's MiG. Realizing that he was not in a good situation, Lê Thanh Đạo requested permission to break off the engagement and return to base, landing at Gia Lâm airfield at 1252 hours.

Meanwhile, Nguyễn Thắng Được had engaged in a dogfight with the F-4s and had been hit by an enemy missile. He was able to eject successfully, but he fell into a tree branch, breaking both arms and seriously damaging two vertebrae in his spine. Even though he was found and given medical treatment, because his injuries were so severe, he died on 20 August 1972.

Based on available information, it was likely that an F-4E flown by Capt. Sammy C. White and 1st Lt. Frank J. Bettine from the 4th TFS/366th TFW was the aircraft that fired an AIM-7E-2 missile that hit the MiG's tail. According to statements provided by the two American pilots, they saw the MiG pilot ejecting from his aircraft.[63]

26 August 1972: A USMC F-4J is Killed by a MiG-21

Based on received information from many sources and the enemy reconnaissance activities during the two previous days, the AF HQ concluded that the USAF would send more than fifty aircraft to attack the area west of Hanoi and Route 1 North. A large percentage of the aircraft would be fighters assigned to escort the bombers and to provide MiG suppression, both over the bombing area and also over Vụ Bản, Hòa Lạc, Miếu Môn, and Tam Đảo.

The AF HQ ordered the 921st and 927th FRs to launch fighters to protect Hanoi and Route 1 North by attacking the enemy aircraft beyond the AD umbrella provided by SAM and AAA units.

The flight of Nguyễn Đức Soát and Lê Văn Kiển was ordered to take off at 1011 hours and fly on a heading of 270 degrees, then turn to a heading of 120 degrees and climb to an altitude of 25,000 feet. MiG No. 1 spotted two F-4s turning to the right 30 degrees to the front at a range of nine miles. These F-4s were two U.S. Marine F-4Js, assigned to carry out the BARCAP mission under the direction of the Teaball airborne control system. However, it was highly probable that on this day the Teaball experienced a "system failure," and it failed to provide direction and guidance to the F-4s when the MiGs were approaching. The American research documents later stated that the battle of 26 August was a prime example of the price that they had to pay when the Teaball system failed, and on that day the air-to-air radio communications relay system also experienced a malfunction.[64]

Taking advantage of the situation, the MiG lead ordered his wingman to drop auxiliary fuel tanks, switch on afterburners, and attack the F-4 No. 1 while he did the same and attacked the F-4 No. 2. The failure of the Teaball system caused the USAF to shift air control direction to the Navy radar net (Red Crown), but by then it was too late and the shift did not take place. The MiG-21s were closing in on the F-4Js and were already in a favorable position to make their attacks. Nguyễn Đức Soát as the leading MiG targeted the F-4 No. 2, and when the range was 1.8 miles he adjusted his target designator but the F-4 was still turning hard to the right. Nguyễn Đức Soát continued to stick on the F-4's tail. He adjusted his target designator again and waited until the distance between him and the F-4J was down to 0.9 miles before firing his first missile. It flew straight and hit the F-4, setting it on fire. The pilot of the F-4 Motion Alpha 01 saw that the F-4 No. 2 had been hit by a missile fired by a MiG. The F-4J that was hit was flown by 1st Lt. Sam Gary Cordova and 1st Lt. D. L. Borders of VMFA-232, Marine Air Group 15 (MAG-15). The F-4J burst into flames and both crewmen ejected. After his parachute opened, 1st Lt. Sam Cordova had time to use his radio to inform other aircraft in the area of his location after he landed on the ground (later it was learned that he was in an area near Sop Hao in Laos). First Lieutenant Cordova was listed as killed in action. The navigator, First Lieutenant

Borders, was fortunate enough to be rescued. The U.S. Marines listed this aircraft as the only U.S. Marine F-4J Phantom aircraft shot down by a MiG in air engagements over North Vietnam. The Vietnamese pilot who scored this victory was Lieutenant Nguyễn Đức Soát of the 927th FR.[65]

After firing his missile, Nguyễn Đức Soát pulled his stick back to break off, radioed to No. 2 to climb to an altitude of 32,000 feet, and heard No. 2 reply, "I am already flying at 32,000 feet." The two MiG-21s flew back to Đa Phúc and landed there at 1036 hours.

Air Engagement on 28 August 1972

After a series of losses inflicted by MiG-21s on the previous days, the USAF had been forced to make a number of changes to their tactics. More fighters were assigned to the MiGCAP mission to fly in ahead of the chaff-dropping aircraft and the bomber strike formation, rather than keeping too many aircraft in the holding areas. At 0935 hours on 28 August, the radar picked up a target group over the Luang Prabang area and tracked the target as it flew past Sầm Tấu to Mộc Châu, Yên Châu, Phú Yên, and Tuyên Quang. Even though the AF HQ did not yet have complete strategic intelligence information, based on the enemy flight path and other indications, and with its very precise ability to "read the enemy's intentions," the AF HQ concluded that the USAF was probably planning to attack transportation targets along Route 2 and on the outskirts of Hanoi.

Phạm Phú Thái and Bùi Thanh Liêm of the 921st FR took off at 0947 hours from Gia Lâm airfield and then flew on a heading of 230 degrees to the area south of Hòa Bình. When the command post informed the pilots that the target was 20 degrees to the left at a range of five miles, the two MiG pilots spotted two U.S. aircraft on the left that were flying a combat weave, from left to right. The target was a flight of F-4Ds assigned to a MiGCAP mission. The F-4Ds probably were being directed by the airborne air control system to intercept the MiGs, but on that day the Teaball system may have suffered a breakdown so air control direction had to be shifted to the USAF air early warning net (Disco). The MiG lead turned in to get on the tail of the lead aircraft of the F-4 formation. When the range was right and he had a stable sight picture, Phạm Phú Thái pressed the firing button to fire one missile, then quickly turned away.

At the same time, Bùi Thanh Liêm was being chased by four F-4s. At 1006 hours, the 921st FR's command post heard MiG No. 2 report that his aircraft had been damaged and he requested permission to eject. At 1006 hours all radio communication with MiG No.2 was lost. Based on information about this air engagement, the F-4D No. 1, flown by Capt. Richard S. Ritchie and Capt. Charles B. DeBellevue, had gotten on the tail of MiG No. 2 and had launched two AIM-7E-2 missiles at a range of about four miles, but MiG No. 2 had managed to evade both missiles. The F-4D moved in closer and launched two more AIM-7E-2 missiles. The second missile went through the right wing of MiG-21 No. 2, damaging it and forcing its pilot to eject.[66] Bùi Thanh Liêm landed safely.

The command post ordered Phạm Phú Thái to break off the engagement. He switched to full afterburner, climbed to an altitude of 28,000 feet, then turned back and landed safely at Gia Lâm airfield at 1017 hours.

2 September 1972: The First Use of MANPAD on a MiG-19

On 2 September 1972, Vietnam's independence day, the AF HQ believed that the USAF and USN would conduct a major strike against important targets, particularly the airfields. With regard to tactical tricks, they would strive to "lure" the MiGs out to the area of Vạn Yên–Hạ Hòa to engage them. Facing this situation, the AF HQ ordered the FRs to use MiG forces to protect the airfields and key important targets.

At 1025 hours, two MiG-19s of the 925th FR were placed on combat alert duty. On that day and as a test, beside the three 30-mm guns with which each MiG-19 was originally equipped, the two MiG-19s were each armed with an additional two A-72 MANPAD shoulder-launched missiles. When the radar net picked up a group of twelve enemy aircraft flying from east of Sam Neua (in Laos) toward Mộc Châu, a flight of MiG-19s flown by Hoàng Cao Bổng and Phùng Văn Quảng was ordered to take off at 1127 hours and fly toward Phả Lại. At this point the group of twelve U.S. aircraft were flying in from Mộc Châu, passing Thành Sơn and heading straight for Đa Phúc airfield. When the MiG-19s were just east of the airfield, No. 2 spotted two F-105s on the left. MiG No. 1 also spotted two F-4s headed straight toward them from the opposite direction, and he gave the order to drop external fuel tanks. This was a composite USAF flight consisting of two F-105Gs and two F-4Es that were assigned to a SAM suppression mission near Đa Phúc airfield. This flight was controlled by the airborne early warning and control system, which had informed the American pilots of the presence of the MiG-19s.

According to the tactical plan that had been prepared, in order to attack the primary target—the U.S. bomber aircraft (F-105)—and avoid the threat from the U.S. fighters, the MiG-19 lead swept in to attack the F-4s while MiG No. 2 turned to attack the F-105s. Hoàng Cao Bổng made a hard left turn and got on the tail of the F-4 No. 2. When the range was right, he squeezed his trigger, firing a total of three bursts. When he saw his shells hit the top of the F-4's fuselage and the F-4 burst into flames and crashed in the Tam Đảo mountains, he shouted: "He's hit!" While conducting a bombing mission, this aircraft was on its third bombing run on the target when the aircraft behind it saw the F-4 burst into flames. Both pilots ejected from the aircraft, but both pilots were killed.

As he was flying over the western end of the airfield, Hoàng Cao Bổng spotted two aircraft flying from west to east and immediately turned to chase them. The F-4 that MiG No. 1 was chasing rolled over and then pulled into a climb. Hoàng Cao Bổng pulled into a climb to pursue him. When the range was right he decided to fire two more bursts from his guns. Right after firing his guns, he felt that his aircraft was unstable and that it dove toward the ground. Unable to control his aircraft, he decided to eject. His parachute brought him safely down to the ground in Phúc Yên village.

Meanwhile, Phùng Văn Quảng in MiG No. 2 turned hard to chase the F-105s when they split up, and decided to pursue the F-105 No. 2. After closing in on the F-105, Phùng Văn Quảng fired one of his A-72 missiles, but the missile missed, falling to the rear of the target, because the range had been too great when he fired. Phùng Văn Quảng decided to continue to chase this target. At a range of 0.37 miles he fired two bursts from his guns, but he saw that his shells had missed. At that moment he decided to fire his second A-72 missile, but this missile also missed. While flying rear cover for his lead, the F-105G No. 2 pilot reported seeing an R-3S missile that had been fired at the F-105 No. 1, but the missile missed (in fact, the missile he saw was an A-72 missile fired by MiG-19). The MiG-19 immediately closed in on the F-105 and used his guns to attack. Learning from his earlier attacks, Phùng Văn Quảng decided to get to a very close range. He then fired a long burst and saw his shells hitting the F-105, after which the F-105 dove toward the ground. The GCI post then ordered No. 2 to break off and he landed at Kép airfield at 1158 hours.

Based on the data on the air engagement and on observations by witnesses on the ground, the VNPAF credited Hoàng Cao Bổng with shooting down one F-4 and credited Phùng Văn Quảng with shooting down one F-105. However, one MiG-19 was lost.

9 September 1972: Three Types of MiG Combined to Fight

It was predicted that on this day the U.S. aircraft would go on with their attacks as they had done on the two previous days, and it was most likely that the USAF would send large strike forces with many aircraft to attack Route 1 North, Route 3, and Thái Nguyên, while the USN would continue to attack the Hải Phòng area. The AF HQ, therefore, issued a general combat plan and sent mission orders to all FRs to launch fighters to intercept the enemy aircraft approaching from both the west and the east.

The weather over the airfield was good, with 20 percent cumulus cloud cover at an altitude of 2,000 feet and visibility of more than twelve miles. Between 1005 and 1010 hours the radar net picked up several groups of U.S. aircraft in both sectors. At 1022 hours, two MiG-21s piloted by Lương Thế Phúc and Đỗ Văn Lanh, took off from Đa Phúc airfield and then flew on a heading of 230 degrees. It was still not yet known from which direction the American aircraft would make their approach. A short time later, based on indications provided by the enemy electronic jamming signals and on the fact that radar station C-53 had picked up a group of eight aircraft approaching from Cửa Ông, the AF HQ agreed with the 921st FR's assessment and ordered the two MiG pilots to turn to a heading of 360 degrees. The pilots were ordered to drop their auxiliary fuel tanks, switch on afterburners, and attack a group of twelve enemy aircraft that were exiting Vietnamese airspace. A little more than two minutes later Lương Thế Phúc spotted four aircraft 30 degrees on the left at a range of twelve miles. Looking to the right, he saw four more aircraft flying in a parallel line formation at a range of five to six miles. This was a composite flight consisting of two F-4Es equipped with the Combat Tree system (but not mounting cannon) and two F-4Ds carrying 20-mm gun pods. All of the F-4s were armed with AIM-9J missiles (a new variant that had just replaced the AIM-9G) and were assigned to the MiGCAP mission. It was possible that this F-4 flight had been directed by the airborne control system to the area of one of the airfields in order to intercept and attack MiG-21s that were almost out of fuel and were making their final approach to land.

In such a situation, the MiG lead maneuvered quickly to get in behind the tail-end enemy aircraft. He stabilized his target designator on the target and, when the range was 1.1–1.2 miles from the target, he fired the missile under his left wing. After firing, he saw the F-4 nose over and dive toward the ground. At that moment he heard No. 2 shout, "They're firing 20-mm guns! Turn hard immediately!" MiG No. 1 immediately turned to the right and pulled up into a climb to break away. The AF command post ordered Lương Thế Phúc to break off the engagement and return to land at Kép airfield. Because he had 120 gallons of fuel left, he made a direct approach to land, but just after he lowered his landing gear and his flaps he heard a voice shouting over the radio, "Retract your landing gear and flaps, turn back and make a counterattack!" The CO on duty in the airfield control tower (K-5) at Kép airfield who gave this timely verbal order to Lương Thế Phúc to turn back to counterattack enemy aircraft was First Lieutenant Nguyễn Xuân Hiển, a pilot who, twenty-eight years later, would become the president and CEO of Vietnam Airlines.[67] The MiG lead quickly obeyed the verbal order and turned his aircraft around to counterattack. When he turned to get on the tails of two F-4s behind him, his fuel tanks ran dry and his engine stopped in mid-air. When the two F-4s fired more missiles at him, he made a hard turn to avoid the missiles, after which he checked his aircraft and tried to restart his engine. However, because his MiG was flying at such low altitudes, he was forced to eject. Lương Thế Phúc parachuted safely to the ground in Lạng Giang District, Bắc Giang Province. At this time the F-4D No. 3 closed in and launched two AIM-9J missiles, but they also missed because the range was too short. The F-4D then moved in closer and fired its M-61A1 20-mm gun, hitting the MiG-21's wing. In his interview, Senior Colonel Lương Thế Phúc said that the American missiles did not hit his MiG and he abandoned his aircraft only because he ran out of fuel.

Đỗ Văn Lanh was sticking on the right side of his lead, and he had a clear view of MiG No. 1's attack on the F-4s. When he spotted two F-4s closing in to fire M-61A1 20-mm guns at MiG No. 1, he shouted a warning to his lead and at the same time fired one R-3S missile at the two F-4s to frighten them. His missile missed because the two F-4s were making a hard turn to the right. Đỗ Văn Lanh decided to chase one of the F-4s that was turning to chase his lead. When the range was one mile and with a good sight picture, he fired his second missile. This one flew straight as an arrow and hit the tail of the F-4, causing it to burst into a huge ball of flames and dive toward the ground. Đỗ Văn Lanh quickly pulled his stick to the left and climbed to an altitude of 40,000 feet. He heard his No. 1 remind him not to climb so high that his aircraft would leave a vapor trail. He quickly dove back down to an altitude of 30,000 feet, then continued his descent to return to Gia Lâm airfield.

At 1040 hours AF HQ ordered a MiG-19 flight, with Nguyễn Tử Dung and Phạm Cao Hà, to take off to fight against the USAF aircraft. Two minutes later the pilots were ordered to turn right and were informed, "The target is 45 degrees on your left at a range of ten miles." While the pilots were flying past Chèm, they spotted four F-4s 90 degrees on their right at an altitude of 4,500 feet. MiG No. 1 gave the order to drop auxiliary fuel tanks and turned in to dogfight against the F-4s. This was an F-4 flight that had already clashed with MiG-21s and that was returning to its assigned air holding position. The F-4s had probably been informed by the airborne early warning system that two MiG-19s were closing in on them. The F-4s turned and met the MiG-19s head-on but at a lower altitude than the MiGs. When the two MiGs flew over their heads, the F-4 formation made a hard turning climb to get on the tails of the MiGs. While Phạm Cao Hà was maintaining the flight formation and covering his lead during the attack on the four F-4s, he suddenly felt his aircraft shake, and then it became uncontrollable. Knowing that his aircraft had been hit by a missile fired by an F-4, he decided to eject and parachuted safely to the ground. The F-4 that chased and fired the missile at Phạm Cao Hà's MiG-19 was probably flown by Capt. John A. Madden and Capt. Charles B. DeBellevue of the 555th TFS/432nd TRW. Before he had a chance to see the missile explode, Captain Madden turned hard to target MiG-19 No. 1. He launched another AIM-9J missile at an angle of 50 degrees and while in a 5-G turn (these figures would have been beyond the firing parameters of the old type of missiles). He reported that the missile tracked properly and exploded right on the tail of MiG-19 No. 1.

For Captain Madden, these were his first and second victories, but for Captain DeBellevue, these were his fifth and sixth victories. This made DeBellevue the top scorer of all American airmen in this war.[68]

However, according to the 925th FR's combat log, of the two MiG-19s that took off and clashed with F-4s on 9 September 1972, the one flown by Nguyễn Tử Dung returned and landed safely. This means that in this air battle the American pilots shot down only one MiG-19.

11 September 1972: An Unusual Engagement

Early in the morning, USN aircraft flew in to attack Niệm Bridge and the Kiến An ferry crossing in the area of Hải Phòng, and the USAF sent sixty aircraft to attack the Hóa River Bridge and transportation targets along Route 1 North. Meanwhile, groups of enemy fighters assigned to MiGCAP missions flew in holding patterns over Lục Nam, Kép and Yên Bái airfields, and Bắc Sơn.

The AF HQ prepared a combat mission that ordered the FRs to use MiG-21s in both the eastern and southern sectors to protect Route 1 North and to attack formations of chaff-dropping aircraft. The weather at the Đa Phúc airfield was 60 percent cumulus cloud cover at 2,000 feet, with good long-range visibility. Soon the radar net spotted eight enemy aircraft flying in two groups south of Sam Neua and one group of twelve aircraft in the east flying over Bạch Long Vĩ Island. The AF command post ordered Lê Thanh Đạo and Trần Văn Năm to take off at 1014 hours from Đa Phúc airfield and they were directed to fly on a heading of 50 degrees at an altitude of 1,600 feet. Very soon after, the pilots were ordered to drop their auxiliary fuel tanks, switch on afterburners, and climb to 20,000 feet. Under the direction of the GCI, Lê Thanh Đạo saw four aircraft on his right and below and four more aircraft farther away. The four aircraft in the lead were in fact chaff-dropping aircraft (it was very likely that because of poor coordination the chaff-dropping formation had arrived before their escort fighters).

Quickly looking over the U.S. formation, Lê Thanh Đạo decided to make the maximum use of this opportunity by quickly attacking the formation on the right, before the F-4 fighter escorts had time to arrive. He ordered his wingman to attack the F-4 No. 3 while he attacked the F-4 No. 4. Lê Thanh Đạo got on the tail of the F-4 and when the range was one mile and his target designator was fixed on the target, he fired the missile under his left wing, which flew straight into the F-4, causing it to explode and burst into flames. This was an F-4E flown by Capt. Brian M. Ratzlaff and Capt. Jerome Donald Heeren of the 335th TFS/4th TFW.[69] Both pilots ejected and were captured. Both of the pilots were very experienced. By the time they were shot down, Captain Ratzlaff had flown a total of four hundred combat missions and Captain Heeren had a total of 312 combat missions. Lê Thanh Đạo quickly pulled into a climb to break off, and then rolled his aircraft upside down to observe the results of his attack. After seeing that no American aircraft were chasing him, he quickly broke off the engagement, reminded his No. 2 to keep his eyes peeled, then returned and landed safely at Đa Phúc airfield.

After seeing No. 1's missile hit the F-4, Trần Văn Năm saw that the other three F-4s were making a left turn. He decided to chase the F-4 No. 3. When he had his target designator stabilized on the target and the range was down to 1.1 miles, he calmly pressed the missile-firing button. However, he did not see the missile warhead detonate. When he pulled up into a climb to break off the engagement, he saw two aircraft on the left and at a higher altitude, so he decided to pursue and attack those two aircraft. He got on the tail of the aircraft on the right, and when the range was one mile he fired his second missile. When he pulled up into a climb he saw the missile fly straight into the F-4. The F-4 began to trail smoke and caught fire. Trần Văn Năm quickly broke off the engagement by climbing to an altitude of 30,000 feet, then flew back and landed safely at Đa Phúc airfield.

In the late afternoon of 11 September 1972, two U.S. Marine F-4Js assigned to MiGCAP duty near Đa Phúc airfield were directed in by the Red Crown air control system to attack a UMiG-21 combat training aircraft being flown by Major Đinh Tôn and a Soviet pilot named Vashili Motlov. The aircraft was conducting a requalification flight for Đinh Tôn over Đa Phúc airfield, and the aircraft was not armed with missiles.

During the training flight, Major Đinh Tôn (in the front seat) spotted the F-4s coming in to attack. Knowing that the UMiG did not carry any missiles, he used maneuvering skills to avoid the F-4's missiles. Đinh Tôn courageously and successfully avoided the missiles fired from the two F-4Js. Maj.

Lee T. Lasseter and Capt. John D. Cummings of Marine Squadron VMFA-333 of the USS *America* were credited with shooting down the UMiG-21. But in fact, when the aircraft ran out of fuel and the airfield was still being covered by F-4s, Đinh Tôn and the Soviet expert decided to eject on their own initiative. Both parachuted safely back to the ground.[70] This was only a single engagement in which Soviet specialist pilots attended passively, and all air combat maneuverability was done by the VNPAF's most skillful pilot Đinh Tôn (not Nguyễn Toon). After trying to attack Đinh Tôn's UMiG, the two F-4Js flew through Hải Phòng's AD zone on their way back to the sea and were shot down by SAMs and antiaircraft guns.

12 September 1972: A Great Score for MiG-21s

With information from the AF HQ about the intention of the USAF and USN to attack targets in Hanoi and along main transportation roads, the 927th FR placed two MiG-21 PFMs on combat alert duty at Kép airfield to be ready to take off and intercept groups of American attackers.

During the early morning, the USN attacker groups attacked the Hà Lầm Mine in Quảng Ninh. Between 0900 and 1030 hours, sixty-four USAF aircraft attacked Kép airfield and the Route 1 North, Lâm Thao, and Phú Thọ areas. The U.S. fighter aircraft flew in a holding pattern in preselected battle areas to cover and suppress air operations at the airfields. Nguyễn Tiến Sâm and Nguyễn Văn Toàn were ordered to take off at 0941 hours and fly on a heading of 50 degrees. Right after the pilots leveled out on the 180-degree heading, the AF command post ordered the pilots to drop their auxiliary fuel tanks and climb to an altitude of 16,000 feet, and informed them that the target was 10 degrees to their left at a range of twelve miles. Just after receiving the information, the two MiGs immediately spotted the eight F-4s. Apparently, it was very likely that at this time the Teaball system had broken down, so the F-4 flight assigned to escort the chaff-dropping aircraft did not hear the warning that MiGs were approaching them. Because of this, the two MiG-21s were able to unexpectedly appear in the rear of the American formation. Although the U.S. escort fighters turned back to engage, the two MiG-21s, from their tactically superior position, switched on afterburners and swept forward straight into the formation of the chaff-dropping aircraft.

The MiG lead Nguyễn Tiến Sâm decided to target the four tail-end aircraft. He saw both flights of enemy aircraft drop their auxiliary fuel tanks and make a hard right turn. Not wasting a second, he quickly got on the tail of the F-4 No. 4 in the trailing flight. However, he had made too sharp a turn so that he got inside the enemy aircraft's turn and ended up too close to his target. Unable to stabilize his target designator on the F-4 No. 4, he quickly shifted his target to the F-4 No. 3. When the range was 0.8 miles, his speed was 760 mph, and he had a stable sight picture, he fired a missile, which flew straight into the F-4 No. 3, causing it to burst into flames. Nguyễn Tiến Sâm quickly rolled his aircraft upside down and dove sharply down to an altitude of 6,400 feet, then turned back to Đa Phúc airfield, where he landed safely.

The F-4E chaff-dropping aircraft that was shot down by MiG No. 1 was flown by Capt. Rudolph V. Zuberbuhler and Capt. Frederick Charles McMurray of the 336th TFS/4th TFW.[71] The aircraft crashed twenty-five miles northwest of Hải Phòng. Both crewmen ejected and were captured.

While he was continually scanning the sky to keep watch and cover No. 1 during his attack, Nguyễn Văn Toàn spotted four U.S. aircraft ahead of him that were chasing MiG No. 1. He decided to target the F-4 No. 2 in the trailing section. When he was in range and preparing to fire he saw the F-4 suddenly make a hard turn away, so he shifted his target to the F-4 No. 1. At a range of 0.7 miles he adjusted his target designator and pressed the firing button. The missile sped away and flew straight into the F-4, causing it to burn. After firing the missile, Nguyễn Văn Toàn quickly pulled his stick over to break away. When he looked around, he saw that two enemy aircraft were chasing him, so he switched his afterburner to full power and pulled into a climb to 22,000 feet, then flew back toward Kép airfield. As he was approaching the airfield and was descending past 13,000 feet, he felt his aircraft suddenly shudder. Looking back, he saw that there were two F-4s behind him. Since he could no longer control his aircraft, he decided to eject and parachuted to the ground safely at the far end of Kép airfield. The F-4E that chased and attacked MiG No. 2 was assigned to escort the chaff-dropping formation, and was probably flown by Lt. Col. Lyle L. Beckers and 1st Lt. Thomas M. Griffin of the 35th TFS /388th TFW.

At 0947 hours radar station C-53 picked up a group of twelve aircraft south of Sam Tau, approaching at an altitude of 16,000–17,500 feet. The 921st FR command post ordered Phạm Phú Thái and Lê Khương to take off from the south end of the runway. A few minutes later, the flight switched on afterburners, climbed to an altitude of 21,000 feet, and then turned right to a heading of 340 degrees. The command post ordered the pilots to drop their auxiliary fuel tanks and watch for targets 30 degrees to their left. Looking out, Lê Khương spotted four F-4s split into two two-aircraft sections at an altitude of 19,000 feet, flying 30 degrees to the left at a range of ten miles.

Meanwhile, the MiG lead also spotted the enemy aircraft and accurately identified them as a flight of F-105s flying in an extended trail formation. When MiG No. 1 decided to pursue these aircraft, he suddenly spotted four more aircraft making a hard turn to the left. Seeing that the situation had suddenly become complicated and that he no longer had the advantage, Phạm Phú Thái decided to break off the attack. As he pulled his aircraft up into a climb he heard No. 2 shout, "Enemy aircraft behind us!" Phạm Phú Thái turned to look back and saw two aircraft behind them firing missiles. However, the range was too great so the missiles did not scare him. At this time, the command post ordered the flight to break off the engagement. Phạm Phú Thái pulled up into a climb to 32,000 feet and turned back to land at Gia Lâm airfield at 1026 hours.

When Lê Khương saw the four F-4s split up into two sections and chase MiG No. 1 to get into position to fire missiles, he swept in at them and fired one missile in front of the noses of the F-4s to scare them off. He was climbing to get to a higher altitude when he heard the ground command post shout, "Enemy to your rear, 150 degrees!" In his rear-view mirror, he saw that the tail elevator of his aircraft had been damaged and that the section where his aircraft's braking parachute was stored had been cracked wide open. His aircraft then began losing speed and tilting down to the left. The F-4D that fired the missile that damaged the MiG-21 was flown by Capt. Michael J. Mahaffey and 1st Lt. George I. Shields. When his aircraft descended to an altitude of 800 feet, Lê Khương pressed the ejection seat button. How-ever, his parachute brought him down so fast that he hit the ground on a mountainside with a 70-degree slope near Yên Bái. As a result, Lê Khương suffered a spinal injury that took a long time to heal.

30 September 1972: The MiG's 300th Victory

From very early in the morning on 30 September, the AF command post informed its FRs it anticipated that, within the day, the USAF would send forty to fifty aircraft to attack targets along Route 1 North. As predicted, in the early morning hours the USAF sent a reconnaissance aircraft in from the west and up along Route 1 North. The 921st FR was ordered to intercept and attack the enemy attacker groups to protect the targets. In particular, they resolved to reach the goal of shooting down the three-hundredth American aircraft (by the VNPAF's own MiGs).

Between 0946 hours and 1031 hours, the B-1 net and the regiment's own radar picked up many target groups operating over northern Laos and flying in the direction of Mộc Châu. The AF HQ agreed to allow Trần Việt and Đỗ Văn Lanh to take off at 1031 hours, then they turned to a heading of 270 degrees and climbed to an altitude of 16,000 feet. Less than thirty seconds later, the pilots spotted four F-4s 30 degrees to the left at a range of eight miles. After instructing his wingman to keep a close eye on their rear, Trần Việt turned his aircraft to get on the tails of these four F-4s. When the range was four miles, the four F-4s split into two sections, with two F-4s turning left while the other two F-4s turned right. While he was chasing the two F-4s that had turned right, Việt saw these two aircraft level their wings to fly straight ahead. He quickly increased his speed to get on their tails, placed his target designator on the tail-end aircraft, and when the range was approximately 1.2 miles he fired a missile from under his left wing.

As soon as he saw that the missile had missed, Trần Việt heard his wingman shout, "56, break off now! There are four aircraft on our tails!" However, after quickly assessing the situation and realizing that the F-4 in front of him was a very good target to attack, Trần Việt decided that he was not going to miss this opportunity. The MiG lead kept his target designator steady on the target for three to four more seconds, and when the range was down to 0.9 miles he fired a second missile, which sped straight into the F-4; it burst into flames and crashed on the spot. This was the three-hundredth U.S. aircraft that was shot down in the skies over North Vietnam by the VNPAF MiGs.

After launching the second missile, Trần Việt quickly pulled up in a climb to break away. He heard his No. 2 shout, "He's firing a missile!" Trần

Việt quickly pulled into a sharp climb up to an altitude of 35,000 feet, but the regiment's command post again warned him to keep his eye on his rear. The F-4D No. 1 that chased him fired four AIM-7E-2 missiles and four AIM-9 missiles, but all of the missiles missed. The F-4D No. 1 then ordered the F-4E No. 2 (which was armed with a 20-mm gun) to take over the attack, but Trần Việt skillfully slipped into the clouds and disappeared. Continually keeping a close watch out for the enemy aircraft, Trần Việt then descended to an altitude of 13,000 feet and headed for Gia Lâm airfield, landing safely at 1058 hours with only one hundred liters of fuel left.

When he heard the command post issue the warning to keep a keen eye on the rear, Đỗ Văn Lanh turned to look back and saw four aircraft on after-burner chasing the MiGs, so he decided to counterattack. But because the four F-4s had lost sight of their target and knew that the MiG was alert to their presence and would turn back to counterattack them, they broke off the attack by increasing speed to flee. Đỗ Văn Lanh turned back again and joined up with his lead, then landed at Gia Lâm airfield at 1059 hours. In summary, the shooting down of the American F-4 aircraft by Trần Việt on 30 September 1972 brought the total number of American aircraft that the VNPAF pilots themselves had shot down over North Vietnam until that time to three hundred.[72]

Pilot Trần Việt later became a major general and was appointed vice commander in chief and chief of staff of the AD and AF Service. With three victories during wartime, Trần Việt was given the honorable title VNP Armed Forces Hero.

Air Engagement on 1 October 1972

Having predicted that the USAF and USN would send large strike groups to attack targets deep inside North Vietnam, the AF HQ concluded that the USAF's primary targets on that day would still be Route 1 North, Route 2, Route 3, and Yên Bái and Kép airfields. The AF HQ ordered the 927th FR to prepare a flight to attack the enemy bomber strike groups, which were approaching from both the east and the west.

At 1444 hours Lê Thanh Đạo and Mai Văn Tuế took off and were navigated to fly on a heading of 330 degrees. Less than a minute later, No. 1 spotted four aircraft 20 degrees to the left at a range of eight miles, and four more aircraft farther away. Guessing that this was a group of eight aircraft flying in extended formation with the individual flights separated by three miles, and that the enemy's goal was to "lure the MiGs" to attack one of the flights so that the other flight could immediately turn and get on the tails of the MiGs, Lê Thanh Đạo decided to use the enemy's tactical ruse against himself by "luring the F-4s." When he saw the lead flight turn left to reverse direction (apparently this flight had dropped its guard because it thought that the two MiGs were moving in to attack the four trailing F-4s), the MiG No. 1 told his wingman to keep his eyes peeled for enemy aircraft and then quickly turned to chase two F-4s that were in a dive.

When the two F-4s realized that there were MiGs chasing them, they made sharp evasive maneuvers and then resumed their diving turn. Lê Thanh Đạo continued to stick tight on their tails. When the two F-4s had just pulled up to a 10-degree angle with a range of 0.9–1.1 miles and a stable sight picture, he fired a missile that flew straight as an arrow and hit the F-4. Lê Thanh Đạo saw the F-4 shudder for a split second and then burst into flames. Pieces of the aircraft broke off and tumbled toward the ground. Apparently the F-4 had experienced a radio failure and had not heard a warning to turn hard, so it was hit by the MiG's missile. Lê Thanh Đạo turned right and pulled up into a climb, then descended to 320 feet and headed back to land at Gia Lâm airfield. While he was preparing to land, he heard No. 2 request permission to make a direct landing approach because he had only three hundred liters of fuel left. Lê Thanh Đạo decided on his own initiative to make a go-around for another landing approach in order to allow his wingman to land first. Lê Thanh Đạo touched down at 1510 hours, ending a successful air combat engagement.

5 October 1972: A Successful Day for the MiG-21

On the two previous days, badly affected by a tropical storm in North Vietnam, the USAF did not send air strike groups against the targets. On the other hand, it did increase its use of reconnaissance aircraft, including an SR-71 to conduct reconnaissance of Hanoi, Hải Phòng, Routes 1, 2, and 5, and the main airfields of the north. When the radar net picked up a number of enemy aircraft formations approaching from the east, the AF command post ordered the 927th FR's Bùi Đức Nhu and Nguyễn Tiến Sâm to take off and fly to the Đồng Mỏ area, to attack enemy attack bomber groups in order to protect the Route 1 North area. However, the activity of the MiG flight was just a deception: the AF command post ordered the two aircraft to return and land at Đa Phúc airfield. This was only the diversionary action to deceive the enemy. After the pilots lowered their landing gears in preparation for landing at Đa Phúc airfield, the command post immediately ordered the pilots to retract their landing gears, fly to Yên Bái at a low altitude, and land there to stand combat alert duty at that airfield, in order to create the element of surprise and to attack the enemy targets approaching from the west. At 1330 hours a group of enemy aircraft was detected south of Sam Neua, and at 1345 hours a target group was picked up over western Sơn La. The AF HQ concluded that the USAF aircraft were approaching to attack Thái Nguyên.

The flight of MiG-21s took off at 1353 hours and was directed to fly on a heading of 270 degrees. The MiG pilots spotted a group of sixteen aircraft at a range of seven miles, and saw two more aircraft in front of the formation and flying toward the MiGs head-on. Perhaps at this moment the American pilots did not know that there were MiGs in the area, and they continued to fly straight and level. As the MiGs flew past the American formation, when the enemy formation was at an 80-degree angle the MiG lead gave the order to make a sharp turn to the left to intercept the target. MiG No. 1 planned to attack the two tail-end F-4s, but because his speed was so great, he shot past his intended target. He quickly decided to turn and attack the lead aircraft in the first flight in the enemy formation. For some unknown reason, at this time an F-4 was continuing to fly straight and level. Bùi Đức Nhu stabilized his target designator and, when the range was 1.1 miles, he fired a missile that sped straight at the target, causing the F-4 to burst into flames and dive toward the ground. The terrified pilots of the three remaining American aircraft in the flight turned in two different directions. Bùi Đức Nhu pulled into a climb to break off the engagement, returned and landed at Đa Phúc airfield at 1403 hours.

When he saw two F-4s flying behind MiG No. 1, Nguyễn Tiến Sâm quickly gave a warning to his lead and then dove to chase these two aircraft. After making one circle chasing the target, he heard the command post informing him, "Watch out for enemy aircraft to your right rear." Nguyễn Tiến Sâm decided that it would not be a good idea to continue to chase the two F-4s so he decided to turn right and continue to look out for the enemy aircraft. When he spotted four additional enemy aircraft at six o'clock, he decided to make a hard inside turn to attack the F-4 No. 4 in this flight. For some unknown reason the four F-4s did not know that there was a MiG chasing them and continued to fly straight and level. Nguyễn Tiến Sâm calmly adjusted his target designator and when the range was 0.7 miles he pressed his missile-firing button. Nguyễn Tiến Sâm recalled that for some reason in this engagement he had placed his weapons system on the "two missile" firing mode. The first R-3S missile flew straight into the F-4, causing it to shudder. Then the second missile hit, causing the F-4 to make a full 360-degree roll and then burst into flames and dive toward the ground. Nguyễn Tiến Sâm saw the F-4 burning like a sky-rocket in a fireworks display and he shouted, "He's burning!" Flying along the Tam Đảo mountains, he pulled up into a climb to break off the engagement, then returned and landed safely at Đa Phúc airfield at 1406 hours.

The F-4D that was hit by Nguyễn Tiến Sâm's missiles was flown by Capt. Keith H. Lewis and Capt. John Hardesty Alpers of the 335th TFS/4th TFW. The two pilots ejected twelve miles north of Yên Bái and both were quickly captured.[73] Captain Lewis had previously flown combat missions from the air base at Cam Ranh Bay, while Captain Alpers had previously been a B-52 navigator and had just converted to the F-4.

6 October 1972: An Active Day for the MiG-21 and the MiG-19

During the first days of October the weather was quite poor, so U.S. aircraft conducted virtually no operations. However, on 5 October the weather was good and the sun was bright, so the USAF and USN aircraft again conducted intense attacks on key, vital transportation targets. The AF HQ predicted that on 6 October the United States would send large strike groups (thirty USN aircraft and sixty USAF aircraft) to conduct mass attacks on targets in the Thái Nguyên and Thanh Hóa areas, while the U.S. fighters would again strive to suppress air operations at North Vietnam's main airfields. At the same time, formations of eight fighters each would fly in holding patterns in three areas—Hòa Bình–Xuân Mai, Yên Bái, and Nhã Nam, and eight aircraft would drop chaff from Mường Lát to Hòa Bình.

In order to fight against this mass attack, the AF HQ issued the following combat order to the FRs: "Concentrate on attacking enemy strike bomber groups in order to protect Route 1 North. In the east and the southeast, intercept and attack bomber groups to protect Hanoi." The 927th FR's primary attack flight, piloted by Nguyễn Văn Nghĩa and Trần Văn Năm, took off at 0849 hours and was directed to fly on a heading of 30 degrees. Five minutes later, the pilots were directed to drop their auxiliary fuel tanks and turn left to a heading of 360 degrees. As he spotted four enemy aircraft 20 degrees to the left at a range of twelve miles, Nguyễn Văn Nghĩa gave the order to attack. When the MiGs had closed to a range of six miles, the four F-4s began their routine tactic of splitting up into two sections. Nguyễn Văn Nghĩa got on the tail of the F-4 No. 2, adjusted his target designator properly, and when the range was 1.1 miles he pressed his missile-firing button. The missile dropped off the missile pylon and then sped forward. Because he did not see the warhead explode, Nguyễn Văn Nghĩa decided to launch a second missile, but then he saw that his first missile had hit the F-4. Seeing the F-4 burst into flames and dive toward the ground, Nguyễn Văn Nghĩa quickly broke off the engagement and flew back to Đa Phúc airfield, where he landed safely at 0909 hours. It was most likely that the F-4E that Nguyễn Văn Nghĩa shot down was flown by Capt. J. P. White and Capt. A. G. Egee of the 307th TFS/31st TFW.[74] Captain White tried to get his aircraft back across the border, but it crashed just after crossing the Laos–Vietnam border. The crewmen ejected and were rescued.

Trần Văn Năm maintained a separation of about 0.9 miles from his flight lead. When he spotted six more aircraft flying in the opposite direction and passing beneath his aircraft, he decided to dive and pursue a single aircraft that had become separated and was making a left turn. When the range was 0.7 miles and he had a stable sight picture, he fired his missile, which flew past the nose of the F-4 and exploded in front of it. While turning to break away, he saw a single F-4 that was making a rolling dive and then pulling up into a climb, so he decided to pursue this target. When the range was 0.9 miles and he had a good sight picture he fired his second missile. As soon as the missile left the missile pylon he immediately pulled the stick back to break away, so he did not see the missile warhead detonate. Trần Văn Năm landed safely at Đa Phúc airfield at 0912 hours.

A number of USAF reports stated that the F-4E flown by Lt. Col. Robert Dale Anderson and 1st Lt. George Francis Latella of the 25th TFS/8th TFW was shot down by a SAM while it was conducting an attack mission near Sơn Tây.[75] But based on the details of the report on the air engagement, it is very likely that this was the aircraft that Trần Văn Năm attacked. The F-4 crew ejected over an area twenty-four miles south of Yên Bái. First Lieutenant Latella was captured as soon as his feet touched the ground. Lieutenant Colonel Anderson was listed as killed in action.

After radar station C-53 picked up a group of twelve aircraft approaching over southern Sơn La and heading toward Bắc Yên, the command post ordered a MiG-19 flight, piloted by Nguyễn Hồng Sơn (A) and Nguyễn Hùng Việt, to take off at 0850 hours and fly on a heading of 90 degrees. By then, the USAF bomber group had reached a point six miles north of Thái Nguyên. The command post ordered the pilots to go to full afterburner, climb to an altitude of 14,500 feet, and then turn to a heading of 330 degrees. As soon as the MiGs leveled off, No. 1 saw two F-4s ahead of them and saw, farther away, four more enemy aircraft that were heading straight at the MiGs. In fact, this was a composite flight consisting of two F-4Es and two F-105Gs, which were flying a SAM suppression mission. By this time this composite flight had probably been warned by the Disco system that MiGs were closing in on them. The two F-105s turned away while the two F-4Es turned to confront the MiGs head-on.

When the lead MiG gave the order to drop auxiliary fuel tanks and attack the two enemy aircraft on the left, No. 2 spotted four aircraft at his six o'clock. He called a warning to No. 1 and then turned to counterattack. Nguyễn Hồng Sơn (A) continued to pursue the two aircraft on the left. He fired one burst from his guns but the range was still too great, so his shells missed. He made a hard turn to the left and steadied on a heading of 180 degrees to break off the engagement. From that time on he lost radio contact with his wingman. He then landed safely at Gia Lâm airfield at 0917 hours.

According to local residents who witnessed the air battle, when turning to make his counterattack, Nguyễn Hùng Việt fired two or three bursts from his guns. After that the witnesses heard a loud explosion and then saw the MiG diving toward the ground. The MiG was not burning. At the same time, the witnesses saw another aircraft chasing the MiG. At that same time, north of Route 1 one American aircraft was seen trailing smoke and diving toward the ground.

The MiG-19 No. 2 crashed on the peak of a mountain 1,000–1,200 feet high near Khuôn Nang Hamlet, Liêm Ninh Village, Võ Nhai District, Thái Nguyên Province. After the VNPAF search team arrived to study what had happened, the team found that Nguyễn Hùng Việt's aircraft had only a small number of cannon shells left and that the barrels of his guns were still smoking. Combining this fact with the statements of the local residents, the search team concluded that it was likely that MiG No. 2 had fired his guns at a U.S. aircraft. The aircraft that chased the MiG-19 No. 2 were two F-4Es, one crewed by Capt. Charles D. Barton and 1st Lt. George D. Watson from the 34th TFS/388th TFW, and the other by Maj. Gordon L. Clouser and 1st Lt. Cecil H. Brunson from the 35th TFS/388th TFW.[76] Each crew was credited with half a kill. Lieutenant Nguyễn Hùng Việt was the last MiG-19 pilot who was killed during the war, and this was also the last air engagement that MiG-19s fought during the war.

During the war, pilot Nguyễn Văn Nghĩa became a VNPAF ace with five victories (he never had to parachute) and was given the honorable title VNP Armed Forces Hero. In the postwar period, he was appointed general director of the Vietnam Civil Aviation Academy in Ho Chi Minh City. In the VN/U.S. veteran pilot meeting in October 2018, two pilots who had engaged each other on 24 June 1972, Nguyễn Văn Nghĩa and Charles A. Jackson, had a very meaningful reunion in Hanoi. Both pilots said that they were now friends and that they hoped there would be no more war, and stressed the fact that our children should follow the path to friendship, cooperation, and peace. That was also the meeting's slogan.

12 October 1972: A Combat Flight of Two Aces

With reports from many sources, the AF HQ was sure that on 12 October 1972 the USAF would send sixty aircraft to attack against logistic warehouses and vital transportation arteries in the Route 1 North and Route 2 areas, and that large numbers of enemy fighters would fly in to suppress air operations at the airfields and counter the MiGs. As such, the AF HQ ordered the 927th FR to launch aircraft to attack the enemy strike bomber groups that might appear in the western and southwestern sectors, as well as in the east and the southeast.

Two combat flights of the 927th FR were given this combat mission. The weather was very bad on that day as the northeast monsoon moved into North Vietnam, with a cloud ceiling of only 450–600 feet, so the regimental command post decided to send the two No. 2 pilots back to their barracks and combined the two No. 1 pilots, Nguyễn Đức Soát and Nguyễn Tiến Sâm, two VNPAF aces, into a new combat flight.

When radar station C-43 picked up a group of sixteen U.S. aircraft north of Sơn Động, the command post ordered the flight of two MiG-21s to take off at 1001 hours. After lifting off the runway, the pilots maintained a tight formation, kept their afterburners on, and flew off on a heading of 40 degrees at an altitude of 1,600 feet. The AF command post then ordered them to climb to an altitude of 16,000 feet, drop their auxiliary fuel tanks, and increase speed to 620 mph. As the pilots were turning to a heading of 240 degrees, Nguyễn Đức Soát spotted four F-4s 40 degrees to the right at a range of twelve miles. He quickly leveled out from his turn and informed his wingman of his sighting. When Nguyễn Đức Soát radioed that he had spotted four F-4s, the GCI officer, Lê Thiết Hùng, radioed the following message to him from the command post: "There are a total of twelve aircraft!" The MiG lead told the wingman not to attack right away but instead to stay at a higher altitude in order to watch for enemy aircraft and cover and support No. 1. To be alert to the tactical tricks used by the F-4s, Nguyễn Đức Soát carefully scanned the air all around to make sure that there were only the four F-4s that were out in front of him. He decided to pursue and attack this flight of four F-4s.

Just as he had begun his turn to attack, No. 2 radioed that there were four more F-4s off to the left. Just after Nguyễn Đức Soát rolled his aircraft back to a level position, he saw eight F-4s flying beneath his aircraft. Six of the F-4s turned to the left and the two other F-4s turned to the right, then turned back into a left turn. When this group of enemy fighters reached the battle area, the air early warning net informed the pilots that two MiG-21s had taken off from Nội Bài to intercept the USAF bomber strike group. While the formation of U.S. escort fighters were concentrating on chasing the MiG-21 No. 2, the MiG lead slipped past them and got in behind a group of attackers.

After quickly scanning the situation, Nguyễn Đức Soát decided to pursue the two tail-end aircraft below him as they were making a sharp turn. Because of his speed advantage and because he made a high-G turn, he was able to cut inside the group of F-4s. Waiting until the two F-4s had just leveled out, he quickly adjusted his target designator and when the range was 0.7 miles he pressed the button to fire a missile. At this time, there were still four F-4s chasing behind him. Nguyễn Tiến Sâm shouted to him to break away immediately, so Nguyễn Đức Soát pulled hard on his stick without waiting to see the missile detonate. When he turned to the left and rolled his aircraft upside down to have a look, he saw that the F-4 was on fire. Nguyễn Đức Soát quickly turned to a heading of 180 degrees and dove into the clouds. When he came out of the clouds, and spotted Yên Tử Mountain, he descended down to an altitude of 1,000 feet and landed safely at Đa Phúc airfield at 1029 hours.

The F-4 that was hit by young pilot Nguyễn Đức Soát's missile was the F-4E No. 4 in an attacker flight. It was flown by Capt. Myron A. Young and 1st Lt. Cecil H. Brunson, of the 469th TFS/388th TFW.[77] The F-4E crashed in an area eighteen miles northeast of Kép. The two pilots ejected and both were captured. Captain Young was a very experienced pilot who had flown a total of 379 combat missions.

When Nguyễn Tiến Sâm saw four F-4s flying below him, he turned back and dove to pursue the two trailing aircraft, but then he noticed two more aircraft chasing him. He decided to pull into a climb so he could make another diving attack. At that moment he felt his aircraft suddenly began to spin rapidly and for a moment he blacked out. Nguyễn Tiến Sâm decided to try to straighten his aircraft up but he found that he could not control the aircraft. He then decided to eject.

During this engagement the GCI officer monitored the USAF formation very well in order to provide timely information and warnings to the MiG pilots. Thanks to this information, when Nguyễn Đức Soát decided to attack he told his wingman not to descend to attack but instead to stay at a higher altitude in order to keep watch on the situation. From this position Nguyễn Tiến Sâm was able to give a timely warning to his lead to look around first and not to make his attack too hastily. Because of that the pilot spotted the additional eight F-4s in time so that not only did he not put himself into a bad situation, he gave himself an opportunity that enabled him to shoot down an F-4.

Air Engagement on 13 October 1972

By analyzing the situation following each of the enemy air actions, the AF HQ predicted that the USAF and USN aircraft (and possibly also Marine aircraft) would approach from two directions to make their attacks, coming in from the east over the sea and also up from Thailand and then turning to enter North Vietnam from the west. The AF HQ ordered the 927th FR to launch MiG-21s to protect the targets along Route 1 North against the enemy attacks from both directions. At 1317 hours a flight of two MiG-21s piloted by Lê Thanh Đạo and Mai Văn Tuế took off and then proceeded on a heading of 360 degrees at an altitude of 10,000 feet. A little more than one minute later, the flight was instructed to drop auxiliary fuel tanks, switch on afterburners, and climb to an altitude of 21,000 feet. The pilots intensified their scan of the sky and spotted a flight of F-4s five miles away at an altitude of 19,000 feet. From their altitude of 26,000 feet, Lê Thanh Đạo ordered a dive down at the flight of F-4s, which was flying in an extended trail formation with the two lead aircraft 1.2–1.8 miles from the second pair of aircraft.

Lê Thanh Đạo decided to make a sharp left turn to cut in and get on the tails of the two F-4s in the rear. However, he saw that the range was too great and that there were two more aircraft speeding in from behind, so he decided not to make the inside turn. At that moment, from the corner of his eye he saw two green streams of flame from two missiles angling in from behind his aircraft. He shouted a warning to his No. 2. Simultaneously, he also saw the explosion of a missile warhead about two miles behind his aircraft. Both the command post and MiG No. 1 called to No. 2 but neither received any reply. Radio contact with MiG No. 2 was lost at 1331 hours, so First Lieutenant Mai Văn Tuế was killed. MiG No. 1 decided to break off the engagement. He dove down sharply to a low altitude, flew back to Đa Phúc airfield, and landed there at 1338 hours.

The F-4D that was believed to have attacked MiG-21 No. 2 was flown by Lt. Col. Curtis D. Westphal and Capt. Jeffrey S. Feinstein, of the 13th TFS/432nd TRW.[78]

15 October 1972: The Last Air Battles of Linebacker I

After analyzing reports from the B-1 net on the USAF planned activities for that day, and being informed that between 1330 and 1430 USAF aircraft would attack targets on the 3rd and 1B roads, the AF HQ issued combat orders to the 921st and 927th FRs to use MiG-21s to make a concerted attack in the same sector, with the goal of intercepting and disrupting the USAF attackers' strike formations in order to protect the targets.

Phạm Phú Thái and Trần Sang of the 921st FR took off at 1412 hours and then flew off on a heading of 270 degrees in order to slip past a group of enemy fighters. As the pilots reached the area north of Hòa Bình, they were ordered to drop their auxiliary fuel tanks, switch on afterburners, and climb to an altitude of 26,000 feet. A few minutes later, the MiG lead spotted four F-4s 60 degrees to the right at a range of four miles. The F-4s were flying in formation but one of the F-4s was lagging far behind. Phạm Phú Thái ordered his wingman to attack the pair on the right while he attacked the pair on the left. When Phạm Phú Thái turned to pursue this target, the F-4 formation accelerated and disappeared. He then decided to break off the engagement, climbed to an altitude of 32,000 feet, and was flying at a speed of 680 mph when he saw two aircraft 60 degrees off to his right, and decided to turn inside to chase them. When the range to the target was 0.7 miles, his speed was 745 mph, and he had a stable sight picture, he pressed the button to fire one missile. He then pulled his stick quickly to turn away. When he rolled his aircraft over to see the results of his attack, he saw that the F-4 was on fire.

Phạm Phú Thái had just pulled up into a climb to break off the engagement when his aircraft was hit by a missile fired by an F-4 that was behind him. The MiG rolled to one side and Phạm Phú Thái realized that his left arm had been wounded. He decided to eject. Just at the moment when his parachute opened he saw some F-4s speeding at him and firing their guns. He used his right hand to control his parachute to make himself descend faster in order to avoid being shot and killed. He landed safely on the ground and was taken to Tuyên Quang.

A flight of F-4Es was assigned to a MiGCAP mission to support the attack bombers. When the F-4s were directed in to intercept MiGs, the F-4E No. 3

fired two AIM-7 missiles but both missiles missed. Seeing that the range was very close, the pilot of the F-4E No. 3 decided to use his M-61A1 gun. Firing at a range of 0.22 miles, he damaged the MiG No. 1, forcing the pilot to eject. It was thought that the MiG might have been previously damaged by the missiles and therefore was unable to make any evasive maneuvers.

Meanwhile, Trần Sang pursued the two F-4s that were flying on the right. However, the two F-4s realized that they had a MiG behind them so they turned and began a dogfight with MiG No. 2 at an altitude of 19,000 feet. Seeing that he would not be able to attack the F-4s, Trần Sang requested permission to break off the engagement and landed at Gia Lâm airfield.

About one hour later, two MiG-21s piloted by Lê Thanh Đạo and Trần Văn Năm took off then were vectored to fly to Ba Vì. When the flight formed up after climbing through the top of the cloud layer, the MiG pilots suddenly saw several enemy aircraft flying above them. Lê Thanh Đạo shouted to his wingman to break off the engagement. When MiG No. 1 spotted two F-4s in front of his aircraft, he decided to chase them. Lê Thanh Đạo recalled that when the range was about 1.2 miles and he wanted to press the button to launch a missile, he felt his aircraft shaking strongly. Then he didn't know what happened. When he came to consciousness he found himself lying at the Central Military Hospital in Hanoi, with only vague memories of why and how he had been able to bail out.

It was most likely that the F-4E that fired a missile at Lê Thanh Đạo's MiG was flown by Maj. Robert L. Holtz and 1st Lt. William C. Diehl of the 34th TFS/388th TFW. While this F-4 was flying near Việt Trì it encountered a flight of MiG-21s at an altitude of 3,000 feet. Seeing that the MiG-21 attempted to break off the engagement, the F-4E No. 3 got on its tail and fired a single Sidewinder that flew straight up the MiG's tailpipe, forcing the pilot to eject.[79]

7

December 1972
LINEBACKER II AND THE
"ĐIỆN BIÊN PHỦ IN
THE AIR" CAMPAIGN

The Nixon administration had limited success in achieving its strategic objectives after six months or so of carrying out the Linebacker I operation. On 23 October 1972, the United States was forced to declare the end of Linebacker I and a halt to its bombing north of the twentieth parallel.[1] However, the United States was also quietly preparing a plan to conduct a new phase of strategic bombing in case the peace negotiations in Paris broke down.

From August 1972, USAF headquarters began to work out a plan to conduct air strikes in all weather patterns against strategic targets in NVN including Hanoi and Hải Phòng. They planned to use destructive airpower and about 50 percent of the B-52 fleet, from Strategic Air Command (SAC) units deployed in the Andersen AFB in Guam and in the U-Tapao AB, Thailand.

Meanwhile, Hanoi had known from very early on of the U.S. scheme and its preparations for the biggest, most brutal, and probably the last campaign it could conduct in the Vietnam War. Under the direction of General Võ Nguyên Giáp, the minister of national defense, and General Văn Tiến Dũng, the chief of the General Staff, the AD and AF Service had completed many preparatory works for this strategically significant campaign. By mid-1972, the AD and AF Service had put all its units on a high combat alert duty level, to be ready to successfully fight against all U.S. strategic attacks. The AD and AF Service had formed study groups that had worked out special plans for the SAM forces to fight against the B-52 strategic bombers with the *Manual for the SAM units to Fight B-52s*. This "Red Manual" was prepared with the contribution of experienced SA-2 regiments operating in the battle areas in central Vietnam, southern Laos, and in Quảng Bình, Quảng Trị, and Thừa Thiên-Huế Provinces. The general combat plan of the VNPAF to fight against B-52s should they attack Hanoi from five directions (the Five-Star Plan) was approved by General Văn Tiến Dũng, chief of the VNPA General Staff.[2] Some Vietnamese sources, having assessed the AD system of NVN before the launch of Linebacker II, mentioned that NVN had 9 regiments with 95 missile battalions. During almost 8 years of war NVN AD had 7,658 SAMs and launched 5,858 SAMs, shooting down 788 U.S. aircraft.[3] Some U.S. authors assessed that NVN had seven years to build up its defenses. By 1972 it had become the strongest and most extensively integrated air defense system in the world. NVN's defense forces included 145 MiGs and 26 SAM Guideline surface-to-air missile sites.[4]

In fact, in preparation for the fight against the B-52s, as early as 1968 a number of VNPAF's high-ranking commanders and skilled fighter pilots had been sent to MZ4 to observe and study how to fight B-52 formations. Two years later, the MiG-21 pilots had completed the special training course with Soviet Union–made IL-28 and IL-18 aircraft standing in for B-52s. Some simulated B-52s had also been built for MiG pilots to conduct attacking exercises. And pilots with nighttime skills, like Đinh Tôn, Hoàng Biểu, Trần Cung, Vũ Đình Rạng, Phạm Tuân, and Vũ Xuân Thiều, were in combat alert duty shifts.[5]

On 26 November 1972, the U.S. Tactical Air Command (TAC) held a very important conference to discuss the topic of tactical measures and how to deal with MiGs. Meanwhile, thousands of miles away, at Trầm Pagoda eighteen miles northwest of Hanoi, the AD and AF Service Command held an important meeting of high-ranking commanders (both AD and AF units), experienced fighter pilots, and GCI officers to discuss how to fight against the USAF and USN strategic air bombing attack should it happen.

On 14 December 1972, National Security Advisor Henry Kissinger returned to Washington after the Paris negotiations broke down. Early in the afternoon of that day, President Richard Nixon held a meeting of the National Security Committee and entrusted Adm. Thomas Moore to order the start of the bombing of NVN and Hanoi using B-52s, the first phase of which would last three days with a possible extension should the objectives not be achieved.[6] The United States decided to bomb at night to avoid the MiG day-time pilots, who counted for 90 percent of all MiG pilots and who had already threatened the B-52s' aircrews.[7]

The other TAC support forces (fighter escorts, chaff-dropping F-4s, low-level attackers, all-weather fighter-bomber F-111s, EW EB-66s, and Wild Weasel F-105s) and others based in Thailand were also ready for missions. In order to arrange the campaign, one combat bomber operations center was established at Andersen AFB.[8] Operation Linebacker II—or "The Eleven Days of Christmas" as some Americans called it, and "Điện Biên Phủ in the Air" as the Vietnamese called it—began the last U.S. airpower campaign in the Vietnam air war, and it lasted for twelve days.[9]

18 December 1972: The First Night

The day began with a lot of unusual and questionable signs. At 1015 hours, many reconnaissance aircraft flew over the skies of Hanoi, then at 1046 hours several reconnaissance aircraft flew over Hải Phòng. At exactly 1200 hours two armed RF-4 reconnaissance aircraft flew past Hanoi. These activities from the United States were enough for Senior Colonel Lê Văn Tri, the very experienced commander in chief of the AD and AF Service, to recognize the threat of an air bomber strike. He immediately convened a meeting at the command post HQ to assess the situation. The AD and AF Service Command's duty watch team unanimously agreed that it was very likely that in the evening the USAF would send B-52s to bomb Hanoi.[10]

Under the general combat plan that had been approved by the VNPA's General Staff, the AD and AF Service HQ sent cables to all regiment and division commanders to bring their units to the highest level of combat readiness. The ground-based air defense units started their electrical generators to check their equipment, and the combat alert MiG flights were ready for takeoff.

At 1441 hours, twenty-eight B-52s of the Eighth AF took off from Andersen air base in Guam and flew on a heading toward Hanoi. At 1718 hours, another twenty-one B-52Ds took off from U-Tapao air base in Thailand then also flew on a heading toward Hanoi.

At 1600 hours, the VNPA's General Staff received the following intelligence report: "A total of thirty-two B-52s have taken off from Andersen air base." In fact, according to the U.S. combat plan, the first night's sorties would consist of fifty-four B-52Gs and thirty-three B-52Ds from Andersen, plus forty-two B-52Ds from U-Tapao, divided into three different waves with four to five hours between waves.[11]

The AD and AF Service Command immediately sent the following alert notice to all combat units: "At or after 1800 hours on 18 December 1972 B-52s will attack Hanoi, approaching the city from the northwest. All units must complete all preparations for combating B-52s by 1700 hours."[12] At exactly 1700 hours Hanoi issued an air raid warning. All of the General Staff's emissaries (headquarters officers responsible for monitoring specific units) were ordered to conduct inspections to check the combat readiness of the SAM units and AAA units. Six MiG-21s on alert at Hòa Lạc, Nội Bài, and Gia Lâm airfields were ordered to a condition of Combat Alert Duty Level 1.

At 1850 hours, all command posts of the entire AD and AF Service were ordered to be ready on Combat Alert Duty Level 1. At the AD and AF Service Command, all the staff were present: Senior Colonel Lê Văn Tri, the service commander; political commissar Senior Colonel Hoàng Phương; deputy service commanders Nguyễn Văn Tiên and Nguyễn Quang Bích; deputy service political commissar Nguyễn Xuân Mậu; deputy AF commander Trần Mạnh; and deputy AF Chief of Staff Nguyễn Phúc Trạch. At the AF HQ (F-371) command post, AF Commander Đào Đình Luyện, Deputy Commander Trần Hanh, and the duty watch officers were all standing by at their combat positions.[13] The MiG-21 flights assigned to combat missions were all at the highest level of combat alert. Although the night of 18 December fell during the northeast monsoon season, the weather was very good and the moon was very bright at altitudes above 10,000 feet. On that night, high-volume alerts from loudspeakers on the tops of the National Bank building, Hàng Cỏ Railway Station, and Nhân Dân Newspaper building informed all of Hanoi that the enemy aircraft were coming and that all the people in the city should immediately get in the shelters.

At 1928 hours, MiG-21 pilot Trần Cung was ordered to take off from Hòa Lạc airfield. The GCI officers at the AF command post, Phạm Minh Cậy and Tạ Văn Vượng, directed Trần Cung to fly toward the Hòa Bình–Suối Rút area to attack B-52s flying from south of Mộc Châu up to Vạn Yên.

As he closed in, when the range to the target was down to eight miles the electronic jamming was so powerful that the radar could not detect the target. The AF command post ordered the pilot to break off the engagement, and Trần Cung returned and landed at Đa Phúc airfield.

At Đa Phúc airfield, Phạm Tuân was ordered to take off at 1947 hours. Even though Đa Phúc airfield had just been bombed by F-111s and A-6s and many sections of the runway had been damaged, Phạm Tuân resolutely took off in spite of the damage. After takeoff, he was directed to fly to the Hòa Bình area. A few minutes later he spotted the target, switched on his afterburner, and sped toward the cell of B-52s. Phạm Tuân saw that there was a tremendous number of F-4 fighter escorts around the B-52s. When the F-4s realized that there was a MiG in the area they turned and fired four missiles at Phạm Tuân's MiG. He made several turns to evade the missiles and continued to pursue the B-52s. However, after evading the missiles he found that he could no longer see the navigation lights of the B-52s. When he switched on his onboard radar all he could see was electronic jamming signals. Meanwhile the number of F-4s that had turned to pursue him steadily grew. The AF command post ordered Phạm Tuân to break off the engagement and return to land.

Seeing that he did not have enough fuel to reach any other airfield, Phạm Tuân decided to land at Đa Phúc airfield. Even though the airfields of Đa Phúc, Kép, Gia Lâm, Hòa Lạc, and Yên Bái had been savagely bombed by ninety U.S. aircraft at 1940 hours, and even though many sections of the runway had been destroyed, and the ground command post had ordered him to eject three times, Phạm Tuân was determined to land. As he was descending over the outer marker beacon, he saw a big, bright fire lighting up the sky beyond the far end of the runway. This ball of fire was the first B-52 that was shot down. The B-52 then crashed in a field at Chuôm Hamlet, Phủ Lỗ Village, on the eastern side of Đa Phúc airfield. The nearness of the ball of fire to the airfield helped Phạm Tuân to see the airfield more clearly for landing. After his aircraft touched down and rolled for several hundred feet, it ran into a bomb crater in the runway. The aircraft rolled on its side, the wing broke off, and the aircraft hit the far edge of the bomb crater, causing the aircraft to flip completely upside down. However, the aircraft did not burn because its fuel tanks were completely dry. Phạm Tuân climbed out of the cockpit through a fragment of the cockpit canopy, completely unhurt.

When the long-range radar picked up a big group of B-52s flying in from a point south of Sam Neua at 0443 hours on 19 December 1972, Vũ Đình Rạng was ordered to take off from Gia Lâm airfield to intercept this bomber group. After taking off, he flew on a heading of 130–140 degrees at an altitude of 1,600 feet, after which he climbed to 10,000 feet and headed toward Chương Mỹ. Three minutes later, the AF command post ordered him to drop his auxiliary fuel tank, switch on his afterburner, and climb to an altitude of 21,000 feet. One minute later, when he spotted two F-4s 30–35 degrees to his right, he quickly turned his aircraft to the left to follow them. Vũ Đình Rạng closed in on his target, placed his target designator on the F-4 No. 2, and when the range to the target was 1.4 miles and his speed was 680 mph, he launched both of his missiles. However, the range was too great and both missiles missed their target. He made a quick right turn to break off. As the runway at Đa Phúc had been heavily damaged, Vũ Đình Rạng was directed to land at Gia Lâm airfield.

As the airfield's runway landing lights had been knocked out, Vũ Đình Rạng landed using his aircraft's spotlight. After the aircraft touched down, it hit a bomb crater, breaking its landing gear struts. When the mechanics inspected the aircraft later, they found that it had numerous shrapnel holes from the missile that had been fired at it during the pilot's return flight to the airfield.

After these first engagements with B-52s, the Vietnamese pilots learned a lesson from this experience. The American fighters assigned to escort the B-52s were using the following tactical trick: when they encountered a MiG, they would switch on their afterburners so that the MiG would see and chase them. Meanwhile, the B-52s would turn off all of the navigation lights on their wings and fuselages. During this engagement it was likely that Vũ Đình Rạng had chased two F-4s that had switched on their afterburners and turned to run in order to lure away the MiG.

On the night of 18 December the tail gunner of a B-52, tail number 56–0676 of the 307th SW, reported that after returning from this bombing mission he shot down one MiG-21. The American side stated that tail gunner

SSgt. Samuel O. Turner had fired the M-60 machine gun mounted in the B-52's tail at a MiG that was headed straight for his B-52, and had hit the wing of the MiG. Turner's claim was supported by another tail gunner in the B-52 cells.[14]

However, all three of the VNPAF MiG-21s that took off to attack B-52s on the night of 18 December and early morning of 19 December 1972 returned and landed at airfields.[15] Therefore the claimed "victory" of tail gunner Turner is not accurate.

19 December 1972: Day Two

In the morning, USAF tactical attackers continued to attack SAM units, airfields, and other important targets. Four flights of MiG-21s took off to intercept and attack them. Fierce air battles took place but no victories were won. In the afternoon, Nguyễn Đức Soát and Nguyễn Thanh Qúy of the 927th FR took off in two MiG-21s. Although the pilots did not shoot down any U.S. aircraft, they did force the American attack aircraft to jettison their bomb loads before they reached their targets.

During the nights of 18 and 19 December 1972, almost all of North Vietnam's airfields were heavily damaged by American bombs. Local people were mobilized to help the engineer troops to quickly repair the airfields so that MiGs could again take off from them. However, because the damage to the runways at Đa Phúc and Kép airfields was so severe, the pilots decided to take off and land using the taxiways, which were only 54 feet wide.

20 December 1972: Day Three

At 1927 hours, a MiG-21 took off from the Đa Phúc airfield taxiway and then flew toward Việt Trì–Phú Thọ. Five minutes later a second MiG took off from Gia Lâm airfield and flew to Mộc Châu–Suối Rút to attack a group of B-52s that was approaching from the northwest. With excellent ground control directions, both MiGs were able to spot their targets. However, when they were about four to five miles from the B-52s, both MiG-21s saw the B-52s suddenly turn off their navigation lights. Meanwhile, the onboard radars of the two MiG-21s were covered with heavy electronic jamming. Both MiG pilots lost sight of their targets and were unable to move in close enough to attack the B-52s, so both pilots were forced to return to land.

Although neither of the two MiGs was able to open fire, they disrupted the formation of B-52s and escort fighters, which reduced the intensity of the enemy's jamming efforts (both active and passive). This caused problems for the B-52s in trying to carry out their planned bombing attacks, and it enabled the SAM guidance operators to more easily and more accurately identify the different jamming signals being emitted by the actual B-52 bomber formations.

On the night of 20 December 1972, the third night of the bombing campaign, the USAF lost six B-52s. This was one of the nights in which the B-52s suffered the heaviest losses. Later, many studies and analyses were written about the USAF's failures (even including criticism of the tactics the B-52s used) during the first three nights of the bombing campaign.

21 December 1972: Day Four

A group of thirty B-52s from U-Tapao air base in Thailand flew in to bomb targets in the Hanoi area on the night of 21 December 1972. When they were forced to defend against MiG-21s, the B-52s had to take evasive action and get out of their predetermined flight paths, so they were no longer protected by the "chaff corridor." Because of this, the SAM units were able to shoot down two B-52s. The aircrews parachuted and were captured.

22 December 1972: Day Five

This was the twenty-eighth anniversary of the founding of the Vietnamese People's Army (VNPA), a day of great significance for all Vietnamese people. On this day, the USAF sent a large number of B-52s to bomb targets in the Hanoi area, including Bạch Mai airfield, Văn Điển, and Thường Tín. Tactical aircraft bombed targets along Route 1 North and Route 2. At night A-6s, A-7s, and F-111s continuously bombed the airfields and a number of important targets.

Around noon Nguyễn Đức Soát and Nguyễn Thanh Qúy of the 927th FR took off from Đa Phúc airfield and were vectored to Thái Nguyên to attack a group of American attack bombers. As the runway at Đa Phúc was severely damaged, the two aircraft had to take off one at a time from the taxiway, which was just 54 feet wide and was lined with bomb craters along both sides. After climbing through the top of the cloud layer and reaching an altitude of 32,000 feet, the flight was directed to attack a group of F-4s over Việt Trì. Suddenly, another group of eight F-4s appeared from the direction of Kép airfield and headed toward the two MiGs. This was a formation of F-4s that had flown in at low altitudes to escort a bomber formation attacking Kép airfield, so it had not been detected by the radars.

When the F-4s were informed by the air early warning net (Red Crown) that MiGs were in the air, the F-4D No. 1, crewed by Lt. Col. James E. Brunson and Maj. Ralph S. Pickett, gave the order to drop auxiliary fuel tanks, increase speed, and climb to intercept the MiGs by coming in from the direction of the sun to attack them. MiG No. 1 Nguyễn Đức Soát initially spotted two F-4s and intended to attack them. Then he saw four more F-4s behind the first pair and two more farther away, also heading toward the MiGs. Nguyễn Đức Soát decided to meet the first two groups of F-4s head-on, planning that as he passed the F-4s he would turn in and get on the tails of the last group of F-4s. Just as he had turned back to get behind the two trailing F-4s, the two F-4s in front were also turning back and diving sharply. When he got behind them and the range to the target was about two miles, he saw two F-4s coming in head-on firing missiles at his wingman. Nguyễn Đức Soát immediately shouted, "Turn hard! They're firing missiles!" However, Nguyễn Đức Soát did not hear any reply from his wingman Nguyễn Thanh Quý.

Also at this time, the two F-4s being chased by MiG No. 1 made a very sharp turn. Realizing that he would not be able to attack them, Nguyễn Đức Soát decided to break off the engagement. The two F-4s that were coming at the MiG head-on also fired four missiles at him. Nguyễn Đức Soát made a hard turn, flew into the clouds, made more turns, and then, after he was over the lowlands passing Hải Dương, he dropped down below the clouds and landed at Đa Phúc airfield.

The MiG wingman Nguyễn Thanh Quý, who had been hit by the F-4 missiles, ejected successfully and parachuted safely to the ground in the Sơn Dương area of Tuyên Quang Province. Based on the reported details of the air engagement, we can assume that the F-4D that chased and fired four AIM-7E-2 missiles at Nguyễn Thanh Quý was the aircraft flown by Lt. Col. James E. Brunson and Maj. Ralph S. Pickett from the 555th TFS/432nd TRW.[16]

Meanwhile, an F-4D flown by Capt. Gary L. Sholders and 1st Lt. Eldon D. Binkley of the 555th TFS/432nd TRW, which had been assigned to the

MiGCAP mission to support the B-52s, was directed to pursue a single MiG-21 that was approaching to land at Yên Bái airfield. After this engagement the MiG-21 crashed and the pilot was forced to eject.[17] However, the VNPAF has no record of any MiG that was lost and its pilot forced to eject in the early morning of 22 December 1972.

23 December 1972: Day Six

At 0018 hours of 23 December 1972, a 921st FR MiG-21 took off from Miếu Môn airfield then flew to Nho Quan in Ninh Bình Province to find and attack B-52s, but the MiG pilot was unable to find the target, so he turned back to land at Đa Phúc airfield. Between 1320 hours and 1430 hours, sixty USAF tactical aircraft attacked the Đông Anh, Hòa Lạc, Việt Trì, and Cầu Diễn areas. F-4 fighters assigned to the MiGCAP mission waited over five different holding pattern areas, with four F-4s waiting in each area to suppress MiG operations. At the AF command post, Colonel Đào Đình Luyện decided to implement the plan for a daylight attack. The 921st FR would send up a MiG as a diversion in order to draw enemy fighters up north of Tam Đảo, while a flight of two MiGs from the 927th FR would take off to make the main attack against enemy aircraft over southern Hòa Bình Province.

The 927th FR ordered Nguyễn Văn Nghĩa and Lê Văn Kiển to take off from Đa Phúc airfield at 1340 hours and then directed them to turn right to a heading of 200 degrees. When the pilots reached Phủ Lý, they were ordered to climb up through the top of the cloud layer, turn to a heading of 290 degrees, drop their auxiliary fuel tanks, and increase speed to 745 mph. The flight was directed to climb to an altitude of 27,000 feet in order to avoid a group of enemy fighters, and to intercept a U.S. attacker group flying from west of Sầm Tơ to Suối Rút. The command post informed the pilots, "Black crows, six flights 45 degrees to the right, range fourteen miles." At that time the American escort fighters discovered that two MiGs were chasing them, so they fired a number of missiles at the two MiGs. The GCI officer at the AF HQ command post informed the pilots, "Target 30 degrees on the left, range twelve miles, four F-4s!" Immediately after, Nguyễn Văn Nghĩa spotted four aircraft 30 degrees to the right at a range of twelve miles. He quickly informed the command post and his wingman of his sighting.

Just as had been predicted, when the range to the F-4s was six miles, the four F-4s began the traditional combat weave maneuver used by American fighter aircraft, meaning that two aircraft made a sharp turn to the left while the two other aircraft made a gradual turn to the right to try to "lure" the MiGs in to attack them. The MiG lead decided to use the enemy's own tactics to quickly close in to attack before the enemy had a chance to react. He shouted, "I will attack the guys on the right" and ordered his No. 2 to attack the section on the left. Nguyễn Văn Nghĩa turned inside the F-4 and when the range was 0.8 miles and he had his target designator stabilized on the target, he pressed the missile-firing button. After seeing that the missile warhead explosion totally enveloped the F-4, he quickly pulled his stick over to break away because before firing he had seen two U.S. fighters at his six o'clock, getting into a position to prepare to fire missiles at him. At that time, MiG No. 2 shouted, "The target is burning!" When Nguyễn Văn Nghĩa pulled over hard to the left to break away, he saw an aircraft that was turning in the same direction. After looking around and being sure that there were no F-4s behind him, he decided to chase this F-4. When the range was 0.7 miles, while both aircraft were still turning, he launched his second missile then he quickly turned to break away. Nguyễn Văn Nghĩa then dove to an altitude of 600 feet to fly back and land safely at Đa Phúc airfield at 1402 hours.

So, during the air engagements on 23 December 1972, Nguyễn Văn Nghĩa from the 927th FR shot down one F-4 over Hòa Bình Province. This was the fifth U.S. aircraft that he shot down and was the first F-4 that was shot down by the VNPAF during the twelve days of the "Điện Biên Phủ in the Air" campaign.[18]

24 December 1972: Day Seven

The night of 24 December 1972 in the Western calendar was Christmas Eve. The USAF reduced the intensity of its bombing attacks and concentrated them primarily on the outer perimeter, but they still sent thirty B-52s from U-Tapao to attack the Thái Nguyên railroad line, Kép airfield, and Bắc Giang City. In addition, thirty-nine USAF tactical aircraft attacked Yên Bái and Kép airfields, and the Vĩnh Tuy area on the outskirts of Hanoi. Also, the tail gunner of B-52 No. 55–0083, A1C Albert E. Moore of the 307th SW, reported that he used his M-60 .50-caliber machine gun to shoot down a MiG-21. Moore's "victory" was witnessed by another B-52 tail gunner named Clarence W. Chute, who said that he saw the MiG-21 on fire and falling away.[19]

However, VNPAF had no records of any combat flight sorties or any MiG losses on the night of 24 December 1972. Therefore, the B-52 tail gunner's claim of victory is not accurate.

25 December 1972: Day Eight

Anticipating that on the night of 24 December and morning of 25 December 1972, the USAF and USN would reduce the intensity of their attacks, in the morning of 25 December, the AD and AF Service held a conference, with high-ranking officers and experienced combat pilots in attendance, to assess the result of the first phase of the campaign and to formulate the battle plan for the second phase. At the conclusion of the conference, the AD and AF Service Command HQ issued the following directive:

> Although the enemy has suffered a painful defeat, he will continue to attack targets in Hanoi. The enemy will attack SAM sites and will change his tactics. He will increase his electronic jamming efforts to jam our radars and our radio communications. He will attack from both the southwest and the northeast and will attack the center of the city in order to put maximum pressure on us. Therefore, the AD and AF Service Command HQ requests all forces to review and learn lessons from the battles of the first phase and prepare battle plans designed to increase combat effectiveness. Particular emphasis is to be placed on making an all-out effort to enable our AF fighters to shoot down B-52s.[20]

26 December 1972: Day Nine

This date was Boxing Day in the Western countries, but in Hanoi and other areas of North Vietnam, innocent people still suffered from cruel bomb attacks by the B-52s' strategic bombing. After a thirty-six-hour bombing halt, at 1300 hours on 26 December 1972, the USAF used fifty-six air combat sorties of TAC to attack SAM units and other targets on the outskirts of

Hanoi. The basic plan for the 26 December raid, unlike the earlier maximum efforts, was using 120 aircraft to strike nine different target complexes in ten separate bomber waves. The support forces for this night raid were 113 combat mission sorties, not counting the refuel mission sorties of tankers. It was apparent that this attack mission was the most ambitious raid to date. It was also the most savage bombing attack during Linebacker II. Leading the formation of B-52s on that night was Col. James. R. McCarthy, commander of the 43rd SW (in Major Stocker's aircraft as airborne mission commander, ABC).[21] Learning lessons from the first phase of the campaign, on that night, the USAF changed their tactic when flying in to attack the targets. The bombing tactics, the spacing between cells, the altitudes for different cells, and the attack directions were changed significantly (some U.S. authors said that, on the night of 26 December, the B-52s were sent in from seven directions simultaneously), and were modified in each wave.[22] At 2200 hours, the USAF used 105 B-52 bombing sorties and 110 TAC aircraft to strike targets in Hanoi, Hải Phòng, and Thái Nguyên. On the night of 26 December 1972, B-52s dropped bombs on Khâm Thiên Street, a very populous street in Hanoi, damaging seventeen blocks of civilian buildings and killing hundreds of innocent people.

On the night of 26 December 1972, the AD and AF Command's SAM units and AAA units shot down sixteen American aircraft, including eight B-52s and one HH-53 helicopter. Four of these aircraft crashed on the spot and numerous U.S. crew members were captured. The battle fought on the night of 26 December 1972 was extremely savage and was of key and decisive significance because it accelerated the Vietnamese forces' progress toward achieving total victory in the "Điện Biên Phủ in the Air" campaign. VNPAF's MiG units continued their preparations for coming battles.

27 December 1972: Day Ten:
The First B-52 Shot Down by a MiG-21

While the Nixon administration was under extreme pressure from the press and from public opinion over the bombing of Hanoi, the United States received the news that, on 26 December 1972, former president Harry Truman had died. Still, the B-52 bombing and TAC fighter attacks over North Vietnam continued. According to strategic intelligence reports, on

27 December 1972 the USAF would send sixty bomber aircraft to attack Hanoi, Thái Nguyên, targets along Routes 2 and 3, and the airfields.

The commanding officers on duty at the AF HQ command post were AF Corps: Commander Đào Đình Luyện, political commissar Văn Duy, and deputy AF commander Trần Hanh. The GCI officer at the AF HQ was Lê Thành Chơn, the GCI officer at the AF command post was Lê Kiếu, and the GCI officer at the Mộc Châu command post was Lương Văn Vóc. At the 927th FR, the commanding officer on duty was deputy regiment commander Nguyễn Nhật Chiêu and the duty GCI officers were Hoàng Đức Hạnh and Phạm Công Kim. The GCI officers at the B-1 command post (at Thọ Xuân airfield) were Đinh Văn Nghĩa and Hoàng Trung Thông. Analyzing the situation and the probability of attacks by the USAF and USN that day, the AF HQ ordered two MiG-21 FRs to mount attacks against the enemy bomber strike groups in order to protect targets in all sectors, and especially to protect the SAM launch sites, and also to resolutely attack and shoot down B-52s at night and on the spot.

On 27 December 1972 the weather over NVN was good. The USAF and USN sent a large-scale strike group to attack both Hanoi and Hải Phòng areas, using both standard (dumb) bombs and laser-guided bombs to attack the SAM launch sites and the radar ground control stations. During this attack raid, U.S. bombers used a new tactic, which was that they split the wave coming in from the northeast into three smaller streams, attacked separate targets, and then reformed into one wave after post-target turn (PTT).[23]

Đỗ Văn Lanh and Dương Bá Kháng were ordered to take off at 1334 hours and then proceeded on a heading of 50 degrees at an altitude of 1,600 feet. One minute later, the command post informed the pilots, "Enemy aircraft 90 degrees to your left, range ten miles." As he was concentrating on looking for the enemy, Đỗ Văn Lanh heard a voice over the radio say, "Enemy aircraft 1.8 miles behind you!" At the same time No. 1 heard his wingman shout, "Make a hard right-hand turn!" When No. 2 saw two F-4s behind them that were speeding toward the MiGs, he informed his lead and then pulled back his throttle to allow the F-4s to fly past him. The two F-4s were conducting a combat weave maneuver. Dương Bá Kháng decided to chase the F-4 No. 1. When the range was down to 0.9 miles, he fired his missile, which sped straight into the F-4, causing it to burst into flames and dive nose-first toward the ground. Dương Bá Kháng quickly made a left turn to break away. He formed up with his lead, flew back to Đa Phúc airfield, and landed safely at 1354 hours.

At the 921st FR, a flight of two MiG-21s was on combat alert duty at Đa Phúc airfield and was assigned to fly a "diversionary" mission, while pilot Trần Việt who was on combat alert at Miếu Môn airfield was assigned to carry out the primary attack. A large number of American aircraft were operating over Hòa Bình Province, and it was considered likely that these were aircraft assigned to search for and rescue a downed U.S. pilot. Early in the afternoon the command post ordered the flight of two diversionary aircraft, flown by Trần Sang and Bùi Thanh Liêm, to take off and fly at a high altitude to Việt Trì to try to lure the F-4s into chasing them. Then, at 1410 hours, the single MiG-21 piloted by Trần Việt that was waiting in ambush at Miếu Môn airfield took off (at that time all of the inner-line airfields had either been rendered unusable by American bombing attacks or were under surveillance and pressure by American fighters). Trần Việt was ordered to fly under the cloud layer on a heading of 90 degrees to a point south of Phủ Lý, so that he could then turn back to come in behind a group of F-4s. A few minutes later, Trần Việt was informed that the target was 45 degrees to his right at a range of twelve miles. He was ordered to drop his auxiliary fuel tank and climb to an altitude of 22,000 feet. One minute later he spotted two F-4s 45 degrees to his right and below him at a range of five miles. Trần Việt decided to switch on his afterburner, accelerated to more than 620 mph, and made a sharp right turn to get on the tail of the F-4 No. 2, which was in a dive. After centering his target designator, at a range of 0.9 miles and a speed of 680 mph he fired a missile from under his left wing. He felt his MiG shudder slightly and saw the missile drop off the missile pylon and then speed straight at the target, making it burst into flames.[24] Trần Việt quickly turned to break away and landed at Đa Phúc airfield at 1432 hours.

This F-4E was flown by Maj. Carl H. Jeffcoat and 1st Lt. Jack R. Trimble of the 13th TFS/432nd TRW. The F-4 was flying a MiGCAP mission to support aircraft searching for an F-111 that had been shot down the night before. The F-4E crashed thirty-five miles northwest of Hanoi. Both pilots ejected and were quickly captured.[25]

Toward the end of the day, the Supreme Command issued the following instructions to the AD and AF Service: "You must protect our SAM units and enable our AF aircraft to take off from the outer ring of our airfields to intercept and attack the B-52s outside of the range of our missiles and enable us to engage the enemy in the northwestern sector and shoot down B-52s." Taking advantage of the time when U.S. aircraft were exiting North Vietnam after completing their strike missions, the AF HQ ordered Phạm Tuân to fly from Nội Bài to Yên Bái airfield in order to wait there in ambush and be ready to take off to attack the B-52s. As Yên Bái airfield had been heavily damaged some days earlier by the American attacks, the Americans did not think that the airfield could be quickly restored to operational status. However, thanks to the participation of the local people, by the afternoon of 27 December the airfield had been repaired sufficiently to allow a MiG to land and take off at Yên Bái airfield. Phạm Tuân secretly flew to Yên Bái and landed there safely.

At 2212 hours, radar station C-22 at Mộc Châu (where the duty GCI officer was Lương Văn Vóc) picked up a number of B-52s flying from Sốp Khao to Sam Neua. At the AF command post, the chief of the duty ground control section Lê Liên, duty officer Đặng Dũng, GCI officer Nguyễn Đăng Điền, and short-range plotting board plotter Nguyễn Văn Tý quickly collated the reports and decided to direct Phạm Tuân to attack the tail-end group of B-52s. The radar ground control officer was ordered to focus his tracking efforts on this B-52 group. Phạm Tuân's MiG-21 was fully prepared and ready. The head of the technical team that checked and maintained Phạm Tuân's MiG was mechanic Nguyễn Văn Lân.

At 2222 hours Phạm Tuân took off from Yên Bái airfield, climbed through the cloud layer, and turned to fly on a heading of 230 degrees. At 2224 hours the Mộc Châu ground control station ordered him to turn to a 190-degree heading. At that time the group of B-52s was about twenty-four miles from the Mộc Châu ground control station, and radar station C-22 was experiencing Level 3 electronic jamming. The AF command post informed the pilot that the target was 20 degrees to the pilot's right at a range of forty-eight miles. Just to make it certain, Phạm Tuân asked, "Is it a big one or a little one?" The command post replied, "Big!" The atmosphere inside the command post grew quiet. Everyone was very calm, as if an important moment in history was about to occur.

At about 2226 hours, Phạm Tuân was ordered to drop his auxiliary fuel tank, increase speed to 600 mph, and turn to a heading of 70 degrees. When the B-52s flew directly past the Mộc Châu control station, the command post calculated the estimated flight path to direct the MiG precisely to intercept the B-52s. At 2229 hours and 30 seconds Phạm Tuân reported that he could see the navigation lights of the B-52s. The command post informed him that the target was six miles in front of him and ordered him to increase his speed to 870 mph. As Phạm Tuân was chasing the B-52s the command post continuously provided him with reports on the range to the target and reminded him to fire both of his missiles at the target. Phạm Tuân viewed the line of B-52 navigation lights both with his naked eyes and with his optical sight. When the range was down to 1.2 miles, he requested permission to fire his missiles. He adjusted his target designator and pressed the firing button when the range was just a little more than 0.7 miles. The two missiles left their missile pylons and sped straight for the B-52 in front of the MiG. It was 2234 hours.

After launching his missiles, Phạm Tuân quickly broke off the engagement by pulling his aircraft into a sharp climb. He then rolled his aircraft upside down to look around. He clearly saw a ball of flames enveloping the B-52 and lighting up the sky. He quickly dove down to an altitude of 6,500 feet and turned to a heading of 360 degrees to return to Yên Bái. At 2239 hours the Yên Bái airfield control tower made contact with the aircraft and brought the MiG in to a safe landing at 2246 hours. At that same moment, the 921st FR command post ordered Nguyễn Khánh Duy to take off and be ready to make another attack on the B-52s in the area over Thái Nguyên–Phú Thọ.

So within the first ten days of fighting against Linebacker II during which the U.S. B-52s dropped bombs on Hanoi and Hải Phòng and other areas of Vietnam, a VNPAF MiG, coordinating with SAM units, for the first time in history shot down a B-52, one of the USAF's so-called "flying fortresses," which had been thought to be invulnerable.[26]

On the night of 27–28 December 1972 the USAF acknowledged the loss of two B-52s and one F-4.[27] One B-52D, flown by Capt. John Mize and a crew of six men from the 28th BW (Bomber Wing), attached to the 307th SW, which had taken off from U-Tapao air base and was part of a formation of sixty B-52s assigned to bomb targets in Hanoi, was hit by a missile. Capt. John Mize and his crew managed to fly the heavily damaged B-52 back across the border, but the aircraft caught fire and crashed in an area fifteen miles southwest of Nakhon Phanom. The second B-52 that was shot down during the night of 27 December was a B-52D flown by Capt. Frank Douglas Lewis and a six-man crew. The B-52 was assigned to the 7th BW but was attached to the 43rd SW. Based on the reported details of the air engagement, this was the B-52 that Phạm Tuân pursued and hit with his two R-3S missiles.[28] The cell of three B-52s that Phạm Tuân attacked was Ivory Cell, the tail-end cell in a formation of four B-52 cells that had flown in to bomb targets in North Vietnam.

After the war, Lieutenant General Phạm Tuân was appointed political commissar of the VNP AD and AF Service, and then was appointed head of the General Department of Defense Industry of the VNP Army. He was the first Vietnamese astronaut (1980) and was twice awarded the honorable title VNP Armed Forces Hero.

28 December 1972: Day Eleven

On the eleventh day of Linebacker II, the AD and AF Service received a directive from the General Staff that stated that, because of the heavy losses it had suffered, the United States might be forced to end the bombing campaign. The directive instructed the AD and AF units to continue to strike hard blows to force the United States to end the conflict quickly.

On that day, the commanding officers on duty at the AF command post were the deputy Air Force Corps commander, Trần Hanh, and the political commissar Văn Duy, while the on-duty GCI officers were Phạm Minh Cậy and Tạ Văn Vượng. The officers on duty at the 927th Regiment command post were the commander, Nguyễn Hồng Nhị, and the GCI officer, Vũ Đức Bình; the GCI officer at radar station C-43 was Đào Văn Thành. Based on the analysis of the intelligence reports and on the activities of the U.S. reconnaissance aircraft during the early morning hours, the AF HQ concluded that on 28 December the USAF would most probably send large strike groups to attack targets in the Hanoi area, along Route 2, Miếu Môn airfield, and the Xuân Mai intersection. Meanwhile, the USN would continue to attack Hải Phòng and targets along the coast. In addition, the attacks might come from two different directions: one from the mouth of the Đáy River–Phủ Lý to attack Xuân Mai, and the other from the Bà Lạt inlet and flying up the

Red River to attack Văn Điển. In fact, on 28 December the USAF sent sixty B-52 bombers from Andersen and U-Tapao air bases to bomb important targets in Hanoi and Hải Phòng.

Large numbers of American fighters assigned to MiGCAP duty flew fighter escort missions and also flew in holding areas over Sơn Động, Yên Tử, Chợ Bến, and Xuân Mai. The VNPAF had learned that the USN's standard operating procedure was that, after the attack bombers completed their attacks, RA-5C reconnaissance aircraft accompanied by F-4J fighter escorts would be sent in to take photographs to assess the results of the bombing attacks.

Based on this analysis and assessment of the Americans' intentions, the AF HQ issued an order to the 927th FR to launch aircraft to fight independently by attacking bomber strike groups within the perimeter of the SAM umbrella to protect Hanoi. The regiment was also instructed to be prepared to fight enemy strike groups in both the southeast and the west. The weather in the battle area was as follows: visibility six to nine miles, 90 percent cumulus cloud cover at an altitude of 1,800 feet.

The 927th FR assigned the daylight combat alert mission to Lê Văn Kiển (MiG-21 PFM No. 5023) and Lieutenant Hoàng Tam Hùng (MiG-21 PFM No. 5013). This would be the first MiG-21 combat mission for young pilot Hoàng Tam Hùng. Aircraft technician Bùi Văn Cơ (who at that time was the commander of the mechanical maintenance company and was in charge of maintenance for the combat alert aircraft) had just signed the log certifying that the aircraft were ready for flight when pilots Lê Văn Kiển and Hoàng Tam Hùng arrived to sign for their aircraft. Company commander Bùi Văn Cơ, who was standing next to the team of mechanics assigned to MiG No. 5013, mentioned to Hoàng Tam Hùng the Western superstition related to the number thirteen. Hoàng Tam Hùng insisted that he was not afraid of thirteen. He said that all he needed was for the aircraft to be properly prepared and ready for action. If that was done, he said that he would take off and successfully accomplish the mission.

At 1110 hours a number of large USN strike groups appeared on the B-1 net. They were approaching from the sea over southern Thanh Hóa and flying in at low altitudes, headed toward the area southeast of Hanoi. At 1117 hours the command post ordered Lê Văn Kiển and Hoàng Tam Hùng to start their engines and take off, then the flight was directed to fly left-hand circles in a holding pattern directly over the airfield. At 1119 hours first radar station C-50 and then radar station C-43 picked up the targets and tracked a formation of twelve aircraft in a USN strike formation headed in to attack the Mễ Trì radio transmitting station. There were also F-4J fighters assigned to MiGCAP duty, which flew in circles in a holding pattern at an altitude of 10,000 feet, forty-six miles south of Hanoi, waiting to intercept any MiGs.

A few minutes later, the command post ordered the flight to turn to a heading of 150 degrees, drop auxiliary fuel tanks, switch on afterburners, and climb to an altitude of 3,500 feet. At that time, Hoàng Tam Hùng reported that he had spotted three enemy aircraft 40 degrees to the right at a range of nine miles. This was a composite formation made up of one RA-5C flying a photographic reconnaissance mission and two F-4J escort fighters. At that time there was a large number of F-4s in the area, and a savage unequal air battle began between the two MiG-21s and twelve F-4s. When the RA-5C completed its mission of photographing fuel storage tanks and missile launch sites, the two F-4s warned the RA-5C pilot of "MiGs at eight o'clock." The two F-4s shouted for the RA-5C to head out to sea to escape, while the F-4s turned back to engage the MiGs. However, it was too late. Using well-practiced movements, the pilot of the MiG No. 2 cleverly and skillfully got on the tail of the RA-5C.

When he spotted four more enemy aircraft 90 degrees to the left at a range of four to six miles, MiG No. 1 immediately turned left to chase those four aircraft. When he had closed to a range of 2.5–3 miles, the four F-4s made sharp turns and then turned and disappeared into the clouds. At that moment No. 1 felt his aircraft shake. He looked back to the rear and saw two F-4s roar right under the belly of his MiG. He decided to make a hard turn to chase the tail-end F-4. However, by the time he had closed the range to 2.4–3 miles, the two F-4s in front had turned back and made a sharp turn to get behind him. Seeing that this situation was not to his advantage, Lê Văn Kiền requested permission to break off the engagement then returned and landed safely at Nội Bài at 1134 hours.

On that day an F-4J flown by Lt. (jg) Scott H. Davis and Lt. (jg) Geoffrey H. "Jeff" Ulrich of VF-142 of the USS *Enterprise* was assigned to fly fighter escort for an RA-5C conducting a photographic reconnaissance mission.

When the flight reached Phủ Lý it was probably informed by the air early warning net (Red Crown) that MiGs were headed toward the F-4s. Two MiGs and twelve F-4s fought a ferocious dogfight, becoming so intermingled that the F-4s were unable to identify the MiGs with their radars and did not dare to fire their missiles indiscriminately. The MiGs turned and maneuvered to get on the tail of the RA-5C. Lt. Cdr. Alfred Howard Agnew, the RA-5C pilot, was warned by the F-4s of the presence of the MiGs and was told to make a sharp turn immediately. The RA-5C pilot made very violent evasive maneuvers at a speed of over 620 mph when he realized that he had a MiG on his tail (while two F-4Js were sticking behind them, waiting for an opportunity to fire missiles at MiG). Hoàng Tam Hùng figured out the RA-5C's pattern of evasive maneuvers. He waited until the RA-5C leveled its wings for a moment to check on the other aircraft in its formation before rolling his aircraft over to make a sharp turn back in the other direction. Hoàng Tam Hùng quickly placed his target designator on the target and fired a missile. The missile dropped slightly and then sped straight at the RA-5C, causing it to burst into a ball of flames and crash south of Hanoi. The RA-5C shot down by Hoàng Tam Hùng was flown by Lt. Cdr. Alfred Howard Agnew and Lt. Michael Firestone Haifley of RVAH-13, aircraft carrier USS *Enterprise*. The pilot, Lieutenant Commander Agnew, ejected and was captured.[29] The burning RA-5C crashed southeast of Hanoi.

At the 927th FR's command post, the radio communications between the command post and the pilot were very poor because there was such heavy enemy electronic jamming that day. The GCI officers heard only the pilot's request for permission to make an attack and then the pilot's shout, "He's burning!" After that, all radio communications were lost.

After shooting the RA-5C down, Hoàng Tam Hùng broke off the engagement and turned back to land at his base. At that time there was a large number of F-4s chasing Hoàng Tam Hùng's MiG. An F-4J (possibly flown by Lt. (jg) Scott H. Davis) closed in and turned into the MiG at an angle of 75 degrees, then fired an AIM-9 missile in front of the MiG's nose to try to prevent the MiG from escaping into the clouds. Hoàng Tam Hùng had planned to escape into the clouds in order to return to the airfield, but when he saw so many F-4s chasing him he decided to turn back to make a counterattack.

The MiG-21 and the F-4s fought a ferocious dogfight. After flying a number of turning circles in the dogfight, Hoàng Tam Hùng got on the tail of one F-4 and launched his second missile, which shot down an F-4.[30] The F-4's crew both ejected. As the USAF was transmitting powerful electronic signals to jam the air-to-ground communications channels, the command post was unable to hear the pilot's report on the battle or provide supporting command instructions to the pilot.[31] After firing the missile at one F-4, the MiG immediately turned away and dove through a hole in the clouds down to a low altitude. The F-4s chased the MiG. When they emerged from the clouds, the aircraft of the two sides were only 100–150 feet above the ground. At the very moment that Lieutenant Davis pressed his missile-firing button the MiG suddenly made a sharp turn back in the other direction, causing the missile to miss its target.

The MiG and the F-4s continued to chase one another at extremely low altitudes. They flew right over the rice paddies of the Red River delta that had recently been harvested. Many people standing on the Red River dikes and soldiers assigned to AAA positions in the area of Thường Tín District, Hanoi City, witnessed the heroic air battle between the MiG and a dozen F-4s. After several sharp turns at extremely low altitudes, just at the moment the MiG leveled its wings, the F-4 fired another AIM-7E missile. Hoàng Tam Hùng was able to avoid the missile, but because he had made such a sharp maneuver at an extremely low altitude (or perhaps because one portion of the MiG's control system had been damaged by one of the F-4's missiles), his MiG went into a stall. The aircraft suddenly pitched up into a 20-degree nose-high position, and then nosed over into a 50-degree dive. The aircraft hit the ground and exploded. Hoàng Tam Hùng's MiG-21 crashed in Tự Nhiên Village, Thường Tín District, Hanoi City, less than 330 feet from the banks of the Red River.

On 13 January 1973, the *Quân Đội Nhân Dân* newspaper published a story about the combat achievements of Lieutenant Hoàng Tam Hùng in the air battle fought on 28 December 1972: "In just a few short minutes of courageous and clever fighting, Hoàng Tam Hùng had accomplished the incredible feat of shooting down two American aircraft that both crashed on the spot."[32] The Navy RA-5C that Hoàng Tam Hùng shot down was the first aircraft of this type shot down by the VNPAF. Lieutenant Hoàng Tam Hùng and Senior Lieutenant Vũ Xuân Thiều (who also scored a victory and was killed on the night of 28 December 1972) were the last Vietnamese pilots killed in the glorious air battles fought by the VNPAF to defend the skies of the Fatherland. Hoàng Tam Hùng died shortly before the day of victory and just twenty-eight days before his twenty-fourth birthday. Later, Lieutenant Hoàng Tam Hùng was posthumously awarded the honorable title VNP Armed Forces Hero.

The Night Air Battle Fought by Vũ Xuân Thiều

After Phạm Tuân's victory on the night of 27 December 1972, on 28 December the AD and AF Service held a conference to review the battle at the command post at Trầm Pagoda. The AD and AF Service commander in chief, Lê Văn Tri, and political commissar Hoàng Phương presided over this meeting. Minister of National Defense General Võ Nguyên Giáp attended the meeting and told the participants to "aggressively study and gain a firm understanding of the enemy's new tricks so that you can fight even more successful battles in the future." It was a great honor for the AD and AF Service command post to be visited by Supreme Commander Võ Nguyên Giáp, who gave his advice and guidance and stayed at the AD and AF Service Command post for the entire day of 28 December 1972.[33]

The AD and AF Service HQ and the AF Corps decided to position the MiG-21 to be used in the nighttime battle at Cẩm Thủy airfield (located in Thạch Thành District, Thanh Hóa Province). The pilot selected to fly the aircraft to the new airfield and to stand combat alert duty that night was Vũ Xuân Thiều, of the 927th FR. At 1530 hours Deputy AF Commander Trần Mạnh sent a message from the AF's forward command post at Thọ Xuân airfield to the AF HQ command post, recommending that Vũ Xuân Thiều be authorized to take off to fly to Cẩm Thủy. Vũ Xuân Thiều took off and then followed Route 1 at an altitude of 660 feet, using a flight plan in which strict radio silence was maintained. He landed safely at Cẩm Thủy airfield and immediately went on combat alert duty as he stood by, ready to fight.

With information provided by the strategic intelligence net that, between 2130 and 2350 hours on the night of 28 December, fifty B-52s would attack Hanoi and Hải Phòng. the AF HQ ordered all command posts and all combat alert units to closely monitor the developments and to be ready to take off to fly combat missions. Pilot Vũ Xuân Thiều, assigned to combat alert duty at Cẩm Thủy airfield, and pilot Đinh Tôn, assigned to combat alert duty at Đa Phúc airfield, were both ready for action. The AF HQ paid particular attention to the combat readiness preparations of the command post at Thọ Xuân airfield and the MiG-21 flight on combat alert at Cẩm Thủy (XB-90 airfield). From 2100 to 2222 hours radar stations C-26, C-22, C-50, C-53, and C-43 were ordered, one by one, to switch on their radar transmitters.

At 2138 hours a second B-52 cell, and then a third B-52 cell, were detected fifty-five miles southeast of Paksane. At the frontline command post, Deputy AF Commander Trần Mạnh concluded that these were B-52 cells assigned to bomb Hanoi. Trần Mạnh ordered his ground control and military intelligence officers to closely monitor these target groups. He also ordered Vũ Xuân Thiều to prepare for take off. The MiG-21 that Vũ Xuân Thiều would fly on this mission was carefully and meticulously prepared for this combat mission by a team of mechanics headed by Nguyễn Mạnh Nỏ. At 2130 hours the Thọ Xuân command post ordered Vũ Xuân Thiều to go to Combat Alert Condition Level 1. Seven minutes later, the AF HQ command post ordered Đinh Tôn, waiting at Đa Phúc airfield, to go to Combat Alert Duty Level 1.

The commanding officer on duty at Cẩm Thủy airfield was Hoàng Biểu, a very experienced night fighter pilot, and the GCI officers were Trần Đức Tụ and Trần Xuân Mão. At 2141 hours Vũ Xuân Thiều was ordered to take off from the Cẩm Thủy rough military airfield. At the frontline command post, Deputy AF Commander Trần Mạnh and the duty watch team concluded that the B-52 formation flying north from Thailand would turn toward Mộc Châu when it reached Sam Neua and then fly down to bomb Hanoi. The duty ground control team made calculations and then decided to guide the MiG in to intercept and attack the B-52s after they made their turn.

At 2152 hours the B-1 command post (at Thọ Xuân) ordered Vũ Xuân Thiều to turn right to a heading of 360 degrees and informed him that his target was in front of him at a bearing of 50 degrees and a range of nine miles. However, because the enemy's electronic jamming was powerful Vũ Xuân Thiều was still not able to detect the target. At this time the radar ground control officer in the command post was Trần Xuân Mão. Using his wealth of experience, he found a dirty white spot that appeared through the jamming signals that covered his screen and was certain that this was a B-52 return signal. The B-52s had changed course and were flying to Sơn La, after which they would turn south to attack Hanoi. The command post immediately ordered Vũ Xuân Thiều to make a sharp right-hand turn to a heading of 90 degrees. After he reached Sam Neua, he would be directed to turn north to follow the B-52s that were heading toward Nà Sản in Sơn La Province.

The command post was exactly correct. At 2158 hours, when Vũ Xuân Thiều was over Sơn La, he spotted the target. He immediately reported his sighting to the command post and accelerated to pursue the target. The entire duty watch team was excited when they received Vũ Xuân Thiều's report. In the black of night and with his aircraft radar affected by heavy enemy jamming, it was difficult to determine the range to the target, but Vũ Xuân Thiều calmly made a visual estimate of the range by looking at the line of navigation lights on the B-52s. At this time Deputy AF Commander Trần Mạnh in the frontline command post transmitted the following verbal reminder to the pilot: "046, remember to switch your weapons system to fire all your missiles at once in order to be sure to destroy the enemy." Vũ Xuân Thiều replied, "Roger." When he heard the audible tone indicating that his missile's heat-seeker had a good lock on the target and when it was in the firing range, he fired both of his missiles. The two R-3S missiles sped forward and hit the B-52, which was by then very close to his MiG. The B-52 burst into flames and crashed near Cò Nòi hamlet in Sơn La Province. The command post then lost radio contact with Vũ Xuân Thiều. The B-1 command post repeatedly broadcast radio messages saying, "046, is everything all right?" They received no response from him. The entire command post was silent as everyone anxiously waited for a reply from him. However, the silence was eternal. With their experience and their sixth senses as commanders, deputy AF commanders Trần Mạnh and Trần Hanh understood that something unusual had happened. The same thought occurred to both men: because it was very hard to estimate distances to targets at night, after firing his two missiles that hit the target, Vũ Xuân Thiều's aircraft most probably collided with the B-52.[34]

Vũ Xuân Thiều died heroically after shooting a B-52 out of the skies over Cò Nòi in Sơn La Province. The AD and AF Service confirmed the victory and credited pilot Vũ Xuân Thiều with shooting down one B-52.

Later, Senior Lieutenant Vũ Xuân Thiều was posthumously awarded the honorable title VNP Armed Forces Hero.

RECOLLECTIONS OF PILOT NGUYỄN ĐỨC SOÁT

At 2300 hours on 28 December 1972 the FR's commander, Nguyễn Hồng Nhị, called me in to the command post and turned on our air-to-ground radio channel [recorder] so we could listen to the air battle. The next day [29 December 1972], after holding the morning staff meeting and working out the battle plan for the next day, Lieutenant Colonel Nguyễn Hồng Nhị said that the AD and AF Service HQ had informed him that on the night of 28 December Vũ Xuân Thiều had shot down one B-52 while flying at an unfavorable altitude. The report said that he had estimated the range visually by looking at the navigation lights and had not used his radar. One minute later radio contact with Vũ Xuân Thiều had been lost. It was feared that he had gotten too close and had either collided with a B-52 or flown into a mountain. In addition, the report said, during interrogation the crew of an F-4 that had been captured stated that they had been shot down by a MiG-21. Based on the interrogation report, the Service now credited Hoàng Tam Hùng with shooting down two enemy aircraft.[35]

29 December 1972: The End of Linebacker II

The United States followed virtually the same attack pattern on the last day of Linebacker II, which was that during the day they sent tactical aircraft to conduct reconnaissance and to attack any targets that survived the B-52 bombing attacks of the previous night, and also to attack SAM launch sites.

The AD and AF HQ received information that, on the night of 29 December, fifty B-52s would conduct two waves of attacks against Hanoi and Hải Phòng. The first attack wave would consist of six cells (a total of eighteen B-52s) and the second wave would consist of nine cells (twenty-seven B-52s). They would approach following a flight path from Sam Neua to Nà Sản, then to Bảo Hà, Tam Đảo, and finally Hanoi. There would be a total of twenty-four support aircraft (F-4s and F-105s).

The AF HQ ordered nighttime fighter pilots of the 921st FR to wait in ambush at the airfields outside of the AD umbrella (Kép, Yên Bái, and Miếu Môn airfields), to be ready to take off to intercept the attackers. MiG-21 pilots of the 5th Night Fighter Company were ordered to be ready to take off to attack B-52s and tactical attack bombers approaching in three different sectors.

The B-1 net picked up four B-52 cells approaching from the west and three cells approaching from the east and heading into the sky northeast of Hải Phòng. They also picked up three flights of enemy fighter aircraft operating over the Thành Sơn area. Nguyễn Khánh Duy was ordered to take off from Đa Phúc airfield at 2300 hours, then flew toward the Yên Bái–Tuyên Quang area to intercept a target group approaching from the west. However, it was very difficult to track the target, because the enemy jamming was too intense, so Nguyễn Khánh Duy's aircraft was unable to intercept the group of B-52s outside of the range of the air defenses (outside the range of SAMs). After the target was inside the range of the air defenses, the GCI ordered Nguyễn Khánh Duy to make a left-hand turn to break away and then to return to Đa Phúc airfield, where he landed safely.

MiG pilot Bùi Doãn Độ was ordered to take off from Kép airfield at 2328 hours, then was directed to fly on a heading of 300 degrees. Four minutes later, while Bùi Doãn Độ was flying past Phú Lương, the HQ turned the ground control command over to the Thọ Xuân command post. The Thọ Xuân command post ordered Bùi Doãn Độ to turn right, fly toward Chợ Đồn, and climb to an altitude of 32,000 feet. At 2348 hours the Thọ Xuân command post ordered him to turn left to intercept the target. At that moment Bùi Doãn Độ spotted dim green lights in the distance, 25 degrees to his right. He reported that he had spotted the target and requested permission to attack. He quickly increased speed to get on to the tail of an F-4, then he calmly stabilized his target designator, and when the range was 0.9 miles he fired his two missiles at the same time. He then quickly turned to break away. This was the first F-4 that MiGs shot down at night. Lieutenant Bùi Doãn Độ landed safely at Đa Phúc airfield at 2358 hours.

This last day of the 1972 air battles, 29 December 1972, was also the last day MiG-21s fought in battle during the Linebacker II campaign, and almost the last of the entire American air war of destruction against North Vietnam. At 0700 hours on 30 December 1972 the Nixon administration was forced to announce the end of the bombing north of the twentieth parallel, and requested a meeting with the Vietnamese delegation in Paris to negotiate the terms of a peace agreement.

The year 1972 was the fiercest year of the Vietnam air war, with the participation of the U.S. SAC units. During that year, the VNPAF launched nearly 4,000 air combat sorties, fought 142 air battles, and shot down 80 U.S. aircraft, including 2 B-52s and 4 UAVs. Meanwhile, the VNPAF acknowledged the loss of 49 MiGs, and 23 MiG pilots were listed as killed in action.

Early 1973: The Last Air Battles of the War

Even though the Nixon administration announced on 30 December 1972 an end to the bombing of NVN, the United States continued to conduct reconnaissance missions and bombing attacks against targets south of the twentieth parallel up until 27 January 1973, when the Paris Agreement was officially signed. During that period, the VNPAF launched aircraft on combat missions thirty times, two of which were night missions.

On the night of 8 January 1973, pilot Bùi Doãn Độ of the 921st FR took off from Đa Phúc airfield and flew to the Lang Chánh area. While he was searching for his target over the Lang Chánh area, his aircraft was hit by a missile fired by an F-4. Bùi Doãn Độ ejected and parachuted to earth safely. The F-4D that pursued and attacked him was flown by Capt. Paul D. Howman and 1st Lt. Lawrence W. Kullman from the 4th TFS/432nd TRW. While flying a MiGCAP mission in Route Package 3, this aircraft was directed in by the Navy's air control network (Red Crown) to intercept and attack the MiG. When he was three miles from his target, Howman launched two AIM-7E-2 missiles. The second missile hit the MiG, setting it ablaze. Lieutenant Bùi Doãn Độ was the last MiG pilot who shot down a U.S. F-4 and also the last MiG pilot who was shot down by a U.S. aircraft's missile, and who parachuted during the air battle.

So the air battle on 8 January 1973 between a MiG-21 and a USAF F-4D was the last one in the longest air war in history.

Recapitulation
LINEBACKER II AND THE "ĐIỆN BIÊN PHỦ IN THE AIR" CAMPAIGN

Linebacker II was one of the most important and strategic air campaigns for U.S. airpower, with the purpose of forcing NVN to return to the negotiating table in Paris and sign the Paris Agreement on Ending the War and Restoring Peace in Vietnam, with conditions, as the United States had predicted earlier. During Linebacker II, the USAF mobilized 206 B-52s (more than half of SAC's entire inventory of the type), which flew 729 sorties against 34 targets in NVN,[36] but their main strategic objectives were not achieved.

Throughout Linebacker II, a total of about two hundred of SAC's KC-135 tankers were mobilized to carry out the mission of airborne refueling of the B-52s, and more than one thousand tactical aircraft were deployed to cover and support these B-52s as they attacked essential targets like SAM sites and MiG airfields. At the same time, six U.S. Navy aircraft carriers with more than four hundred combat aircraft were also mobilized to participate in Linebacker II.

The Vietnamese side announced that, during the twelve days and nights of the "Điện Biên Phủ in the Air" campaign (known as Linebacker II in the United States), all three branches of the Vietnamese armed forces and the militia force, whose core was the VNP AD and AF Service, shot down eighty-one U.S. aircraft of many types, including thirty-four B-52s (of which sixteen were shot down on the spot), five F-111s, twenty-one F-4s, twelve A-7s, four A-6As, one F-105, two RA-5Cs, one HH-53, and one reconnaissance aircraft.[37] Some statistics show that during the campaign, VNP AD launched 239 to 335 SAMs, shot down 29 B-52s (9.2 SAMs for every U.S. downed aircraft), and the remaining five B-52s were shot down by MiGs and AAA units. During only twelve days and nights, VNP AF's MiGs shot down two B-52s, and six tactical aircraft. Meanwhile, the VNPAF acknowledged the loss of three MiGs, and two MiG pilots were killed.[38]

At the same time, some American sources reported that during the twelve days and nights the VNP's AD fired about 884 to 1,285 SAMs, shot down 15 B-52s (9 of series D and 6 of series G), seriously damaging 3 and slightly damaging 6. During the campaign more than 1,300 B-52 air crewmembers participated in air attacks against NVN. The 307th SW (U-Tapao AB) lost 7 B-52s and 4 of its B-52s were damaged. The 43rd SW (Andersen AB) lost 2 B-52s, and 5 were damaged. The 72nd SW lost 6 B-52s, and 1 was damaged. According to one American author, there were 92 crewmembers on board the 15 downed B-52s, and 61 of these 92 were in the B-52s that crashed on the spot. Of those 61 crewmembers, 28 were listed as KIA or MIA, and 33 became POWs. There were also 31 crewmembers on the five B-52s that crashed in Thailand and Laos. Of these, 26 were rescued, 4 were killed, and 1 remains missing.[39] The tactical wings/squadrons lost 3 F-4s, and the USN lost one RA-5C. Meanwhile, the USAF shot down 6 MiGs including 2 shot down by B-52 tail gunners.[40]

In relation to the results of the campaign, the Vietnamese side and the U.S. side produced different results and, therefore, different assessments. It is common knowledge that on 27 December 1972, the American side sent a message signaling its readiness to go back to the negotiating table in Paris.[41] On 27 January 1973, the Agreement on Ending the War and Restoring Peace in Vietnam was signed in Paris. So the Vietnam air war, with its historic confrontations between the VNPAF and U.S. airpower, one of the longest (lasting nearly eight years) and fiercest air wars in the history of aerial warfare, came to a close, leaving many meaningful lessons for the warring parties.

On 12 February 1973, Operation Homecoming began at Gia Lâm airport in Hanoi. Fifty-four USAF C-141A flights carried 591 American POWs to the Philippines and then back to the United States.

8

Other Enemy Targets Attacked by the VNPAF

Most sections of this book focus on air-to-air battles between the VNPAF and U.S. airpower from 1965 to 1973. But during the war the VNPAF's MiGs also conducted attacks on U.S. unmanned drone aircraft, and crews of the 923rd FR and the 919th Military Air Transport Regiment (MATR) attacked the enemy's ground and sea targets, including a very strategical and meaningful attack on Tân Sơn Nhất airport conducted by pilots of the 923rd FR on 28 April 1975. These attacks all contributed to the victories of the VNPAF in general. Therefore, the authors deem it necessary to devote certain exclusive pages of this chapter to these attacks.

MiG Attacks on U.S. Drones

During the Vietnam air war, the USAF used Ryan Firebee UAVs and the next variant, the Ryan Model 147 Lightning Bug, to conduct reconnaissance missions over the skies of North Vietnam, including high- and low-altitude reconnaissance drone missions. According to some American publications, a total of 3,435 UAV sorties were launched to conduct reconnaissance flights during nearly eight years of war, during which the United States lost a total of 554 UAVs.[1] Usually the UAVs were launched in mid-air from DC-130s and flew the planned path to take photos of important targets. As soon as a UAV appeared over the skies of North Vietnam, the VNPAF's MiG-17 and MiG-21 units were assigned missions to find and shoot down the U.S. UAVs. Finding and shooting down UAVs was an important mission of

VNPAF fighters. During the nearly eight years of the air war, MiG-17s and MiG-21s launched 102 combat sorties, fought 52 engagements against UAVs, and shot down 38 UAVs, of which MiG-17s fought 12 engagements and pursued and shot down 10 UAVs while MiG-21s fought 40 engagements, and pursued and shot down 28 UAVs. The VNPAF acknowledged that in those air battles against the UAVs, five MiG pilots were killed.[2]

In terms of tactics, in the first stage, the UAVs usually flew in at very high altitudes, sometimes higher than 32,000 feet. The high-altitude Model 147H could operate at 69,000 feet. In the first battle of 4 March 1966, pilot Nguyễn Hồng Nhị's MiG-21 shot down the first UAV at an altitude of 55,000 feet. Later, the UAVs usually flew in to conduct their reconnaissance missions at low altitudes and along riversides to avoid MiG intercepts. At low altitudes, it was difficult for MiGs to find them out and shoot them down. In some circumstances, when maneuvering at a low altitude, MiG pilots even got lost and flew into terrain. During the period of time when the United States was forced to limit its bombing north of the twentieth parallel (1968–1970), the USAF intensified its use of the UAVs to carry out reconnaissance missions. During that time the number of UAVs that were shot down by MiGs was the greatest (more than a half of the total that were shot down).

Even though the UAVs were not equipped with missiles or cannon, the air battles against the UAVs were good chances for the newly graduated pilots of the VNPAF to train and exercise their air combat skills (including their firing skill) and acquaint themselves with fierce fighting conditions. MiG-21 pilots of the first and second groups shot down sixteen UAVs, and those of the third group shot down nine UAVs. Some of the VNPAF's MiG pilots each shot down two or three UAVs.

The Air-to-Sea Attack by MiG-17s

During almost eight years of war, beside the primary mission to intercept the U.S. attackers and fighters, the pilots of the 923rd FR also accomplished some important air-to-ground and air-to-sea attack missions. From early 1967, they were assigned extra training to be ready to carry out this type of mission.

In order to push the USN carriers away from Vietnamese territorial waters, the AD and AF HQ assigned the 923rd FR to take further training and be ready to attack the U.S. ships when they got closer to the coast. One Cuban pilot-instructor (Captain Ernesto Delapaz Palomo) was invited to conduct a training course for Vietnamese pilots to teach them how to apply the "slippery bombing" technique in attacking U.S. ships.[3] A group of ten of the most experienced MiG-17 pilots were selected to attend the training course. On 12 April 1972, three MiG-17 pilots—Lê Xuân Dy, Nguyễn Văn Lục, and Nguyễn Văn Bảy (B)—were assigned to carry out this mission and were moved to Gát airfield (west of Quảng Bình Province). At 1545 hours on 18 April 1972, two MiG-17s from the 923rd FR, flown by pilots Lê Hồng Điệp and Từ Đễ, secretly took off from Kép airfield, landed at Gia Lâm airport, then flew to Vinh airfield. After filling up the fuel tanks, they secretly took off and were directed to fly to Gát airfield without radio communication and landed there safely. All pre-combat mission works were quickly accomplished and two MiG-17s were ready to take off.

At 1605 hours on 19 April 1972, the C-43 radar company picked up a target only ten miles from the coast. Two MiG-17s flown by Lê Xuân Dy and Nguyễn Văn Bảy (B) were ordered to take off from Gát airfield and fly toward the sea, where a group of USN ships were waiting to support USN aircraft that were due to attack targets inside North Vietnam. Ten minutes later, the flight spotted the target, Lê Xuân Dy dove to an altitude of 180 feet and, as planned, dropped two 550-pound bombs using the "slippery bombing" technique. Some intelligence sources stated that the U.S. ship that was attacked and damaged by Lê Xuân Dy's MiG-17 was the USS *Higbee*. Meanwhile, the MiG No. 2 Nguyễn Văn Bảy (B) continued to fly until he spotted the group of U.S. ships a minute later, when he dove and attacked the second ship at an altitude of 180 feet with the "slippery bombing" technique. The U.S. ship that was attacked and damaged by Nguyễn Văn Bảy (B)'s MiG-17 was the USS *Oklahoma City*. The two MiG-17s flew back and landed safely at Gát airfield.[4] Two U.S. ships were damaged and the USS *Higbee* had to move to Subic Bay in the Philippines for repair.

Only three days later, the United States discovered Gát airfield and sent a large number of aircraft to bomb it. One MiG-17 was destroyed and another slightly damaged. This was the first and only air-to-sea attack by MiG-17s during the war. The two MiG-17 pilots were given the honorable title of VNP Armed Forces Hero.

Victory-Minded Squadron: The Air Attack on Tân Sơn Nhất Airport, 28 April 1975

On 28 April 1975, the 923rd FR conducted an air-to-ground attack on Tân Sơn Nhất airport using a number of American A-37 aircraft that had been captured by the VNPAF when some of the provinces in SVN with air bases were liberated. The attack on Tân Sơn Nhất airport took place when the Saigon puppet government was about to collapse.

After Đà Nẵng was liberated, a group of the 923rd FR's MiG-17 pilots was assigned to take a short training to convert to flying American aircraft. On 22 April 1975, five experienced MiG-17 pilots arrived at Đà Nẵng airport. They were Lieutenants Từ Đễ, Nguyễn Văn Lục, Hán Văn Quảng, Hoàng Mai Vượng, and Trần Cao Thăng. In only three days, from 23 to 26 April, with the assistance of some captured pilots and technicians of the South Vietnam puppet army, they completed an extremely short training course with only one or two flights in A-37s for every pilot. And from 27 April 1975 they were ready to take off to carry out the mission. At 0930 hours on 28 April the flight of five A-37s moved from Phù Cát airfield to Thành Sơn airfield, where they completed the preparation and stood on combat alert duty. At 1300 hours Senior Colonel Lê Văn Tri, commander in chief of the AD and AF Service, Colonel Trần Mạnh, vice chief of staff of the AD and AF Service, Colonel Trần Hanh, commander in chief of the VNPAF, and Colonel Nguyễn Hồng Nhị, vice commander of the 371st Air Fighter Division, directly assigned the mission to the flight and gave the flight the code name (call sign) "Victory-minded Squadron."[5]

At 1625 hours Colonel Trần Hanh, the commanding officer on duty, ordered the flight to take off. After flying past Hàm Tân, the flight turned right, climbed to a higher altitude, and approached Tân Sơn Nhất airport. At 1705 hours the pilots attacked the parking area of the enemy's combat aircraft. According to the intelligence report, twenty-four aircraft were destroyed and more than one hundred soldiers of the ex-SVN puppet army were killed. This was the only battle during the entire Vietnam air war where MiG pilots used trophy American aircraft to accomplish an air-to-ground attack.

When assessing the victory of the VNPAF's Victory-minded Squadron in the attack on Tân Sơn Nhất airport on 28 April 1975, General Văn Tiến

Dũng, VNPA chief of general staff, said: "This is the perfect air-to-ground battle, with excellent coordination of all branches of the VNP Army at the extremely important point of time, which gave great impetus to our campaign and drove the enemy to a new panic, leading to the rapid collapse of the puppet government in South Vietnam."[6] Later, in the postwar period, each of the five members of the Victory-minded Squadron were given the honorable title VNP Armed Forces Hero.

Epilogue

Ending the War

On 27 January 1973, the Paris Agreement on Ending the War and Restoring Peace in Vietnam was signed, ending more than twenty years of U.S. involvement in Vietnam and Southeast Asia. The agreement stipulated that there would be a total withdrawal of U.S. troops, and those of other foreign countries allied with the United States, from South Vietnam within sixty days, along with the simultaneous return of captured military personnel and foreign civilians of all parties.

The VNPAF had started the eight years of the fierce air war as just one fighter regiment with thirty antiquated MiG-17s, but with pilots who had fought staunchly, with courage and great skill. With experience gained in the air battles, the VNPAF had steadily grown to become a big and powerful force that would contribute to the firm defense of the fatherland's territorial airspace.

The relationship between the two countries changed in the postwar period, until it came to a new chapter of diplomatic history. On 12 July 1995, President Bill Clinton of the United States and Prime Minister Võ Văn Kiệt of Vietnam signed a document announcing the normalization of relationships between Vietnam and the United States of America. The first postwar ambassador to Vietnam was Ambassador Douglas Brian "Pete" Peterson, who had a vivid image of the mission to put aside the past and move forward to the future. After many activities in re-establishing relations in diplomacy, economics, culture, and tourism, military relations between the two countries were also gradually improved. High-level delegations from both sides have exchanged visits, and some U.S. ships have come to Vietnam. In this peaceful and positive atmosphere, many U.S. veteran pilots have visited Vietnam, and veteran pilot delegations from both sides have organized meetings in Hanoi (2016 and 2018) and in San Diego (2017). These meetings were very meaningful, and they manifested the veteran pilots' aspirations to the development of a Vietnam—U.S. friendship and comprehensive cooperation between the two countries, to which they would contribute a part.

Vietnam Air War: Statistical Figures and Analysis

The Vietnam air war lasted nearly eight years, with approximately four hundred engagements between the VNPAF and the USAF and USN in the skies over North Vietnam. (The number of air engagements only represents engagements in which aircraft of either or both sides fired their missiles or guns and caused damage or fatality to the other.) This was the first air war in history where both sides used jet fighters and air-to-air missiles as the main weapons in battle. During these air battles, hundreds of aircraft from both sides were shot down or badly damaged. Furthermore, hundreds of fighter pilots and aircrews from both sides were shot down, captured, rescued, or listed as KIAs and MIAs.

It should be noted that, from the earlier days of the air war, both sides started to keep statistical records. The U.S. side had Project Red Baron, which systematically collected and incorporated all records related to air combat factors during the Vietnam air war. The Vietnamese side, from the AD and AF Service Command down to AF FRs also had a project to archive and summarize all factors that related to the air engagements with the USAF and USN. In this epilogue, I have tried to consider and review some of the statistical results produced by both sides.

Some Vietnamese authors have tried to gather the statistical figures on the results of the air battles between the VNPAF and U.S. airpower during the eight years of war.[1] They have reviewed, collected, and incorporated figures, and provided the following: For nearly eight years of the air war, the VNPAF flew 7,132 mission sorties and took part in more than 400 air engagements with 587 firing and shooting attempts (365 missile firing attempts, and 222 cannon shooting attempts using 34,400 shells), shot down 320 U.S. aircrafts of 19 types (including U.S. aircraft that were shot down by North Korean AF units and UAVs). To be specific, the Vietnamese side's records mention that the VNPAF's MiG-21s made a total of 365 missile firing attempts and shot down 166 U.S. aircraft. Meanwhile, MiG-17s and MiG-19s fired a total of more than 34,400 cannon shells at U.S. aircraft, resulting in 127 kills.

At the same time, the VNPAF also acknowledged that there were probably 125 MiGs lost in the air-to-air battles with the USAF and USN aircraft. These figures did not include aircraft that were broken down by non–air-combat causes, like training accidents, air accidents, getting killed by one's own defense forces (friendly fire), running out of fuel, forced landings, and so forth. The number of MiG pilots killed in action during air engagements was 58 (among the 125 MiGs lost). It should be noted that, of the number of MiG-21 pilots who parachuted, 90 percent did it successfully, while the percentage of MiG-17 pilots who successfully parachuted is 76.1 percent.

According to some U.S. publications, during the war a total of 800,000 tons of bombs were dropped on North Vietnam by about 350,000 attacking sorties (not including those from the USN).[2] But some others give different figures, saying that during the war U.S. aircraft flew 1,992,000 combat sorties.[3] About the statistical result of air engagements between the USAF/USN and VNPAF, some American sources mention that during the air war in Vietnam, USAF and USN aircraft conducted a total of 1,577 air attacks, including 361 attacks with guns, 1,127 attacks with air-to-air missiles, and 89 attacks with other types of weapons. Of these, 319 got results, including shooting down 189 MiGs (142 with missiles and 47 with guns).[4]

In the process of gathering and studying documents for this project, I also found some differential figures from other U.S. documents that show that, during the Vietnam air war, the USAF and USN were credited with destroying two hundred NVN aircraft (including two Soviet-built propeller AN-2s).[5] Some others mention that during the war the USAF and USN lost ninety aircraft to MiGs, but these figures do not include thirty-eight UAVs that were shot down by MiGs.[6]

Although there are several figures on the results of air combat compiled by various documents, in order to make the analysis and the comparison easier to understand in this epilogue and in the appendixes of this book, I use the statistical figures produced by numerous U.S. authors, which indicate that 197 MiGs were shot down in air battles.

In the postwar period, many books and articles on the Vietnam air war have been published by authors in the United States and other countries. In some of these books and articles, U.S. authors mention the USAF and USN aerial victories in the Vietnam air war in general, and especially refer to the accounts of U.S. and VNPAF aces and their claims of victories.[7] The causes of the differences in statistical figures are stated in the preface of this book, with the hope that U.S. readers will have one more view from the Vietnamese sources of information, which appendixes IV, V, and VI present in this book. These appendixes show that, of the 197 MiGs that the U.S. pilots claimed to have shot down, there were in fact 83 MiGs that were not shot down. These 83 MiGs returned and landed safely after the battles (according to the VNPAF records, daily combat logs, battle reports, and according to accounts by witnesses). There were even a number of U.S. reports of successes in some air battles, but the VNPAF records reveal that MiGs did not even take off to fight these battles. So in another way it can be said that 42.13 percent (83/197) of U.S. pilots' claims are not correct. In addition, during my compilation of this book, I found there was a number of aircraft shot down by one side, but the opposite side did not record them.

In the final analysis, in reality, the number of MiGs that the USAF and USN shot down and the number of MiGs that the VNPAF confirmed as lost in air battles (125 MiGs) are more or less the same.

Similarly, of the seventeen MiGs that U.S. aces claimed to have shot down, there were in fact seven MiGs that were not shot down, or were only "probably" shot down because there may have been a case, or some cases, in which only one MiG was shot down but it was simultaneously claimed by two or three U.S. air crews. So again it can be said that 41.17 percent of the U.S. aces claims were incorrect or were only "probable victories" (see appendix V).

More than fifty years have passed, as we all know, and these statistical figures have gone down into historical archives, and they only make sense for history scholars to study, so let's put them aside and together we move forward.

Development of the MiG's Intercept Tactics

The opponent of the VNPAF was the modern USAF and USN, with pilots well trained in operations and hands-on air combat experiences gained from the two earlier wars (World War II and the Korean War). So in order to fight and win such an enemy air force, the VNPAF pilots had to apply clear and good operational and tactical thinking, besides having the courage, skills, and good techniques for air combat. Then they had to intelligently apply the combat tactics in such a way that was suitable to the Vietnamese conditions, to their level of proficiency, and to the technical specifications of the weapons they were armed with.

MiG-17 TACTICS
Through many air engagements the MiG-17 pilots understood that they had to maximize their aircraft's potential and outstanding horizontal maneuverability at medium and low altitudes. Therefore, MiG-17s could appear as a surprise to the enemy attackers, chase them at a close distance, then launch direct and sudden attacks on them. The close engagement and the aircraft's strong maneuverability with its small circle's radius could force the U.S. pilots into a dogfight, then the MiG-17 pilots could instantly obtain a good position to fire at enemy aircraft at a close or very close range of about 0.15–0.25 miles. Some U.S. publications named MiG-17 ambush tactics "guerrilla," while some others called it "Wagon Wheel" at low altitudes.[8] These tactics were very effective when applied against F-105 strike forces and F-4 fighters.

MiG-21 TACTICS
Considering those factors related to the MiG-21's operation capabilities, in the first stage of its use in combat, a number of MiG-21 pilots used to engage in dogfights, just as MiG-17 pilots did, in the airspace near the airfields or near the targets to be protected. As a result, they experienced difficulties, suffered losses, and were unable to take advantage of the MiG-21's superiorities such as high speed and very high maneuverability at medium and

higher altitudes. In joint endeavors to improve such a situation, the VNPAF commanders and pilots thought it was necessary to develop a new theory of intercept tactics for the MiG-21. They decided to conduct research and studies, and draw experiences from the battles they had courageously fought. After several seminars with open discussions and practical experiences from many bloody air battles where a number of VNPAF pilots had lost their lives, a theory on intercept tactics for MiG-21s, suitable to the conditions of the Vietnamese air front, was finally formulated.

The core elements of this theory was that the MiG-21 was the intercept aircraft, that it could not engage in dogfights and in battles over the airfields as the MiG-17 did, and that the MiG-21 should fight in such a way as to take the utmost advantage of its superiority. As such, the new intercept theory included three components, namely: (1) Clear thinking by commanders and pilots, to take advantage of the full play of the MiG's technical advances, together with the combined power of the entire air defense system; (2) The achievement of a tactically advantageous position, of superiority in speed, in flying at high altitudes, and in gaining the attacking angle over the enemy before attacking them; (3) Well-trained pilots with high-level technical and tactical skills and an ability to foresee what would happen in the battle and how to handle it.

The necessary and sufficient conditions for the success of the air battle were: to have accurate information from the GCI about the enemy, to take off on time (neither too early nor too late), to focus on the main target— enemy attackers (not fighters), to achieve a favorable entry angle and the ability to spot the enemy very soon, before they could realize the MiGs' presence, and to form secret elements of surprise in the attack against the enemy.

These main elements of the new theory on intercept tactics would help MiG-21 pilots approach the enemy formations far from the protected targets, and would also help them easily select the enemy groups for attack before the latter could deploy their combat formation. Furthermore, should conditions become unfavorable, the MiG pilots could easily take the initiative to break off. The new theory on intercept tactics had been successfully applied by VNPAF pilots of the MiG-21 since 1967. In the second stage of the war (1972), there were updates and modifications to the theory contributed by many new and young flight leaders who had good tactical thoughts, which helped MiG-21 pilots respond very well to all battle developments with their good flying and attempt-firing techniques, resulting in high combat effectiveness.[9] These main elements of the MiG-21 intercept tactics have also been mentioned by some American authors in their written works, where they called MiG-21 tactics "ambush" tactics, "fast attack, fast withdrawal" tactics, "high-speed, one-pass" tactics, or "hit-and-run" tactics.[10]

The VNPAF commanders and pilots fully understood that one of the laws of survival in war was that tactics are the most flexible element and are meant to be applied in specific battle situations, knowing that the enemy will always try to find new ways to counter new tactics. Therefore, they constantly analyzed their past successes and failures so as to learn how to fight new battles with secret elements of surprise. Tactics and techniques must be constantly studied, modified and improved in order to be able to deal with the opponent's new tactics and new weapons.

From the Vietnam Air War to a New Airpower Doctrine

Gradually, the lessons learned from the Vietnam air war helped build, step by step, a heroic and mighty VNPAF. Moreover, this experience even forced the USAF and USN to draw lessons for improving tactical techniques for new generations of fighter aircraft, weapons, pilot training programs, and operational and tactical theory.

The Vietnam air war left many lessons for the high-level strategic planners of both countries, and for interested historians and researchers. It can be said that these lessons have, to some extent, helped the high-level strategic planners to form a new airpower doctrine in modern warfare. Several air war researchers and historians have mentioned that these lessons have generated many ideas for air force strategists and planners to make a new strategic plan for the AF's development and operation in a modern air war. For many high-ranking AF officials in many countries, including those in the USAF, the air war in Vietnam constituted a turning point, illustrating a myriad of doctrinal, organizational, force-structure, and training deficiencies.[11] In addition, many modern technological advances in tactics, and in both aircraft and weapon design, have been partly made with consideration of the results of the Vietnam War.[12]

Regarding the topic of air combat tactics, literature on the world's aerial warfare abounds as to the ways air battles were fought. The first air engagements fought in World War I were conceived as a type of dogfight air combat. This meant that pilots from both sides encountered each other mostly with dogfight tactics, they could see each other in the range of their guns, which were effective to about 0.2–0.3 miles or even closer. This air combat tactic was used on a large scale during World War II, especially in dogfights between the Soviet AF and the Nazi AF (Luftwaffe).

The Vietnam air war marked the beginning of a new era of air combat when pilots from both sides encountered each other in a broad visual range and with the use of jet aircraft equipped with air-to-air missiles. That type of air combat was documented as within-visual-range (WVR) air combat. From the 1990s on, after the air campaigns of the 1990s air wars in Kosovo and Iraq, many Western air theories proposed a new concept of airpower. The main idea of this was that the air force should no longer be used as a substitute for its military predecessors that airpower must connect directly to "strategic end games."[13] Together with the advent of fifth-generation fighters came a new theory of air-to-air combat operation and tactics in the modern air war, which was called beyond-visual-range (BVR) air combat. The foundation of this type of air combat was the appearance of a new generation of fighter aircraft, equipped with air-to-air missiles that could be launched from a range of beyond the pilot's visual range. These aircraft also had a new generation of radars, including a new onboard radar system that was able to track and block multiple targets from a distance of 120–150 miles, even to 240 miles in narrow beams.

Today, air battles can take place in all weather conditions and involve modern aircraft and more powerful weapons, which are used with such high degrees of accuracy that are measured in centimeters and at a range of hundreds of kilometers. Advanced technology has dramatically improved not only aircraft details but also the sensors used to find, fix, track, and target.[14] A new theory about airpower has been formulated, with a picture of revolutionized modern air battle, the initial steps of which were related to the Vietnam air war.

It has been more than fifty years since the end of the Vietnam air war. Things have changed, and air forces in general have experienced rapid developments in airpower, theory, and weapons, with the fifth and even the sixth generation of multi-mission fighter aircraft. But from the lessons of the Vietnam air war it can be confirmed that the human factor is the decisive element in victory.

From Dogfight to Détente

History has changed and moved forward. Diplomatic relations between Vietnam and the United States of America have been fully normalized and have developed comprehensively. At the initiative of Lieutenant General Nguyễn Đức Soát of the VNPAF and Col. Charles Tutt of the USMC, there have been three meetings between Vietnamese and U.S. veteran pilots, held in Hanoi (2016 and 2018) and San Diego (2017). The information that we received from the participants in these meetings has helped us to add more details to this book.

What is important now is for the veteran pilots of both sides to put aside the past and come together to build a peaceful future. During these three meetings, many Vietnamese and American veteran pilots had the chance to meet their former opponents. Many felt deeply moved when they met each other. Lieutenant General Nguyễn Đức Soát met U.S. pilot Capt. John Cezak, whom he shot down. Lieutenant General Phạm Phú Thái met Navy pilot Lt. Roy Cash, who shot him down in July 1968, and also met pilot Capt. Thomas J. Hanton, whom he shot down in the battle of 27 June 1972. Brig. Gen. A. J. Lenski met Senior Colonel Vũ Ngọc Đỉnh, who fifty-one years earlier had encountered and shot down his wingman, Capt. Joe Abbott. Col. David R. Volker even met MiG-21 pilot Vũ Đình Rạng who, on the night of 20 November 1971, chased and fired an Atoll missile at his B-52. Other VNPAF pilots such as Nguyễn Văn Bảy (A), Mai Đức Toại, Đồng Văn Song, Nguyễn Văn Thọ, Lương Thế Phúc, Nguyễn Công Huy, and Nguyễn Văn Nghĩa also had the chance to meet their former opponents. The main theme of these meetings was the idea that was written in a slogan when the two delegations met in the USS *Midway* in San Diego: "From dogfight to détente." These three Vietnam/U.S. meetings got the attention of the media and of many enthusiasts from both countries. Some media mentioned that these were historic meetings, where the old enemies now became friends.[15] We do hope that more meetings between veteran pilots, and even young pilots, of the two countries will be held in years to come.

In the USS *Midway* meeting, when Mr. Scott McGaugh, the marketing director of the USS *Midway* Museum, asked Colonel Lê Thanh Đạo, the MiG-21 ace, to say something brief about that historic meeting, he said, "I firmly believe that this meeting will become a very special landmark event that is beyond the usual meetings. It will be evidence for a new phase in the relations between the two countries. To conclude, I would like to say: 'We cannot change the past but we have to build the future together!'"

We remember the past, but we must move forward!

APPENDIX I

Key Organizations and Personnel of VNPA and AD and AF Service 1963–1975

No.	Unit/Title	Rank/Name	Period of time in office
1	Minister of National Defense	General Võ Nguyên Giáp	1946–76
2	VNP Army Chief of General Staff	General Văn Tiến Dũng	1953–79
3	VNP AD and AF Service Commander in Chief	Senior Colonel Phùng Thế Tài Senior Colonel Đặng Tính Senior Colonel Lê Văn Tri	1963–67 1968–70 1971–77
4	VNP AD and AF Service Political Commissar	Senior Colonel Đặng Tính Senior Colonel Hoàng Phương	1963–71 1971–74
5	VNP AD and AF Service Chief of Staff	Senior Colonel Nguyễn Quang Bich Senior Colonel Đỗ Đức Kiên Senior Colonel Lê Văn Tri Senior Colonel Hoàng Văn Khánh Senior Colonel Hoàng Ngọc Diêu	1963–65 1966 1967 1968 1969–74
6	VNP Air Force Corps Commander in Chief	Senior Colonel Nguyễn Văn Tiên Colonel Đào Đình Luyện	1967–69 1969–74
7	VNP Air Force Corps Chief of Staff	Colonel Đào Đình Luyện Lieutenant Colonel Trần Mạnh	1966–69 1969–74
8	VNPAF 921st FR Commander	Lieutenant Colonel Đào Đình Luyện Lieutenant Colonel Trần Mạnh Lieutenant Colonel Trần Hanh	1963–66 1966–69 1969–72

No.	Unit/Title	Rank/Name	Period of time in office
9	VNPAF 923rd FR Commander	Lieutenant Colonel Nguyễn Phúc Trạch	1965–67
		Lieutenant Colonel Lê Oánh	1968–70
		Lieutenant Colonel Lâm Văn Lích	1970–73
10	VNPAF 925th FR Commander	Major Lê Quang Trung	1969
		Lieutenant Colonel Mai Đức Toại	1970–73
11	VNPAF 927th FR Commander	Lieutenant Colonel Nguyễn Hồng Nhị	1972–73

Note: The rank was held and the title was conferred during wartime (1965–73). Ranks of officers in the VNP Army (from low to high): first lieutenant, lieutenant, senior lieutenant, captain, major, lieutenant colonel, colonel, senior colonel, major general, lieutenant general, three-star general, and general (four stars). The tenure of the defense minister (1946–80) and the chief of the general staff (1953–79) is the total time they held the office. The remaining titles only count the time of the air war (1963–75).

APPENDIX II

VNPAF Aces' Victories in the Vietnam Air War
1965–1973

No.	Rank/Name	Unit/Type of aircraft	Number of victories/ Type of enemy aircraft destroyed
1	Lieutenant General Nguyễn Văn Cốc	921st FR/MiG-21	9 (2 F-4s, 5 F-105s, 2 UAVs)
2	Major General Mai Văn Cương	921st FR/MiG-21	8 (2 F-4s, 3 F-105s, 3 UAVs)
3	General Phạm Thanh Ngân	921st FR/MiG-21	8 (2 F-4s, 3 F-105s, 1 RF-101, 1 F-102, 1 UAV)
4	Major General Nguyễn Hồng Nhị	921st FR/MiG-21	8 (1 F-4, 1 RF-4, 1 F-8, 3 F-105s, 1 RF-101, 1 UAV)
5	Senior Colonel Nguyễn Văn Bảy (A)	923rd FR/MiG-17	7 (4 F-4s, 1 F-8, 2 F-105s)
6	Captain Đặng Ngọc Ngự	921st FR/MiG-21	7 (3 F-4s, 1 F-105, 3 UAVs)
7	Senior Colonel Lưu Huy Chao	923rd FR/MiG-17	6 (2 F-4s, 2 F-8s, 1 F-105, 1 C-47)
8	Senior Colonel Nguyễn Nhật Chiêu	927th FR/MiG-17/ MiG-21	6 (5 F-4s, 1 F-105)
9	Senior Colonel Lê Thanh Đạo	921st FR/MiG-21	6 F-4s

No.	Rank/Name	Unit/Type of aircraft	Number of victories/ Type of enemy aircraft destroyed
10	Senior Colonel Vũ Ngọc Đỉnh	921st FR/MiG-21	6 (5 F-105s, 1 CH-53)
11	Major General Nguyễn Ngọc Độ	921st FR/MiG-17/ MiG-21	6 (2 F-4s, 3 F-105s, 1 RF-101)
12	Major General Nguyễn Đăng Kính	921st FR/MiG-21	6 (2 F-4s, 1 F-105, 1 EB-66, 2 UAVs)
13	Senior Colonel Lê Hải	923rd FR/MiG-17	6 (4 F-4s, 1 F-8, 1 F-105)
14	Lieutenant General Nguyễn Đức Soát	927th FR/MiG-21	6 (4 F-4s, 1 A-7, 1 UAV)
15	Captain Võ Văn Mẫn	923rd FR/MiG-17	5 (3 F-4s, 1 F-8, 1 F-105)
16	Lieutenant Nguyễn Phi Hùng	923rd FR/MiG-17	5 (2 F-4s, 1 F-8, 2 F-105s)
17	Senior Colonel Nguyễn Văn Nghĩa	927th FR/MiG-21	5 (4 F-4s, 1 UAV)
18	Senior Colonel Nguyễn Tiến Sâm	927th FR/MiG-21	5 F-4s
19	Major Lê Quang Trung	923rd FR/MiG-17	5 (1 F-8, 2 F-105s, 1 A-4, 1 A-1H)

Note: A total of 124 MiG pilots were credited with shooting down enemy aircraft, including 19 Aces, who each shot down 5 or more. Of the 19 Aces, 7 never parachuted during the war. The pilots are listed according to the highest rank each one achieved.

APPENDIX III

Ordnance Firing Effect

	Type of ordnance	Total firing attempts	Malfunctions	Total confirmed enemy kills***	Success rate (not counting failures/ malfunctions)
1	MiG-21's air-to-air missile (R-3S Atoll)	365	N/A	166	2.1 missiles/ 1 kill = 45.5 percent
2	MiG's guns/ cannon	34,329	N/A	127	270.03 shells/ 1 kill = 0.37 percent
3	Air-to-air missile AIM-4D/Falcon	61	* N/A	5	12.2 missiles/ 1 kill = 8.2 percent
4	Air-to-air missile AIM-7 Sparrow*	612	404	56	3.7 missiles/ 1 kill = 26.9 percent
5	Air-to-air missile AIM-9 Side-winder*	454	213	81	2.9 missiles/ 1 kill = 33.6 percent
6	U.S. aircraft guns**	361		47	7.68 attempts/ 1 kill = 13 percent
7	U.S. miscellaneous	89		1	89 attempts/ 1 kill = 1.12 percent

* The success rate of U.S. AIM-4/7/9 missiles does not include the number of missiles that did not function properly.

** From May 1967 onward, a number of the USAF's F-4s were equipped with M61 Vulcan 20-mm cannon, in order to fight MiGs at close quarters, but for some technical reasons the USN F-4s did not carry the centerline cannon.

*** The number of MiGs that the United States claimed to have shot down (listed in this appendix) is 190, which may not include the two Soviet-built propeller A/C AN-2s.

APPENDIX IV

Statistical Disparity

No.	Date	U.S. pilot's claims of shooting down MiGs	MiG actual losses, confirmed by VNPAF	Statistical disparity
1	20.6.1965	2 MiG-17s	1 MiG-17 lost, others landed safely	1
2	6.10.1965	1 MiG-17	No MiGs lost	1
3	23.4.1966	2 MiG-17s	1 MiG-21 lost, no MiG-17 lost	1
4	29.4.1966	2 MiG-17s	1 MiG17 lost, others landed safely	1
5	12.5.1966	1 MiG-17	U.S. F-4 most likely engaged with Chinese AF	1
6	12.6.1966	2 MiG-17s	All MiG-17 s that took off landed safely	2
7	21.6.1966	2 MiG-17s	1 MiG-17 lost, others landed safely	1
8	29.6.1966	1 MiG-17	All MiG-17s landed safely	1
9	16.9.1966	1 MiG-17	All MiG-17s landed safely	1
10	21.9.1966	2 MiG-17s	1 MiG-17 lost, others landed safely	1
11	2.1.1967	7 MiG-21s	5 MiG-21s lost	2
12	10.3.1967	2 MiG-17s	No MiG-17 lost	2
13	19.4.1967	4 MiG-17s	All MiG17s that took off landed safely	4
14	24.4.1967	2 MiG-17s	All MiG17s that took off landed safely	2

No.	Date	U.S. pilot's claims of shooting down MiGs	MiG actual losses, confirmed by VNPAF	Statistical disparity
15	26.4.1967	1 MiG-21	No MiG-21s lost	1
16	28.4.1967	2 MiG-17s	All MiG-17s that took off landed safely	2
17	30.4.1967	1 MiG-17	No VNPAF MiG-17s took off	1
18	1.5.1967	3 MiG-17s	1 MiG-17 lost, others landed safely	2
19	12.5.1967	1 MiG-17	All MiG-17s that took off landed safely	1
20	13.5.1967	7 MiG-17s	No MiG-17s lost	7
21	14.5.1967	3 MiG-17s	2 MiGs-17s lost	1
22	20.5.1967	5 MiG-17s, 2 MiG-21s	2 MiG-21s lost, but no VNPAF MiG-17s took off	5
23	22.5.1967	2 MiG-21s	1 MiG-21 lost, others landed safely	1
24	21.7.1967	4 MiG-17s	No engagements between VNPAF MiG-17s and USAF or USN aircraft	4
25	18.10.1967	1 MiG-17	No VNPAF MiG-17s took off	1
26	27.10.1967	1 MiG-17	No MiG-17s lost	1
27	19.12.1967	2 MiG-17s	All MiG-17s that took off landed safely	2
28	3.1.1968	2 MiG-17s	1 MiG-17 lost, others landed safely	1
29	18.1.1968	1 MiG-17	No MiG-17 lost	1
30	5.2.1968	1 MiG-21	All MiG-21s that took off landed safely	1
31	12.2.1968	1 MiG-21	No VNPAF MiGs took off	1
32	14.2.1968	2 MiG-17s	1 MiG-17 lost, others landed safely	1
33	9.5.1968	1 MiG-21	No MiG-21s lost	1
34	19.1.1972	1 MiG-21	No MiG-21 or MiG-17 lost	1
35	21.2.1972	1 MiG-21	No MiG-21s lost	1
36	30.3.1972	1 MiG-21	No MiG-21s lost	1
37	6.5.1972	2 MiG-21s, 1 MiG-17	1 MiG-21 and 1 MiG-17 lost, others landed safely	1
38	8.5.1972	1 MiG17, 1 MiG-19	All MiG-17s and MiG-19s landed safely	2

No.	Date	U.S. pilot's claims of shooting down MiGs	MiG actual losses, confirmed by VNPAF	Statistical disparity
39	10.5.1972	7 MiG-17s, 4 MiG-21s	3 MiG-17s lost, others landed safely; 2 MiG-21s lost, others landed safely	4 2
40	12.5.1972	1 MiG-19	All MiG-19s that took off landed safely	1
41	23.5.1972	3 MiG-17s, 1 MiG-19, 1 MiG-21	2 MiG-17s and 1 MiG-19 lost; no MiG-21s lost	2
42	31.5.1972	2 MiG-21s	1 MiG-21 lost, others landed safely	1
43	11.6.1972	2 MiG-17s	No MiG-17 lost, but 2 MiG-19s lost	0
44	21.6.1972	2 MiG-21s	1 MiG-21 lost, others landed safely	1
45	29.7.1972	2 MiG-21s	1 MiG-21 lost, others landed safely	1
46	9.9.1972	2 MiG-19s	1 MiG-19 lost, others landed safely	1
47	11.9.1972	1 MiG-21	1 MiG-21 lost by fuel running out, not caused by air combat	1
48	11.9.1972	2 MiG-19s	1 MiG-19 lost, others landed safely	1
49	12.9.1972	3 MiG-21s	2 MiG-21s lost	1
50	5.10.1972	1 MiG-21	All MiG-21s that took off landed safely	1
51	15.10.1972	3 MiG-21s	2 MiG-21s lost	1
52	18.12.1972	1 MiG-21	All MiG-21s that took off landed safely	1
53	22.12.1972	2 MiG-21s	1 MiG-21 lost, others landed safely	1
54	24.12.1972	1 MiG-21	No MiGs lost	1
	Total			**83**

Note: The number of MiGs the U.S. pilots claimed to have shot down is 197. The above appendix shows the battles where the statistical figures of the two side were different. Of the 123 MiGs U.S. pilots claimed to have shot down during these battles, 83 were in excess of the actual number of MiG losses.

APPENDIX V

Statistical Differences between
U.S. Aces' Claims and Actual MiG Losses

No.	Date	USAF/USN aircraft type/Call sign/Unit	U.S. claim	VNPAF MiG actual losses
1	19.1.1972	F-4J/Showtime 112 VF-96, USS *Constellation*	1 MiG-21	No MiG-21s lost, all MiG-21s that took off landed safely
2	16.4.1972	F-4D/Basco 03 13th TFS/432nd TRW	1 MiG-21	Confirmed by Vietnamese side
3	8.5.1972	F-4J/Showtime 112 VF-96, USS *Constellation*	1 MiG-17	No MiG-17s lost, all MiG-17s that took off landed safely
4	10.5.1972	F-4J/Showtime 100 VF-96, USS *Constellation*	3 MiG-17s	3 MiG-17s lost, but beside R. Cunningham's claims, 3 more U.S. aircrews also claimed to have killed 4 MiGs
5	10.5.1972	F-4D/Oyster 03 555th TFS/432nd TRW	1 MiG-21	2 MiG-21s lost, but 4 U.S. aircrews claimed victories
6	31.5.1972	F-4D/Icebag 01 555th TFS/432nd TRW F-4E/Gopher 03 13th TFS/432nd TRW	2 MiG-21s	1 MiG-21 lost, but 2 U.S. ace aircrews claimed victories
7	8.7.1972	F-4E/Paula 01 555th TFS/432nd TRW	2 MiG-21s	Confirmed by Vietnamese side

8	18.7.1972	F-4D/Snug 01 13th TFS/432nd TRW	1 MiG-21	Confirmed by Vietnamese side
9	29.7.1972	F 4D/Cadillac 01 13th TFS/432nd TRW	1 MiG 21	Confirmed by Vietnamese side
10	28.8.1972	F-4D/Buick 01 555th TFS/432nd TRW	1 MiG-21	Confirmed by Vietnamese side
11	9.9.1972	F-4D/Olds 01 555th TFS/432nd TRW	2 MiG-19s	Only 1 MiG-19 lost, others landed safely
12	13.10.1972	F-4D/Olds 01 13th TFS/432nd TRW	1 MiG-21	Confirmed by Vietnamese side

Note: The above appendix shows in detail that the number of MiGs the U.S. aces' aircrews claimed to have shot down is 17 MiGs, but 7 claimed cases were either incorrect or only "probable."

APPENDIX VI

Vietnam Air War (1965–1973)
Results of Air Battles*

Years	Type of a/c that killed enemy a/c	Number and type of U.S. aircraft that MiG pilots claimed to have shot down	VNPAF MiG losses
1965	T-28	1 C-123K	
	MiG-17	14** (5 F-4s, 2 F-8s, 4 F-105s, 2 A-1Hs, 1 CH-47)	8
1966	MiG-17	33 (6 F-4s, 6 F-8s, 10 F-105s, 4 A-4s, 3 A-1Hs, 1 A-1E, 2 C-47s, 1 UAV)	9
	MiG-21	21 (3 F-4s, 13 F-105s, 5 UAVs)	8
1967	MiG-17	49 (28 F-4s, 2 F-8s, 13 F-105s, 4 A-4s, 2 A-1Hs)	22
	MiG-21	47 (16 F-4s, 2 RF-4Cs, 1 F-8, 23 F-105s, 3 RF-101s, 1 A-4, 1 EB-66)	17
1968	MiG-17	8 (3 F-4s, 3 F-8s, 2 UAVs)	4
	MiG-21	22 (5 F-4s, 1 F-8, 4 F-105s, 1 F-102, 1 EB-66, 10 UAVs)	6
1969	MiG-17	2 UAVs	0
	MiG-21	8 UAVs	0
1970	MiG-17	2 UAVs	0
	MiG-21	2 (1 F-4, 1 CH-53)	1
1971	MiG-17	1 UAV	0
	MiG-21	2 (1 F-4, 1 OV-10)	0
1972	MiG-17	9 (7 F-4s, 1 A-7, 1 UAV)	7
	MiG-19	9 (8 F-4s, 1 F-105)	9
	MiG-21	62 (51 F-4s, 1 RF-4H, 1 RF-4C, 1 F-105, 2 A-7s, 1 RA-5C, 2 B-52s, 3 UAVs)	33

1973	MiG-17	1 UAV	
	MiG-21	2 UAV	1
Total		294 (134 F-4s, 15 F-8s, 69 F-105s, 3 RF-4s, 3 RF-101s, 1 F-102, 9 A-4s, 3 A-7s, 1 A-1E, 7 A-1Hs, 1 RA-5C, 2 EB-66s, 1 OV-10, 2 B-52s, 2 C-47s, 1 CH-47, 1 CH-53, 1 C-123, 38 UAVs) Total: 294 + 26 NKAF**** = 320	125***

*   The figures in this chart were recorded by the VNPAF on results of air battles by year and by aircraft type.

**   The number of MiG-17 victories in 1965 includes two F-105 "probable" kills, one on 20 June 1965, and one on 14 October 1965.

***   The 125 MiGs that were lost in air combat included 50 MiG-17s, 9 MiG-19s, and 66 MiG-21s.

****The number of victories claimed by the North Korean AF unit stationed at Kép airfield.

GLOSSARY

(A), (B), (C): used to differentiate Vietnamese pilots with the same names

ace: Unofficial term for an airman with five or more aerial victories over enemy aircraft

AGM-45 Shrike: Air-to-ground missile, antiradiation type

Atoll: Soviet-built air-to-air, heat-seeking missile

Bạch Mai airport: An airport nine miles south of Hanoi's center

Black Crown: VNPAF's code name for an enemy aircraft

Cẩm Thủy airfield: A rough frontline airfield forty-three miles west of Thanh Hóa City

Combat Tree: A highly classified radar attachment for some F-4 radars, which allowed them to separate MiG radar returns from American aircraft radar returns

C-22/26/41/43/53: Radar stations of the AD and AF Service's radar network

Đa Phúc (Nội Bài) airport: VNPAF's main base, nineteen miles north of Hanoi

Disco: Radio call sign for College Eye, the EC-121 aircraft that provided airborne navigational assistance, border warnings, and MiG warnings

Drink beer: Code phrase used by MiG pilots to report to GCI after they launched their missiles

Feather Duster: USAF and USN tactic to cope with MiG-17s

F-371: Code name of the first fighter division of the VNPAF

Gát airfield: A small, rough airfield located in the western part of Quảng Bình Province

Gia Lâm airport: International airport near Hanoi

Hanoi Hilton: An unknown U.S. prisoner of war's nickname given to a prison in Hanoi, where he and many other POWs were detained.

Hòa Lạc airport: A VNPAF airfield northwest of Hanoi

Iron Hand: Code name of USAF aircraft assigned to SAM suppression mission

Kép airport: A major airport of the VNPAF, mostly used by 923rd FR

Kiến An airport: An airport located near Hải Phòng City

Linebacker I and II: U.S. bombing campaigns against North Vietnam, 1972

MiG Valley: An area south of Tam Đảo Mountain that was the location of Đa Phúc and Kép airfields, the VNPAF's main MiG bases

Operation Bolo: A U.S. air campaign with the purpose of killing MiGs in January 1967

pop-up: The pull-up point, a USAF tactical maneuver by which the aircraft ascends from a low altitude to a higher one and attacks enemy aircraft

Rolling Thunder: Code name for a major U.S. bombing campaign against North Vietnam, from 1965 to 1968

route package: Geographical division of North Vietnam for the purposes of air strike targeting

Teaball: A highly classified system established to collate all signal intelligence on North Vietnamese air activity gathered by all sources

Tết: Vietnamese Lunar New Year holiday

Thọ Xuân airport: A VNPAF airport located in Thanh Hóa Province

Thud: American nickname for the F-105 fighter-bomber aircraft

Thud Ridge: American nickname for a prominent geographical feature in North Vietnam, one the eastern edge of the Tam Đảo mountain range northwest of Hanoi

Top Gun: A training program of the USN, stationed at Miramar NAS, California, to prepare USN pilots for Operation Linebacker, 1972

VNP Armed Forces Hero: The most honorable title in the VNPA

Wagon Wheels: Nickname given by U.S. pilots to a MiG-17 tactic formation that increased the defensive capability of the MiG when it was engaged with and outnumbered by enemy aircrafts

Yên Bái airfield: An airfield located in Yên Bái Province, mostly used by the 925th FR

Notes

Notes from Vietnamese and Russian sources are shown only in English.

PREFACE

1. Futrell et al., *Aces and Aerial Victories*, v, vi; McCarthy, *MiG Killers*, 21.
2. Futrell et al., *Aces and Aerial Victories*, vi; Sayers, "The Vietnam Air War's Great Kill-Ratio Debate"; Sayers, "'Shooting Down' the Enemy's Aces"; Pedersen, *Topgun*; Momyer, *Air Power in Three Wars*, 158.

INTRODUCTION

1. This information is corroborated by the USAF's official aerial victory tables held at the Air Force Historical Research Agency.

CHAPTER 1. PRELUDE

1. Thompson, *To Hanoi and Back*, 19; Dorr and Bishop, *Vietnam Air War Debrief*, 135; Olsen, *Global Air Power*, 99.
2. Thompson, *To Hanoi and Back*, 18; Boniface, *MiG over North Vietnam*, 161.
3. Tài, *Uncle Hồ*, 57.
4. Hưng et al., *Air Engagements over the Skies of Vietnam*, 44.
5. Hải, *Fighter Pilot*, 50. According to pilot Lê Hải, a flight student had to complete an average of 180–200 hours of flight to graduate, and flying hours for a pilot on combat alert duty were about 250–300.
6. Ethell and Price, *One Day in a Long War*, 13, 205; Boniface, *MiG over North Vietnam*, 171–72.
7. Hưng et al., *Air Engagements over the Skies of Vietnam*, 46.

8. Soát and Hưng, *Air War over North Vietnam*, 149–52.

9. A number of U.S. documents have acknowledged the fact that there was no attack by the North Vietnamese navy's torpedo boats on 4 August 1964. See "McNamara Meets Former Foe," *Washington Post*, 10 November 1995. In the meeting between McNamara and General Võ Nguyên Giáp, when McNamara asked General Giáp, "What really happened in the Tonkin Gulf on 4 August 1964?" the general replied clearly: "Absolutely nothing happened!" Capt. Jim Stockdale wrote in his memoir: "Our destroyers were just shooting at phantom targets. There were no PT boats there." Stockdale, *In Love and War*, 23, 25. See also Greenspan, "The Gulf of Tonkin Incident, 50 Years Ago"; Paterson, "The Truth about Tonkin."

10. Thompson, *To Hanoi and Back*, 21, endnote 31, where Thompson was quoted in LeMay, *Missions with LeMay*, 565; see also LeMay and Smith, *America Is in Danger*.

11. Soát, "General Đào Đình Luyện, the Eldest Brother of the Vietnam People's Air Force," *60th Anniversary of the Vietnam People's Air Force*, 12.

CHAPTER 2. 1965: THE AIR FRONT OPENED UP

1. Soát, "General Đào Đình Luyện, the Eldest Brother of the Vietnam People's Air Force", *60th Anniversary of the Vietnam People's Air Force* 13.

2. Major General Phạm Ngọc Lan, interviewed by the author, Hanoi, 12 August 2012, and Senior Colonel Hồ Văn Qùy, interviewed by the author, Đà Nẵng, 11 September 2012.

3. Some U.S. documents stated that the F-8 was hit by cannon in the air battle on 3 April 1965 but was only damaged and landed at Đà Nẵng air base. Mersky, *F-8 Crusader vs MiG-17*, 34–35; Weaver, "An Examination of the F-8 Crusader through Archival Sources," 77.

4. The losses of two F-105Ds to MiG-17s in air battles on 4 April 1965 were acknowledged in Chris Hobson's book *Vietnam Air Losses*, 17.

5. Nghị, *History of Air Navigation*, 51.

6. Lieutenant General Trần Hanh, interviewed by the author, Hanoi, 14 June 2012.

7. Hobson, *Vietnam Air Losses*, 17.

8. McCarthy, *MiG Killers*, 23.

9. Tri, *The Ground and the Sky*, 96; Phạm Phú Thái, "Recollections of the former political commissar of the VNPAF, Lieutenant General Chu Duy Kinh," in *60th Anniversary of the VNPAF*, 18–19.

10. This is a type of conference in which all commanders and pilots can discuss openly their experiences in past air engagements and the results, in order to find new ways to fight the enemy. During wartime, both sides from time to time

conducted, at different levels, weapons and tactics conferences. For the VNPAF, at the regimental level, these conferences were called open tactic discussing seminars, and at a higher level, they were called summary conferences.

11. Colonel Hồ Văn Qùy, interviewed by the author, Đà Nẵng, 11 September 2012.

12. In *MiGs over North Vietnam*, 21, author Roger Boniface says that pilot Lê Trọng Long shot down one F-4 over Nho Quan. He says that another F-4 was shot down at the same time but does not identify the pilot of the MiG that shot the second F-4 down.

13. Nghị, *History of Air Navigation*, 54.

14. Hưng, *Air Engagements over the Skies of Vietnam*, 100–101.

15. Davies, *USN F-4 Phantom II Units of the Vietnam War*, 48, 49.

16. Senior Colonel Mai Đức Toại, remark in the Vietnam/United States veteran-pilots meeting, 13 April 2016, Hanoi.

17. According to Mai Đức Toại's remark in the Vietnam/United States veteran-pilots meeting on 13 April 2016, Nguyễn Văn Lai was killed because he flew into a mountain while making hard turns at low altitudes.

18. McCarthy, *MiG Killers*, 27.

19. The information about two MiGs killed by USAF F-4s in air battles on 10 July 1965 was recorded in McCarthy, *MiG Killers*, 28, 29.

20. Hưng et al., *Air Engagements over the Skies of Vietnam*, 110.

21. Tài, *Uncle Hồ*, 142.

22. Trần Danh, "S-75 (SAM-2): Effectiveness of Surface-to-Air Missile," VGP News, 29 November 2012, https:// baochinhphu.vn; "S-75 Dvina SAM-2, Main Armament to Destroy B-52," *Tiền Phong* (Hanoi), 18 December 2017.

23. Hưng et al., *Air Engagements over the Skies of Vietnam*, 116.

24. The losses of Cdr. J. Stockdale and Lt. Col. R. Risner were acknowledged in Hobson, *Vietnam Air Losses*, 31, 32.

25. Hưng, "Nguyễn Nhật Chiêu: A Legendary Pilot," in *60th Anniversary of the VNPAF*, 89.

26. Senior Colonel Nguyễn Văn Bảy (A), interviewed by the author, Ho Chi Minh City, April 2012.

27. Hobson, *Vietnam Air Losses*, 35.

28. Hưng et al., *Air Engagements over the Skies of Vietnam*, 127–28.

29. McCarthy, *MiG Killers*, 24–30; Hobson, *Vietnam Air Losses*, 17, 23, 35, 41.

CHAPTER 3. 1966: THE DEPLOYMENT OF MiG-21s

1. Huy, *Memoirs of Night-time Flights*, 23–24.

2. Huy, *The Sword and the Sky*, 136–39.

3. Tài, *Uncle Hồ*, 182.

4. Hưng et al., *Air Engagements over the Skies of Vietnam*, 154.

5. McCarthy, *MiG Killers*, 33.
6. Futrell et al., *Aces and Aerial Victories*, 30.
7. Futrell et al., 34.
8. Senior Colonel Nguyễn Văn Bảy and Senior Colonel Lê Hải, interviewed by the author and other members of Editorial Board, Ho Chi Minh City, 3 April 2012.
9. McCarthy, *MiG Killers*, 36.
10. Nghị, *History of Air Navigation*, 68.
11. Hobson, *Vietnam Air Losses*, 62.
12. McCarthy, *MiG Killers*, 37.
13. Tài, *Uncle Hồ*, 184–85.
14. Hưng, "General Trần Mạnh: The Main Architect of the MiG's Tactical Mind," in *60th Anniversary of the VNPAF*, 41–43; Soát and Hưng, *Air War over North Vietnam*, 311–16.
15. McCarthy, *MiG Killers*, 38.
16. Nghị, *History of Air Navigation*, 69.
17. Senior Colonel Nguyễn Nhật Chiêu, interviewed by the author, Hải Dương, 3 August 2012.
18. Hobson, *Vietnam Air Losses*, 65.
19. Futrell et al., *Aces and Aerial Victories*, 31.
20. Soát and Hưng, *Air War over North Vietnam*, 297–98.
21. Hobson, *Vietnam Air Losses*, 68.
22. Nghị, *History of Air Navigation*, 77.
23. Nghị, *History of Air Navigation*, 79.
24. Hobson, *Vietnam Air Losses*, 73.
25. Senior Colonel Nguyễn Văn Bảy (A), interview by author, Ho Chi Minh City, 3 April 2012.
26. Hưng, "From Dogfight to Détente."
27. McCarthy, *MiG Killers*, 41.
28. Senior Colonel Hồ Văn Qùy, interviewed by the author, Đà Nẵng, 11 September 2012.
29. Hobson, *Vietnam Air Losses*, 75.
30. Hobson, 76.
31. Phạm Thanh Ngân, interviewed by the author, Hanoi, 10 June 2012; Hưng, *Air Engagements over the Skies of Vietnam*, 215–16.
32. Hobson, *Vietnam Air Losses*, 77; McCarthy, *MiG Killers*, 43.
33. Senior Colonel Đồng Văn Song, interviewed by the author, Hanoi, 14 June 2012.
34. Futrell et al., *Aces and Aerial Victories*, 76.
35. Thompson, *To Hanoi and Back*, 104; Boniface, *MiGs over North Vietnam*, 35.
36. Hobson, *Vietnam Air Losses*, 82.

37. Tài, *Uncle Hồ*, 192. In his memoirs, General Phùng Thế Tài recalled this nickname coined by some unknown U.S. pilots.

38. During an interview conducted on 23 July 2012, Lieutenant General Nguyễn Văn Cốc said that his MiG virtually "climbed onto" the F-105's back when he fired his rockets, but unfortunately he missed.

39. Senior Colonel Vũ Ngọc Đỉnh, interviewed by the author and members of VNPAF Pilots Editorial Advisory Board, Ho Chi Minh City, 3 April 2012.

40. Hobson, *Vietnam Air Losses*, 82.

41. Bell, *100 Missions North*, 131.

42. Of the eight MiG-21 pilots who participated in the 14 December 1966 air battle, six were later awarded the honorable title of VNP Armed Forces Hero.

43. Bell, *100 Missions North*, 132.

44. Bell, 132.

45. Hưng et al., *Air Engagements over the Skies of Vietnam*, 237–38.

46. Hobson, *Vietnam Air Losses*, 268–69.

47. McCarthy, *MiG Killers*, 148–49.

48. Lieutenant General Nguyễn Văn Cốc, interviewed by the author, Hanoi, 23 July 2012.

CHAPTER 4. 1967: AIR BATTLES OVER MiG VALLEY AND MiG INTERCEPT TACTICS

1. Olds, *Fighter Pilot*, 270.

2. Olds, 272–74.

3. Futrell et al., *Aces and Aerial Victories*, 38.

4. McCarthy, *MiG Killers*, 48.

5. Futrell et al., *Aces and Aerial Victories*, 40.

6. Futrell et al., 41.

7. Colonel Vũ Ngọc Đỉnh, interviewed by the author, 3 April 2012, Hồ Chí Minh City.

8. Michel, *Clashes*, 74; Futrell et al., *Aces and Aerial Victories*, 41.

9. Cốc, *Valiant Pilots and the Sky*, 136; Hưng, "General Trần Mạnh: The Main Architect of the MiG-21 Intercept Tactical Mind."

10. Futrell et al., *Aces and Aerial Victories*, 43.

11. Senior Colonel Vũ Ngọc Đỉnh, Lieutenant Colonel Lê Thành Chơn, and Lê Thiết Hùng, interviewed by the author, 3 April 2012, Ho Chi Minh City.

12. Hobson, Vietnam Air Losses, 87.

13. Tài, Uncle Hồ, 196.

14. Hobson, *Vietnam Air Losses*, 93.

15. McCarthy, *MiG Killers*, 56.

16. The information about the loss of an F-105 and an A-1E to MiGs in air battles on 19 April 1967 was acknowledged in Hobson, Vietnam Air Losses, 96.

17. Futrell et al., *Aces and Aerial Victories*, 46 , 47.

18. Hải, *Fighter Pilot*, 15.

19. Hải, 15–16.

20. Hobson, *Vietnam Air Losses*, 96.

21. McCarthy, *MiG Killers*, 59–60.

22. Nghị, *History of Air Navigation*, 105.

23. Hobson, *Vietnam Air Losses*, 97.

24. Hobson, 97.

25. Tài, *Uncle Hồ*, 198.

26. Hobson, *Vietnam Air Losses*, 97.

27. Michel, *Clashes*, 96.

28. Broughton, *Thud Ridge*, 161.

29. Bell, *100 Missions North*, 224.

30. Cốc, *Valiant Pilots and the Sky*, 155–56.

31. Hobson, *Vietnam Air Losses*, 98.

32. Bell, *100 Missions North*, 224.

33. Michel, *Clashes*, 89, 112.

34. Futrell et al., *Aces and Aerial Victories*, 51.

35. McCarthy, *MiG Killers*, 268–69.

36. Tài, *Uncle Hồ*, 22–25.

37. Drendel, *. . . And Kill MiGs*, 12.

38. Hobson, *Vietnam Air Losses*, 99–100.

39. Message from Colonel Vipperman, December 2018, after the VN/U.S. veteran pilot meeting of October 2018 in Hanoi and Hồ Chí Minh City.

40. Futrell et al., *Aces and Aerial Victories*, 53; Bell, *100 Missions North*, 233.

41. Michel, *Clashes*, 104.

42. Senior Colonel Lưu Huy Chao, interviewed by the author, 14 June 2012, Hanoi; and Senior Colonel Hồ Văn Qùy, interviewed by the author, 11 September 2012, Đà Nẵng.

43. McCarthy, *MiG Killers*, 70.

44. Futrell et al., *Aces and Aerial Victories*, 58–59; Drendel, *. . . And Kill MiGs*, 13; Davies, *F-4 Phantom II vs MiG-21*, 38.

45. McCarthy, *MiG Killers*, 72.

46. McCarthy, *MiG Killers*, 71–75; Davies, *F-4 Phantom II vs MiG-21*, 37–38, 41–42.

47. Hải, *Fighter Pilot*, 40; Chao interviewed by the author; Qùy interviewed by the author.

48. The presence of North Korea's air force unit during the first phase of the war (1966–67) has been written about in Tài, *Uncle Hồ*, 22, 23.

49. Hobson, *Vietnam Air Losses*, 102.
50. McCarthy, *MiG Killers*, 73.
51. Davies, *F-4 Phantom II vs MiG-21*, 38; Colonel Vũ Ngọc Đỉnh, interviewed by the author, 3 April 2012, Ho Chi Minh City.
52. Hải, *Fighter Pilot*, 37.
53. Hưng et al., *Air Engagements over the Skies of Vietnam*, 330.
54. Futrell et al., *Aces and Aerial Victories*, 64.
55. McCarthy, *MiG Killers*, 81–83.
56. Hải, *Fighter Pilot*, 40. After losses in air combat in early June 1967, the MiG-17s were ordered to stop fighting until the end of July, in order to gain additional experience and training.
57. Hợp, "The Story of 14 North Korean Pilot Graves in Bac Giang"; Tài, *Uncle Hồ*, 22.
58. McCarthy, *MiG Killers*, 83.
59. Thompson, *To Hanoi and Back*, 86, and endnote no. 43 of chapter 3 of this book.
60. Michel, *Clashes*, 128; Hobson, *Vietnam Air Losses*, 115.
61. Hobson, *Vietnam Air Losses*, 115.
62. Hobson, 115.
63. Olds, *Fighter Pilot*, 331–32.
64. Senior Colonel Nguyễn Nhật Chiêu, interviewed by the author, 3 August 2012, Hải Dương; also remark given by Chiêu at the 921st FR meeting on the 45th anniversary of the 23 August 1967 air battle.
65. Futrell et al., *Aces and Aerial Victories*, 65.
66. Senior Colonel Nguyễn Văn Chuyên, interviewed by the author, Hanoi, 26 Decem-ber 2012.
67. Hobson, *Vietnam Air Losses*, 117.
68. Hobson, 119.
69. Hobson, 120.
70. Hobson, 120.
71. Michel, *Clashes*, 132.
72. Futrell et al., *Aces and Aerial Victories*, 68.
73. Futrell et al., 68.
74. McCarthy, *MiG Killers*, 86.
75. Hobson, *Vietnam Air Losses*, 123.
76. Hobson, 124.
77. Michel, *Clashes*, 134.
78. The information about the loss of two F-105s to MiGs in air battles on 18 November 1967 was acknowledged in Hobson, *Vietnam Air Losses*, 126.
79. Cốc, *Valiant Pilots and the Sky*, 352–53; Major General Nguyễn Đăng Kính, interviewed by the author, 14 June 2012, Hanoi.

80. Senior Colonel Nguyễn Văn Chuyên, interviewed by the author, Hanoi, 26 Decem-ber 2012.

81. The information about the loss of two F-4Bs to MiGs in air battles on 19 November 1967 was acknowledged in Hobson, *Vietnam Air Losses*, 126.

82. Lê Hải, "Memoirs of Three Air Battles," *65th Anniversary of the VNPAF*, 76–78; Senior Colonel Lê Hải, interview by author, Ho Chi Minh City, 3 April 2012.

83. Hobson, *Vietnam Air Losses*, 127.

84. Chao interview.

85. McCarthy, *MiG Killers*, 90.

86. Thompson, *To Hanoi and Back*, 111.

87. Futrell et al., *Aces and Aerial Victories*, 73.

88. Michel, *Clashes*, 139–40.

89. Tài, *Uncle Hồ*, 219–20.

90. McCarthy, *MiG Killers*, 149–51.

91. Thái and Hưng, "Some Thoughts on Weapons and Tactics in Three Air Wars (Korean War, Six-Day War, and Vietnam War)," in *60th Anniversary of the VNPAF*; Hưng, "General Trần Mạnh: The Main Architect of the MiG-21 Inter-cept Tactical Mind"; Hưng, "A New Theory of MiG-21 Intercept Tactics."

CHAPTER 5. 1968–1971: CLASHES WITH THE USN OVER THE SKIES OF MILITARY ZONE 4

1. Tài, *Uncle Hồ*, 222.

2. Hải, *Fighter Pilot*, 84.

3. Michel, *Clashes*, 188.

4. Futrell et al., *Aces and Aerial Victories*, 75.

5. Senior Colonel Lưu Huy Chao, interviewed by the author, Hanoi, 14 June 2012.

6. Hobson, *Vietnam Air Losses*, 131.

7. Senior Colonel Đồng Văn Song, "Reminiscence of a Battle," in *60th Anniver-sary of the VNPAF*, 166–69; Senior Colonel Đồng Văn Song, interviewed by the author, Hanoi, 14 June 2012.

8. The losses of EB-66 and F-105 aircraft to MiGs in air battles on 14 January 1968 were acknowledged in Hobson, *Vietnam Air Losses*, 133.

9. Senior Colonel Nguyễn Văn Chuyên, interviewed by the author, Hanoi, 26 December 2012; Thompson, *To Hanoi and Back*, 98.

10. Chấp et al., "In Memory of the VNPAF's Martyrs," 114.

11. General Phạm Thanh Ngân, interviewed by the author, Hanoi, 10 June 2012.

12. Hobson, *Vietnam Air Losses*, 135.

13. Hobson, 136.

14. Major General Nguyễn Ngọc Độ, interview by author, Hanoi, 7 November 2012.

15. Cốc, *Valiant Pilots and the Sky*, 219.
16. Hobson, *Vietnam Air Losses*, 148.
17. O'Connor, *MiG Killers of Yankee Station*, 123–28.
18. Lieutenant General Phạm Phú Thái, "The Air War in Vietnam: Many Mysteries Are Continuing to Be Clarified," in *65th Anniversary of the VNPAF*, 511.
19. Hải, *Fighter Pilot*, 72–74.
20. Hobson, *Vietnam Air Losses*, 159.
21. Hobson, 162.
22. Hobson, 197.
23. McCarthy, *MiG Killers*, 101.
24. *Trận không chiến đầu tiên giữa MiG-21 và B52- 47 năm nhìn lại* [The first air engagement between MiG-21 and B-52: Looking back 47 years], Vietnam National Assembly TV, 5 October 2018, https://quochoitv.vn; Cường, "From Dogfight to Détente."
25. Senior Colonel Lê Thanh Đạo, interviewed by the author, Hanoi, 12 August 2012.
26. Hobson, *Vietnam Air Losses*, 217.

CHAPTER 6. 1972: TACKLING LINEBACKER I

1. Ethell and Price, *One Day in a Long War*, 16–17.
2. Thompson, *To Hanoi and Back*, 220–21.
3. McCarthy, *MiG Killers*, 102.
4. Thái, *The Airman Soldier*, 237–38.
5. Hobson, *Vietnam Air Losses*, 218.
6. Futrell et al., *Aces and Aerial Victories*, 89.
7. Hobson, *Vietnam Air Losses*, 223.
8. The victories of F-4s from USS *Oklahoma City* and USS *Kitty Hawk* over MiGs in air battles on 6 May 1972 were recorded in McCarthy, *MiG Killers*, 108, 109.
9. Thái, *The Airman Soldier*, 301.
10. McCarthy, *MiG Killers*, 102, 154.
11. Ethell and Price, *One Day in a Long War*, 34.
12. Ethell and Price, 21.
13. Some documents indicated that launching AIM-9 missiles at low altitudes was not effective. See Michel, *Clashes*, 154–55. At that time MiG pilots had also been instructed to try to maneuver with high Gs at low altitudes, to limit the effectiveness of U.S. missiles.
14. Email exchange between author and Curt Dose, November 2019; Ethell and Price, *One Day in a Long War*, 43.
15. McCarthy, *MiG Killers*, 155.
16. Thompson, *To Hanoi and Back*, 236.
17. Drendel, . . . *And Kill MiGs*, 64–65; McCarthy, *MiG Killers*, 110–14.

18. Ethell and Price, *One Day in a Long War*, 122.

19. Ethell and Price, 189–90; Cunningham and Ethell, *Fox Two*, 107.

20. Drendel, . . . *And Kill MiGs*, 66; Ethell and Price, *One Day in a Long War*, 189–90.

21. W. A. Sayers wrote that "there is solid evidence to suggest that Lt. Randall H. Cunningham was shot down by [a] MiG-21 piloted by Vũ Đức Hợp." Sayers, "'Shooting Down' the Enemy's Aces."

22. Ethell and Price, *One Day in a Long War*, 21, 122; "46 năm và nước mắt của một cựu chiến binh Mỹ" [46 years and the tears of an American veteran], *Báo Khánh Hòa* [Khanh Hoa newspaper], 24 April 2019, https://baokhanhhoa.vn.

23. Thái, *The Airman Soldier*, 322; Hưng et al., *Air Engagements over the Skies of Vietnam*, 625–26; Hải, *Fighter Pilot*, 127.

24. Hưng et al., *Air Engagements over the Skies of Vietnam*, 622.

25. Ethell and Price, *One Day in a Long War*, 174–78, 187.

26. McCarthy, *MiG Killers*, 110–12; Ethell and Price, *One Day in a Long War*, 174–75.

27. The losses of an F-105G and an F-4D to MiGs in air battles on 11 May 1972 were acknowledged in Hobson, *Vietnam Air Losses*, 226.

28. The 927th FR's Battle Report No. 183/TC, 11 May 1972; Michel, *Clashes*, 215; Hobson, *Vietnam Air Losses*, 226.

29. Hobson, 226.

30. Hobson, 226.

31. Hobson, 227; Soát, *Diary of a Fighter Pilot*, 260.

32. The two victories over MiG-17s on 23 May 1972, of the F-4B from VF-161 of the USS *Midway* and the F-8J from VF-121 of the USS *Hancock*, are mentioned in McCarthy, *MiG Killers*, 116.

33. Soát, *Diary of a Fighter Pilot*, 260–61; Lieutenant General Nguyễn Đức Soát and Senior Colonel Nguyễn Tiến Sâm, interviewed by the author, Hanoi, 8 August 2012.

34. Futrell et al., *Aces and Aerial Victories*, 96.

35. Hobson, *Vietnam Air Losses*, 227; Thái, *The Airman Soldier*, 351.

36. McCarthy, *MiG Killers*, 122. In this book, the author stated that two MiG-17s were shot down by U.S. pilots on 11 June 1972, but in fact these were two MiG-19s that were downed.

37. Lieutenant Colonel Phạm Phú Thái, iinterviewed by the author, Hanoi, 8 August 2012; Thái, *The Airman Soldier*, 370.

38. Senior Colonel Lương Thế Phúc, interviewed by the author, Ho Chi Minh City, 16 August 2012.

39. Hobson, *Vietnam Air Losses*, 229.

40. Nghĩa, "Sky and Love," in *60th Anniversary of VNPAF*; Senior Colonel Nguyễn Văn Nghĩa, interviewed by the author, Ho Chi Minh City, 2 January 2013.

41. Michel, *Clashes*, 237.
42. Soát, *Diary of a Fighter Pilot*, 268; two F-4s downed by MiG-21s in air battles on 24 June 1972 were acknowledged in Hobson, *Vietnam Air Losses*, 229.
43. Nghĩa, *Air Combat*, 548–49; Senior Colonel Nguyễn Văn Nghĩa and Lt. Charles Allen Jackson met each other in the VN/U.S. veteran pilots meeting in Hanoi, October 2018.
44. Michel, *Clashes*, 239.
45. Soát, *Diary of a Fighter Pilot*, 272.
46. The losses of four F-4Es from the 308th TFS/31st TFW and the 366th TFW to MiGs in air battles on 27 June 1972 were acknowledged in Hobson, *Vietnam Air Losses*, 230.
47. Michel, *Clashes*, 239.
48. Thái, *The Airman Soldier*, 396.
49. The loss of two F-4s downed by MiGs on 5 July 1972 was acknowledged in Hobson, *Vietnam Air Losses*, 231.
50. Senior Colonel Nguyễn Tiến Sâm, interviewed by the author, Hanoi, 8 August 2012; Soát, *Diary of a Fighter Pilot*, 282; Hobson, *Vietnam Air Losses*, 231.
51. Senior Colonel Nguyễn Tiến Sâm and Lieutenant General Nguyễn Đức Soát, interviewed by the author, Hanoi, 8 August 2012.
52. Futrell et al., *Aces and Aerial Victories*, 98.
53. Hobson, *Vietnam Air Losses*, 231.
54. Futrell et al., *Aces and Aerial Victories*, 98.
55. Futrell et al., 99.
56. Soát, *Diary of a Fighter Pilot*, 287; Hobson, *Vietnam Air Losses*, 231.
57. McCarthy, *MiG Killers*, 127.
58. Hobson, *Vietnam Air Losses*, 233.
59. One loss to a MiG and one victory over MiGs by USAF F-4s in air battles on 29 July 1972 were mentioned in Hobson, *Vietnam Air Losses*, 233, and in McCarthy, *MiG Killers*, 128.
60. McCarthy, *MiG Killers*, 128.
61. Soát, *Diary of a Fighter Pilot*, 293.
62. McCarthy, *MiG Killers*, 129.
63. Futrell et al., *Aces and Aerial Victories*, 102.
64. Michel, *Clashes*, 256.
65. Hobson, *Vietnam Air Losses*, 256; Soát, *Diary of a Fighter Pilot*, 314–15.
66. McCarthy, *MiG Killers*, 156.
67. Senior Colonel Lương Thế Phúc (who later became an executive vice president of Vietnam Airlines), interviewed by the author, Ho Chi Minh City, 16 August 2012. During the war Nguyễn Xuân Hiển served as a pilot with the 923rd FR.
68. McCarthy, *MiG Killers*, 132.

69. Hobson, *Vietnam Air Losses*, 235.

70. Thái, *The Airman Soldier*, 435–36.

71. Nghĩa, *Air Combat*, 586. The information about the USAF victories and the loss of a U.S. F-4 to a MiG on 12 September 1972 is confirmed in McCarthy, *MiG Killers*, 134, and in Hobson, *Vietnam Air Losses*, 236.;

72. Nghĩa, *Air Combat*, 590.

73. Thái, *The Airman Soldier* , 446; Hobson, *Vietnam Air Losses*, 238.

74. Hobson, 238.

75. Hobson, 238.

76. McCarthy, *MiG Killers*, 135.

77. Soát, *Diary of a Fighter Pilot*, 345; Hobson, *Vietnam Air Losses*, 238.

78. McCarthy, *MiG Killers*, 137.

79. McCarthy, 138.

CHAPTER 7. DECEMBER 1972: LINEBACKER II AND THE "ĐIỆN BIÊN PHỦ IN THE AIR" CAMPAIGN

1. Thompson, *To Hanoi and Back*, 253.

2. Tri, *The Ground and the Sky*, 160–61.

3. Danh, "S-75 (SAM-2): Effectiveness of Surface-to-Air Missile."

4. Boyne, "Linebacker II."

5. Huy, *Memoirs of Night-time Flights*, 126–30.

6. Michel, *The 11 Days of Christmas*, 53–55.

7. Momyer, *Air Power in Three Wars*, 241.

8. McCarthy et al., *Linebacker II*, 26.

9. Michel, *The 11 Days of Christmas*, 53–56.

10. Tri, *The Ground and the Sky*, 168–69.

11. McCarthy et al., *Linebacker II*, 41.

12. Tri, *The Ground and the Sky*, 167.

13. Tri, *The Ground and the Sky*, 167, 168.

14. Futrell et al., *Aces and Aerial Victories*, 111–12.

15. Tri, *The Ground and the Sky*, 169.

16. McCarthy, *MiG Killers*, 140.

17. McCarthy, *MiG Killers*, 140.

18. Nghĩa, *Air Combat*, 633.

19. McCarthy, *MiG Killers*, 141; Futrell et al., *Aces and Aerial Victories*, 114.

20. Tri, *The Ground and the Sky*, 173.

21. McCarthy et al., *Linebacker II*, 122.

22. McCarthy et al., *Linebacker II*, 121; Thompson, *To Hanoi and Back*, 264.

23. McCarthy et al., *Linebacker II*, 146.

24. Khyupenen, *The Battles Fought by Vietnam's Air Defense and Air Force Troops in December 1972, U.S. SAC in Operation Linebacker 2*; Drenkowski and Grau, *Patterns and Predictability*, 31–32.

25. The 28 December 1972 issue of the *People's Army* newspaper carried the Supreme Command's commendation sent to the VNPAF for shooting down two USAF combat aircraft; Hobson, *Vietnam Air Losses*, 245.

26. Tri, *The Ground and the Sky*, 181; Huy, *Memoirs of Night-time Flights*, 144–45.

27. Hobson, *Vietnam Air Losses*, 245, 246.

28. Huy, *Memoirs of Night-time Flights*, 144.

29. Hobson, *Vietnam Air Losses*, 246.

30. Soát, *Diary of a Fighter Pilot*, 385. In his book, *The Battles Fought by Vietnam's Air Defense and Air Force Troops in December 1972, U.S. SAC in Operation Linebacker 2*, A. I. Khyupenen wrote that, based on reports by local militia troops, antiaircraft gunners, and local residents, the AD and AF Service Command determined that Hoàng Tam Hùng shot down one RA-5C and one F-4.

31. Hưng et al., *Air Engagements over the Skies of Vietnam*, 830.

32. Nhưỡng, "8 Minutes to Shoot Down Two American Aircraft"; Hưng, "The Last Pilots to Give Their Lives in the Skies over Hà Nội."

33. Tri, *The Ground and the Sky*, 182.

34. Huy, *Memoirs of Night-time Flights*, 154.

35. Lieutenant General Nguyễn Đức Soát, interviewed by the author, including examination of his combat diary, Hanoi, 15 July 2012; Soát, *Diary of a Fighter Pilot*, 384.

36. McCarthy et al., *Linebacker II*, 171.

37. Tri, *The Ground and the Sky*, 183.

38. Hà, "USAF's B-52 losses and a Victorious Điện Biên Phủ in the Air Campaign"; Hưng et al., *Air Engagements over the Skies of Vietnam*, 849.

39. Hưng et al., *Air Engagements over the Skies of Vietnam*, 849–51; Michel, *The 11 Days of Christmas*, 239–40; Nalty, *Tactics and Techniques of Electronic Warfare*, 113–14. Michel lists 28 MIA or KIA and 34 POWs, but this adds up to 62, not 61. In the author's opinion, the cause of this mismatch is that one of the 34 POWs later died, and that number was added to the number of MIA/KIA to equal 28, but the author did not subtract from the number of captured (which should have been 33, not 34).

40. McCarthy, *MiG Killers*, 139–42, 157.

41. Karnow, *Vietnam, A History*, 654.

CHAPTER 8. OTHER ENEMY TARGETS ATTACKED BY THE VNPAF

1. Schuster, "Lightning Bug War over North Vietnam"; Axe, *Drone War Vietnam*.

2. Hưng et al., *Air Engagements over the Skies of Vietnam*, 855–60.

3. Senior Colonel Từ Đễ, interviewed by the author, Ho Chi Minh City, 3 April 2012; Thành, "The deep love as brothers of one family."

4. Senior Colonel Lê Xuân Dy, interviewed by the author, Hải Dương, 18 August 2012; Senior Colonel Từ Đễ, interviewed by the author, Ho Chi Minh City, 3 April 2012.

5. Senior Colonel Từ Đễ, interviewed by the author, Ho Chi Minh City, 3 April 2012; Senior Colonel Nguyễn Văn Lục and Senior Colonel Hán Văn Quảng, interviewed by the author, Hanoi, April 2015.

6. Dũng, *The Complete Victory of the Resistance War against the United States*, 248.

EPILOGUE: ENDING THE WAR

1. Hưng et al., *Air Engagements over the Skies of Vietnam*, 897, 899–900; Soát and Hưng, *Air War over North Vietnam*, 96–98.

2. Thompson, *To Hanoi and Back*, 301.

3. Davies, *F-4 Phantom II vs MiG-21*, 71.

4. Michel, *Clashes*, 153–59, 287–89.

5. McCarthy, *MiG Killers*, 148–57; Boniface, *MiGs over North Vietnam*, 172.

6. Hobson, *Vietnam Air Losses*, 271.

7. Sayers, "'Shooting Down' the Enemy's Aces"; McCarthy, *MiG Killers*, 148–57.

8. Michel, *Clashes*, 88–90, 112; Futrell et al., *Aces and Aerial Victories*, 78, 170–71.

9. Soát and Hưng, *Air War over North Vietnam*, 358–59.

10. Michel, *Clashes*, 130; Dorr and Bishop, *Vietnam Air War Debrief*, 101; Sayers, "The Vietnam Air War's Great Kill-Ratio Debate."

11. Olsen, *Global Air Power*," 97; Soát and Hưng, *Air War over North Vietnam*, 379–80.

12. McCarthy, *MiG Killers*, 145.

13. John A. Warden, "Smart Strategy, Smart Airpower," in *Airpower Reborn*, ed. John A. Olsen, 127.

14. Olsen, *Global Air Power*, 412; Soát and Hưng, *Air War over North Vietnam*, 389–90, 402, 418, 423.

15. Interviews of Lieutenant General Nguyễn Đức Soát, Lieutenant General Phạm Phú Thái, Senior Colonel Lê Thanh Đạo, Senior Colonel Hà Quang Hưng, and Senior Colonel Nguyễn Thanh Qúy aired on Vietnam National Assembly TV, October 2018; Hưng, "From Dogfight to Détente."

Bibliography

Ashubeily, Igor Rauphovich. Воздушно Космическая Оборона. Третья Сфера обороны: Зарождение и Становление [Aerospace Defense. Third air theatre in modern war: Building up and growing]. Moscow: Asgardia, The Space Nation, 2015.

Axe, David. *Drone War Vietnam*. Annapolis: Naval Institute Press, 2021.

Báo QĐND [People's Army newspaper], 11, 15, 20, 28, 30 December 1972 and 13 January 1973.

Bell, Kenneth H. *100 Missions North: A Fighter Pilot's Story of the Vietnam War*. Washington, D.C.: Potomac Books, 1993.

Bodansky, Yossef. "Air War Vietnam: What the Soviets Learned." *Air University Review* 34, no. 2 (January–February 1983): 84–91.

Boniface, Roger. *MiGs over North Vietnam: The Vietnamese People's Air Force in Combat, 1965–1975*. Manchester, UK: Hikoki Publications, 2008.

Boyne, Walter J. "Linebacker II." *Air Force* Magazine, November 1997, p. 52.

———. *Phantom in Combat*. Atglen, PA: Schiffer Publishing, 2004.

———. "*The Teaball Tactic*." *Air & Space Forces* Magazine 91, no. 7 (July 2008).

Broughton, Jack. *Thud Ridge: F-105 Thunderchief Missions over Vietnam*. Manchester, UK: Crecy Publishing, 2009.

Chao, Lưu Huy. *MiG-17 và chúng ta* [MiG-17 and us]. Hanoi: People's Public Security Publishing House, 2010.

Chấp, Hà Văn, Nguyễn Văn Quang, Vũ Đình Rạng, Lâm Hồng, Lê Thế Hưng, Nguyễn Xuân Át, Lê Đình Cảnh, Nguyễn Chiêm, and Trần Ngọc Hiệp. *Nhớ ơn các Liệt sỹ Không quân* [In memory of the VNPAF's martyrs]. Hanoi: People's Army Publishing House, 2010.

Clodfelter, Mark. *The Limits of Air Power: The American Bombing of North Vietnam.* New York: Free Press, 1989.

Cốc, Nguyễn Văn. *Dũng sỹ bầu trời* [Valiant pilots and the sky]. Hanoi: National Culture Publishing House, 2010.

Coonts, Stephen, and Barrett Tillman. *Dragon's Jaw: An Epic Story of Courage and Tenacity in Vietnam.* Boston: Da Capo Press, 2019.

Correll, J. T. "Rolling Thunder." *Air & Space Forces* Magazine 88, no. 3 (March 2005): 58–65.

Cunningham, Randy, with Jeff Ethell. *Fox Two: The Story of America's First Ace in Vietnam.* Mesa, AZ: Champlin Fighter Museum, 1984.

Cường, Nguyễn Việt. "Từ không chiến đến hòa giải:họ từng gặp nhau trên không" [From dogfight to détente: they met in the air]. *Báo Quân Khu 7* (Ho Chi Minh City), October 2018.

Danh, Trần. "Tên lửa đất đối không hiệu quả" [S-75 (SAM-2): Effectiveness of surface-to-air missile]. Government of the Vietnamese Socialist Republic, 29 November 2012, https://baochinhphu.vn.

———. *F-4 Phantom II vs MiG-21: USAF & VPAF in the Vietnam War.* Oxford, UK: Osprey Publishing, 2008.

———. "S-75 Dvina SAM-2, main armament to destroy B-52." *Báo Tiền phong ngày* (Hanoi), December 18, 2017.

Davies, Peter. *F-105 Thunderchief Units of the Vietnam War.* Oxford, UK: Osprey Publishing, 2010.

———. *USN F-4 Phantom II Units of the Vietnam War, 1969–1973.* Oxford, UK: Osprey Publishing, 2018.

Dorr, Robert, and Chris Bishop. *Vietnam Air War Debrief: The Story of the Aircraft, the Battles, and the Pilots who Fought.* London: Aerospace Publishing, 1996.

Drendel, Lou. *. . . And Kill MiGs: Air to Air Combat in the Vietnam War.* Carrollton, TX: Squadron/Signal Publications, 1984.

Drenkowski, D. A. "The Tragedy of Operation Linebacker II." *Armed Forces Journal International*, July 1997, 24–27.

Drenkowski, Dana, and Lester W. Grau. *Patterns and Predictability: The Soviet Evaluation of Operation Linebacker II.* Fort Leavenworth, KS: U.S. Army Foreign Military Studies Office, January 2007.

Dũng,Văn Tiến. *Cuộc kháng chiến chống Mỹ toàn thắng* [The complete victory of the resistance war against the United States]. Hanoi: Trust Publishing House, 1991.

Ethell, Jeffrey, and Alfred Price. *One Day in a Long War: May 10, 1972, Air War, North Vietnam.* New York: Random House, 1989.

Futrell, Robert Frank, William H. Greenhalgh, Carl Grubb, Gerard E. Hasselwander, Robert F. Jakob, and Charles A. Ravenstein. *Aces and Aerial Victories: The United*

States Air Force in Southeast Asia, 1965–1973. Edited by James N. Eastman, Walter H. Hanak, and Lawrence J. Paszek. Maxwell AFB, AL: Air University, 1979.

Giáp, Võ Nguyên. *Tổng hành dinh trong mùa xuân Đại thắng* [VNPA General Staff in the great spring victory]. Hanoi: National Political Publishing House, 2000.

———. *Hào khí trăm năm* [One hundred years of pride]. Hanoi: Young Publishing House, 2011.

Greenspan, Jesse. "The Gulf of Tonkin Incident, 50 Years Ago." History.com, 31 August 2018. https://www.history.com/news/the-gulf-of-tonkin-incident-50-years-ago.

Hà, Hoàng. "USAF's B-52 Losses and a Victorious Điện Biên Phủ in the Air Campaign." *Báo QĐND* [People's Army newspaper], 16 December 2017.

Hải, Lê. *Phi công tiêm kích* [Fighter pilot]. Hanoi: People's Army Publishing House, 2007.

Hải, Lê. "Kỷ niệm về ba trận *đánh*" [Memoirs of three air battles]. In *65th Anniversary of the VNPAF*. Hanoi: People's Army Publishing House, 2020.

HKVN 50 năm: biên niên sự kiện [Vietnam Civil Aviation 50th anniversary: A chronology of fifty years of events]. Hanoi: People's Army Publishing House, 2005.

Hobson, Chris. *Vietnam Air Losses*. Hinckley, UK: Midland Publishing, 2001.

Hợp, Tuấn. "Chuyện về 14 ngôi mộ phi công bắc Triều tiên ở Bắc giang" [The story of 14 North Korean pilot martyrs' graves in Bắc Giang]. *Dân Trí* (Hanoi), 5 March 2019. https://dantri.com.vn/xa-hoi.htm.

Hưng, Nguyễn Sỹ. "The Last Pilots to Give Their Lives in the Skies over Hanoi." *World Security* (Hanoi), no. 1,224, 19 December 2012.

———. "Thiếu tướng Trần Mạnh: Kiến trúc sư chiến thuật MiG-21" [General Trần Mạnh: The main architect of the MiG-21 intercept tactical mind]. *World Security* (Hanoi), no. 77, June 2014.

———. "MiG-21 thanh gươm báu, huyền thoại bầu trời" [MiG-21 the legendary air sword in the sky]. *World Security* (Hanoi), no. 1549, March 2016.

———. "Từ không chiến đến hòa giải" [From dogfight to *détente*]. *Vietnam's Quintessence* (Hanoi), no. 65, December 2017, and *Vietnam–USA* Magazine, March 2018, 49–61.

———. "Nguyễn Nhật Chiêu: Một phi công huyền thoại" [Nguyễn Nhật Chiêu: A legendary pilot]. In *65th Anniversary of the VNPAF*. Hanoi: People's Army Publishing House, 2020.

———. "Lý thuyết mới về Chiến thuật MiG-21" [New theory of MiG-21 intercept tactic]. *Military Culture* Magazine (Hanoi), no. 175, March 2020.

Hưng, Nguyễn Sỹ, Nguyễn Nam Liên, Nguyễn Văn Quang, Lữ Thông, Hà Quang Hưng; Từ Đễ, Nguyễn Công Huy. *Những trận không chiến trên bầu trời Việt Nam (1965–1975), Nhìn từ hai phía*, [Air engagements over the skies of Vietnam (1965–1975), as viewed from both sides]. Hanoi: People's Army Publishing House, 2013.

Huy, Nguyễn Công. *Thanh kiếm, bầu trời* [The sword and the sky]. Hanoi: Labor Publishing House, 2012.

———. *Ngày dài không chiến* [10 May 1972: A long day of air battles]. Hanoi: People's Army Publishing House, 2016.

———. *Ký ức trời* đêm [Memoirs of Night-time Flights]. Hanoi: Hồng Đức Publishing House, 2020.

Karnow, Stanley. *Vietnam, A History: The First Complete Account of Vietnam at War.* London: Century Publishing, 1983.

Kháng, Đinh Trọng, Nguyễn Phương Diện, Nguyễn Văn Sửu, Nguyễn Hữu Ngọ, Hoàng Thảo. *65 năm Không quân nhân dân Việt Nam* [65th anniversary of the VNPAF]. Hanoi: People's Army Publishing House, 2020.

Khôi, Nguyễn Kim. *C-15, E-921 ngày xưa* [Weapon Company C-15, 921st FR, during wartime]. Ho Chi Minh City: Young Publisher, 2014.

Khyupenen, A. I. "*Вьетнамская Война: как она была, воздушные бои СРВ зенитных и ВВС в Декабре* 1972; США *Стратегическая Авиация в Операций Лаунебакер* 2" [The battles fought by Vietnam's air defense and air force troops in December 1972, U.S. SAC in Operation Linebacker 2]. Moscow: *Military Historical Journal*, February 2005, 30–33.

LeMay, Curtis E., with MacKinlay Kantor. *Mission with LeMay*. New York: Doubleday, New York, 1965.

LeMay, Curtis E., and Dale O. Smith. *America Is in Danger*. New York: Funk & Wagnalls, 1968.

Lenski, Albert J. *Magic 100*. Nashville: Turner Publishing, 1995.

McCarthy, Donald J. *MiG Killers: A Chronology of U.S. Air Victories in Vietnam, 1965–1973*. Manchester, UK: Crecy Publishing, 2009.

McCarthy, James R., and George B. Allison. *Linebacker II: A View from the Rock*. Edited by Robert E. Rayfield. Washington, D.C.: Office of Air Force History, USAF, 1985.

"McNamara Meets Former Foe." *Washington Post*, 10 November 1995. https://www .washingtonpost.com/archive/politics/1995/11/10/mcnamara-meets-former -foe/cb4a9a55-ea9b-4fb1-8e0d-5d5db68870dd/.

Mersky, Peter. *F-8 Crusader Units of the Vietnam War*. Oxford, UK: Osprey Publishing, 1998.

———. *F-8 Crusader vs MiG-17: Vietnam 1965–1972*. Oxford, UK: Osprey Publishing, 2014.

Michel, Marshall L., III. *Clashes: Air Combat over North Vietnam 1965–1972*. Annapolis, MD: Naval Institute Press, 1997.

———. *The 11 Days of Christmas: America's Last Vietnam Battle*. New York/London: Encounter Books, 2002.

———. *Operation Linebacker I, 1972: The First High-Tech Air War.* Oxford, UK: Osprey Publishing, 2019.

Mintier, Tom. "Two Former Enemies Meet in Friendship." CNN, 9 November 1995. http://www.cnn.com/WORLD/9511/vietnam_mcnamara/11-09/.

Momyer, W. William. *Air Power in Three Wars.* New York: Arno Press, 1980.

Nalty, Bernard C. *Tactics and Techniques of Electronic Warfare: Electronic Countermeasures in the Air War against North Vietnam, 1965–1973.* Washington, D.C.: Defense Lion Publications, 2013.

Nghị, Vũ Chính, Nguyễn Văn Nhâm, and Lương Quốc Bảo. *Lịch sử dẫn đường Hàng không* [History of air navigation]. Hanoi: People's Army Publishing House, 2007.

Nghĩa, Nguyễn Văn. *Bầu trời và tình người* [The sky and love]. In *60th Anniversary of the VNPAF.* Hanoi: People's Army Publishing House, 2015.

———. *Không chiến* [Air combat]. Hanoi: People's Army Publishing House, 2019.

Nguyên, Đồng Sỹ. *Trọn một con đường* [All along the road]. Hanoi: People's Army Publishing House, 2012.

Nhưỡng, Hà Bình. "Tám phút bắn rơi hai máy bay Mỹ" [8 minutes to shoot down two American aircraft]. *Báo QĐND* [People's Army newspaper], 13 January 1973.

O'Connor, Michael. *MiG Killers of Yankee Station.* New York: New Past Press, 2003.

Olds, Robin. *Fighter Pilot.* New York: St. Martin's Griffin, 2010.

Olsen, John. *Global Air Power.* Washington, D.C.: Potomac Books, 2011.

———. *Airpower Reborn: The Strategic Concepts of John Warden and John Boyd.* Annapolis, MD: Naval Institute Press, 2015.

Paterson, Pat, Lt. Cdr., USN. "The Truth about Tonkin." *Naval History* 22, no. 1 (February 2008).

Pedersen, Dan. *Topgun: An American Story.* Paris: Hachette Books, 2020.

Pokruskin, A. I. Тактика истребительной авиации [Fighter Tactics]. Novosibirsk, Siberia: Gornisia, 1999.

Sayers, William A. "The Vietnam Air War's Great Kill-Ratio Debate." *Vietnam Magazine,* June 2018.

———. "'Shooting Down' the Enemy's Aces." *Vietnam* Magazine, June 2019, 34–36.

Schuster, Carl O. "Lightning Bug War over North Vietnam." *Vietnam* Magazine, February 2013.

Soát, Nguyễn Đức. "Thượng tướng Đào Đình Luyện-Người anh cả của bộ đội Không quân" [General Đào Đình Luyện, the eldest brother of the VNP air force]. In *60th Anniversary of the VNPAF.* Hanoi: People's Army Publishing House, 2015.

———. *Nhật ký Phi công tiêm kích* [Diary of a fighter pilot]. Hanoi: Young Publishing House, 2020.

Soát, Nguyễn Đức, and Nguyễn Sỹ Hưng. *Chiến tranh Trên không ở Việt Nam, Phía sau những trận không chiến* [Air war over North Vietnam, 1965–1973: Behind the air engagements]. Hanoi: People's Army Publishing House, 2017.

Song, Đồng Văn. "Kỷ niệm một trận đánh" [Reminiscence of a battle]. In *60th Anniversary of the VNPAF*. Hanoi: People's Army Publishing House, 2015.

Stockdale, Jim and Sybil. *In Love and War: The Story of a Family's Ordeal and Sacrifice during the Vietnam Years*. New York: Harper & Row, 1984.

Summers, Harry G. *On Strategy: A Critical Analysis of the Vietnam War*. Novato, CA: Presidio Press, 1995.

Tài, Phùng Thế. *Bác Hồ, những kỷ niệm không quên* [Uncle Hồ, unforgettable memories]. Hanoi: People's Army Publishing House, 2002.

Thái, Phạm Phú. *Lính bay* [The airman soldier]. Hanoi: Vietnam Writers' Association Publishing House, 2016.

———. "Mấy ký ức của cựu Chính ủy không quân Trung tướng Chu Duy Kính" [Memories of the former political commissar of the VNPAF, Lieutenant General Chu Duy Kính]. In *65th Anniversary of the VNPAF*. Hanoi: People's Army Publishing House, 2020.

———. "Chiến tranh trên không ở Việt Nam, nhiều bí ẩn *đang* tiếp tục tìm lời giải" [The air war in Vietnam, many mysteries are continuing to be clarified]. In *65th Anniversary of the VNPAF*. Hanoi: People's Army Publishing House, 2020.

Thái, Phạm Phú, and Nguyễn Sỹ Hưng. "Một số suy nghĩ về chiến thuật và vũ khí trong 3 cuộc chiến" [Some thoughts on weapons and tactics in three air wars (Korean War, Six-Day War, and Vietnam War)]. In *60th Anniversary of the VNPAF*. Hanoi: People's Army Publishing House, 2015.

Thành, Nguyễn Trọng. "Nghĩa tình keo sơn-anh em một nhà" [The deep love as brothers of one family]. *Báo Nhân chứng và sự kiện* [Events and Witnesses newspaper], 11 December 2020.

Thompson, Wayne. *To Hanoi and Back: The U.S. Air Force and North Vietnam, 1966–1973*. Washington, D.C./London: Smithsonian Institution Press, 2000.

Tilford, Earl H., Jr. *Setup: What the Air Force Did in Vietnam and Why*. Ann Arbor: University of Michigan Library, 1991.

Tri, Lê Văn. *Mặt đất và bầu trời* [The ground and the sky]. Hanoi: People's Army Publishing House, 2006.

Weaver, Michael. "An Examination of the F-8 Crusader through Archival Sources." *Journal of Aeronautical History*, February 2018. http://www.aerosociety.com/media.

Index

About the Author

Lieutenant Colonel **Nguyễn Sỹ Hưng (Đồng Sỹ Hưng)** is a former MiG-21 pilot with the 921st FR, 371st Air Force Fighter Division. He is the son of General Đồng Sỹ Nguyên, VNPA, the commander in chief of the Ho Chi Minh Trail during the Vietnam War. Nguyễn Sỹ Hưng received his BA from the Political Sciences Academy in Moscow (1981), received his doctoral degree at the Moscow Military Political Sciences Academy (1988), and his bachelor's degree in the English language at Hanoi University of Foreign Studies (1994). Nguyễn was the head of faculty of the Vietnam People's Air Force Academy (1988–1991). He later worked in the aviation industry and was the chairman and CEO of Vietnam Airlines from 1998 to 2011.

Nguyễn Sỹ Hưng is a researcher and the author of several books on the air force and the Vietnam air war. He has written and translated (from English and Russian into Vietnamese) several books, and has written articles on the subject of the air war in Vietnam. His previous books include: *Scientific Foundations of Flight Safety*; *Aviation Psychology: Applied Problems*; *Air Engagements over the Skies of Vietnam (1965–1975), as Viewed from Both Sides*; and *Air War over North Vietnam: Behind the Air Engagements*.